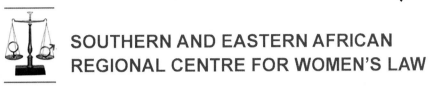

SOUTHERN AND EASTERN AFRICAN REGIONAL CENTRE FOR WOMEN'S LAW

WOMEN & LAW

Innovative approaches to teaching, research and analysis

Edited by

AMY S. TSANGA and JULIE E. STEWART

NORTH-SOUTH
LEGAL PERSPECTIVE
SERIES NO.5

WEAVER
PRESS

Acknowledgements

The regional Masters in Women's Law and the publication of this book as part of the women's law north–south series, would not be possible without the continued financial support provided by the Norwegian Government. The programme has from its inception in Oslo and since its commencement and development in Zimbabwe been wholly funded by the Norwegian Government. Very special thanks go to the staff of the Norwegian Embassy in Harare, who have been, over the last 20 or more years, unwavering in their support to the programme, especially when the social, economic and political going became tough. We can do little more than express our most sincere gratitude for their steadfast support towards the advancement of women's rights in the region.

The writing of this book has also been made possible by the contributions of chapters by all colleagues who teach on the masters programme who have spared time to share valuable insights. Appreciation is extended to Professor Sylvia Tamale who played a significant role in formulating the core issues to be focused on in examining issues of gender, sexuality and power relations. The same can be said for Professor Patricia Kameri-Mbote for formulating the critical issues to be addressed in linking legal form to lived realities. Our deep thanks are extended to Margo Bedingfield for her sterling editorial work on the book as a whole and for making suggestions for an innovative layout and helping us shape its overall perspective. She really shook us out of our traditional academic comfort zones and challenged us to walk our talk in terms of communication paradigms and writing styles.

Gratitude is also extended to Professor Cynthia GrantBowman at the University of Cornell Law School who provided a no strings attached, visiting scholar award to one of the editors, Amy Tsanga, who spent an uninterrupted month working on the book, a very rare privilege indeed.

Very special thanks too to our past students whose input undoubtedly provided the necessary fodder for crafting a book on teaching methodologies.

The publishers would like to acknowledge the following sources of materials:

Maria Nicolo and the A Woman's Place team for the thumbnail of Tandaswa Ndita from the video, *A woman's place* (1998) on page 15; Zimbabwe Women's Resource Centre and Network and Chiedza Musengezi for the poem 'Try again' on pages 20 and 21; Malula Nkanyemba and Sakina Sinda for photo extracts from their dissertations on pages 101 and 103; UNICEF Mozambique for the photo on page 213; Joseline Kabasiime Masigye and EQUINET for the photo on page 232; Mark Parisai for the Gingerbread man cartoon on page 286; Zapiro for the cartoon on page 292; www.cartoonstock.com for the cartoon on page 300; Ed Wilmsen for photos on pages 415, 417 and 422

We reproduced thumbnails of the covers of the following valuable resources:

The video *Neria*, produced by Media for Development Trust (1993); the book *Venia Magaya's sacrifice*, published by WLSA (2001); the video *Stolen childhood*, produced by GEM TV, Ethiopia (2003); the book series *Training for Transformation*, revised edition, published by ITDG (1984); the video *Monday's girls*, produced by Lloyd Gardner (1993); the book, *Reclaiming our lives: HIV and AIDS, women's land and property rights and livelihoods in southern and east Africa, narratives and responses*, produced by HSRC Press (2006)

We also reproduced some headlines and brief extracts from newspaper articles in *The Herald* (Zimbabwe) on pages 205 and 212 and current page extracts from *Google scholar* and *Training for law* on pages 138 and 139.

© SEARCWL, 2011

ISBN: 978 1 77922 144 5

WEAVER
PRESS

Published by Weaver Press
38 Broadlands Road,
Emerald Hill, PO Box A1922
Avondale, Harare
Mobile phone:
+263 4 308330, 339631

In association with:
Southern and Eastern African
Regional Centre for Women's
Law (SEARCWL)
30 Mount Pleasant Drive,
Mount Pleasant, Harare,
Zimbabwe
Phone: + 263 4 745365/6
Email: tsomondo@law.uz.ac.zw
OR rudo@law.uz.ac.zw

Publishing consultant:
Margo Bedingfield
Illustrated by Mashet Ndhlovu
Printed by MPG Biddles Ltd,
United Kingdom

Contents

About the editors...

Amy Tsanga
Editor

Amy Tsanga teaches law at the University of Zimbabwe and is the Deputy Director of the Southern and Eastern African Regional Centre for Women's Law (SEARCWL). She graduated in law from the University of Zimbabwe in 1986 and also holds postgraduate qualifications from the University of Oslo, University of Warwick and University of Zimbabwe. She started her legal career as one of the few lawyers then to work extensively with rural communities in African settings. She joined academia in 1994. Among her publications is *Taking law to the people: gender, law reform and community education in Zimbabwe* (Weaver Press, 2003). Her academic and research interests are in the fields of the development of African feminist theory, human rights, gender, social justice and development issues.

Combining activism and academia, she has worked extensively on issues of women and access to justice. She has also been recognized by the Zimbabwe Women Lawyers Association for her contribution to women's legal and human rights activism in Zimbabwe. She currently serves on the Board of the International Law Schools Association.

Julie Stewart
Co-editor

Julie Stewart is a Professor of Law at the Faculty of Law, University of Zimbabwe and the Director of SEARCWL. She was instrumental in conceptualizing, setting up and shaping the Masters in Women's Law which is the subject of this book. She has been organizing and running SEARCWL since 2002 and prior to that she set up and ran the Postgraduate Diploma in Women's Law at what was previously styled the Women's Law Centre. She has researched and written on a variety of legal topics including how women are affected by the application of law in all its forms, by the gendered and sexed deficiencies in law and by the problems and barriers that specifically affect women and the girl child's access to and positive benefits from human rights initiatives.

The Masters in Women's Law programme has led her to spend a considerable amount of time devising flexible and viable methodological approaches which raise the key questions about how women are affected by, use and implement laws and human rights norms and conducting research in this field.

Like other authors in this book she has been active in the quest for women's rights and improving women's legal situation and has won a number of awards recognizing the significance of this work.

About the contributors...

Elize Delport

Elize Delport is an independent human rights lawyer and gender activist. She is an Extraordinary Lecturer at the University of Pretoria Centre for Human Rights. She is a member of Solidarity for African Women's Rights (SOAWR) and serves on the governing council of the African Centre for Democracy and Human Rights Studies (Banjul) and on the steering committee of the African-Spanish Women's Network for a Better World.

Anne Griffiths

Anne Griffiths holds a personal Chair in the Anthropology of Law at the School of Law at Edinburgh University. Her research focuses on anthropology of law, comparative and family law, African law, gender, culture and rights. Her most recent project is a study on the gendered dynamics of land tenure in southern Africa, funded by the Leverhulme Trust (United Kingdom). She has held visiting appointments at various institutions, including Distinguished Visiting Professor, Faculty of Law, University of Toronto, the Max Planck Institute for Social Anthropology, Halle/Saale, Germany, the International Institute for the Sociology of Law Oñati – Gipuzkoa, Spain, the University of Texas at Austin School of Law and SEARCWL. She is a former President of the Commission on Legal Pluralism (2003-2009).

Munyaradzi
Gwisai

Munyaradzi Gwisai is a lecturer in the Faculty of Law at the University of Zimbabwe where he teaches labour law and jurisprudence. He has an LL.B from the University of Zimbabwe and an LL.M from University of Columbia. In addition to his academic career he is a leading member of the International Socialist organization (ISO) and a founder member of the Zimbabwe Labour Centre which works with trade unions.

Anne Hellum is a lawyer and anthropologist holding a Doctor Juris Degree from the University of Oslo. She is Professor in the Department of Public and International Law at the University of Oslo and Director of the Institute of Women's Law, Child Law, Discrimination and Equality Law. She was the first leader of the University of Oslo's diploma course in women's law, the forerunner of SEARCWL's regional masters programme. Her research, which cuts across human rights law, discrimination law and anthropology of law, has focused on the relationship between human rights and legal pluralism in Zimbabwe, South Africa, Pakistan and Norway. She currently holds a grant at the Centre for Advanced Studies as part of the international research project, 'Why states ratify human rights', where she is directing the CEDAW project.

Anne Hellum

Chuma Himonga

Chuma Himonga obtained her LL.B from the University of Zambia in 1977 and taught there until 1988. She obtained her LL.M and Ph.D. (1978 and 1985) from the University of London. She also worked in the *Sonderforschungsbericht 214: Identität in Afrika – Prozesse ihrer Entstehung und Veränderung* at the University of Bayreuth, Germany and is now Professor of Law at the University of Cape Town. She holds the South African National Research Foundation Research Chair in Customary Law. She also worked for WLSA for many years and, in addition to teaching African customary law, she sustains her research interests in comparative African family law, women and law in southern Africa and children's rights.

Patricia
Kameri-Mbote

Patricia Kameri-Mbote is Professor of Law at Strathmore University. She was previously an Associate Professor of Law at University of Nairobi where she served as Chair of the Department of Private Law and Acting Dean at the School of Law. She is an Advocate of the High Court of Kenya. She studied law in Nairobi, Warwick, Zimbabwe and Stanford and served as a Policy Scholar at the Woodrow Wilson International Center for Scholars. She was the Director of Research and Policy Outreach and Acting Executive Director at the African Centre for Technology Studies, Nairobi, and has been identified by the World Conservation Union (IUCN) as a Renowned Thinker in the global environment and sustainable development field. She has published widely in the areas of international law, environmental law, women's rights and property rights.

Sheillah
Kanyangarara

Sheillah Kanyangarara is a researcher in international trade and criminal law. Her research interests in trade include translating the benefits of regional trade agreements to the economic empowerment of ordinary people. She focuses on justice delivery in sexual offences in her criminal law research. Sheillah is an entrepreneur who has developed a line of personal care products for the lower end market. Her products are distributed through direct marketing by rural women with the aim of economically empowering women.

Ngeyi Ruth
Kanyongolo

Ngeyi Ruth Kanyongolo is a lecturer in the Faculty of Law, Chancellor College at the University of Malawi. She is also Head of the Practical Legal Studies Department. She has an LL.B (Hons) (Malawi), LL.M (London) and Ph.D. (Warwick). She specializes in labour, social security, women and law. She is a visiting lecturer on the SEARCWL Masters in Women's Law programme. She is currently the President of the Women Lawyers Association and has previously served as Vice President of the Malawi Law Society. She serves as a director on a number of boards in Malawi. Her recent research has focused on social security, labour and trade unions in Malawi. She is also involved in developing policies on refugees and care work in Malawi.

Rosalie Kumbirai
Katsande

Rosalie Kumbirai Katsande holds an LL.B and a Masters in Women's Law (SEARCWL). She is a lecturer and a doctoral candidate at SEARCWL. Prior to joining SEARCWL, she was a lecturer and Executive Dean of the Faculty of Law at the Midlands State University in Zimbabwe where she also teaches a 'Gender and the law' module. At SEARCWL, Rosalie is the course convener of the 'Women, commerce and the law in Africa' course. Her research interests are on women's economic empowerment, particularly focusing on the development of theoretical and methodological approaches to the analysis of the socio-legal aspects of women's participation in commercial activities in Africa.

David Kaulemu

David Kaulemu is the Regional Coordinator for the African Forum for Catholic Social Teaching, based at Arrupe College, the Jesuit School of Philosophy and Humanities in Harare. He was previously a lecturer of philosophy and Chair of the Department of Religious Studies, Classics and Philosophy at the University of Zimbabwe. He has taught, researched, facilitated workshops and published on African philosophy, social and political philosophy, social justice, human rights, social transformation, human development and Christian social teaching. He has been an International Visiting Scholar in the Department of Philosophy and Centre for Sustainable International Development at the University of Aberdeen, the Woodstock Theological Centre at Georgetown University and the Council for Research in Values and Philosophy at the Catholic University of America.

Thembani
Malapela

Thembani Malapela is the Acting Deputy Librarian at the University of Zimbabwe. From 2007 to 2010 he managed the Law Library at the University of Zimbabwe. He is also the Chair of the University of Zimbabwe Libraries' Open Access Initiatives Committee. Since 2005 he has been researching around the issues of free access and open access to law. In 2009 he was an intern at the Southern African Legal Information Institute where he compiled an index to Zimbabwean Judgments (2002-2009) accessible via the Saflii website. His current research interests are on adapting Free Open Source Software (FOSS) in library and information services.

Cecilie
Butenschøn Mariri

Cecilie Butenschøn Mariri graduated from the Norwegian College of Librarianship (*Statens bibliotekskole*) in 1976. She worked in various academic and specialist libraries in Norway before moving to Zimbabwe in 2000. She also set up a Documentation Centre for the (then) SADCC Energy Secretariat in Luanda, Angola in 1987-89. She has worked for SEARCWL since 2001 and enjoys running a library with a focus on gender studies and women's rights, as well as working with students and researchers at all academic levels.

Sesedzai
Munyaradzi

Victor Nkiwane

Pauline
Nyamweya

Oliver Phillips

Sesedzai Munyaradzi holds a Bachelor's degree in Business Management and Information Technology and is currently working towards her Masters in Computer Science. She has technical certification in Computer Programming and Systems Analysis and Design. She has trained adults since 1996, working with two different universities and training students in information technology. She has also trained adults in a community project where people come in with no knowledge of computing at all. She has thus developed expertise in working with information technology for different target groups. She currently works at SEARCWL as the Information and Technology Manager.

Victor Nkiwane is a Zimbabwean national currently lecturing in the Faculty of Law at the University of Kwa-Zulu Natal, teaching family law and property law. He holds a Bachelor of Law degree and a Postgraduate Diploma in Women's Law from the University of Zimbabwe and an LL.M from Warwick University. His research interests include family law and gender and law, with particular interest in law and masculinities. He previously held the post of Dean and taught law in the Law Faculty at the University of Zimbabwe. He has also taught at Vista University in South Africa and at the National University of Lesotho. He was also a long-standing member of the WLSA Board.

Pauline Nyamweya holds a first class LL.B from the University of Nairobi and an LL.M from the University of Cambridge. She has over twenty years experience in teaching law and legal practice and in participating in legal and constitutional reforms, and governance and human rights advocacy in Kenya. She currently lectures in the School of Law, University of Nairobi. She has served as Secretary of the Kenya Capital Markets Tribunal, Deputy Secretary of the Constitution of Kenya Review Commission and as Director of Programmes at the Public Law Institute in Kenya. She has undertaken professional consultancy assignments in the areas of governance, gender and human rights for the Kenyan government and various development partners.

Oliver Phillips is currently a Reader in the School of Law, University of Westminster. He has an LL.B from the University of Cape Town and a Ph.D. in Criminology from the University of Cambridge. He has been a Rockefeller Fellow at the Program for the Study of Sexuality, Gender, Health and Human Rights at Columbia University and has taught at Birkbeck and Goldsmiths Colleges of the University of London, at Keele University and at the Universiteit van Amsterdam. He has published numerous articles on sexuality, HIV/AIDS, human rights and the law in southern Africa and has worked with both regional and international advocacy organizations for political and sexual rights, as well as for access to treatment for HIV/AIDS in southern Africa. He is on the advisory board of the International Gay and Lesbian Human Rights Commission and is a founding trustee of the Friends of the Treatment Action Campaign.

Sylvia Tamale

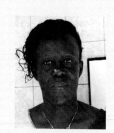

Lillian Tibatemwa-
Ekirikubinza

Sylvia Tamale is a leading African feminist lawyer and scholar based in Kampala, Uganda. She holds an LL.B from Makerere University, an LL.M from Harvard Law School and a Ph.D. in Sociology and Feminist Studies from the University of Minnesota. She is the immediate outgoing Dean of Law at Makerere University and has been a Visiting Professor at several academic institutions around the world. In combining academia with activism, she adopts a critical approach to the law that aims at enhancing students' transformative personal growth and action. In 2006 she founded the Law, Gender and Sexuality Research Project at Makerere University. She has won several awards for defending the human rights of marginalized groups such as women, sexual minorities, people living with HIV/AIDS and refugees.

Lillian Tibatemwa-Ekirikubinza is the first Deputy Vice-Chancellor (Academic Affairs) and Professor of Law at Makerere University. She holds a Ph.D. in Law from University of Copenhagen, an LL.M (Commercial Law) from University of Bristol, an LL.B (Hons) from Makerere University and a Diploma in Legal Practice from the Law Development Centre, Kampala. She is enrolled as an Advocate of all Courts of Uganda's Judicature. Professor Tibatemwa-Ekirikubinza has engaged extensively in academic and policy impact research in areas of criminal law, criminology and gender, comparative criminal jurisprudence, children's rights, juvenile justice, women's rights, human rights perspectives of criminal law, rights of people with disabilities, e-evidence and computer crime and transnational crime. She is widely published in refereed journals.

Introduction

Why a book on teaching women's law?

At the Faculty of Law at the University of Zimbabwe, women's law as an academic discipline has been explored and taught since the first diploma programme was run in conjunction with the Institute for Women's Law at the University of Oslo in 1991. Since that first course the teaching and researching in women's law has evolved from a paradigm-challenging and hectic postgraduate diploma programme run over two semesters which commenced in 1993, into a masters programme run over three intense semesters.

Reflecting on more than 20 years of the programme's development in the eastern and southern African context, the academic staff collectively determined that there was merit in turning our reflections into a book that documents what we do, how we do it and why we do it. Most importantly it gave us all a chance to consider the implications of teaching and researching using a truly grounded, human rights influenced exploratory framework that maps and interrogates women's experiences with the law in its many different forms and manifestations. We have also been asked on numerous occasions how we shape, conduct and develop the courses we offer and the end products – our graduates. This book aims to answer those questions.

...the academic staff collectively determined that there was merit in turning their reflections into a book that documents what we do, how we do it and why we do it.

The objectives of the book

The book shares experiences and reflections on strategies, methods and approaches to developing women's law in Africa, drawing from the teaching of the Masters in Women's Law across all three semesters. It is targeted at four main audiences, namely, academics, students, researchers and trainers. For academics who teach similar courses, it is hoped that the book will provide reflective insights and promote dialogue on teaching and learning experiences across continents. For students undertaking similar programmes, it provides insights into how such courses are taught within contexts that are either different from or similar to their own. For researchers in the field of gender studies and women's law, the book addresses important concepts of doing 'women's law' research as well as the inter-linkages between academic conceptualizing of issues and doing grounded research. For gender practitioners and trainers, the book is a significant resource in highlighting issues that can be dialogued with some suggestions as to how this can be accomplished on various themes that have to do with women, gender and the law. The book could also serve as a blueprint to assist anyone intending to set up a similar programme.

Background and thrust of women's law as an academic discipline

Women's law as an academic discipline rests on the premise that although sex and overt gender discrimination have largely been addressed by the law and it is common to find laws that purportedly apply equally to both men and women, in reality the consequences of gender-neutral laws are felt in a very sex and gender specific manner.[1] The reason lies in the different conditions and needs that women experience as compared to men in their daily lives. In-depth and detailed research into women's 'lived realities' has been instrumental in unearthing the differential impact of laws on the lives of women when compared to men. A crucial point of departure in women's law is that through researching women's lived realities and crafting situation-specific responses, the position of women in law and in society can be improved. Women's law also emphasizes scrutinizing areas that have not traditionally fallen under legal purview from a gender perspective (Dahl, 1987).

As a jurisprudential field within the eastern and southern African contexts, women's law has its origins in a diploma course initially offered by the University of Oslo in 1987 which was offered until 1989. The primary thrust of the diploma was to provide theoretical and methodological perspectives in women's law, drawing on the Norwegian tradition of women and the law, and combining it with input from scholars from Africa, in particular from Zimbabwe, Mozambique and Tanzania.[2]

The early diploma programmes were also influenced by the research approaches and methodologies that had evolved in the late 1980s through the Women and Law in Southern Africa (WLSA) regional research initiatives and the later the Women and Law in East Africa (WLEA) research group. In 1998 a research methodology and methods book, *Pursuing grounded theory in law: south–north experiences in developing women's law* (Bentzon *et al.*, 1998) was produced. It combined the research experiences from the Institute

> *A crucial point of departure in women's law is that through researching women's lived realities and crafting situation-specific responses, the position of women in law and in society can be improved*

---

[1] See Tove Stang Dahl, *Women's law: an introduction to feminist jurisprudence* (Norwegian University Press, 1987) The Faculty of Law at the University of Oslo was the first to introduce women's law as a specific discipline in 1975.

[2] Among the Norwegian scholars were the late Tove Stang Dahl and Anne Hellum who still teaches at the University of Oslo and who has given invaluable advice, academic support and encouragement to SEARCWL as it has developed its programmes and scholarship. Among the African scholars were Rose Migiro (now Deputy Secretary General of the United Nations) who was then with the University of Dar es Salaam. She contributed as a visiting lecturer, as did Albie Sachs (former judge of the Constitutional Court of South Africa) who was then in exile in Mozambique, working with the Department of Research and Legislation in the Ministry of Justice in Mozambique. Mary Maboreke, now secretary to the African Commission on Human and People's Rights and the first women's law masters student from the University of Zimbabwe also played a key role as a visiting scholar.

of Women's Law (University of Oslo), WLSA and the early programmes at University of Zimbabwe. The book served and its later chapters continue to serve as a key text on the programme.[3]

The initial diploma course that was run in Oslo drew its student body from female lawyers and activists from eastern and southern African countries that were among the main development partners with Norway at that time. These included Botswana, Kenya, Tanzania, Mozambique, Zambia and Zimbabwe. Right at the outset, there was a strong sense that the course should relocate to Africa for it to develop more fully and to take into account the realities and challenges that face different countries on the continent. It moved to the University of Zimbabwe in 1990 as part of an ongoing partnership agreement between the universities that had commenced in 1985. The University of Zimbabwe ran several diploma courses in women's law until 2003 when the programme upgraded to a fully-fledged masters programme in women's law.

Methodologies that exposed the interlink between law and lived realities have made it possible to use the jurisprudence of women's law outside its original Norwegian foundations. It is important to emphasize that the programme is not a transplant; it is an independent and autonomous programme. The programme has responded and continues to respond in its character and shape to continental stimuli as illustrated in the chapters in this book. The book addresses two major aspects of the current Masters in Women's Law development, namely, what has been taught and how it has been taught.

The programme has responded and continues to respond in its character and shape to continental stimuli

Though largely targeted at lawyers, the programme also includes non-lawyers working in the field of women's law thereby emphasizing the value of interdisciplinarity in understanding law in context. It is also open to men who generally constitute about a quarter of the class.

When the masters programme was launched in 2003, it was premised on new second semester optional courses and on establishing a regional network of partner universities and academics. These partners form a core of academic staff with diverse experience and profound regional insights which greatly enrich the teaching on the programme. Thus there are now partnerships not just with the University of Oslo but initially with five universities in the eastern and southern African region, namely, University of Cape Town, Makerere University, Chancellor College, University of Malawi and the Nairobi and Strathmore universities in Kenya. Two more universities have recently become partners – the University of Zambia and the Open University

---

[3] As a teaching tool we now try to restrict students to using chapters 6 –14 of *Pursuing grounded theory* (PGT as it is known). The first six chapters have passed their conceptual sell-by date. Concurrent with the publishing of this new book, those still useful chapters will be available for downloading from the SEARCWL website: www.searcwl.com or www.uz.ac.zw/law/women

of Tanzania. Partnering with comparable law faculties from the region has helped to strengthen the regional nature of the master's programme. Outside official university cooperation, staff are also drawn from other universities in both the north and south.[4]

This book therefore also speaks to the experiences of using faculty across borders and the realities of building academic liaisons among universities in an age that fosters interaction and mutual interdependence in the experiences of humankind.

Students continue to be drawn from countries such as Kenya, Uganda, Tanzania and Ethiopia, in eastern Africa, and Zambia, Malawi, Namibia, Zimbabwe, Lesotho and Mozambique, in southern Africa. In a few instances students have also come from as far afield as Cameroon in West Africa. Its focus on drawing on students from a range of eastern and southern African countries brings a comparative approach to issues and increases the value among students of learning from other jurisdictions with similar problems. The students arrive with pre-existing knowledge and experience of their own legal systems. As such the main thrust is to provide them with insights about the areas of law that are problematic for women and the tools to tackle them.

The structure of the masters programme

The masters programme has three semesters spread over an 18 month period.

In the first semester students focus on women's issues through compulsory core courses. These are 'Theories and perspectives in women's law', 'Research methods and methodologies in women's law' and the 'Practical paper' which includes group field research and a report writing phase. As of 2011, 'Human rights and women' has become a compulsory core course in the first semester. In past years it was a part of a compulsory short module in the theories and perspectives course in the first semester and a more in-depth approach was taken in an optional full course in the second semester.[5] The first semester comprises a combination of participatory lectures, seminars, fieldwork and research methodology practicals. Teaching is normally carried out in thematic or course blocks. Timing of the blocks in the first semester is based on a curve of inculcating understanding and skills as and when they seem to be needed in the intellectual development of the students.

---

[4] At the end of every programme there is a colloquium in which all teaching is reviewed, suggestions for changes in the programme are made and innovations both in teaching and research explored.

[5] As will be seen from the discussion of the optional courses, human rights are an integral component of most optional courses.

In the second semester, students select two optional courses from eight possible choices. These are normally grouped into two groups of four courses from which students select one. The four courses run simultaneously over a six-week period. This period includes a reading week and an exam week. The students then do their second course from the second group of four courses.

The choices of optional courses are:

Block 1
● Women, commerce and law in Africa
● Women, law reform and social justice strategies
● Women and the criminal justice system
● Women, family, social realities and the law

Block 2
● Women, access to resources and law
● Masculinities, gender and the law
● Gender, sexuality and the law
● Women, labour and social security and the law

During the second semester students determine their dissertation topic for the third semester and develop their dissertation proposal and field work methodology and methods under the guidance of SEARCWL supervisors.

In the third semester each student conducts field research and works on a 20,000-25,000 word dissertation in a selected field in human rights and women's law in their own country. The programme remains cognizant of the value of country level experiences as exemplified by the requirement that students do detailed women's law oriented research in their own countries. This also gives students the opportunity to engage with law in the real world and to appreciate its potential as well as its limits for changing women's lives.

Requiring students to do research in their own environments is also crucial to them engaging with their own specific realities. Students are visited for hands-on supervision during the course of their field work. The detailed data analysis and writing up processes are conducted at SEARCWL.

Requiring students to do research in their own environments is also crucial to them engaging with their own specific realities

The structure of the book

The book has four main themes with courses that are offered providing the relevant backdrop for the discussions in the various chapters.

The first theme is 'Laying the conceptual foundations and devising effective legal research skills and methods'. The five chapters under this theme cover the core courses that all students did in the first semester up to 2011. The dissertation that is researched and written up in the third semester is also discussed under this theme.

The second theme, 'Gender analysis of legal frameworks' draws on experiences from four courses that aim to enhance students' skills in gender analysis of legal frameworks. These include the former 'Human rights' course, 'Women and the criminal justice system', 'Women, family, social realities and the law' and 'Women, law reform and social justice strategies'. These chapters bring to the fore issues relevant to teaching critical aspects of women, gender and legal frameworks. These include the need to appreciate the character and nature of human rights and legal frameworks that are core to analyzing their gendered nature. The plurality of factors that shape legal frameworks, such as common law, general law, living and official customary laws and religious laws, provide the context of the teaching experiences under this theme. How gendered inequalities create and perpetuate crime is the backdrop for analyzing the implications for teaching a course on women and the criminal justice system. Courses map the gap between human rights norms and lived realities of women. They also explore how such gaps can be narrowed by different interventions, including law reform, working with custom and human rights interventions. Skills to analyze law from a gendered perspective and the ability to integrate human rights into social and cultural contexts that women as well as men live in, are further honed.

Courses map the gap between human rights norms and lived realities of women

The third theme is that of 'Power relations and transformation'. There are two courses discussed in this theme that surface gendered assumptions, inequalities and the law: 'Gender, law and sexuality', which is covered in two chapters and 'Masculinities, gender and the law'. The critical questions and issues raised in this part include the ways in which specific areas of enquiry such as sexuality and masculinities reflect unequal social and power relations. This theme explores linkages between the law, whether statutory, customary or religious, and hierarchical gender power relations. Also key to the discussions are the ways in which various legal mechanisms, including statutes, conventions and policies, among others, hinder or facilitate social change or transformation. The chapters also discuss examples that can be used to highlight marginalized groups as actors and active agents in transformation processes.

The fourth theme in the book is that of 'Linking legal form to lived realities'. Under this theme courses that examine the experiences of women in plural legal settings by exploring the convergences, divergences and other linkages between law (statutory, religious and customary) and the lived realities of women's lives are discussed. The courses are: 'Women, and access to resources', 'Women, labour and social security' and Women, commerce and law in Africa'. Each chapter documents experiences in addressing, interpreting and conceptualizing plural legal norms and how these impact on women's lives. Each course identifies and analyzes international and national legal norms, customs and semi-autonomous social fields that generate rules for regulating behaviour and, in particular, women's behaviour.

Most significantly, the chapters illustrate how legal form in and of itself gives an incomplete picture of women's experiences of law in their lives. They point to the need to explore the interface between laws, policies and people's lives to excavate lived realities and thus facilitate effective encounters with the legal form. Linking legal form to lived realities is all about fleshing out legal and policy skeletons with people's stories and lives. It enables instructors to interrogate law thoroughly using their lives and those of others.

In the classroom context, this leads to blurring roles between the students and the instructors as experiences are shared and each side takes responsibility for both learning and sharing. In all the chapters, it is clear that the methodological approaches for delivery are expanded and new territories are mapped as the course progresses. With regard to labour, the discourse on what comprises work unmasks the realms of women's engagement in the domestic sphere through care work which in law is 'non-work'. Women's engagement in commerce and search for access to resources is also nuanced by gender roles and definitions of productive and reproductive roles.

...the chapters illustrate how legal form in and of itself gives an incomplete picture of women's experiences of law in their lives

ONE

Laying the conceptual foundations and devising effective legal research skills and methods

1

Pedagogical reflections

from teaching theories and perspectives in women's law across disciplines

Amy Shupikai Tsanga

> *'Women's law knows no formal limitations other than the feminist perspective....No legal issue, in theory, is without relevance for women's law before it has been examined.'*
>
> Stang Dahl, 1987

Part I: Introduction

Locating myself as a feminist teacher

In sharing my experiences on laying conceptual foundations, in this chapter I draw largely on teaching a course on feminist theories and perspectives on law to a multidisciplinary class of students. The student body consists mainly of women and some men[1] who represent different professions. They include legal practitioners, magistrates, prosecutors, social scientists, non-governmental organization activists and the police. They come to the table with different levels of exposure as regards their experiences with feminism and feminist theorizing. What they share in common, however, is a desire to engage with issues of women and the law at a deeper level and in a manner that they can relate to in their practical worlds. This is their reason for pursuing a Masters in Women's Law. Whilst open and eager for new insights, ultimately the guiding issue for them is what is applicable out there. This can make engagement with theory a complex methodological terrain. Theory can seem abstract for some people and it can alienate and frustrate practitioners unless they engage with it in such a way that they can constantly make the connections with their day to day realities.

Theory can seem abstract for some people and it can alienate and frustrate practitioners unless they engage with it in such a way that they can constantly make the connections with their day to day realities.

---

[1] We generally take on between 30 to 36 students for the Masters in Women's law. Of these, on average six to eight are male students.

I am reminded of an incident from my postgraduate student days when a fellow student (a practising lawyer) confronted a professor about his excessively abstract approach to the subject of criminal law. After attending several lectures in the chosen course, in which she could not make sense of what the professor was saying, she bravely went to complain to him. She articulated her standpoint that she had not paid her money to pursue a course which she had deemed from its title, to be most relevant to her professional grounding but which was turning out to be incomprehensible jargon. In my own case, as a lawyer then working with grassroots communities, I knew that I was in an academic setting for the specific purpose of finding new critical insights into law, given my disillusionment with the law, particularly as far as the poor were concerned. Therefore postgraduate students, at least from the practical world, come to academic settings with expectations of what they hope to gain out of their decision to examine any given field in some greater depth. Nebulous academic encounters, I can attest, are certainly not among them – at least for the majority. Hence in this chapter, I mainly seek to share how I have addressed the challenges of grappling with feminist theories with a student body that is grounded in the very real world in terms of their professional encounters with women's issues.

A large part of our standpoints and pedagogical approaches, as feminist teachers or teachers in any field, are no doubt influenced by the academic and practical fountains that we have drunk from. As a teacher of feminist legal theory to postgraduate students from eastern and southern Africa, what has shaped my knowledge and pedagogical approach to this course has been a crucial mixture of working in the real world with grassroots communities on the law, postgraduate training in the north and south with specialist leanings towards women and the law, and a continuing healthy amalgamation of activism and academia in today's world where women's rights are part of the global agenda. I am conscious of the fact that my work in community legal education on leaving law school is what led me to appreciate the need to embrace innovative and participatory approaches to teaching the law.[2] I am also conscious that the content of what we teach must be relevant to the lived realities of the people whom we seek to benefit if we are to achieve impact.

...my work in community legal education on leaving law school is what led me to appreciate the need to embrace innovative and participatory approaches to teaching the law

My interest with interrogating legal frameworks arises from one of those insights that continues to captivate the mind long after it has been digested. I first had an opportunity to study women's law in depth as a postgraduate course at the University of Oslo in 1988. I was particularly struck then by

---

[2] When I worked as a lawyer for a non-governmental organization working with grassroots communities, I also had the opportunity to attend training courses on adult communication methods and running workshops with clearly defined expectation in terms of output objectives. So when I later joined the university as a lecturer, I had shaken myself loose from black-letter lawyering.

Stang Dahl's call to scrutinize all areas of the law to assess their impact on women. I had the honour of being taught by Stang Dahl herself and saw first hand how she, together with Anne Hellum, structured the diploma course we were undertaking to effectively combine the theoretical constructs with women's lived realities. The discussion of women's undervalued work in the home, for example, was neatly followed up with a guest speaker who had been actively involved in a campaign to get the state to recognize women's unpaid work in the home. The grounded research by Anne Hellum and Marianne Fastvold (1988) on money and work in marriage, aptly entitled, 'We have researched to have women's voices heard', was key to appreciating the value of research in understanding the links between law and lived realities. We have expanded women's law by embracing other theoretical standpoints such as human rights and developmental jurisprudence. But even as we have done so, Stang Dahl's assertion that no area is without relevance for women's law until it has been examined, has continued to hold tremendous potential for a thorough analysis of these frameworks beyond that which is generally obvious to the legal eye.[3]

I was particularly struck then by Stang Dahl's call to scrutinize all areas of the law to assess their impact on women.

Dinner with Stang Dahl (left) and Ingunn Birkeland, the wages for housework campaigner (right), Oslo, 1988

[3] The need to interrogate the legal system from the lived realities of men and women was generally not the guiding principle in our learning when I studied law at the University of Zimbabwe between 1983 and 1986. However, to some extent courses such as family law, with regard to divorce, custody rights and guardianship, and succession law in terms of entitlements, particularly under customary law, drew attention to the law's differential treatment of men and women. Most legal courses tended to embrace the law's seeming gender neutrality without analyzing the factors that may contribute to the law taking on different meanings for specific groups of people. A select breed of African scholars who had joined the university at independence also infused marxist perspectives in the subjects that they taught, such as jurisprudence, property law and customary law. It enabled us to appreciate the structural foundations of laws and the crucial factors that are often brought to bear upon the law. Undertaking the postgraduate diploma in women's law presented a shift of seismic proportions in my perspectives on law.

The realities of existing in a time and space where activism on issues of law, gender, human rights and development are central, has added further impetus to the need to constantly interrogate legal frameworks so as to better appreciate the ways in which law can be effectively used to bring about change in the lives of both women and men.

How and what do I conceptualize across similarities and differences? In engaging with theory, how do I keep it real? How do I keep it all relevant to lived realities yet at the same time progressive?

In this chapter, I focus on how I use feminist theories to develop course content that speaks to the realities of mature and experienced students who come from varying legal systems and diverse academic disciplines. How and what do I conceptualize across similarities and differences? In engaging with theory, how do I keep it real? How do I keep it all relevant to lived realities yet at the same time progressive? I also highlight and illustrate some of the teaching methodologies that I adopt that are especially suited to achieving the objectives and outcomes of the course. These centre on developing students' skills in spotting feminist and human rights arguments and being able to use them effectively in researching, writing, analyzing, articulating and advocating for women's rights and empowerment. Given the students' grounding in practical work on women's issues, it is crucial to engage teaching methodologies that maintain a healthy balance between illustrating theory and linking it to lived realities. The combination of the teaching methods used include: tutor-led explanation, discussion and demonstration, largely to clarify concepts; visual imagery; personal study and research by the students; guest lecturers or speakers on selected topics; group discussions; and practical assignments and seminars on selected topics.

The chapter is divided into four main parts. The first part is the introduction. The second part examines the foundations and parameters that provide for our engagement with feminist legal theorizing. These centre on what students need to appreciate at the outset to make their journey with feminist theories smoother. In the third part, I select liberal, radical and existentialist feminism to illustrate how I engage with these in class and to outline their impact on feminist legal reasoning within the African context. I also discuss how these often act in unison to produce interlocking oppressions. I deliberately zero in on only three so as to more effectively illustrate the methodologies in the space available.[4] In the final part, I draw some conclusions about the implications of this course for developing African feminism.

---

[4] In this chapter I have omitted the discussion on marxist and socialist feminism, for example, as the tenets of these are adequately captured in chapter 14. The human rights aspects of the course are addressed in chapter 6.

Part II: Laying the foundations for engaging with feminist legal theorizing

The foundations for moving towards African feminist legal theory

I draw substantially on western feminist thought as a point of departure.[5] One might ask why a course on feminist theory in African contexts takes its point of departure from western feminist theoretical standpoints. Are these not fundamentally elements of a transplant, embodying a reactive as opposed to a proactive approach? There are various reasons why I take the approach of seeing African feminism as part of the global picture.

The first reason is that feminist theory greatly influences feminist legal theory and African legal systems have been shaped by western legal systems due to colonial contact. This is an inescapable fact especially at the level of official state law. A common frame of reference for all the students is that they come from countries where the legal systems have been shaped by Africa's colonial history. Another area of mutual experience for the student body in question is the existence of customary law as a parallel legal system and the challenges that often exist in the development and interpretation of customary law to address contemporary challenges. Whilst family laws under customary law remain highly influential in people's lives, it is largely the content of formal state laws which is used as the yardstick for inroads into customary laws. In this regard, whether taking their cue from English law, common law or Roman Dutch law, substantive aspects of the legal system share important characteristics with western legal systems thereby rendering strands of western feminist thought that impact on legal theory relevant in African settings.

Secondly, most women's rights activism on the continent takes place through donor-funded programmes. While programmes often operate within local contexts, issues have more often than not taken their cue from dominant western ideological trends on the issues in question. For example, the specific interest in interrogating culture and custom has an ideological basis in liberal notions of equality. Moreover, to effectively draw on the concerns of African women, students need to grasp the potential and the limits of those theoretical frameworks that have impacted so strongly on the continent. This does not mean that African feminism is reactive but that unearthing Africa's stifled experiences must of necessity be a process that fully understands what has influenced its current complex realities. Also, given African sensitivities to cultural impositions, it is imperative for informed discussion to know

... to effectively draw on the concerns of African women, students need to grasp the potential and the limits of those theoretical frameworks that have impacted so strongly on the continent ...

---

[5] A starting piece for introducing students to feminist theories is the book by Rosemarie Tong, *Feminist thought: a more comprehensive introduction* (1994).

exactly what is being objected to in western thought. On closer scrutiny, it often emerges that while there are indeed points of difference, there are many more areas of commonality than one might initially acknowledge without an understanding of the content of dominant ideologies. This is especially so in the field of feminist legal theory.

Students as theory builders

Getting students to understand what feminist theory is and why we need it is a key part of my introduction to feminist theorizing in general and feminist legal reasoning in particular. Charlotte Bunch (in Humm, 1992:170-175), for instance, whose arguments I draw from, points out that feminist theory is a study of the situation of women which brings insights from the movement and from female experiences. She argues that theory is not just a body of facts or set of opinions but involves explanations and hypotheses that are based on available knowledge and experience. As the student body comes with lots of experience from different vantage points that contribute to the women's movement, it is particularly significant for them to appreciate, right at the outset, the role that their own insights can play in shaping theory in our settings. If what shapes theories and assumptions are lived realities and experiences then, from the beginning, students are imbued with the empowering notion that their grounded experiences in working with women's issues are crucial in shaping African feminist theory.

As the student body comes with lots of experience from different vantage points that contribute to the women's movement, it is particularly significant for them to appreciate, right at the outset, the role that their own insights can play in shaping theory in our settings.

Their observations matter, especially since, as Bunch argues, thinking about women's oppression forces us to ask critical questions, to examine issues from new angles and to seek explanations of why things work or are not working. Their insights are also important for another reason in the development of African feminism. Because they come from different countries and different societies, this makes it easier to see points of connectedness as well as points of variance in the causal factors for women's situation. Since theory is also a particularly fertile ground for the development of strategies that lie behind why we think women are oppressed, the strategic links between theory and practice need to be understood. In the same vein, theories provide a framework for evaluating whatever strategies may have been adopted and also for shaping new theories when the ones we have worked with have not produced the desired results. It is on this latter aspect that the potential for developing African feminist theory further emerges.

Why question the law: engaging with Stang Dahl

Stang Dahl's justifications for women's law provide an excellent foundation for students with different exposures to understand, in the initial instance, the need to interrogate the law from a gender perspective. The essence of her argument is that 'women's law' is necessary because equal laws in themselves do not preclude discrimination. She opines that men and women follow different paths in life and are affected by laws differently. Taking this point further, she observes that law is one-sided and that it is the male norm which we find in the law, hence the need to take women's lives or a grounded approach as the starting point in our understanding of laws and the different impact that they have on women as compared to men. She summarizes the ultimate purpose of women's law as being to describe, explain and understand the legal position of women with the specific aim of improving the position of women in law and society. Getting students to interrogate these concepts from their own experiences is useful. Questions that inform this dialogue are captured in the box on the right.

ACTIVITY

Lived realities of women and men

● What are your experiences as regards the lives of men and women in your society?

● Are the experiences you describe affected by the law? If so, how? If not, why not?

● Do you think that the 'differences' approach is a useful framework for interrogating the law?

Understanding the meaning of feminist legal reasoning

Feminist legal theories take their cue from the broad range of feminist theories that exist on why women are oppressed. They are not separate from them. Thus, for example, liberal feminist theories have given legal theorists insights into how liberalism impacts on or is reflected in the law. Feminist legal theorizing also emanates from the recognition that traditional legal jurisprudence has generally not looked at law from a feminist perspective. As such, a core aim of feminist legal theory is to cast a feminist eye on law in general. What is critical therefore is that students have the tools for feminist legal reasoning at the outset. As feminist theories are examined, they can use these as a springboard for analyzing the place of law in these theories. Authors such as Dahl (1987) and Barnett (1998:19–27), for example, have offered sound theoretical and practical approaches that can be used to equip students with foundational skills in interrogating legal frameworks, especially from a woman-centred perspective.

… a core aim of feminist legal theory is to cast a feminist eye on law in general

In terms of feminist legal reasoning, Stang Dahl, for instance, suggested a three-pronged feminist perspective to law; namely starting by describing and evaluating existing law – analyzing existing law critically – then moving on to identifying areas of strong legal support, weak legal supports and judicial voids (see the relevant activity in the box on the next page) and lastly discussing

ACTIVITY
Applying feminist perspectives to law

Using Stang Dahl's feminist perspective to law and as far as the legal system in your country is concerned, what would you say are the areas of:

- Strong legal support
- Weak legal support
- Judicial voids

whether and how the body of law ought to be expanded, contracted or replaced (Dahl, 1987). Principally therefore the critical elements in each of these stages are review, critique and reform.

From a legal perspective, we also discuss and analyze the challenges of taking equality with men as the frame of reference. These include, as Judy Fudge (1995:139) has pointed out, the ways in which anti-feminist groups have relied on equality clauses to challenge affirmative action, to win fathers a say in abortion issues, to protect the rights of the foetus, to secure more rights for those accused of sexual offences, to challenge legislation providing benefits to sole support mothers, to challenge child support provisions and to challenge procedures regulating the adoption of children born to single women. In our context, students have also been able to illustrate how Africa's plural legal context often means that semi-autonomous social fields such as culture and religion limit the law's efficacy.

The distinction between positive and negative discrimination is also a necessary tool of analysis in reflecting on the gendered nature of laws

The distinction between positive and negative discrimination is also a necessary tool of analysis in reflecting on the gendered nature of laws, particularly in getting students to realize the basis upon which legislative reforms that seek to improve women's lives are being undertaken. The ways in which women have benefited (positive discrimination) because of their inferior position in society (negative discrimination) are highlighted. Special measures such as quotas are also placed within the framework of positive discrimination.

In a similar vein, in outlining feminist methods for legal reasoning, Hilaire Barnett (1998) zeroes in on four feminist legal methods. The first of these, feminist consciousness-raising, centres on the need to understand the substantive and procedural legal disabilities that women have suffered. Women too need to be aware of their own and others' situations, otherwise there will be no pressure to change. The second method is that of 'asking the woman question' which she describes as demanding explanations for women's exclusion from those who perpetuate it. The third method is looking at law's gendered nature, in particular understanding the gender neutrality of the law and the effect of this on women's lives. An example is gender neutrality in criminal law, especially in matters such as rape and domestic violence. The fourth method, feminist practical reasoning, centres on unearthing juridical techniques employed by the courts. To what extent do these techniques further women's inequality? For example, male reasoning is often said to focus on objectivity, rationality and deductive logic and that if these dominant perspectives are applied, injustice may result. Understanding the meaning of gender bias within the court system is also critical (Wikler, 1993:98).

It is useful to unpack students' own understanding and application of the core concepts of feminist legal reasoning (see box below).

Grasping the significance of interlocking oppressions

An integral feature of this course is getting students to understand the multiple oppressions that are often brought to bear upon African women's lives and that further complicate legal frameworks in addition to gender. In this regard, the course moves beyond a simple gender analysis of legal frameworks, as this is only a part of the broader picture. Poverty, culture, race, patriarchy and class are some of the factors that complicate the lives of women in different settings. It is important for students to understand that women's positioning in society emanates from interlocking factors as opposed to one single explanation.

...women's positioning in society emanates from interlocking factors as opposed to one single explanation

Therefore although each of the feminist theoretical debates we explore contributes its own explanation of why women are oppressed, in the real world the factors more often than not interlock. I generally choose to use videos that are based on women's lived realities as a backdrop for discussing and reflecting more deeply on interlocking oppressions.

If carefully used to draw out questions for discussion, visual imagery can result in powerful perceptions and insights by students often at a very personal level. In terms of my use of visual imagery, the examples of videos or films I use in this chapter are those that have been available to me. I am alive to the reality that there are probably many others in existence that are just as powerful if not more so in portraying multiple oppressions. Consequently, it is the methodology of incorporating visual imagery to unearth or project into interlocking oppressions in a course on feminist jurisprudence that I particularly wish to highlight. An important aim in writing this piece is to generate an exchange of useful information on methods and methodologies including the use and types of visual imagery among those of us engaged in teaching feminism on the continent and beyond.

...visual imagery can result in powerful perceptions and insights by students often at a very personal level

---

SUMMARY

Core elements of feminist legal reasoning

- Feminist consciousness raising in terms of substantive and procedural disabilities faced by women

- Asking the woman question centred on the exclusion of women from those who perpetuate the law

- Understanding the gendered nature of the law

- Feminist practical reasoning in terms of understanding how the courts apply the law, gender bias, and so on

Part III: Turning feminist theories into feminist legal theories

Engaging with liberal feminism and the law

In terms of theories and their linkages to law, it is useful to start with liberal feminism. In liberal theory, women's subordinate position as compared to that of men emanates from customary and legal constraints. Translating to feminist legal theory, the solution for equalizing the rights of women vis à vis men lies predominantly in equalizing the playing field by removing whatever customary and legal constraints stand in the path of equality. In modern liberal philosophy, the notion of equality is not in the abstract sense but in terms of the lived experiences of men and women. Gender justice is a core objective, as is freeing women from oppressive gender roles that have been used as excuses or justifications for giving women a lesser place or no place at all.

Gender justice is a core objective, as is freeing women from oppressive gender roles that have been used as excuses or justifications for giving women a lesser place or no place at all

The ways in which different legal systems exhibit the influence of liberal feminism through the legislative changes that have been made to equalize the rights of men and women is easier for students to grasp once they understand the core tenets of liberal feminism. As already highlighted, particularly striking in the sub-Saharan context is the extent to which the quest for equality for women has largely been influenced by the liberal frameworks that are informed by removing legal constraints to equality whether in official state or customary laws.

I give students activities to enable them to assess how liberalism has impacted in their contexts (see box on page 13).

At the beginning of the course, I find that cultural practices and socialization are isolated in student discussions as being primary among the factors that often contribute to making the arena of rights a complicated space for women. Ogundipe-Leslie (2001) indeed sees one area of African feminist activism as cultural transformation. The challenge, as she sees it, is to decide which cultures must go and which must stay. More critically, who should make those important decisions? Who speaks for whom? How do we go beyond the rural/urban and tradition/modernity dichotomies in advancing African causes?

Among the cultural concerns mentioned is that women generally occupy a subordinate role within families. There are culturally defined roles that generally go with womanhood in different cultural contexts on the continent. Where bride price exchanges hands, it is often regarded as adding to the complications of wifehood for women. The importance placed on marriage is also regarded as playing an important role in women's image of themselves. The values that women are brought up with, within different cultural contexts, are also considered important to understand if we are to appreciate the limits and potential of law in bringing about change. Cultural practices such as early marriage or even giving away young girls in marriage to appease spirits are also seen as problematic. Where female circumcision is practised, it is regarded as a cultural practice that impacts on women's status in society. It is also seen as one through which women may be unwittingly perpetuating the male values of controlling women's sexuality since the women carry out the practice as part of their socialization.

I have also found, for instance, that students understand the influence of liberal feminism and the quest for equality, particularly in the arena of constitutionalism and human rights activism as undertaken by non-governmental organizations in Africa. There is an appreciation of the fundamental influence of liberal feminism in the engagement with customary law as evidenced by the way law reform as well as litigation have often been used to challenge customary laws that discriminate against women.

...students understand the influence of liberal feminism and the quest for equality

The ways in which women lawyers' organizations in particular have used advocacy for legislative and policy reforms in areas such as proprietary rights in marriage, guardianship rights, inheritance rights and access to land, to mention a few, as well as in test case litigation, are seen by students as evidence of the deep permeability of liberal feminist influences in African legal settings. These activities are also seen as examples of feminist consciousness raising on gaps in the substance and application of the law. The fact that there are a significant number of organizations on the continent concerned with women's awareness of their rights is seen as yet another indicator of liberal feminist influence on the continent.

ACTIVITY

Unearthing the influence of liberal feminism in the African context

Students are divided into country groups so as to more accurately reflect on and share their country's experiences vis à vis the constraints that women encounter. Questions that are used to analyze each country's experiences with liberal feminism include:

- What are the facts on the ground regarding women's customary and legal situation?

- Given liberal feminism's focus on removing customary and legal constraints that impede women's rights, is there any evidence of this influence in the way your country has sought to address women's situation? If so, how?

- From your observation, what other factors have influenced the way women's issues have been dealt with in your country?

The exercise raises students' feminist consciousness and awareness of problems that women suffer. It also enables them to appreciate gaps in the law and how they can be addressed.

...despite the vigorous liberal agenda that has manifested itself on the continent, the lives of African women ... cannot change for the better overnight.

There is also an understanding that, despite the vigorous liberal agenda that has manifested itself on the continent, the lives of African women, like the lives of women elsewhere, cannot change for the better overnight. It is in this regard that students often see the significance of the influence of other feminist theories, such as those dealing with undervaluing women's work and the concept of women as the 'other', as adding on to the tapestry of explanations in terms of women's continued subordinate status.

Attractive and useful as liberal feminist concepts are to understanding women's position in law and in society, I am also alive to the need for students to appreciate at the very onset, as a tool to legal analysis, the issue of diversity among women's experiences so as not to reduce women to a monolithic group. In this regard we explore the arguments made by Deborah Rhode (1995:61–72), for instance, that the differences among women brought on by race, class, age, ethnicity and sexual orientation need to be taken into account so as to appreciate diversity as well as commonalities among women.

I have also used the article by Obioma Nnmaemeka (2004:357-383), 'Nego-feminism: theorizing, practising and pruning Africa's way', in terms of unearthing key debates on how we can usefully build theories on African 'feminisms' in ways that are relevant, locally driven and geared towards social change. For example, she reflects on the concept of nego-feminism which she describes as a 'concept of negotiation or no ego feminism' as a term that names African feminism (2004:361). She talks of shared values, attitudes and institutions that can be used as organizing principles in talking about Africa. She also highlights the need to build on the indigenous in constructing African feminist theory and the need to be driven by theoretical and practical discourses that will bring about social change, as opposed to being lured by their attractiveness on the scale of sophistication. She emphasizes that the indigenous is not the traditional but whatever people consider important in their lives. Developmental change should be linked to values, interests and aspirations. She argues that our theory is in 'narrative forms, in the stories we create, in the riddles and proverbs, in the play with language, since dynamic rather than fixed ideas seem more to our liking' (Nnmaemeka, 2004: 365). Her argument is that it is not to western feminism that we should look in developing African feminism but the African environment itself. Since this course is ultimately about the impact of feminist theory in the legal arena, the reasons for engaging with western feminist theories has already been explained. Nonetheless, the practical implications of these arguments are explored with the students.

Using visual media to illustrate liberal feminism

I have made use of visual media to illustrate liberal feminism at play within the African context. The video, *A woman's place*, is one I use to examine questions of gender egalitarianism or more appropriately the lack thereof in legal frameworks, as well as to illustrate how interlocking oppressions may affect the efficacy of laws. It discusses distinct legal issues such as inheritance, marriage and divorce and domestic violence using the experiences from three countries, namely South Africa, India and the United States. Each story focuses on a woman in the legal profession who is exploring strategies for using the law to create meaningful change for women in their communities. The overall point of departure of this hour-long video is that social and political movements all over the world have created legal equality between men and women but it asks the crucial question whether this is translated to *de facto* as opposed to *de jure* equality in the real world.

What I find particularly appealing about this video as a tool for interrogating legal frameworks, is that it goes beyond changing the laws, to the complex terrain of attitudes to the law and in particular attitudes of the legal system to women. The video can be used in whole or in part. I have chosen to use it for different themes to illustrate theoretical frameworks more clearly. For example, under liberal feminism, the first case study from the video, which is on inheritance, is ideal for examining the gap between constitutional ideals and grounded realities. Centred on South Africa's post-apartheid constitution and its emphasis on equality, the case study focuses on the real-life experience of a magistrate in the remote rural areas of South Africa who struggles to get people to understand why some of their traditions and customary ways of doing things are being challenged by concepts in the new constitution.

This example is extremely powerful in terms of illustrating the limits of liberal feminism and the gap that often exists between law and the people. From a perspective of feminist legal reasoning, it is also useful to project into the substantive and procedural challenges that women encounter with the law. It also helps in understanding how the exclusion of women from inheritance is framed by those who exclude them. What emerges as a core theme for further exploration is that steps in getting people to see the positive elements of new legislation that seek to level the playing field are incremental and require communication, participation, ongoing dialogue and persuasion.

> VIDEO
> **A woman's place**
>
>
>
> © A Woman's Place
>
> In the episode on 'law and custom', Tandaswa Ndita, a magistrate (now a judge) in rural South Africa, uses the new constitution with its guarantee of equal rights for all to combat traditional laws declaring all women perpetual legal minors. Her partnership with community leaders and tribal chiefs slowly changes attitudes about women's right to inherit property.

...getting people to see the positive elements of new legislation that seek to level the playing field are incremental and require communication, participation, ongoing dialogue and persuasion

Using a feature film for a more detailed exercise:
The example of Neria

I have used the Zimbabwean film, *Neria*, on inheritance to illustrate the challenges that are presented for women in Africa who exist in plural legal contexts (see below). As it is a full feature film, I tend to make it an afternoon activity. In addition, I use it to illustrate how film can be a tool for communicating not just legal messages but dialoguing important theoretical foundations concerning women's issues. The film depicts one woman's struggle in challenging her brother-in-law who dispossessed her and her two children of property after the husband's death. It is a powerful film which forces students to address critical issues such as whose interests are being served by customs that exclude, rather than include, on gendered lines.

© Media for Development Trust

The film was also available with a special training pack designed for community workshops on inheritance rights

FILM ANALYSIS

Analysis framework for the film *Neria*

Awareness

● What awareness did you get from the film concerning inheritance under customary law?

● What did you consider to be the most important messages conveyed by the film?

Knowledge

● What knowledge have you acquired about women's rights or women's struggles from the film?

● How effective was the film as a tool for imparting knowledge about legal issues?

● Is film a useful tool for creating legal awareness?

● What were the strengths?

● What were the weaknesses?

Attitudes

● From the film what attitudes surrounding the issue of inheritance did you consider most problematic and which need to be addressed?

Behaviours

● What concrete steps that give rise to new behaviour need to be taken to address some of the issues that emerge from the film?

FILMS

Other recent films and documentaries that speak to the experiences of women in Africa and make for excellent critical feminist dialogue include:

1   *The witches of Gambaga* by Yaba Badoe about a community of outlaw women in Ghana accused of being witches (documentary, 2010)

2   *The greatest silence: rape in the Congo* by Lisa F. Jackson. This documentary uncovers women's experiences of sexual violence as a weapon of conflict in the Democratic Republic of Congo (documentary: 76 minutes, 2007)

3   *I want a wedding dress* by Tsitsi Dangarembga, a story addressing multiple themes of marriage, poverty, infidelity, cross generational relationships and sexual networks in the era of HIV/AIDS (film, 2010)

(As some of these are fairly long they can be used for film evenings or shown when convenient and then aspects discussed in class).

In using visual media such as video or film to interrogate legal frameworks, it is helpful to have a set of questions for students to bear in mind as they watch the video which makes for more meaningful dialogue and sharing of perceptions after the viewing. These centre on issues of awareness, knowledge, attitudes and behaviours.

Neria raises core issues for analysis from a feminist perspective. These include issues such as: culture as both a negative and positive force for women in Africa; the meaning of empowerment for women; male dominance in decision making and the range of masculinities depicted in the film; and the implications for behavioural change.

Interrogating legal frameworks through student voices and insights

I have used student-led lunch-time seminars as a practical approach to analyzing legal frameworks and giving voice to their experiences within their own cultural and legal contexts. The topics that students have discussed are shown as an appendix to this chapter. These seminars help to shape critical dialogue on feminist issues within the continent. Students work in country teams of three students on a topic that allows them to assess the theoretical frameworks and legal, gender and other dynamics at play. It is crucial that the topics deal with concerns that are relevant to the realities of women and so, in selecting the topics, I have often relied on co-lecturers in the different countries to send me topics that they consider important. In some cases these topics later go on to form deeper dissertation topics for some of the students.

Engaging with radical feminism

Interrogating how legal frameworks within the African context address important gendered issues makes a good entry point. We look at issues such as women's control of their own sexuality in matters like abortion, access to contraceptives, rape and marital rape, and criminalization of willful transmission of HIV/AIDS, with an understanding of the feminist positions on sex and sexuality, as well as on motherhood.

A common starting point with radical feminism is the belief that it is the patriarchal system that oppresses women. Patriarchal control is seen as being particularly evident in culture, religion and control of women's sexuality. With specific reference to matters such as abortion, sterilization, hysterectomies, contraceptives and infertility treatment, these are all seen as greatly influenced by patriarchal control of women's sexuality. Men, rather than society or conditions, have forced women into oppressive gender roles and sexual behaviour. Radical feminists argue that men assert themselves supported by customs and laws denied to women, and that men have physical power which equals power over others. As such, from a radical feminist perspective, the task of feminist analysis is to unravel women's subordination and lack of power. In so far as motherhood is concerned, a radical feminist view is that no matter how much educational, legal and political equality women achieve and no matter how many women enter public industry, nothing fundamental will change for women as long as biological reproduction remains the rule rather than the exception.

... from a radical feminist perspective, the task of feminist analysis is to unravel women's subordination and lack of power

Most students are married with families and have a lot to share in terms of their perceptions of motherhood and sexuality. Most also regard religion as an important influence in their lives. Consequently they are somewhat jarred by those feminist notions that regard motherhood as not without its significant problems for women and that locate liberatory potential for women beyond heterosexuality. Their value systems are challenged by such feminist theories on gender and sexuality. While a few are sufficiently curious to pursue the subject matter further in a more detailed optional course in the second semester, many continue to find comfort in more conservative feminist analyses of legal frameworks. They are able to see the ways in which the laws in different countries clearly control women's sexuality through, for example, the non-recognition of marital rape in some jurisdictions, limited abortion laws that sideline women's experiences and the pervasiveness of domestic violence.

To the extent that radical feminism challenges patriarchy and control of women's sexuality, students have been able to engage with the ways religion and culture can be implicated in this. For example, some students have discussed how and whether practices such as widow cleansing and female genital mutilation are indeed examples of control of women's sexuality. This analysis on patriarchy and control of women and their bodies has also been brought to bear in the light of alarmingly growing incidences of practices such as rape, child abuse, sexual harassment and violence against women. The reality of the existence of specific organizations within some African countries that deal with violence against women and provide shelter, further bolsters the view that issues around patriarchy and control are crucial to understanding women's experiences in this light.

Another legal area where radical feminism on sex and sexuality has been seen to offer useful insights into the situation of African women is that of abortion. The position in many of the countries is that of limited abortion laws against a stark reality of illegal abortions that often take their toll on women's lives. Given the high prevalence rate of HIV/AIDS in sub-Saharan Africa, students consider women's control of their sexuality increasingly important, albeit not with the radicalism that western philosophies of feminism use to project the issue. The ways in which different countries have introduced laws to address wilful transmission of HIV, as well as laws on marital rape, makes for useful engagement on this topic.

The position in many of the countries is that of limited abortion laws against a stark reality of illegal abortions that often take their toll on women's lives

I have also used the poem 'Try again' by Chiedza Musengezi (see the full text on pages 20 and 21) to address the issue of interlocking oppressions, especially when it comes to women's control of their own sexuality and their freedom to decide on the number and spacing of their children. In a context where many of the students are wont to see child bearing as a natural and inevitable consequence and expectation of marriage in African societies, the poem's storytelling vividly illustrates the problematic context within which some of these expectations arise. In terms of using storytelling, for example, Ogundipe-Leslie highlights the need to look for African women's voices in sites (largely rural) that embody their daily lives. As she puts it:

> 'We must look for them in places such as kitchens, watering sites, kinship gatherings; women's political and commercial spaces where women speak often in the absence of men.'

So how do I use this non-legal piece to interrogate and unearth interlocking oppressions when it comes to women's control of their sexuality? Given the multidisciplinary nature of the class, I find the piece an invaluable entry point into women's reproductive rights and a nuanced discussion of who controls those rights within cultural contexts. Emphasizing the right of women to choose the number and spacing of their children and to be equal in marriage is more easily said than done, especially in the context where semi-autonomous social fields have gravitas. The poem also illustrates that culture is not static. Here the woman, though married in a patrilineal context, goes away with her children and she is not challenged. But her going away with the children brings in the issue of whether her husband will contribute to their support and leads us to interrogate women's experiences with maintenance claims in different legal contexts.

Try again

I became pregnant of the first of marriage (sic)
and I gave birth to a baby girl
They danced and ululated
They sang: 'You gave us back our Mother'
Who died when we were young
So they named her after Mother – Sekai (*to laugh at*)
Sekai took first faltering steps
and they asked:
'What are you waiting for?
For your baby to tassle like maturing maize?'
I plucked the breast out of her mouth
and carried another in my womb*

This time they wanted a boy
Who could use his sister's dowry to marry
But another girl came
They named her Hazvineyi (*It does not matter*)
It didn't matter
They would let me try again

When Hazvineyi's gums whitened with teeth
The breast was yanked out of her mouth
Within a month
I was pregnant again
The baby inside disliked the Father
So they said 'It must be a boy'
Extender of the clan

My birth pangs started
The baby arrived with clenched little fists
and a furrowed brow
She felt their cold touch on her skin
When they cradled her in their hands
She was greeted with grunts and sighs
They named her Tryagain

When Tryagain began to smile
Auntie brought me herbal medicine
To turn my womb into a boy's room
Had herbal medicine porridge
Every morning, noon and evening
A chubby baby girl arrived
I named her Hamunyari (*You are not ashamed*)

*   The meanings of the names that have been put in brackets are translations so as to
    give the reader an overview of the gender dimensions of naming.

She unleashed their tongues
'She'll only take medicine sweet on the tongue'
Must be watched like a child when she takes it
She hates traditional medicine
She spits out the herbs
I drank every drop
It stopped my lunar cycle

My womb grew big as a mountain
Felt like I was carrying a calf
The baby kicked and pushed hard
But the birth canal was not big enough
They had to cut me open

Out came a boy
They named him after his father – Chamboko (*beating stick*)
Six months passed
Chamboko could not sit up or smile
Followed by six years of mute drooling
I travelled the entire country
I searched everywhere for help
The medical doctors, healer and shaman
Nothing changed
They all pointed at me
'You're a witch'
You don't want the clan to grow
Outsider, pack your bags and leave
Cast out the evil spirit

My tongue was unglued
I answered back:
'Yes! I will right away
I can't meet your huge expectations:'

I headed home to my parents'
With my baby strapped on my back
My suitcase balancing on my head
and a long line travelling behind me
Me,
   Sekai, (*to laugh at*)
    Hazvineyi, (*it does not matter*)
     Tryagain,
      Hamunyari (*you are not ashamed*)
       Chamboko (*beating stick*)

Chiedza Musengezi

ACTIVITY
Key questions
in analyzing the poem

- What do you learn about women's sexuality from the poem?
- What are the implications that flow from what you observe?
  - Social implications
  - Legal implications
  - Implications for women's empowerment

Source: *Women Plus Magazine* 3 (2)May-July 1998, Zimbabwe Women's Resource Centre and Network

Giving girls names that express displeasure, suffering or disdain is fairly common in many African cultures

I am also interested in discussing how women are often the active custodians of cultural expectations and practices. Thus what issues appear to interlock in shaping this woman's life are expectations that having married she should bear boy children; emphasis that she is an outsider whose role is to extend the clan on marriage, thereby bringing to the fore an example of 'otherness'; and expectations that she is not the one who controls her own fertility or who decides on the number and spacing of her children. The issue of naming is also important. Giving girls names that express displeasure, suffering or disdain is fairly common in many African cultures. Boys on the other hand are often given celebratory names or ones that emphasize power, control and authority as was indeed the case in the poem. I do not seek to use the examples in this poem as standing for all African women's experience with motherhood but rather as one of the many strands regarding their experiences with motherhood. I find the poem useful in its realism and in its portrayal of both the joys and pain of African motherhood.

I have also examined violence against women as an example of understanding patriarchal control. For grounded experiences I have found it useful to bring in a guest lecturer from a non-governmental organization, Musasa Project, which deals with the issue of violence against women.

Part IV: Engaging with existentialist feminism

To the outside world, African women's experiences are too often easily reduced to cultural backwardness, customs, religion and a seemingly heightened degree of patriarchal manifestations compared to experiences in other parts of the globe. Even within cross-cultural communities at the country level, the tendency is to assume that 'African' women are worse off than everyone else. Simone de Beauvoir's notion of women as the 'other' or existentialist feminism is particularly interesting to engage with. It offers insights into the relations between men and women that cut across cultural divides and gives a more nuanced explanation of women's position beyond culture, custom, religion or patriarchy.

de Beauvoir argues that part of the problem is that women have internalized the view of men as the essential in society and their own position as inessential

At the core of existentialist feminism as espoused by de Beauvoir is that women are the second sex: women are oppressed because 'man' has declared himself the self and declared 'woman' the other. She argues that part of the problem is that women have internalized the view of men as the essential in society and their own position as inessential. Added to this, when women try to rid themselves of this position in society, there is a backlash. This explains to a large measure the resistance in society to women's equality. While de Beauvoir singles out two primary roles that she sees as creating or contributing to the 'otherness' of women, namely wifing and motherhood,

CASES

Exploring otherness in case law

All the cases below make for excellent review of the concept of 'otherness' in the African context. They can also be used to project into various feminist theoretical standpoints. For example, customary or legal constraints are at the heart of each case in contributing to women's oppression. Women's work, proprietary rights, women's sexuality, women's empowerment, and so forth, are also underlying themes in these cases. They can be used with the necessary emphasis and to show how feminist theories in fact interlock to provide explanations for women's oppression.

- *Katekwe v Muchabaiwa* (Zimbabwe)

  To what extent is the concept of payment of seduction damages an example of women's 'otherness'?

- *Magaya v Magaya* (Zimbabwe)

  How are the arguments presented in this case for the exclusion of women from inheritance a reflection of 'otherness'?

- *Wambui Otieno v. Joash O. Ochieng* (Kenya)

  What do we glean from this case about the difficulties of using the law to challenge women's 'otherness'?

- *Bhe v Magistrate of Khayelitsha* (South Africa)

  What prospects do constitutionalism and human rights have for challenging women's 'otherness'?

- *Unity Dow* (Botswana)

  The meaning of citizenship?

Overall question for analysis

- Is customary law out of tune and oppressive to women when it comes to its standpoints on each of the issues at stake in the above cases?

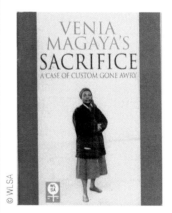

Women and Law in Southern Africa Research and Educational Trust published a book about the Magaya case in 2001

these are clearly debatable within different contexts. In her view the institution of marriage destroys spontaneity between lovers in that feelings are translated into mandatory duties and shrilly asserted rights. Motherhood is also regarded as putting endless demands on women to be at the service of their children.

Of interest in terms of engagement are the ways that de Beauvoir suggests for overcoming 'otherness' as they offer strategies to tackle gendered frameworks outside the law. These include urging women to engage in paid work as this opens up possibilities for women, especially economic freedom, and also encourages women to actively contribute to shaping the world through intellectual engagement in the broad sense of the word. In other words, working towards social transformation is seen as key. From a legal perspective, we often put practices such as polygamy, women's lack of guardianship rights and property rights under the existentialist feminist spotlight of 'otherness'.

From a legal perspective, we often put practices such as polygamy, women's lack of guardianship rights and property rights under the existentialist feminist spotlight of 'otherness'

While students accept that the sum total of the different feminist perspectives weaves a complex mosaic in understanding the oppression of African women, particularly in the field of women and the law, it is perhaps the concept of 'otherness' that most see as directly relevant to African women's lived realities. I suspect that this is because the concept goes beyond legal explanations and has a way of 'gelling' a number of causal factors, such as patriarchy, power and culture under this web of 'otherness'.[6]

Putting it all together: Illustrating interlocking oppressions

I have found the video *Stolen childhood* most apt in terms of visually illustrating the interlocks in a woman's life that emanate from all the theoretical standpoints that we discuss. Set in Ethiopia, *Stolen childhood* is a story of how an eight year old girl, Kebebesh, is married off to an old man because the family is poor. Her parents see marriage as the only option for her. Unable to bear the

VIDEO EXERCISE
Key questions used to discuss *Stolen childhood*

- What factors emerge as interlocking to produce Kebebesh's experiences with life?
- Can you relate her experiences to different feminist theoretical standpoints?
- Are there areas of her experiences to which we can apply feminist legal reasoning?
- In your view what are the overall implications of Kebebesh's experiences for women's equality?

[6] The second case study in the *A woman's place video* is from India and is useful for understanding women's 'otherness' in society.

constraints of child marriage, she ultimately escapes her misery and heads for the city where she finds work as a domestic worker. She is raped by a tenant at the house where she was staying and working as a domestic worker. No action is taken against him. Instead she is chased away and is taken in by a bar owner to work as a barmaid. Her misery finds no respite as her female boss has no sympathy for her situation, requiring her to resume work on the day that she gives birth. She leaves this job in search of a better life and works the streets as a prostitute, exposing herself to physical and mental dangers.

I have used the video to illustrate legal issues of early marriage, the undervaluing of women's work, rape, prostitution and HIV/AIDS. Equally important from a social context, I have used the video to illustrate multiple and interlocking oppressions of poverty, class and patriarchy and culture as they play themselves out in the life of one woman. I do not think these interlocking oppressions would be as evident if I relied on written texts or discussions alone. I ask students to tease out for themselves what they see emerging as interlocking oppressions and we discuss these in some detail. Students clearly find connections with lived realities in the use of a video that addresses real African issues.

Conclusion

The course has provided a valuable opportunity to more fully assess, from a comparative African perspective, what the influences on feminist legal theories have been on the continent. For historical legal reasons, as well as the fact that there are problems that affect all women regardless of where they are, common concerns and overlaps have been identified within western feminist theoretical standpoints. Yet our conversations have also revealed differences that emanate from social, cultural, political and economic contexts. More poignant has been the unearthing of the pervasiveness of legal pluralism and how African feminist legal theory cannot be examined apart from the complexities brought on by this reality.

When it comes to challenges emanating from economic and political realities in women's struggles on the continent, our dialogue also points to the long overdue reshaping of the engagement between southern and northern feminists in ways that go beyond common struggles. Africa's problems are both internal and external to itself. From an internal perspective we have explored how age, location, class and patriarchy impact on women's struggles in our context. We have also examined the opportunities that exist within each society for creating alternative realities. Yet as we have explored the complex challenges that relate to women's realization of their rights from both a theoretical and practical standpoint, it has also become clearer that the shaping of feminist legal theory in Africa is not separate from global

…as we have explored the complex challenges that relate to women's realization of their rights … it has also become clearer that the shaping of feminist legal theory in Africa is not separate from global economic realities

Law alone, even with its pluralist accommodations, falls far short of providing an answer to the challenges

economic realities. Strengthening the development of feminism in Africa must of necessity be multidisciplinary and multisectoral and be rooted in global realities. Law alone, even with its pluralist accommodations, falls far short of providing an answer to the challenges. In fact in many instances law can take its cue from these realities.

From the perspective of the student body, the course has allowed them to appreciate the broader theoretical contexts of the world that women live in. It has provided an underlying core for dissertation topics that range from reproductive and health rights issues and gender violence concerns to family law related matters, to mention only a few. Indeed in some cases students have zeroed in more directly on analyzing the feminist theoretical question underlying women's activism on the continent.[7] These dissertations stand to play a role in our deeper formulation of feminist legal theory on the continent. There is clearly merit in using them as a basis for deeper theoretical engagements.

---

[7] For example, Joyce Siveregi's 'A critical analysis of the pursuit of the feminist agenda through the experiences of women's legal rights organizations in Zimbabwe' (2006).

Bibliography

Barnett H. (1998) *Introduction to feminist jurisprudence*, Cavendish Publishers, London.

Beauvoir S. de (1949, reprinted 1997) *The second sex*, Vintage, London.

Bhavnani K. (ed) (2001) *Feminism and race*, Oxford University Press, Oxford.

Bryson V. (1999) *Feminist debates: issues of theory and political practice*, Macmillan, London.

Bunch C. (1992) 'Not by degrees: feminist theory and education', in M. Humm (ed) *Feminisms: a reader*, Harvester Wheatsheaf, New York

Conaghan J. (1995) 'The invisibility of women in labour law: gender neutrality in model building', in F. E. Olsen (ed) *Feminist legal theory 11: positioning feminist theory within the law*, New York University Press, New York.

Dahl S.T. (1987) *An introduction to women's law*, Norwegian University Press, Oslo.

Fudge J. (1995) 'The effect of entrenching a Bill of Rights upon political discourse: feminist demands and sexual violence in Canada', in F. E. Olsen (ed) *Feminist legal theory 11: positioning feminist theory within the law* New York University Press, New York.

Hellum A. and M. Fastvold (1988) 'We have researched to have women's voices heard', in M. Fastvold and A. Hellum (eds), *Money and work in marriage*, Studies in Women's Law No. 26, University of Oslo, Oslo.

Humm M. (ed) (1992) *Feminisms: a reader*, Harvester Wheatsheaf, New York.

Mohanty C. (1988) 'Under western eyes: feminist scholarship and colonial discourses', *Feminist Review* 30 1988

Nnameka O. (2004) 'Nego-feminism: theorizing, practising and pruning Africa's way in signs', *Journal of Women in Culture and Society* 29(2):357–383 Winter 2004.

Ogundipe-Leslie M. (2001) 'Moving the mountains: making the links', in K. Bhavnani (ed) *Feminism and race*, Oxford University Press, Oxford.

Olsen F.E. (ed) (1995) *Feminist legal theory 11: positioning feminist theory within the law*, New York University Press, New York.

Rhode D.L. (1995) 'The woman's point of view', *Journal of Legal Education*, reproduced in F.E. Olsen *Feminist legal theory 11: positioning feminist theory within the law*, New York University Press, New York.

Schuler M. (1986) *Empowerment and the law*, OEF International, Washington.

Siveregi J. (2006) 'A critical analysis of the pursuit of the feminist agenda through the experiences of women's rights organizations in Zimbabwe', masters dissertation, SEARCWL, UZ, Harare.

Tong R. (1994) *Feminist thought: a comprehensive guide*, Routledge, London.

Wikler N. (1993) 'Exclusion of women from justice: emerging strategies for reform', in K. Mahoney and P. Mahoney (eds) *Human rights in the twenty-first century: a global challenge*, Martinus Nijhoff Publishers, Dordrecht.

Appendix: Student lunchtime seminar topics

TABLE 1: Topics addressed in country groups by 2005 class

Country	Topic
Kenya	The impact of traditional/religious institutions on gender relations and gender discriminative practices and scope for changing the negative trends: A case study of select pastoral communities in Kenya
Uganda	Gender analysis of acid throwing attacks in Uganda or Gender implications of introducing a dress code at Makerere University
Malawi	'I do' means always available for sex: A critique of the decision by the Malawi Law Commission not to recognize rape in marriage. Advocating for reform: Domestic violence in Malawi and the Domestic Violence Bill. Does matrilinity make a difference to women's rights under customary laws? Some select examples from Malawi.
Tanzania	Law as a vehicle for gender inequality: Girl child marriages in Tanzania
Zambia	An analysis of the efficacy of Zambia's law of inheritance under customary law: Has law reform stimulated change in practices? Women's access to health care in Zambia: What are the issues at stake?
Zimbabwe	Revisiting motherhood: A critical analysis of baby snatching incidents in Zimbabwe Women's own political parties? Should we be rethinking our terms of engagement in governance? Should the laws of witchcraft be tightened or loosened? A gendered analysis of the role of belief systems in civil and criminal disputes in Zimbabwe. Analyzing the increase in gender violence in Zimbabwe: A backlash against women's equality?

TABLE 2: Topics addressed in country groups by 2007 class

Country	Topic
Uganda	A critical analysis of the Sexual Offences Bill in Uganda or Exclusion of sexual orientation from the recently passed Equal Opportunities Law
Tanzania	A critical analysis of the call for the recognition of Kadhi's courts in Tanzania as part of the justice system vis à vis the rights of women Changing inheritance laws in a plural legal context: The challenges facing Tanzania
Zimbabwe	Engaging with customary law courts in improving access to justice for women in Zimbabwe: Opportunities and challenges A gendered analysis of key messages in anti-HIV/AIDS campaigns in Zimbabwe The women's question in transitional justice processes: An analysis of democratic politics in Zimbabwe.
Zambia	The role of the police in protecting women's rights in Zambia: An analysis of strengths, constraints and challenges
Kenya	An analysis of Kenya's rejected draft constitution vis à vis the rights of women: Lessons gleaned in shaping the way forward.
Malawi	Emerging experiences with the Domestic Violence Act in Malawi.
Kenya & Mozambique	A comparative analysis of the role of the women's movement in Kenya and Mozambique in bringing about change

2

Breaking the mould
Research methodologies and methods

Julie Stewart

New approaches need transformed students

The first two first semester courses, 'Theories and perspectives in women's law' and 'Research methodologies and methods in women's law,'[1] are designed to actively and beneficially transform students' approaches to women's issues and women's engagement with law and human rights. These two courses, with the practical course, form the platform for the rest of the programme. The approaches in these courses are designed to develop the critical analysis and research capacities of students on the programme. In this chapter I describe and discuss the evolving role and content of the research methodologies and methods[2] course in shaping the intellectual provenance in which the Masters in Women's Law programme is conducted.[3]

In the first semester of the programme, the aim is to remould students from a wide spectrum of professional backgrounds – from orthodox lawyers and legal practitioners or users of the law in the case of 'un-lawyers' – into critical evaluators of the nature and form of law in its myriad manifestations. 'Un-lawyer' is a term coined within the programme to distinguish those who do not have legal training from those who do – non-lawyer seems a rather pejorative term implying a 'lack' in some form or other. Whereas 'un-lawyer' involves an appreciation of someone not being a lawyer; but being competent in other areas. It is extremely important in the context of the programme to stress that the object is not to turn un-lawyers into lawyers but to enhance their capacity

...we seek to remould students from a wide spectrum of professional backgrounds, from orthodox lawyers and legal practitioners or users of the law in the case of un-lawyers, to critical evaluators of the nature and form of law in its myriad manifestations

---

[1] As discussed in the description of the programme these two courses run parallel for the first ten weeks of the course, with the practical course intervening on issues of research design towards the end of the fifth week.

[2] Methods are dealt with in the discussion of the practical course where they are eventually employed.

[3] This chapter also needs to be read with chapter 3 on African philosophy and religion and with the chapter on the practical course and the dissertation.

> **EXAMPLE**
>
> **The WLSA experience**
>
> A good example of this symbiosis of lawyers and un-lawyers is the Women and Law in Southern Africa (Research Trust) (WLSA) work. WLSA is a research organization based in southern Africa that at its outset combined the skills of lawyers and social scientists to undertake local research into the experiences of women with the law in all its pluralities.
>
> Lawyers picked up and were expressly taught social research skills by their social science colleagues and social scientists gleaned how to use and embrace aspects of the law in their work.

to engage with lawyers, understand the potential of law and thus to be able to act largely as critical outside end-users of law as a strategy.

Conversely, lawyers are not expected to displace social scientists but to engage with them and see them as potential partners at a variety of levels – producing mutual professional respect, collaboration and cooperation (see box for WLSA example).

The intention is to make them creative and adept users of innovative legal arguments and insights into the law and its possibilities for improving the lot of women. The hope is that they graduate as informed and effective activists in creating and implementing women-specific rights as human rights and human rights as women's rights. To reach this state, transformative interventions have to be employed in the classroom and in group and individual exercises undertaken by students.

Knowledge: whose knowledge?

There is another challenge that must be met and that is how to conceptualize and handle 'knowledge' and 'sources of knowledge' in the programme. Legal, social and scientific knowledge as 'western' sourced and derived tends to be academically privileged, as is western derived religious and ethical knowledge. Human rights standards are assumed to be western in their content and derivation. The methodology course on the programme, as with the theory course, aims to destabilize this view of knowledge and its legitimate sources. The challenge is not to the knowledge itself but to its privileging and hegemony. The course also seeks to provide the tools that prompt a revisiting and review of indigenous knowledge and indigenous knowledge systems. Although these skills are honed and tested mainly in the other courses.

The course also seeks to provide the tools that prompt a revisiting and review of indigenous knowledge and indigenous knowledge systems

One significant aspect of the methodology course, intertwined with the practical course in the first semester, is demonstrating how to recognize and explore the significance of these systems and their influences. Showing how such influences in people's lives contribute to the understanding of women's needs is a critical component of the skills students need to acquire. There is similar emphasis on ascertaining women's situations and how women use and interact with the law. Students need to be able to explore, interrogate and assess indigenous knowledge and its sources, especially knowledge that is female sex and gender based and derived as these sites of knowledge tend to be even more likely to be dismissed as legitimate sources than those emanating from males.

Students need to be able to investigate women's rights and entitlements under a variety of normative orders. They need to be able to position themselves between seemingly competing orders and make as unbiased an assessment as possible of antagonistic or complementary values that emerge. Juxtaposing western normative values with local or indigenous values should create an opportunity to assess their core commonalities and complementarities. Carrying out such exercises, as discussed later in this chapter, creates a basis for comparison of normative orders within an overarching human rights framework. Perhaps most importantly, garnering this knowledge and understanding lays the groundwork for informed dialogue about human rights compliance and how it can be achieved. Most significantly, the kinds of open analytical approaches that need to be applied across normative orders are revealed.

Common denominators?

Human rights, as global common minimum standards to be complied with universally, direct us to reflect on and consider national and local compliance. Although there is often tension around human rights norms and arguments about their values, they are transcendent and there are international commonalities upon which there can often be basic consensus.

Although there is often tension around human rights norms and arguments about their values, they are transcendent

These approaches, as employed within the programme, have developed from the methodological approach of the late Professor of Women's Law at the University of Oslo, Tove Stang Dahl, who described the methodology of women's law as:

> '[C]ross disciplinary and pluralistic and calls for a rather free use of the available material wherever it can be found' (Dahl, 1988).

This approach fits perfectly into the research and analytical requirements in understanding and improving the lot of women in the eastern and southern African regions. Although the injunction seems somewhat nebulous, as Dahl herself explains, certain key elements can be identified:

> 'We can nevertheless distinguish three distinct methodological bases as fundamental: the ethical, the empirical and the legal doctrinal. We discuss moral and political questions. We deal with empirical material. And we analyze current law. All this is done from the perspective of one looking upwards from below which I shall ... call women's perspective. The term implies that we wish to see law, reality and morality from a women's point of view' (Dahl, 1988).

Human rights, as a gauge for assessing women's progress, were not on the 1988 agenda. They tended to be regarded as a rarified protection component of public international law, not a tool for identifying and responding to grounded

Using the capabilities approach and also recognizing the arguments postulated by Nancy Fraser to grapple with delivery of human rights entitlements were useful additions to our eclectic basket of tools

needs on a day to day basis. We would postulate that stimulating autonomous development and women's self actualization within development paradigms is now a key component of women's law as a legal discipline.[4] In 2009 Amatya Sen and Martha Nussbaum's theorizing on capabilities as a tool for identifying needs as well as capacities was introduced to the class by Dr Reena Patel from the University of Warwick. This became a useful approach which was engaged with methodologies to uncover the realities in the field research at the end of the first semester and in some of the dissertations in 2010. Using the capabilities approach and also recognizing the arguments postulated by Nancy Fraser to grapple with delivery of human rights entitlements were useful additions to our eclectic basket of tools for further development in future courses.[5]

Using international standards, exploring different ways of assessing and implementing compliance with international human rights in national and local contexts is an appropriate way to monitor and stimulate development which effectively benefits women. The ambit of women's law has grown both theoretically[6] and methodologically since 1988. Growth that has, inevitably, led to the development of new and innovative processes especially in contexts which have to engage with legal pluralism, customary, traditional and religious laws and dogma. We must also grapple with changing social and economic norms and with the conceptual canons of international and regional human rights norms.[7] But the critical entry points are still informed by Dahl's exhortation 'that we wish [need] to see law, reality and morality from a women's point of view' (Dahl, 1988).

---

[4] See further on this in chapters 13 and 15 on 'Women, commerce and law in Africa' and 'Women and access to resources'.

[5] This is further developed in chapter 4 in discussions on choosing methodologies to inform field research.

[6] The theoretical development of women's law, the quasi-mirror image of the methodology is described and discussed in chapter 1. I style it a quasi-mirror image as the chapters and content will not be an exact reflection of the methodology chapter but the thrust of each chapter is inextricably linked to the other. It must also be appreciated that the methodology and theoretical courses are taught separately but are intertwined in the first semester, often drawing on the same resources and skills from guest lecturers requiring us to keep the students apprised of how the pieces fit together. As separate courses, they reflect the interests and concerns of the designers and teachers of the courses but we hope they are complementary.

[7] The potential, role and significance of human rights norms in furthering women's rights is discussed in chapter 6 and our concern in this chapter is with the methodological implications and importance of taking such an approach.

Part I: Theory and methodologies: moving forward, looking backward

In taking up the challenge of women's law it is important to recognize that women's situations are never static. There are constant challenges thrown up as we explore the intellectual, empirical and theoretical demands created by the ever growing body of (and need for) scholarship in women's law and related areas. Thus the most exciting aspect of conducting[8] the methodology-related courses on the programme is the constant challenge of devising appropriate methodologies and methods to serve the needs of researchers.

At SEARCWL, we have tried not to be constrained by theories, perspectives, methodologies or methods. Yet at the same time we need to respect and intellectually use their conceptual significance, insights, direction and guidance. Thus it is vital that students are able to develop and critique new methodological and theoretical approaches.

I was fascinated to be informed of the derivation of the word 'method'[9] as 'an after path', something that follows and embellishes a theory. *After path* aptly describe what we have been trying to achieve in developing and evolving methodologies. *After path* also clearly invokes the notion that methodologies and methods should be in a constant state of flux as they evolve and are engaged with research and research findings, and are then retooled in the wake of theorizing and re-theorizing.

Theorizing and re-theorizing and innovatively developing appropriate methodologies can be represented as a cycle (see diagram on the right).

Theory and research methodology cycle

Research need → Methodological challenges → Evolving methodologies and methods to meet needs → Using methodologies and methods → Research outcomes Analyzing data → Assessing methodologies and their impact → Theorizing and re-theorizing → New or continued theorizing and research cycle

THEORY

---

8   Initially I had used the word 'teach' but on reviewing the expression in the chapter, I decided that 'conducted' imparts a notion of participation by all parties and not one of delivery of predetermined tools which are merely 'plugged in' and off you go.

9   For this insight I have to thank Bill Louw of the English Department at UZ for providing this striking derivation of the term 'method'. Bill conducts language and English expression enhancement sessions for our masters students, especially those who come from jurisdictions where English is not one of the official national languages. His assistance to them goes beyond the simplistic matters of grammar into more significant intellectual support around language and comprehension. These services are also used by other students on the programme.

This is an endless cycle, with each stage informing and driving the next. Such a dynamic representation helps students realize that they too can theorize and re-theorize. This might sound condescending but it is not intended as such; not infrequently students are initially afraid of challenging existing hegemonic theories because they have not had the empirical tools to spur their enquiries and the practical proof to begin to question and theorize for themselves. Perhaps their questioning capacity has been dampened by previous non-critical rote teaching and examining methods. For an example of research informed theory challenges, see Stewart (2008).

The whole programme is directed at precisely this skill, coupling it with the ability to identify, adapt and create appropriate methodological tools to test and challenge old and new theories as well as one's own emerging theories. One provocation that seems to dismantle the perception that theory is for academic others is asking: 'Do you have a theory?' This is followed by asking the following question, not necessarily to be answered at that point but as a general encouragement and authorization to think:

> 'Is there an approach – assumption – hypothesis you want to put forward (postulate) and investigate – test – which might help you theorize (think through) about new approaches (advance)? *(They may start in pure guess work or emerge from prior research, empirical or desk research and analysis of that research. However derived, these are ways to move forward.)*

Authority to theorize and challenge is implicit throughout the course but we seem to need to officially license students to do so.

Authority to theorize and challenge is implicit throughout the course but students seem to need to have official licence to do so. There is, however, an endorsement on the licence that you have to have the supporting evidence or at least tenable assumptions to explore empirically.

Having made that first tentative intervention, students need encouragement to take the next step and articulate their assumptions. Then they need to test them empirically through research, then question and re-theorize, re-question, re-test and adjust once again – then off again.

It is important to point out that theories can become rigid and a form of dogma that is fixed and immutable in the minds of uncritical individuals. Also, that theory can be ill-grounded, false and, not infrequently, manipulated and distorted to serve the interests of a select few.

The perpetual theory and research cycle

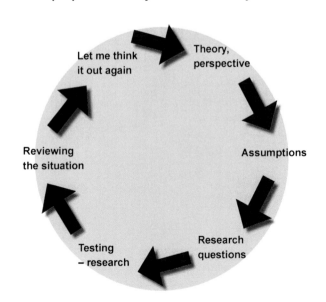

Let me think it out again

Theory, perspective

Assumptions

Research questions

Testing – research

Reviewing the situation

Likewise students must come to appreciate, understand and internalize the intellectual reality that theories are transitory and not fixed. They can be challenged; they need to be and ought to be constantly challenged. Theories are starting points or temporary markers of intellectual progress. Challenges to theories are not necessarily negative, rather, in many instances, they seek to develop the parameters and scope of the theory. For example, the theory of evolution and the big bang theory are constantly being exposed to new scientific findings and thus constantly re-evaluated and shaped, demanding further research, and thus more appropriate methodologies and methods to conduct the new research. Marxist theory and feminist theory are less capable of scientific evaluation but as societies change and respond to external conditions so one re-evaluates the significance, usefulness and changing applications of these theories. Thus how to deal with new issues in the light of these theories is considered and adjusted over time.

> *...students must come to appreciate, understand and internalize the intellectual reality that theories are transitory and not fixed*

The significance of individual theorizing and re-theorizing becomes easier to grasp when it is operationalized in the first semester field work exercise and the dissertation. Usually the homily above and the importance of theorizing are introduced about midway through the first semester but can come earlier or later depending on the class and the opportune moments.[10]

Part II: Breaking moulds

The next part of the chapter describes and discusses the mould-breaking processes I apply to students at the beginning of each new Masters in Women's Law programme. Critical at this stage of the process is developing awareness of sex and gender stereotyping and sexed and gendered perspectives on the world. The awareness process starts with the students doing a self analysis to facilitate an appreciation of the insidious nature of sexing and gendering in the world. The focus then shifts to techniques to develop the students' capacity to undertake multi-faceted and mainstreamed gender analysis as an integral part of theorizing and empirical research.

The majority of our students are law graduates who come from legal education and legal practice backgrounds that are legal centrist in approach. A few may have taken courses on women and the law or gender and the law or similar topics but by and large they have had little exposure to sex and gender informed study and analysis of the law. Some may have worked in non-governmental organizations which focus on women's specific needs

---

[10] I have this on my flash drive and can, thus, if it seems apposite, flip to it during any teaching session. Whenever possible I like to use it reactively to a question or comment in class, the most likely scenario being someone raising an issue and then doubting their capacity to challenge existing theories or ideas.

within the law but even among those there is rarely a deep appreciation of the sex and gender nuanced dimensions of the law as it affects women.

Most of our students arrive with an expectation that we will teach them what the law has to say about women and then dish out pre-ordained responses on how to improve the lives of women. There is some surprise when it becomes apparent that as lecturers we provide the initial tools and the instigating theories but they, as students, will be doing the research and analyzing how the law in its multiple and plural forms affects women. And they will be determining how to respond to their findings. To undertake such work, students must become sharply sex and gender aware. They must develop the capacity to expose and challenge the political, social, religious, economic and legal assumptions that inform the ways in which women and men's roles in life are prescribed and stereotyped. In undertaking research, law reform or any form of action-oriented interventions, including litigation, the women's law practitioner has to question every issue that arises, interrogate every law and every phenomenon from a sex and gender perspective.

...the women's law practitioner has to question every issue that arises, interrogate every law and every phenomenon from a sex and gender perspective

Creating effective proponents of women's law, be they male or female, involves using Dahl's dictum about understanding law in its various manifestations from a woman's perspective.[11] Understanding the contexts in which laws, whatever their form or derivation, operate is critical in tackling the differing ways in which lived realities and their intersections with laws affect men and women and shape the outcomes of their lives. Students need to be brought to the realization that the law in its formal construction is very confining in terms of conceptualizing and resolving problems in a holistic and situation-sensitive manner (Bentzon *et al.*, 1998). Lawyers box and define issues from a strictly legal relevance perspective; they do so because of the strictures and artificially-defined parameters of what 'law' purportedly recognizes as being within its compass. Likewise the 'law' limits the ambit of remedies and its sites of intervention. Yet law is nothing but the product of human intellect and, so far in human history, the emphasis has been mainly on the intellectual engagement of 'man' in the word human. Thus if as *wo*-man's law proponents we seek to balance the intellectual processes and gendered power within conceptualization of law, the female experiences and needs have to be introduced as balancing paradigms in developing law and jurisprudence.[12]

[11] In the masters programme, a course, 'Men, gender and law', was introduced so perhaps we can even lay claim to looking at law from a male perspective, although perhaps the most significant element is to help us all understand from a male perspective the male–female diversities and differences in expectations, treatment and experiences with the 'law'.

[12] Useful readings for the class are drawn from Smart (1998) and Dahl (1988). The choices vary with classes and identified areas of interest.

Opening up the parameters of legal techniques to accommodate a women's law approach requires a 'remoulding' of the traditional legal mindset in which the notion of gender neutrality of law tends to dominate.[13] Un-lawyers need to be given the tools to enable them to engage in questioning the versions of law and legal solutions that are given to them and to demand demystification of the law. They need to obtain sexed and gendered deconstructions of the implications of particular laws and law itself when they interact with lawyers. As Tsanga discusses in her chapter on teaching women, law reform and social justice strategies, un-lawyers in non-governmental organizations and relatively untrained community workers carry out much of the legal information dissemination work. So the ability to interrogate law and lawyers is also critical to their needs.

Thus students need to be enabled – whatever their background or experience – to deconstruct law and laws as a prerequisite to critically analyzing law and human rights norms and re-theorizing and re-conceptualizing laws and the administration of law in an informed manner. The most effective way to make students, both lawyers and un-lawyers, aware of what this requires methodologically is to challenge their preconceptions about law and their perceptions about themselves, their world and their own personal development and engagement with that world in its social, cultural, legal, religious, economic, sexed and gendered formats.

Henceforth, one hopes, they will examine all issues through sex and gender lenses, and investigate and assess the social and economic dynamics that mediate the lives of women and also men. The focus is also on men because if, as women, we do not understand what motivates them and what their perceptions of life, their entitlements and their needs are, we cannot engage in the critical transformative debates about women's rights, entitlements and genuine equality.

The first and most critical step in this process is to develop the students' power of introspection – self-examination and criticism. This is not a breast-beating self criticism but one designed to assist students to assess how they treat others. For example, litigants who come before them, clients who come to consult them or perhaps individuals whom they interview in field research. Introspection is critical in developing the capacity to recognize the gendered and sexed[14] nature of our worlds and engagements with others, as only when

> *Opening up the parameters of legal techniques to accommodate a women's law approach requires a 'remoulding' of the traditional legal mindset in which the notion of gender neutrality of law tends to dominate*

> *The first and most critical step in this process is to develop the students' power of introspection – self-examination and criticism*

---

[13] As this whole book addresses ways to overcome the consequences of such approaches to law, I will not dwell directly any further on this issue in this chapter.

[14] 'Sexed' in this context refers to the realities and practicalities of sex difference and the need for those differences to be catered for as management issues – more of this later. See also Stewart (2003).

there is an awareness of these elements that underpin our lives as individuals, can the process of informed research and exploration of the lives of others begin.

Early in the semester I also carry out feminist-informed exercises to raise awareness about gender roles using as a starting point fairly standard tools such as comparative male and female physiological (sex-based) tables. Having constructed such a table, the next table analyzes assumed male and female social characteristics (gender). From there we can construct the educational paradigms for males and females and then build a table of employment and other life opportunities.[15] What emerges is a pyramid derived from the sex-based life assumptions (gender) applied to individuals. As the pyramid opposite illustrates, for many females, first as girls and then as women, the life opportunities become narrower and more constrained than those for males.[16] Representing the gender dynamics of life as a pyramid also allows one, as the bands become smaller, to factor in other considerations such as race, class, ethnicity, religion, disabilities and economic and educational opportunities for both males and females. Self evidently, the further one climbs up the pyramid, the more constrained the access to opportunities becomes for most people.

ACTIVITY
Using male and female comparative tables

Based on the contributions from the class, we draw up the initial male/female tables on flipcharts. The general content of these tables will eventually be transferred to the sex and gender pyramid. Be warned, this can become a heated exercise as we do it in the early days of the course before the more personal experiential sex and gender exercises, discussed later, have been carried out.

As we compare issues such as relative strength, emotional profiles, social and economic roles in a class of females and males, stereotypical attitudes about male superiority and female inferiority are vigorously aired.

Sometimes women in the class become vociferous in expressing frustration and deep anger about their treatment from men. Some men become defensive and may be reduced to recycling the statement 'but that's the way it is' or, more provocatively, 'that's the way it has to be, because ...' Which fuels even more vigorous and venomous retorts from the women in the class.

Within a few weeks the class dynamics change but that is for later in this chapter.

---

[15] For more on this see Stewart (2003). But the key intervention seems to be the personal biographical exercise.

[16] All these instruments are discussed in other chapters in this book; the use of the instruments in research activities is the focus in this chapter.

Sex and gender pyramid

As the levels move progressively upwards towards power and influence, opportunities become increasingly narrow for everyone but more so for women than men as the dividing line indicates

M

Leadership, decision making

PUBLIC ARENAS OF DISCRIMINATION BECOME MORE EVIDENT

F

Career opportunities

Socially prescribed life roles dominate life choices

DISCRIMINATION BECOMES INSTITUTIONALIZED

Education, training

Gendered perceptions create stereotypical roles and activities for males and females

DISCRIMINATION BECOMES MORE EMBEDDED

Social constructions of male and female roles

(What men should and can do; what women should and can do.)

This also directs gendered approaches to children and their life opportunities

DISCRIMINATION BECOMES PERCEPTIBLE

Social (general societal) perceptions about being male or female

The physical, intellectual, psychological and emotional implications of being male or female

GENDER 'PROFILING' BEGINS

Physiological characteristics

Sex

MALE

FEMALE

BIRTH

The sex and gender pyramid and its implications as regards personal choices and opportunities are not always easy to reconcile with individual perceptions of the organization of societies and their own status and position within that society. What I mean by this is that most people do not distinguish sex from gender and the media persistently presents them as different terms for the same thing. Because they are often seen as synonymous there is a false perception that if one's sex is female then one's gender must likewise be female. Women who have taken up professional careers which are governed by male paradigms sometimes struggle to reconcile their female sex with their seemingly male career and social outlook. This may be more a problem for older women who broke the barriers earlier but may not have broken the pervading perception of the need to fit into the hegemonic male career mould which is at odds with their sex-based reproductive role. Younger women who followed them have found to some extent a more female-oriented environment but may still need to consciously locate themselves in the sex/gender continuum. That more female-oriented environment is a product of the continuing breaking down of barriers to women pursuing what once were regarded as exclusively or largely male careers.

On the page opposite is a description of how I came to grapple with representing this identity issue. There are many more dimensions to this, some of which arise more specifically in the 'Gender, sexuality and law' course in the second semester but this short piece seems to open up the debate effectively, not least because it is autobiographical (Stewart, 2004).

Thus I argue with my students, and often vehemently at the start, that if we accept the reality of biological and physiological difference, and the need to manage their implications as normal and natural issues, we might be able to focus more effectively on what the social, economic and cultural barriers are to mainstreaming women and getting gender concerns on the agenda. It should then be possible to focus on the legal, policy, educational, social, cultural, scientific, economic, medical, agricultural, political (governance) and other paradigmatic changes which need to be made by both men and women as genders and with their gendered definitions of the world and how it works. The end result being management of sex differences which provides a platform for gender equality.

...there is a false perception that if one's sex is female then one's gender must likewise be female

...if we accept the reality of biological and physiological difference, and the need to manage their implications as normal and natural issues, we might be able to focus more effectively on what the social, economic and cultural barriers are to mainstreaming women

Gender – gendered attitudes – what can be changed?

Although there is growing capacity to change one's (apparent) sex, for those who have the resources, the reality is that most of the world's population is consigned to its sex and it is not one's sex that is the problem – it is the construction put on sex–gender. Gender or gender roles are negotiable and if we manage sex, then there is a real possibility of negotiating gender. I have tried to represent my perception of the sex–gender dichotomy in the table below. I do not know whether the table might have the same liberating impact that it had on me when I could finally conceptualize its structure and content. All my life I have been (and am now the post middle aged version of one) what is described as a 'tomboy' – male games, male career choices (as they were in my youth) were what really interested me. Yet I was still female and very comfortably heterosexual. How does one then balance the male aspirations with female emotional and sexual needs? There was continuing tension, or so it was in my experience, until it was possible to see how my two identities, sex and gender could be separated and both fulfilled. The table below is an attempt to represent the sex-gender dichotomy as it appears to me to impact on the reality of our lives.

I found having constructed the table that it was perfectly feasible and in no way contradictory or conflicting to be physiologically female and socially (largely self constructed) veering towards the social construction male.

In using the table I would place myself in the female category for sexual identity and female (heterosexual) for sexual preference but slightly on the male side for gender identity (Stewart, 2004). For what it is worth, in gender profiling tests, I invariably show up as male.

Numbers of students over the years have explained themselves as 'tomboys' thereafter – and specifically in the cultural experiential exercise which is described in this chapter.

So far no male has yet described himself as having female gender aspects but some of them begin to be more comfortable about being empathetic and caring. This reaches a high point for those who take the 'Masculinities, gender and law' course in the second semester. In the first semester report back in 2009 one male student stated, as did others, that he was more empathetic at home and that his wife had noted this. However, he said he felt less of a man when asked how it affected his self perception. I had hoped he would feel as much or more of a man.

In reviewing this comment, I also note that it is socially more acceptable and possible for a woman to display male gendered tendencies in terms of interests and activities than for men to display female tendencies.

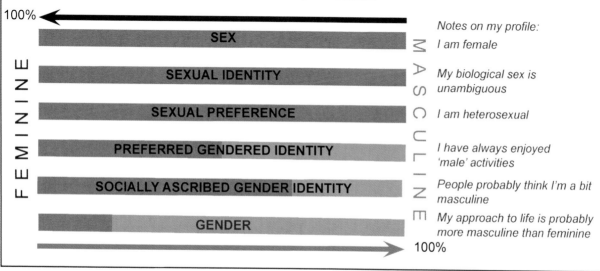

		Notes on my profile:
SEX	M	I am female
SEXUAL IDENTITY	A S	My biological sex is unambiguous
SEXUAL PREFERENCE	C	I am heterosexual
PREFERRED GENDERED IDENTITY	U L	I have always enjoyed 'male' activities
SOCIALLY ASCRIBED GENDER IDENTITY	I N	People probably think I'm a bit masculine
GENDER	E	My approach to life is probably more masculine than feminine

FEMININE 100% ← → 100%

Huh —where is the law in all this?

To the considerable surprise of many students they find themselves in the first weeks of the programme hardly talking or writing about law but exploring their cultural and religious backgrounds and writing autobiographical pieces. Essentially they are asked to cast their minds back to childhood, adolescence or to experiences with their own or other children and to analyze how girls and boys are treated socially, religiously, culturally and educationally.

Students have to consider how this early treatment shapes attitudes of and to males and females and how this creates stereotypical social expectations, behaviour and response patterns in both sexes and thus is a catalyst for the emergence of gender roles and gendered lives. This exercise is reproduced on pages 44 and 45.

The ways in which students tackle this exercise is revealing in itself. Some attempt to write, despite the clear instructions, a theoretical piece, no doubt thinking, based on prior university studies, that this will make it an academic triumph. Others may puzzle over whether they have a culture. One empathetic student of European ancestry, born and raised in an African context, raised the issue that she did not think she had a culture, reflecting the notion of cultural normativity being 'European cultures' and that others have a culture by way of difference. A brief questioning about fairy tales and family practices produced the 'aha' response and an excellent piece of descriptive work emerged that we could also use for comparative purposes with the 'cultural memories' of other class members. Of course even the nomenclature 'European' or 'western' is misleading in this context as there is no general culture or norm. The problem is the otherness that lies in our thinking.

What emerges from the comparisons is the similarity of treatment of and attitudes to male children as distinct from female children regardless of the cultural backdrop. The details might be different but the thrust is the same.

Conducting these autobiographical and personal experience exercises seems effective in bringing about an understanding and realization that gendered patterns of expected behaviour imposed on babies, young children and adolescents shape their personal aspirations,

NOTE
Good food for thought

To stimulate thought processes for this exercise, a number of readings are helpful – Stephanie Garrett's first and second chapters, 'Biology and gender' and 'The socialization of gender roles', in her book, *Gender*, effectively raise these issues. These chapters inspired me to develop the cultural gender identity exercise. Another pertinent and useful text is Viki Holten's, 'An equal chance to succeed'.

John Radford's book, *Why can't a woman be more like a man?*, probes the significance of male and female difference whilst questioning the gendered gloss that develops around physiological sex differences. Radford also highlights the sex–gender continuum and the difficulties in disaggregating sex from gendered roles which is a point that the students need to grasp at an early stage.

the expectations others have of them and their expectations of others. What emerges and is readily identified by the 'authors' is that engendering and defining cultural roles is insidious. The exercise exposes the innate nature of much sexed and gendered discrimination which is not perceived as unacceptable or problematic because it seems to be normal and natural and thus is not questioned or analyzed.

The exercise exposes the innate nature of much sexed and gendered discrimination which is not perceived as unacceptable or problematic

Male students are usually the most profoundly affected by the exercise. They are used to being told that women and girls are discriminated against; being 'shouted at' about patriarchy and patriarchal values but cannot, without further insights, internalize or address the criticism. On their own, they struggle to understand why women or girls have not risen to challenge issues of inequality, why women remain in abusive relationships or why they are not eligible for or are under represented in a range of occupations which are ostensibly open to both males and females. Suddenly, these men have to confront the enabling effect of the 'privilege' in their own development as compared to sisters, female cousins or other girls within their families and communities. There is another 'aha' process.

Monitoring the remoulding process

Quite radical change in attitudes seems to take place within the first month or so of the programme. This, as shown in chapter 4, is later boosted by the practical and field work components of the semester. On the first day of class for any new intake, each student is asked to describe their professional background and their expectations from the course. During this exercise, one very senior male police officer quite openly stated that he 'didn't have much time for this gender stuff' and he couldn't see 'what women's problems were and why they did not change their own lives'. Having written the autobiographical exercise and been exposed to the other aspects of the programme, at the three-week progress review session that I hold essentially to get reactions and changes in expectations and attitudes, he admitted that he 'could now see the problem'. Having identified the difference between how he was treated as a child and how his sister was treated, he had been forced to confront the gendered realities of life through the lens of his own experience. This was for him the breakthrough into understanding the importance of informed sex and gender analysis. He was not the first male to do this. Some years previously a male magistrate gave a similar response and underwent the same conversion. Years afterwards he is regarded as a gender specialist and is known by his female colleagues as 'sister' – in the most complimentary way.

...women who are politicians, judges, lawyers or successful professionals in other fields are often insensitive to or insulated against the realities of the lives of other women

Nor is this an exclusively male insight stimulating exercise – women who are politicians, judges, lawyers or successful professionals in other fields are often insensitive to or insulated against the realities of the lives of other women. They have, by their own assessment, made it by their own efforts.

EXERCISE

Sex and gender analysis – based on your personal experiential data

Read the short selection from Stephanie Garrett's *Gender* and John Radford's *Why can't a woman be more like a man*? Then select *one* of the exercises that follow and type a submission in about 1800 to 2000 words.

In doing the exercise, you will need to cast your mind back to your childhood, adolescence or to your own family or community based experiences. You might also recollect the experiential data from your own experience as a parent or grandparent.

Each paper must indicate:

- Your name (and its meaning in your vernacular or in English)
- Your sex and gender
- Your country
- Your ethnic or religious group (the context of the data)
- Whether it is an urban or rural setting

Format

The following format is not obligatory but may be useful in ordering your presentation and outlines the required content. (Use catchy titles for sections if you so desire.)

A   Introduction/scene setting – a word picture of the community/family setting, the social/economic situation and physical environment. Where appropriate include other pertinent matters such as access to education, transport and health services. (The reader may not be intimate with your country, area or life style.)

B   Experiential data – *your own* recollections, observations and experiences of the practices and processes you present in your answers.

In writing up remember that what you find obvious and commonplace may be exotic and exciting to others. Don't suppress information you think is embarrassing or peculiar. We need the whole truth (as they say). Most importantly, the questions are designed to make you think about your own knowledge base and record your own experiences and impressions. Do not answer in a rote manner but write descriptively and with local colour. (Thus in this section you should address the issues listed in either question 1 OR question 2.)

C   Analysis/conclusions – When you have finished the descriptive section, analyze with hindsight how the practices and processes have affected or may later affect the gender identity and life choices of the person or people concerned.

Choose exercise 1 OR exercise 2

Exercise 1

1. How is a new baby received into a family? Is there any difference between the reception (reactions) for a male baby and for a female baby?

2. Are any special ceremonies performed for new babies; do they differ for male and female babies? Are there any sex-related traditional, cultural or religious practices which take place in relation to a baby or young child? Do these differ between male and female children?

3. Are there different social, feeding or rearing practices dependent on whether a baby or child (up to about the age of five) is male or female? If so, what are they? Are some foods reserved or preferred for male babies and small boys or for female babies and small girls? Are there foods that either group are not supposed to eat?

4. Are male and female babies dressed differently (even if the clothes are minimal)? Are there colours of clothing that are regarded as more appropriate for males than females and vice versa?

5. Are there games, toys (simple home constructed toys are to be included here) that are reserved or preferred for male babies and small boys? Can small girls participate in these games? Repeat the exercise for female babies and small girls and also for boys' participation in those games.

6. Are there traditional tales, 'fairy' stories, legends, books, drawings that depict males and females differently and emphasize male/female characteristics? If so, what are these and how are males and females differently portrayed?

Exercise 2

1. Are there social, cultural, religious or traditional practices that mark the onset of puberty in boys and girls? What are they? Do they differ for boys and girls? How? Do boys and girls attend any ceremonies or educational or religious courses when they reach puberty? What are they? Do they differ for boys and girls? How?

2. Do any sex-related traditional, cultural or religious practices take place for adolescent boys or girls? Do these differ?

3. Do social, eating or communication practices differ depending on whether an adolescent is female or male? How? Are particular foods reserved or preferred for adolescent boys or girls? Are there foods that either group are not supposed to eat?

4. Do adolescent boys and girls dress differently? Are some colours regarded as more appropriate for males or females? Even if clothing is similar, are any items specifically male or female? What are they?

5. Are particular tasks around the home or other spheres regarded as appropriate for male or female adolescents? If so, what are they?

6. Are certain cultural, social or sports activities reserved or preferred for adolescent boys? Can adolescent girls participate? Repeat the exercise for adolescent girls. Are adolescent boys and girls' social activities restricted in any way? How and why?

7. Do adolescent-oriented traditional tales, books, comics and media materials depict males and females differently and emphasize male or female characteristics? What are these differences? (Only describe what applies to the family or community you are portraying.)

They may have had families that were especially supportive of females and the pursuit of personal career options and consequently are not alive to the barriers and difficulties that other females experience. Such women also have an 'aha' experience on doing the exercise and the follow up work described in chapter 3 on African philosophy and religion.

The methodological and theoretical value of this process of creating awareness is that students, regardless of sex or gender, begin to appreciate why women they come into contact with professionally, as clients, litigants, petitioners and as persons seeking help, are often passive. Why they are reluctant to take action against husbands, other family males, male colleagues or men in their social arena. They begin to understand why women are wary of asserting employment rights, why they do not actively participate in governance issues or demand their rights even against other women. They begin to understand why many women do not, in feminist terminology, challenge patriarchy.

[Students] begin to understand why many women do not...challenge patriarchy

One senior politician confessed to the rest of her class at the personal re-evaluation session at the end of the first three weeks that she had 'previously thought women were the problem, because of their lack of action and impetus towards development and legal change'. She admitted that 'it now seems like I am the problem'. On being asked why she came to that conclusion she admitted that she could not previously understand why other women did not embrace and push for change. Clearly she realized that as an activist in future she would need to provide an enabling environment for women to appreciate their rights, their power and their capacity for change and to recognize the barriers to their participation and help them overcome those barriers as a precursor to action.

These might seem like obvious exercises with trivial outcomes, yet you would be surprised at some students' lack of realization of women's or other women's lived realities. Every new intake prompts me to wonder whether I should keep doing the exercise and every intake it becomes clear that it is absolutely essential. The target methodological component of the exercise is the level of personal insight it creates.

...you would be surprised at the lack of realization of women's or other women's, lived realities

The significance of these relatively simple exercises emerges in the second major exercise students undertake – exploring customs, practices, identities and their linkages to laws, usage of laws, law reform, human rights and human rights implementation.

The final part of the chapter deals with the creation and ongoing development of methodologies to promote re-conceptualizing and re-analyzing the law. It also addresses using human rights standards and implementing human rights norms in all matters relating to women and the law, including law in its multiple pluralities as experienced by women in eastern and southern Africa. This part of the chapter also explores methodologies to highlight deficits in human rights frameworks and how we might rectify these deficits.

Part III: Re-casting the mould

The next major phase in the remoulding process is breaking the lawyers' old conservative, boxed, problem-defined and regulated analytical thinking patterns. Lawyers may also arrive with a limited perception of the role and utility of human rights in pushing development and third generation rights issues.

Un-lawyers need to break (overcome) their awe of or, as often the case, frustration with law and appreciate how they can use it to pursue women's rights. And how they can use human rights as a standard against which to assess development initiatives and programme or government performance in development programmes and projects driven by human rights.

Both lawyers and un-lawyers need to see how they can develop a symbiotic relationship that enhances the potential to improve women's rights and deliver human rights and development entitlements across the board.

Given the breadth of issues, the divergence of countries, laws, cultures and religions, there is a need for an overarching standard of what is acceptable in relation to the treatment of women in every sphere of life. There is a need to constantly review, reconceptualize and evolve new measures to implement the minimum standards to be applied to all women, regardless of who they are or where they are located. The standards employed are informed by international and regional human rights norms, mainly but not exclusively, the Convention on the Elimination of all forms of Discrimination Against Women (CEDAW), the Protocol to the African Charter on Human and Peoples' Rights on the Rights of Women in Africa (the Women's Protocol), the Convention on the Rights of the Child and the African Charter an the Rights and Welfare of the Child.[17] Using this transcendent framework allows for useful comparative work between countries, gives a solid reference base on standards, and facilitates incisive and critical assessment of laws, policies and interventions.

There is a need to constantly review, reconceptualize and evolve new measures to implement the minimum standards to be applied to all women

The second exercise for significant marks[18] consists of unpacking, dissecting and challenging stereotypical understandings of the world and its social, economic, religious and legal functioning using human rights norms to further develop the ability to reconceptualize.[19] This exercise is reproduced on pages 48 and 49.

---

[17] There are, as discussed in chapter 5 on ITC skills and library use, short exercises that attract limited marks that contribute to the overall methodology course marks.

[18] By the time this commenced in earlier years, they would have spent a week, as described and discussed in the 'Theories and perspectives in women's law' course, on human rights instruments and human rights implementation structures.

[19] Human rights norms as stimuli to law reform are covered in the human rights chapter. This portion of the work done in semester 1 was part of the course on theories and perspectives.

EXERCISE

Human rights, gender, customary law and customs and practices

Individual work

Your submission must be in the form of a report to your national gender commission or your national human rights commission (or their equivalent). If they don't exist in your country, pretend they do!

You, as an individual, have been commissioned to determine and report on the aspects of customary law (both the formal and informal versions of customary law) and customs and practices on the ground that accord with or violate the provisions of any relevant articles of the following:

- the Universal Declaration of Human Rights
- the African Union Charter
- the Convention on the Elimination of all forms of Discrimination Against Women (CEDAW)
- the Protocol to the African Charter on Human and Peoples' Rights on the Rights of Women in Africa (Women's Protocol)
- any other human rights instrument you consider pertinent

Your report should also assess whether some or all of the aspects of customary law and customs and practices in your chosen area could potentially be used in the quest for the more general application of human rights to the needs of women and girls in your country.

In carrying out this commission you need to examine statutory provisions, received laws, policies and so on, where appropriate. (You might not be able to do this thoroughly if you cannot access the statutes in your home country – but try as far as possible to access them – we are concerned with your approach to the process so the detail can always wait.)

Select one of the following areas of human endeavour for investigation. The areas are influenced by customary law and/or customs and practices in their application and they might have an adverse impact on women and girl's human rights.

1   Women's access to and control of financial resources to enable them to obtain ownership of land in (a) urban areas or (b) rural areas

OR

2   Women's rights to use, enjoy, alienate and bequeath (leave by way of inheritance) the fruits of their own labour freely (for example, material and or financial benefits such as from handwork, traditional healing, salaries, business enterprises and other activities)

OR

3   Women's entitlement and capacity to participate actively and equally in decision making within their local communities

OR

4   Women and girls' entitlement and capacity to pursue educational opportunities to the full extent of their intellectual capabilities

OR

5   Women's rights to independently determine when, how, where and how often they will access health care and other medical services for themselves and their minor children (Ignore finance problems for this section – women's capacity to act within customary frameworks is the issue.)

Once you have selected an area, carry out the following tasks (part 1 and part 2).

PART I

1   Compile the key elements which deal with women and women's rights in the articles in the human rights instruments that appear to apply to the area you have chosen to work on. Ascertain and discuss the social values and legal principles that seem to inform the articles you are working with in the human rights instruments you have identified as relevant to your commission.

2   Identify and outline the content of any relevant national (general/received) laws[20] from your home country which inhibit or facilitate, at this point in time, compliance with the human rights instruments considered in 1 above. Identify and discuss the social values and legal principles that seem to inform these national laws.

3   Outline the relevant 'formal/official' customary law in your country – as 'captured' by the courts in decided cases, in so-called restatements of customary law or in textbooks. Analyze and discuss the social values and legal principles that seem to inform these versions of customary law.

4   Based on your own experiential, previous research or other relevant data, consider and document the general content of the customs and practices on the ground in relation to the identified areas of 'customary law'. Analyze and discuss the social values these customs and practices seem to reflect.

5   Note any significant differences between the customs and practices on the ground and the 'formal/official' versions of customary law identified – using your findings in 3 and 4 above.

6   Building on 3, 4 and 5, assess whether it is possible to distill (extract) any broad underpinning/overarching legal principles from the customs and practices on the ground and the formal/official versions of customary law. (There may be a difference between the official customary law and the customs and practices on the ground in the principles which you distill.)

7   Assess and document the extent to which both the formal/official versions of customary law (question 3) and the customs and practices on the ground (question 4) *comply or do not comply* with the human rights instruments identified in question 1.

8   Assess whether all or some of the broad principles identified in question 6 encourage, develop or further compliance with the human rights instruments identified in question 1 by your national legislature, judiciary or policy makers.

PART 2

Map (illustrate, set out, draw) with explanations, the past, present and possible future influence of actors on structures (collections of actors) and structures on individual actors in the compliance or non-compliance of customary law (formal/official) and customs and practices (in relation to the articles and the topic you have chosen) with the human rights instruments identified in step 1 part 1.

---

20 The detail isn't important at this point – it is appreciating that there is or might be some legislation.

The starting point is to select a recognized problem area for women in terms of the application of what are routinely regarded as retrograde practices in the realms of customary law or religious laws affecting women and girls. Directly engaging human rights, culture, religion and associated practices in a tight analytical framework reveals how one can use human rights norms in research at multiple levels. They can be used as ways of identifying problems, resolving problems and probing societies to understand the impact and significance of local norms on women and girls, and for that matter, on men and boys' lives.[21] This is not an exercise just to be applied to so-called customary law or religious laws; it can be equally effectively used as an interrogative tool when examining the impact of general (received) law on the rights and entitlements of women.

The exercise also provides the necessary information, even where there is poor compliance, to initiate informed dialogued processes. This is important as mere nebulous uninformed criticism of customary or religious norms and values tends to produce spirited and defensive responses, creating rallying points for resistance to change. Likewise, reluctance to 'tread' in customary or religious arenas leads to senseless cultural (in the sense of the patterns that inform daily behaviour) relativism. So one of the critical questions that students have to grapple with is how to identify the positive (for women) aspects of customs, practices and religious norms. Having done this, the task is to use them to advance the arguments for recognizing and implementing women's rights. Students need to be able to analyze how they can, from that same vantage point, identify those customs, practices and religious norms that are inimical to the rights of women. It is then possible to facilitate and negotiate the terrain to bring about informed and meaningful change.

...one of the critical questions that students have to grapple with is how to identify the positive (for women) aspects of customs, practices and religious norms

Based on a wide variety of human rights norms, the exercise demonstrates how human rights can be used as a cut through analytical and state compliance monitoring tool, regardless of the subject matter of the right and irrespective of the normative system being examined.[22] The simple diagram on the left illustrates the milieu in which these issues need to be explored. There are other dynamics that can be added depending on the issues

Human rights and customary laws? A contested or negotiable arena?

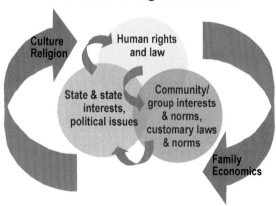

---

[21] It is possible to cover a wide range of issues with the six initial groups. Class presentations also mean useful feedback across all the issues.

[22] It would be folly to assume that general law is always human rights compliant; it frequently is not. The same interrogation is needed on general law, especially in the realm of the family.

NOTE

Creating cohesive groups

When we initially run through the exercise in class we select groups based on professional interests, country perspectives or life experiences. Even country groups can be hit or miss in terms of cohesiveness. Just because students come from the same country does not mean they share a common culture but at least they may have some understanding of other local cultures.[23]

Conversely, using diverse groups in terms of countries and cultures leads inevitably to discourses about the meaning of terms, the nature and forms of customs and practices. As facilitator, ensure that issues of language and meaning are carefully explored on a regional basis. As we use English as the common language for instruction it is important to stress that translating vernacular terms into English frequently obscures their meaning. Local nuances and specificities are lost, complex terms become simplified and realities are masked.

For example, the term 'cleansing ceremony' agglomerates practices in relation to inheritance from many cultures in eastern and southern Africa. These can range from presenting water to a relative of the deceased to complex sexual, religious and traditional rituals. The same goes for the term 'bride price' – they all need to be carefully unpacked and discussed.

---

but for the purposes of this book I have kept this as a simple representation of the potential complexities in dealing with human rights issues. One can also substitute general law for customary law in the same framework and obtain a sense of those complexities. It becomes even more complex when general law and customary law are combined in the same framework.

The exercise forces students to bring together human rights, customary and, where appropriate, religious norms and state laws in a non-confrontational comparative analytical framework. The exercise should force students to thoroughly analyze the content and purpose of the human rights norm being invoked. Then that norm, usually a specific article, becomes an overarching criterion to assess compliance, identify and explore the nature, form and purpose of the invoked custom and practice in context and to juxtapose both of these with general (received) law prescriptions and interventions. The first exercise on personal cultural experiences, discussed earlier, seems to emerge at this point as informing a critical component of analysis. There is awareness of gendered elements in culture and even more subtle gendered nuances that emanate from each cultural setting. Along with Dr David Kaulemu's interventions this exercise has, hopefully, alerted students to the multi-directional impact of culture and religion on their perceptions of gender roles and gendered manipulation of people's lives, literally from cradle to grave.

---

[23] If they don't then this is an initial prompt to start acquiring that understanding.

In doing the exercise it is as important for students to focus on conjunctions and similarities as it is to focus on differences and disjunctions, ultimately they will need to analyze both. An interrogation they need to employ is whether the underlying human rights values are similar to the underlying values in customary laws once you strip away the rule-oriented outcomes? One way of exploring this is to ask: if we juxtapose the core human rights norms relating to an area under investigation and interrogate the underlying values of all normative orders 'playing' into the field, is it possible to ascertain the fundamental norms being embraced?

One can facilitate a similar process with religious prescripts by sending the religious apologist back to the original text, a process which reflects the thrust of much continuing feminist scholarship in religious arenas.[24] Having completed this last exercise, students should be ready to theorize and re-theorize women's legal and human rights position and entitlements. They should also be able to discern potential modes of positive intervention to convert their theorizing into appropriate, measured and feasible practical applications.

Re-tooling for old tasks

The methodology course is designed to culminate in the research design exercises that take place in the practical course and the dissertation. By the time students have to design their research they should be able to 'lay bare' the projected basic social, religious, cultural, economic and legal frameworks they will engage with in their research and in subsequent intervention planning. The deeply embedded context of the programme is the lived reality of women and girls' lives. The aim is to uncover that reality and engage the findings in the quest for beneficial change for women and girls.

I have long struggled to find adequate transmissible and malleable tools for this perennial task. Since 2007, I have begun to postulate personally and rhetorically and more pointedly in specific circumstances, a series of interrogations on how to commence the process of exploring, assessing and addressing women's rights. The interrogations are directed at a series of assumptions that seem to inform the perspectives from which we engage in women's rights discourse. There are subtle, often unarticulated influences and constraints that may limit what we do, what we explore and how we explore it. These same influences and constraints may also limit how we engage in law reform, how we engage with communities: the national and the local.

There is general awareness that customs and practices were distorted in the process of creating customary law in the colonial milieu. Extensive and excellent work has been undertaken on this process, for example the large body

...the challenge for the programme is to harness these religious, anthropological and historical insights and combine them with human rights imperatives in seeking the methodological tools to improve the lives of women

---

[24] See Ali (2007) and Manjoo (2008).

of WLSA work and Chanock(1985) and Woodman's (1988) incisive analyses of the distortions and their evolution. Similarly in the religious arenas is Ali's (2007) work which points to the value in uncovering the sources of religious norms and the origins of distortions of some apparent but spurious religions dogma about women and women's rights. Although we expose students to these debates, the challenge for the programme is to harness these religious, anthropological and historical insights and combine them with human rights imperatives in seeking the methodological tools to improve the lives of women.

Now is a critical moment to take this process forward as there is a growing social and judicial awareness of women's rights, especially in constitutional terms, in the eastern and southern African regions. There are recent and relatively recent decisions in Bhe and Shilubana[25] and there are constitutional provisions mandating equality for women.[26]

Such recognition demands that we equip our students to research and promote these positive developments in customs and practices on the ground. These emerging or recovered norms can then be recognized and applied at all levels of the judicial system and within society at large.

We need a template to use in setting about a systematic process of interrogating the sources and the legitimacy of current customs and practices and so-called religious norms that are translated into legal prescripts. So far the best I have devised is a table that is completed by combining theorizing, methodological insights, human rights compliance needs and indicators of how to engage communities and individuals in transformative agendas. The initial column prompts sex and gender based assessments of the outcomes of the practices for those affected by it. Then you use the appropriate human rights instruments to assess whether the practice, custom or belief violates human rights standards or complies or potentially complies with human rights.

Appropriate methods for intervening that are religiously sensitive but assertive will have to be devised

Having made a preliminary assessment, the next step, usually where there is a violation, is to identify the source of the practice, custom or belief. It is at this point that the researcher has to be aware and alert. One cannot be fobbed off with 'it is our custom' or told that a deity purportedly pronounced on the matter. In the case of religious beliefs, such statements have to be interrogated where possible by examining the chapter and verse. Numerous students have discovered over the years that so-called religious sources often cannot be provided when a polite but insistent interrogation is carried out. In some cases an admission might emerge that religious leaders have not revealed the actual content and form of religious texts. This is especially problematic where

---

[25] *Bhe and others v Magistrate, Khayelitsha and Others, Shilubana and Others v Nwamitwa*

[26] See the South African constitution and the recent Kenyan constitution for examples of equality trumping cultural and religious rights.

TABLE : **Data collection and analysis**

Practice/ Custom/ Belief	Sex-based outcomes		Gendered outcomes		Human rights violations /compliance	Source of practice/ custom/belief	Status of source	Evaluation of practice/ custom/belief	Opportunities/ options for intervention
	F	M	F	M					
Example: *Female genital mutilation (FGM)*									

women's rights are concerned and women cannot access the texts on their own because they cannot read or cannot read the language of the religious text. In some cases women and girls may be excluded wholly or partially from religious services and denied access to religious scholarship. Appropriate methods for intervening that are religiously sensitive but assertive will have to be devised. But awareness of the problem is the first step and an important focus of the programme is to explore such problems.

With customs and practices, we need to cast a fairly wide net in field research to ascertain the sources (discussed in chapter 4). These questions and queries, if the next question technique is thoroughly employed and consistent probing takes place, can reveal the process of distortion that has taken place. Interviews and discussions, especially with the elderly, are revealing.

The table above can be used to inform the data collection and analysis processes outlined here. It facilitates an ordered questioning and analysis of both practices and sources and from there one moves to readdressing the context and content of normative orders.

Human rights and compliance tool

...we may need to retrieve, refurbish and above all recognize women's rights within customary contexts rather than mount premature and sometimes antagonistic human rights creation 'rescue missions'

The very process of asking these questions can prompt revision and review of sources and of content (Hinz, 2008; Stewart, 2008). As Mchaju-Liwewe[27] discovered, women may have significant and superior rights under customary law, especially in matrilineal societies, which have been obscured by notions of male superior rights that pervade development agendas. Thus we may need to retrieve, refurbish and above all recognize women's rights within customary contexts rather than mount premature and sometimes antagonistic human rights creation 'rescue missions'.

---

[27] She was exploring women's rights in irrigation schemes in Malawi which were located in matrilineal areas. Government schemes had tried to create new tenure systems and when these collapsed instead of examining prior tenure schemes, human rights based equality schemes were postulated. However, examining the women's customary rights would have shown their superior rights. Doing so might arguably have revealed that men's rights were in need of positive adjustment. This work is further discussed in chapter 4.

Clearly, we need to seriously reassess the impact of the often unarticulated assumptions that influence the way we begin processes to effect legal and constitutional change to benefit women. We need to re-examine our assumptions about customary law, customs and practices. We should also pursue the process of revisiting our assumptions about women's position under various religious normative orders. Especially as in many settings in our regions these religious norms are muddled up with and obscured by local cultural practices (Stewart, 2008).

A new positioning is required when we consider women's position under these regimes; we need, as I have styled it elsewhere, 'break out assumptions'. We need to formulate assumptions that force us to research and assess women's rights from a more positive perspective than the traditionally negative one of women as marginalized and excluded:

● Women have rights but they do not conform to standard patterns of recognition of rights in the dominant system (Stewart, 2008);

● Women may at times have significant and even superior rights but they are not articulated – as in matrilineal systems (Mchaju-Liwewe, 2008);

● Custom mutates (Stewart, 1998);

● Multilateral social and economic processes shape change and inform the choices people, especially women, make (Stewart and Tsanga, 2007);

● Women's rights in religious normative orders may be potentially beneficial to women (Ali, 2007);

● Women's rights in customary and religious normative orders can or may be human rights compliant (Hellum, 2007);

● Societies and communities may be willing to review women's rights of their own volition or if given the opportunity to do so (Ondieki, 2006).

Each one of these assumptions mandates research, or least dialogue, as to what is actually happening on the ground. To effectively carry out such research the researcher or dialoguer must mentally position herself between male and female and between the normative systems being investigated. Having conducted the research or dialogue there is a critical need to analyze the outcomes from gender and sex perspectives. Such research, driven by breakout assumptions, can reveal that individuals and communities have effected change or are ripe for positive change in favour of women without any further external intervention being required. Assumed resistance may be precisely that, assumed (Hinz, 2008; Stewart, 1998; Hellum, 2007; Mchaju-Liwewe, 2008; Ondieki, 2006). But, and it is as always a strong but, the reality may be of female adverse formulations of entitlements. Nonetheless dialogue and thorough understanding of the terrain of rights entitlements as they exist on the ground is the way forward.

Stages in planning for reform

Area of law Law reform?	Activities	Targets	Methods
REFORM	Devising the reform – content and thrust Thorough research, analysis and understanding Discussions and consultations	Law reformers? Ministry heads and personnel? Ministers? Men? Women? Children? NGOs? Churches?	Research on: comparative provisions Determining human rights standards to be met Informed dialogue with key players on nature and form of reform needed
LOBBYING	Getting parliament to pass reforms	Parliament – women's caucus Cabinet ministers Political parties Targeted known supporters and competent debaters	Personal meetings Donor pressure on government where feasible Regional power pressure – signing frenzies publicity, identifying strategic opportunities
IMPLEMENTING AND USING	Capacitating staff and institutional development Publication and provision of the law to the judiciary, implementers	Non-governmental organizations, trainers, judicial training institutions, bureaucratic users, strategic personnel – chiefs etc – those who need to act or intervene	Preparing materials, forms, monitoring mechanisms Research into appropriate methodologies for implementing and also dealing with the whole organizational structure needed to make the law effective and accessible
DISSEMINATION	Preparing broad-based multi-directional information campaigns	Population at large, community leaders, religious leaders	Radio, popular theatre, TV, cartoons, posters, discussions. Soap operas, basic simple materials for general use

Problems	Potential outcomes	Corrective strategies	Progress assessments
Lack of political will Societal, religious resistance, lack of concern on the issue Accommodating cultural and religious biases demanded in the legislation	Opposition to reform Consensus on the need for legislation Might be a compromise on critical content of the legislation	If there is opposition then renewed efforts are needed for consensus building Review what you are prepared to sacrifice to get the minimum standards in place	Chart progress and spin off This is when you need to review strategies and assess what the barriers to reform are. This is most important for future law reform exercises
Not seen as critical part of political agendas Political backsliding in favour of other interest groups Splitting the female lobby	Passage of legislation, amendments to legislation Postponements and delays, legislation not passed Unsatisfactory version passed	If there are postponements etc, need to determine whether a new lobby is needed and if so what needs to be adjusted Decide minimum standards	Ascertain what the barriers are and strategize for future reform exercises
Absence of professional expertise and understanding of provisions and procedures Absence of forms, lack of access to service providers, financial constraints	Staff and courts (in)capable of implementing reforms Capacitation of staff at NGOs, courts etc to assist the public in using the law Law passed but no capacitation/ people use/ don't use the new law	National training programmes if possible – lobby donors Assess barriers to use and devise appropriate remedies It may be a national governance issue!	Ascertain whether staff are ready and able to implement law reform. Examine staff retention in justice delivery system. Has training been lost by attrition? Is there interest in law reform and its outcomes from communities and leaders?
Lack of resources for dissemination Poor, inadequate community strategies, lack of cultural and gender sensitivity, lack of monitoring and control of materials	Population in general have a basic knowledge of the law Law in place but not known or understood	Need to mobilize broad-based coalitions to spread information May need to revisit campaign contents and strategies	Determine user rates, both increases and decreases Assess general levels of user understanding of the reforms and their import.

Law reform, hurry up change!

Students frequently want to undertake law reform as part of research processes. Non-governmental organizations and government departments want or need to engage in law reform activities. One problem that bedevils these exercises is the failure to anticipate potential problems or barriers in the processes they undertake. Law reform does not lend itself well to donor programme monitoring processes; considerable progress may be made in getting law reform going but then it stalls for lack of political will, changes in governments or fear of adverse consequences from presumed resistant electorates. So to the donor, it seems that nothing has happened.

Law reform may be put in place but implementation problems often arise because the law reform is seen as an end in itself, whereas it is but the first step. Law reform needs to be contextualized from the point of conceptualization to final full-scale effective implementation. The chart on pages 56–57 provides a holistic view of the stages we need to plan for from initiating the drive for reform to effectively implementing the laws and finally targeting communities and individuals using the laws. It can be used as a programming and implementing tool. One advantage if we use the table as a matrix is that we should be able to determine where a law reform process is at any point in time. It can be used as a trouble locator in the sense of tracking what has been done and what has been missed in the process and needs to be rectified.

Conclusion

This chapter outlined and discussed the major stages in the pedagogical enterprise that is the 'Research and research methodologies in women's law' course. Along with Dr Amy Tsanga's 'Theories and perspectives in women's law' course, it is designed to arm students with the intellectual insights and the questioning and analytical tools to re-cover, re-shape, re-form, re-vive and re-view the rights of women and of course the girl child, not just in our catchment regions but in the wider world as well. The processes in this course are crystallized in chapter 4 on the practical and dissertation courses.

Bibliography

Ali S.S. (2007) 'Interpretative strategies for women's human rights in a plural legal framework. Exploring judicial and state responses to Hudood laws in Pakistan', in A. Hellum, J. Stewart, S.S. Ali and A. Tsanga, *Human rights, plural legalities and gendered realities. Paths are made by walking*, Weaver Press, Harare.

Armstrong A. (1992) *Struggling over scarce resources: women and maintenance in southern Africa*, University of Zimbabwe Publications, Harare.

Bentzon A.W., A. Hellum, J. Stewart, W. Ncube and T. Agersnap (1998) *Pursuing grounded theory in law, south–north experiences in developing women's law*, Tano-Aschehoug, Oslo, Mond Books, Harare.

Chanock M. (1985) *Law, custom and social order: the colonial experience in Malawi and Zambia*, Cambridge University Press, Cambridge.

Chimbaru F. (2008) 'The burdened witness: catering for the needs of mothers with small children required to give evidence in criminal trials in Zimbabwe', masters dissertation, SEARCWL, UZ, Harare.

Dahl S.T. (1988) *Towards an interpretive theory of law – the argument for women's law*, Institute of Public and International Law Publication Series 27(7)1988.

Fraser N. (1995) 'From redistribution to recognition? Dilemmas of justice in a "post-socialist" age', *New Left Review* 212 July/August:68-93.

Garrett S. (1987) *Gender*, Routledge, London.

Hinz M. (2008) 'Strengthening women's rights: the need to address the gap between customary and statutory law in Namibia', in O.C. Rippel (ed) *Women and custom in Namibia: cultural practice versus gender equality?*, Macmillan Education, Windhoek.

Holton V. (1998) 'An equal chance to succeed: comparing women and men in management', in J. Radford (ed) *Gender and choice in education*, Routledge, London.

Manjoo R. (2008) *The recognition of Muslim personal laws in South Africa: implications for women's human rights*, International and Comparative Law Colloquium Paper 5, available online at: http/digitalcommons.law.umaryland.edu/iclc_paper/5

Mchaju-Liwewe O. (2008) 'A history of diminishing returns: the paradox of women's customary land rights in small-scale irrigation schemes in matrilineal societies in southern Malawi', masters dissertation, SEARCWL, UZ, Harare.

Nussbaum M. (2000) *Women and human development: the capabilities approach*, Cambridge University Press, Cambridge.

– (2003) 'Capabilities as fundamental entitlements: Sen and social justice', *Feminist Economics* 9(2–3):35-59.

Ondieki E. (2006) 'Culture and traditions among the Abagusii community influence the practice of genital mutilation: grounded notions and perspectives about male and female attitudes on how to maintain cultural identity without a cut', masters dissertation, SEARCWL, UZ, Harare.

Radford J. (1998) 'Why can't a woman be more like a man, or vice versa', in J. Radford (ed) *Gender and choice in education*, Routledge, London.

Smart C. (1989) *Feminism and the power of law*, Routledge, London.

Stewart J.E. and A.S. Tsanga (2007) 'The widows and female child's portion. The twisted path to partial equality of widows and daughters under customary law in Zimbabwe', in A. Hellum, J. Stewart, S.S. Ali and A. Tsanga, *Human rights, plural legalities and gendered realities. Paths are made by walking*, Weaver Press, Harare.

Stewart J.E. *et al.* (1997) *Paving the way forward: a review and research primer of WLSA research methodologies*, WLSA, Harare.

Stewart J.E. (1998) 'Rights, rights, rights: women's rights', in P. Blume and K. Ketscher (eds) *Ret og skonsomhed i en overganstid*, Akademisk Forlag, Copenhagen.

– (1998) 'Why I can't teach customary law', in J. Eekelaar and T. Nhlapo (eds) *The changing family: family forms and family law*, Hart Publishing, Oxford.

– (2004) 'Sex? Gender? So what? Mainstreaming gender concerns', in I. Welpe, B. Thege and S. Henderson (eds) *The gender perspective: innovations in economy, organizations and health within the Southern African Development Community (SADC)*, Peter Lang, Frankfurt.

– (2008) 'Intersecting grounds of (dis)advantage: the socio-economic position of women subject to customary law – a southern African perspective', in O.C. Rippel (ed) *Women and custom in Namibia: cultural practice versus gender equality?* Macmillan Education, Windhoek.

Woodman G. (1988) 'How state courts created customary law in Ghana and Nigeria', in B.W. Morse and G.R. Woodman (eds) *Indigenous law and the state*, Foris, Dordrecht.

3

African philosophy and religion

in the service of women's law

David Kaulemu

Professor J.E. Stewart invited me to offer a seminar series on African philosophy and religion as part of her course on methodologies of studying and developing women's law. The SEARCWL masters programme pays special attention to research on the situation of women in different African societies with the aim of improving it. Having various academic and professional backgrounds and coming from various countries and cultures of Africa, the masters students work towards addressing the concerns of women in their respective communities and societies. The centre realizes that it has to look at those special needs of women in the context of established and especially dominant cultures and religions of society. The section of the course that deals with African philosophy and African religions looks at those aspects of African cultures that affect the development of laws that in turn affect the lives of women.

...we start with the assumption that women are human beings who live in real societies paradoxically characterized by various forms of oppression and opportunities for liberation

In the seminar, we start with the assumption that women are human beings who live in real societies paradoxically characterized by various forms of oppression and opportunities for liberation. Their various situations are affected, if not determined, by people, institutions, cultural practices, and the religious beliefs and philosophical ideas of those surrounding them. But, as human beings, they are capable of influencing the societies they live in and those beyond.[1]

---

[1] Anthony Giddens points out with respect to modernity that, 'The self is not a passive entity, determined by external influences; in forging their self-identities, no matter how local their specific contexts of action, individuals contribute to and directly promote social influences that are global in their consequences and implications' (Giddens, 1991:2). In the seminar we try to encourage students to see themselves as conscious agents of social transformation.

African philosophies, religions and liberation

I was asked to facilitate discussions on the role of African philosophies, African traditional religions and cultures and their implications for how identities are constructed and how the identities and lives of women are thereby shaped. I took up this task with a desire to create contexts for analyzing various African religious and cultural practices which influence and impact on the lives of women in African societies and communities. Our main aim was to identify social and political opportunities within these cultures, practices and philosophies that could be used to positively influence the development of laws, institutions and appropriate practices for the benefit of the marginalized and impoverished, especially girls and women. In directing this process, I was inspired by the methodology used by Anne Hope and Sally Timmel in the four-volume handbook for community workers entitled, *Training for transformation* (Hope and Timmel, 1984 and 1995). I have had opportunities to use these books at the Grail Centre in Cape Town. These handbooks use Paulo Freire's approach to social transformation which links and balances theory with practice. They, in the spirit of Freire's widely influential book, *Pedagogy of the oppressed*, encourage communities to participate in shaping their own social development by sharpening their analytical and political transformational skills. In the preface to the first volume, Hope and Timmel declare that, 'Reflection without action is mere verbalism. Action without reflection is pure activism' (Hope and Timmel, 1984 and 1995). Thus, this approach recognizes the importance of linking theory with practice and analysis with social transformation. Freire's work in encouraging members of communities to be active, critical and political is well known and has influenced the spirit of our seminars at SEARCWL.

In the seminar on religion and philosophy, I encourage students to bring the content of their beliefs and theories of African cultural beliefs and philosophies into the discussion. However, I encourage them to call into play the real social contexts and practices of actual human beings as they struggle to shape their own lives. Rather than starting with idealized rational, egotistic human beings as in many economic and legal paradigms, we start with real beings embedded in cultures and religions characterized by both oppression and possibilities for transformation and liberation.

Students usually demonstrate deep and expansive knowledge about the cultures they come from.[2] The seminar suggests different conceptual frameworks, paradigms, methodologies and analytical tools for self-understanding and for critically assessing the cultural values, institutions,

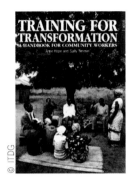

© ITDG

'Reflection without action is mere verbalism. Action without reflection is pure activism'
Hope and Timmel

Rather than starting with idealized rational, egotistic human beings ...we start with real beings embedded in cultures and religions characterized by both oppression and possibilities for transformation and liberation

---

[2] Before commencing the seminar they have carried out the personal experiential data exercise discussed in chapter 2.

processes and practices that affect people's, and especially women's, lives. Self-reflective philosophical skills help to achieve this goal, particularly when focused on the study of ethical principles, virtues and theories which help in interrogating various propositions that have been suggested as standards for social justice for women in African societies. This study of ethical responses to women's condition in societies is supposed to interrogate people's ideas and practices in relation to justice. It is a way of eliciting new responses that express respect for the dignity and rights of all people, especially women and children. It interrogates cultures and traditions in the light of the rights and interests of all members, especially women. It is therefore about social transformation in all its aspects – intellectual, emotional, structural, institutional, legal and procedural. While I have no legal background, I hope that the tools they acquire in the seminar help them to appreciate the social and historical backgrounds of the law. In the seminar, law is treated as a social and political construction which can be both oppressive and yet liberating. The politics of how to make law a liberating force, is what we encourage by identifying the social aspects and backgrounds of law.

...law is treated as a social and political construction which can be both oppressive and yet liberating

In interrogating the religious, philosophical and cultural aspects that affect the development of laws affecting women, we look at different levels of human development. I ask about the concepts and knowledge that people carry *in their heads* and use in their language when they deal with the lives of girls and women. Ideas and concepts that are expressed through language are important as windows through which reality is understood and articulated. As Wittgenstein pointed out, '*The limits of my language* mean the limits of my world' (Wittgenstein, 1922: line 5.6).

We also interrogate their emotional responses and virtues that have been cultivated in them as individuals and also in their various societies. Virtues at the individual level are those qualities that are encouraged and cultivated as good qualities to have. Individuals can cultivate such virtues in themselves, for example, courage, respect for the dignity of others and prudence. Societies can cultivate justice, respect for human rights, appreciation of accountability and the protection of those who are marginalized.

...sometimes, while students may intellectually accept the rights of women, they respond emotionally in ways that undermine that declared respect

I find that sometimes, while students may intellectually accept the rights of women, they respond emotionally in ways that undermine that declared respect. This usually happens when discussing issues of equality in the home and in the church. The other areas which demonstrate this imbalance between intellectual acceptance and emotional response include *lobola* (bride price), female genital mutilation, traditional chieftaincy and authority and in issues of alternative lifestyles. At times too, individual and social qualities that are cultivated in local and world religions have been identified as undermining human rights. Tensions between cultural and religious virtues on the one hand and various ways of understanding social justice and human rights on the other have been one of the most exciting and energy-draining parts of the seminar. In the last session that I facilitated, some strong claims on ethnicity were made. For example, some Kenyan students claimed that the Kikuyu people are only interested in money and business and not in education or charitable activities. They made this claim with so much essentialist conviction that one would have thought they had scientific evidence to support the claim. They appealed to the fact that there was no Kikuyu student on the SEARCWL programme as clear indication that the Kikuyus, by nature, are not interested in education but in money. Of course there have been Kikuyu students on the SEARCWL programme. Some Zimbabwean students made claims to the effect that Karanga men are hard, cruel husbands. These strong sweeping claims were made and defended by students who also believed in the equality and humanity of all human beings. They were on the SEARCWL programme partly because they believe in the possibility of making the world more just and more humane. But here they were making claims that some people are beyond reform and some cultures unchangeable.

In the last session that I facilitated, some strong claims on ethnicity were made

In the seminar, we used these sweeping prejudiced claims as opportunities to handle strongly-held cultural and religious beliefs. We interrogated these strongly felt sentiments using the principles of morality and justice. We asked for the difference between these sorts of sentiments and those prejudices expressed against women, black people and the poor. In group activities, we looked for historical, sociological and religious factors that could have given way to the apparent qualities attributed to the Kikuyus, Karanga men and others. It was exciting to see the process of interrogating culture. And even more exhilarating to see students identifying possible ways of addressing these strongly-held views. The trick was to find beliefs, activities, institutions and persons within a given tradition that could be used to debunk the strongly-held prejudices emanating from that given tradition.

...we used these sweeping prejudiced claims as opportunities to handle strongly held cultural and religious beliefs

Methods and processes used in the seminar

The seminar uses plenary sessions, group work and individual research and reflection. All sessions are meant to be participatory and rely on the knowledge and experiences of the students. We take advantage of the fact that students come from different regions and cultures of Africa to encourage them to share those varied experiences and to reflect on them. Comparative analysis is central to concretely demonstrate how what is considered *normal* by one culture or one group of people may be questioned by another. This helps to assess the *rationality* of cultural and religious practices and to demonstrate the historical and contingent nature of cultural practices.[3] It is important that

Comparative analysis is central to concretely demonstrate how what is considered normal by one culture or one group of people may be questioned by another.

---

[3] See Richard Rorty's *Contingency, irony, and solidarity* (1989).

students consciously learn from each other and help each other to reflect critically about their respective societies. In doing so, they appreciate more that following cultural practices involves individuals making decisions to follow the cultural practices in specific ways.

Thus sometimes group work activities involve discussing and analyzing the cultural practices of some group members' communities. The members whose cultural practices are analyzed invite and lead the other members to appreciate the challenges and opportunities in their communities. I encourage students to respectfully challenge each others' analytical frameworks and ethical responses. The idea is to make people uncomfortable with common practice in order to create conditions for fresh thinking on issues.[4] Philosophy is very good at creating such uncomfortable conditions that help to transform our own personal lives, our communities, our environment and the whole society. In this regard, we take philosophy as critical theory where definitions of terms are not just descriptions of reality but also ideal standards towards which reality can be made to aspire. David Ingram explains philosophy as critical theory in the following terms:

The idea is to make people uncomfortable with common practice in order to create conditions for fresh thinking on issues

> 'Unlike descriptive and explanatory theories, critical theories are chiefly concerned with evaluating the justice and happiness of societies. In this respect they are more akin to philosophy than science. Philosophy, as it is traditionally conceived, involves reflecting on the essential meaning of life and the subordinate activities and terms under which it is carried on. The essential means the most basic, the most necessary and/or the most universal features of some activity or thing. It is what defines something in its innermost identity, relating it to things that are like it and distinguishing it from things that are not. Although this defining activity is similar to the social and political scientist's penchant for constructing classifications, it involves considerably more than the mere description of reality; it prescribes a norm or ideal to which the activity or thing being defined must conform in order for it to be truly what it is. Therefore, the definitions sought by philosophers have a critical edge' (Ingram, 1990:xx).

David Miller (1976), appeals to D.D. Raphael's distinction between 'conservative' justice and 'ideal' or 'prosthetic' justice. He explains this distinction in the following words:

> 'Raphael analogously contrasts conservative justice, whose "object is to preserve an existing order of rights and possessions, or to restore

---

[4] The Socratic method in its general form encourages students to question established definitions, traditions and practices. We encourage students to explain and try to justify specific practices and assess their rationality, morality and possible motivations.

it when any breaches have been made", with prosthetic justice, which "aims at modifying the *status quo*"' (Miller, 1976:25).

Definitional ideals are placed within their historical and social contexts. For example the definition of humanity is not only about what humans are as a matter of fact but also the standard of what it means to be truly human, so that those who fall short can aspire to be more human in the context of their respective societies.[5] We used this approach to interrogate the claims about the Kikuyu and the Karanga men mentioned earlier. The advantage of placing cultural practices in their social and historical contexts is in making it easier to assess the implications of analytical definitions on power relations and in identifying those people who are made to bear the social cost of development. This helps us to be alert to the fact that ethical definitions have political implications. This, however, does not necessarily imply that we should abolish ethics or our appeal to universal criteria for judging morality and justice. Politics should be compatible with some sense of objective morality and the common good. The whole SEARCWL programme is, in a sense, an attempt to create a professional and political practice that is aimed at improving the lives of everyone but especially those who have been historically disadvantaged.

Our main aim is, as Amartya Sen recently put it, 'to clarify how we can proceed to address questions of enhancing justice and removing injustice, rather than to offer resolutions of questions about the nature of perfect justice' (Sen, 2009:ix).

Ethical reference to universal criteria for judging is controversial even within feminism. Feminist critique of modernity, rationality, patriarchy and masculinity has demonstrated how appeals to universality have been used to justify the marginalization and oppression of women and other groups. This has led some feminists to reject any reference to universal concepts and values. This tendency has culminated in what has been termed 'the postmodern turn' which has been critical of Enlightenment philosophical ideals of 'objectivity', 'reason', 'truth', and so on. Yet other feminists have been worried by the dangers of postmodern criticisms of Enlightenment values leading into forms of relativism and nominalism that render feminist politics impossible.

Thus the dangers of postmodernism, as seen by some feminists, are those of both relativism and the abandonment of theory. While many reject the modernist 'view from nowhere', they question whether postmodernism would not lead us to the equally problematic 'view from everywhere'. Are coherent theory and politics possible within a postmodern position (Nicholson, 1990:9)?

The ... programme is...an attempt to create a professional and political practice that is aimed at improving the lives of everyone but especially those who have been historically disadvantaged

---

[5] As Linda J. Nicholson points out, 'Thus, theorizing which is explicitly historical, that is, which situates its categories within historical frameworks, less easily invites the dangers of false generalizations than does theorizing which does not ' (Nicholson, 1990:9).

These kinds of debates form the content of the discussions in the seminar. Students appreciate the implications of taking particular philosophical positions and frameworks. They challenge each other in assessing their usefulness in defending the rights of women and opening up possibilities for human development in very specific cultural contexts. Some social and historical contexts have demonstrated how useful appeals to universal ethical standards can be in dismantling local forms of oppression. International, inter-cultural and inter-religious struggles against local injustices have been waged successfully against apartheid, racism and other injustices in the name of universal standards. Yet appeals to universal ethical standards have also been notorious for inspiring imperialism, paternalism and other social and historical cruelties. Therefore, to decide on the philosophical demands of social liberation is a delicate matter that involves practical wisdom.

Areas covered

The seminars discuss and cover the following key areas:

- the nature of philosophy,
- the nature of religion,
- the nature of cultural traditions,
- concepts as tools for understanding reality.

I encourage students to identify tools for the liberation of women and the marginalized from within given cultural traditions. An analysis of any culture and religion demonstrates that every cultural tradition has possibilities for the liberation of the marginalized. There is no culture without tools for addressing its own injustices and blind-spots.

An analysis of any culture and religion demonstrates that every cultural tradition has possibilities for the liberation of the marginalized

Session 1: What is philosophy?

This session encourages an appreciation of the different ways African philosophies have been understood and the various implications of those understandings. These discussions are meant to demonstrate how philosophy can be practised differently and legitimately. However, the idea of appreciating different approaches to philosophy is not meant to encourage relativism or nihilism but to create rational public discourse. While critical philosophy rightly points out that definitions suggest criteria for judging, it does not offer definite criteria. It therefore allows for rational debate on the criteria offered by different definitions. Each approach that is informed by specific definitions helps to focus on useful perspectives that are ignored by other approaches. The following are some of the different approaches to understanding philosophy.

1   Philosophy as a body of knowledge or system of beliefs

The focus of this definition is on the content of people's beliefs and not so much on how they come to have those beliefs or the logical coherence of the ideas (personal and communal thought – for example, the knowledge content that is attributed to the Shona, Chewa or Kikuyu people as their respective beliefs). This definition encourages us to learn about what a group of people believes, that is, the actual content of their beliefs. But it says little about the correctness or usefulness of the group's beliefs. This logical separation of the fact of having a belief from its correctness or truth can be liberating. Many defenders of cultures give the impression that the truth of beliefs is determined by and within the culture in question.

Many defenders of cultures give the impression that the truth of beliefs is determined by and within the culture in question

2   Philosophy as a way of looking at the world (world outlook, perspective or ideology)

This approach does not so much focus on the content of a philosophy as on its perspective or point from which the philosophy is developed. The assumption of this definition is that people's beliefs are determined by the vantage point from which they look at the world. For example, a feminist perspective or a black perspective is based on the background from which the perspective is given. This raises the debate as to whether a perspective can make sense to a person who is from a different background. If this is impossible, then universal struggles against injustice are impossible. For example, can a man understand and appreciate the feminist perspective? Can a man be a feminist or can a white person fight for black liberation? Indeed, can adults, especially men, fight for the liberation of the girl child?

Can a man be a feminist or a white person fight for black liberation?

3   Philosophy as a rational activity

From this perspective philosophy is not concerned so much with the end result of the philosophical process as in the first definition above. Rather, the definition concentrates on philosophical activity as a rational activity. It asks what sub-activities make up the activity we call philosophy? The useful analogy is the activity of 'gardening' which is made up of the sub-activities of weeding, watering, planting and mulching. Under this definition of philosophy the sub-activities are usually understood in terms of the three Cs, that is *clarity, coherence* and *credibility*. The rational activities of clarifying concepts demand that concepts used in cultural and religious discourse should be defined in such a way that people can clearly see what they mean and what they do not mean. This philosophical activity was exemplified by Socrates' practice of philosophy. Socrates made many powerful people uncomfortable by demanding that they define the fundamental concepts of their professions. The assumption is that if a judge cannot define justice, how can she emit

...if a judge cannot define justice, how can she emit it in the courts?

it in the courts? Coherence as a rational activity is the demand that when a number of concepts are used to explain the nature of reality, the concepts must be consistent with one another. Stories that explain the nature of reality must be coherent in the sense that they do not contain contradictions since contradictions are not true of reality. For example, we know that there cannot be a round square or a triangular circle in the world. We know this *a priori*, that is independently of experience. Now, rational stories that try to explain the nature of reality should not only be coherent but should also be credible in the sense that they are believable, given the best scientific explanations we already have. Hence to understand philosophy as a rational activity is to demand the three Cs in all stories about reality. In this spirit the clarity, coherence and credibility of philosophies that justify oppression of different kinds have been challenged. The struggles for the liberation of women have sometimes been waged as struggles for more rational societies and more rational social arrangements.

4   Philosophy as political discourse versus philosophy as objective universal discourse

This debate on the nature of philosophy centres on the concepts of 'objectivity', 'truth' and 'universality'. For some, philosophy makes it possible for us to have access to certain philosophical truths about reality. For others, the search for such truths is like following mirages.

Women and philosophy

The claim that philosophy is a rational activity has raised deep debates about its relationship to women's lives. This has created an ambiguous relationship between women and philosophy. Traditionally, philosophy has tended to be a male-dominated subject. Some philosophers, mainly women, have argued that 'rationality' has historically been defined to suit male domination. Male rationality in this sense has been identified as a major cause of social injustices, wars and oppression. The rationalization of social life in modernity through the market forces, bureaucratization of institutions and legal systems has been identified as a major cause of modern social alienation, exploitation, marginalization and annihilation. The liberation of women is therefore understood in this context as the de-construction of modern rationality. This raises the question of whether philosophy can be a vehicle for women's liberation even though its history has been not only male dominated but detrimental to women's welfare and development.

Male rationality ... has been identified as a major cause of social injustices, wars and oppression

Law, like philosophy, has been seen as an essentially male institution. Can it serve the liberation of women? Women's self-conscious participation in the development of the law and the collaboration of progressive people can lead to women's liberation. Given that the law will be with us for a long time – that the abolition of the law is virtually impossible – it is the ethical duty of everyone committed to the liberation of women to fight to influence its development and to search for opportunities to do so. This requires an understanding of the issues at stake and an appreciation of the need to transform society in the interest of human social development and the flourishing of the lives of all beings. Philosophy in all its forms can be used to identify such opportunities for the liberation of women and men in the African context.

Philosophy in all its forms can be used to identify … opportunities for the liberation of women and men in the African context

Session 2: Methods of doing African philosophy

One way of bringing out the role of African philosophy is to let students identify different ways in which African peoples have responded to modernity and modern institutions, traditions and principles. In group discussions and participatory plenary sessions the following different kinds of responses usually come up:

- Hostility towards modernity and modern institutions accompanied with attempts go back to traditional ways of life;
- Total embrace of modernity and total rejection of traditional life styles, values and institutions;
- Attempts to find middle ground and combine aspects from both the modern and the traditional.

In the history of African philosophy the following different ways of doing philosophy have been identified by the late Kenyan philosopher Odera Henry Oruka. These methods offer different ways of understanding African philosophy and how to do it. They are explained by Oruka as ethno-philosophy, sage philosophy, professional philosophy and political/ideological philosophy.

1   Ethno-philosophy

This is one of the most popular methods of doing African philosophy which was promoted by colonial anthropology. It also attracted respected African philosophers and anthropologists. It tries to prove that Africans have unique ways of understanding reality. Because of this unique understanding or epistemology, it is argued that Africans have unique cultures and ways of organizing society and unique values and moral criteria for judging actions. This method attributes Africans with unique communal thought systems and values that cannot be reduced to or translated into other cultures.

Also interesting is the question, 'If Africans have a unique epistemology, do women, as women, have their own unique epistemology that cannot be

ACTIVITY

Using ethno-philosophy

Students discuss the advantages and disadvantages of this method. They give special attention to the implications for the lives of women.

Students can be divided into groups that then the groups each organize a skit to illustrate the disadvantages for women of ethno-philosophy.

Some students were excited by the creation of spaces for women through the claim for a unique women's epistemology

...being critical does not necessarily mean being negative about the culture but looking at and finding good reasons for following or rejecting particular cultural practices

reduced into other ways of seeing reality?' Does African philosophy take the feminist perspective seriously? History demonstrates that it has not always done so. But can it be made to do so? Groups can also be asked to discuss ways in which ethno-philosophy can be made to serve the interests of women. Students have in the past illustrated how opportunities in traditional cultural practices can be created to advance the interests of women. These include practices such as 'sitting on the man', a practice in which senior women in traditional societies could confront abusive men. Other areas include traditional practices that recognize and respect women's ownership of property and women's roles as spirit mediums and as queen mothers. Some students were excited by the creation of spaces for women through the claim for a unique women's epistemology. They saw this as an exciting subversion of ethno-philosophy. But others were concerned that the spaces created for women could still be marginalized if they were not in the mainstream of social institutions, the economy and politics.

2   Sage philosophy

This method rejects the idea of a 'communal thought system'. It argues that Africans, and indeed women, are individual persons who think for themselves as individuals. Under this concept, the idea of African communal thought or women's communal thought is seen as oppressive to individuals. So if we want to retrieve African philosophy, we have to pay attention to individual Africans who think independently of European philosophies and independently of the communal thought systems. We have to consider seriously the individuality of women whose thinking can be different from that of fellow women. The definition of philosophy in this approach focuses on independent thinking and critical analysis of one's culture. Here, being critical does not necessarily mean being negative about the culture but looking at and finding good reasons for following or rejecting particular cultural practices. Odera Oruka who promoted this method, looked for African wise people who were least affected by modernity and were experts in their own cultures. The idea was to find individuals who were familiar with their own cultures but were prepared to be critical of them, asking questions and suggesting new ways of proceeding in their cultural practices. One criticism of Oruka was that he tended to interview mainly men, giving the impression that only men were wise. However, Oruka's method does not have to be biased against women. In this course I pay special attention to old wise women rather than to men.

In our class, we do not have time to carry out the interviews.[6] We, instead, divide ourselves into different groups. Students in each group identify what they think a woman sage in their cultures would consider important. What critical comments could she make with regard to a specific cultural organization of her society – paying special attention to the roles given to girls and women in that organization? This analysis is made with conscious attention to the existence of both 'conservative' and 'prosthetic' justice.

3   Political-ideological philosophy

This approach to philosophy focuses on applying African traditional ideas to the political structures of society. They are mainly represented by such ideological movements as *Ujamaa* where Julius Nyerere applied the idea of African traditional familyhood to the political system. Nyerere argued that this approach recommended African socialism. This approach has generally been detrimental to women who have been marginalized in modern African politics. The conceptualization of 'the African family' which has been used to idealize African politics has been tilted against women. Activities to deconstruct this conceptualization and its consequences can be useful. Other political ideologies falling under political-ideological philosophy include Kenneth Kaunda's *Humanism*, Samkange and Samkange's *Hunhuism/Ubuntuism*, Leopold Seda Senghor's *Negritude* and Steve Biko's *Ubuntu* in Black Consciousness. In groups, students can discuss the ways in which, historically, political/ideological philosophy has been disadvantageous to women and ways in which it can be made to work for women.

4   Professional philosophy

Professional philosophers are those who are professionally trained and are employed to do and teach philosophy in modern African universities and colleges. These philosophers believe the profession of philosophy has universal definition and application. While, historically, the practice of professional philosophy has been a disadvantage to women, new avenues for the liberation

ACTIVITY
Interviewing wise people

Students interview a number of (for example, five) old wise women to identify their understanding of their own culture. Wise women are identified by the respect they command in the communities. The women chosen for interview should be those who have as little influence of the modern as possible. They should be women who respect their culture and yet are prepared to identify its weaknesses in order to improve it in the service of women. Special attention should be taken to find out how the old wise women were able to challenge and influence their cultures using the possibilities provided for by these cultures.

The conceptualization of 'the African family' which has been used to idealize African politics has been tilted against women

---

[6] Nor would it be appropriate to interview only Zimbabwean wise women but this is an approach that has to be used at the stage of undertaking field research in the first semester and in the dissertation. It also raises the issue of who to interview on customary matters and also which women to interview – Section editor.

of women can be found. Firstly, professional women philosophers are rewriting the history of philosophy by digging up the work of past women philosophers who have been forgotten in the male-dominated practice of the subject. Secondly, women philosophers are redefining philosophy in the interest of their own lives. Thirdly, women are demanding to participate in the development of the subject with a view to influencing its major issues of concern (Nicholson, 1990). The approach of professional philosophy is to raise philosophical questions with regard to women's lives. Using an eclectic combination of philosophical methodologies, such as conceptual analysis, critical theory, Foucauldian archeology and hermeneutics, I try to shake students from what David Hume called 'dogmatic slumber'. Philosophy in this sense is made to make people uncomfortable in order to create opportunities for wider and more rational discussions.

I try to shake students from what David Hume called 'dogmatic slumber'

Session 3: African traditional religions

African nationalism has tended to encourage Africans to see themselves as one. One way of doing so has been the postulation of African traditional religion as if all Africans have one religion. This approach of seeing Africans as belonging to one traditional religion was encouraged by missionaries and especially anthropologists who studied African cultures. Anthropologists as tools of European imperialism studied African religion in order to find ways of controlling and managing African life. In many ways European modernity tried to banish plurality, ambiguity and ambivalence in African social life for they made colonial control more complex and more difficult. John Mbiti, however, points out that while 'Africans are notoriously religious', it is also true that 'each people has its own religious system with a set of beliefs and practices' (Mbiti, 1969:1). He goes on to explain that: 'We speak of African traditional religions in the plural because there are about three thousand African peoples (tribes), and each has its own religious system' (Mbiti, 1969:1). In our seminar, we recognize this reality.

This approach of seeing Africans as belonging to one traditional religion was encouraged by missionaries

The three major responses to modernity are reflected in students' responses to African traditional religions. Some students tend to be totally against traditional religions. Many of them do this on the basis of having joined world religions such as Islam and Christianity. They reject traditional religions as primitive or evil. Other students take the opposite position of totally embracing traditional religions and rejecting 'foreign' religions. Many, though, try to combine traditional religions with one of the world religions.

In our seminar, we try to respect all religions. We do not encourage students to renounce their religious commitments. We assume that if God exists, and She or He is what religious people say She or He is, then She or He must be in communication with all human beings. Since God is of justice, peace and

TOPICS FOR DISCUSSION

Interrogating religious institutions, practices and values

Group discussions, short stories, pictures, and skits can be used to deal with the following questions that help to interrogate religious institutions, practices and values:

1   Identify the relevant literature that describes the situation of woman in the religious traditions of your society. Discuss especially the attitudes towards women and the behaviours and institutions that support those attitudes. In your discussion, identify the attitudes, behaviours and institutions that undermine women and those that liberate them.

2   Critically discuss the meaning of the following terms:

– within African traditional religious contexts and

– in the context of your own religion/church/synagogue/ mosque:

● human liberation

● respect for human dignity

● human self-fulfillment

● human rights

3*   Discuss exceptional women in your local religious traditions. Identify ways in which they have helped to transform their society.

4*   In what ways do your African religious traditions raise the dignity of women? In what ways do they restrict women from making their full contribution?

5   What can be done in order to make the influence of women more effective in your African religious tradition?

* Questions 3 and 4 have benefited from T*raining for transformation: a handbook for community workers*, Book III, written by Anne Hope and Sally Timmel.

abundant life, then all religions can be assessed on their capacity to promote justice, peace and full lives for all individual human beings. In this sense, any religious arrangements, practices, institutions and rules that undermine justice should, by that account, be rejected as contravening God. Students are therefore encouraged to interrogate their religions in order to find best ways of improving their capacities for delivering justice, especially for women.

Activities: African traditional religions and justice

I encourage groups to discuss how their respective religions can be made to promote justice for girls and women. There are many examples of how African traditional religions have been understood as oppressing the lives of women. This is not difficult to demonstrate. What is more difficult but more exciting is to ask students to find strategies for how those African traditions can renounce the oppression and begin to promote justice while still working within the African traditional religion in question. For example, how can women living in an African traditional society that restricts women's participation in public discourse promote that participation within the framework of the African traditional society in question? It is always refreshing to read Nkiru Nzengwu's article, 'Recovering Igbo traditions: a case for indigenous women's organizations in development' (Nussbaum and Glover, 1995). Nzengwu demonstrates how indigenous Igbo traditions can be used to liberate women. She analyzes traditional Igbo culture in order to identify strategies and institutions that could defend the interests of women even today. She concludes:

> 'Therefore, guided by the belief that development assistance to grassroots women's organizations is often stalled through lack of historical knowledge, I shall follow my general account of Igbo traditions with a description of indigenous women's institutions that are deserving of development support. These associations deserve consideration for several reasons: they seek activities that have social and cultural relevance; they are advantageously positioned to channel resources to women who need more empowerment and autonomy; their existence has been obscured by hostile development policies; and their leadership is not currently in a position to articulate their demands or to argue for them in terms that officials of foreign development agencies expect and demand. My aim is not to invoke outmoded ancestral relics, but to point out enduring administrative structures that have relevance for development at the grassroots level' (Nzengwu, in Nussbaum and Glover, 1995:453).

Session 4: Deconstructing popular approaches to culture, tradition, gender roles and identity

This session stresses the analytically problematic nature of 'culture' and 'tradition' without necessarily rejecting them. While culture and traditions are usually presented as clear and cast in stone, this session introduces a sense of ambiguity and ambivalence in the development and practice of culture. It encourages students to appreciate how culture is always historical and social.

Even if culture and traditions were cast in iron and therefore unambiguous, following them would always raise ambiguities. As Wittgenstein postulated, there are an indefinite number of ways in which a rule can be followed and in which traditions and cultures can develop. Cultural rules are always ambiguous because human beings are human beings and not machines. Attempts to banish ambiguity have been the major drive towards modern forms of oppression, especially the oppression of women. Attempts to define women and their roles have been at the core of the oppression of women in most traditions and religions.

Politics, people's needs, power, corruption and greed are some of the factors that influence the development of cultural traditions. This point is brought out by analyzing cultural rituals and traditional practices. I encourage students to consider the thesis of the 'invention of traditions' developed by people such as Terence Ranger and Leroy Vail.

Students share their experiences of cultural ambiguities during both pre-colonial and post-colonial rituals. If pre-colonial cultures, traditions and identities are understood to be ambiguous, then they must be understood as having possessed possibilities for both the suppression and the liberation of women. This session works to identify such possibilities.

The colonial experience helped to push African cultures in a more monarchical, hierarchical, patriarchal and authoritarian direction. This was possible because the local cultures had the possibilities of developing in that direction. In many ways they already had their own hierarchies, forms of oppression, prejudices and exploitation. But they also had possibilities for developing in many different directions.

> **EXAMPLE**
> **Manipulating tradition?**
>
> Participants were asked to remember their experiences of attending traditional rituals such as funerals, burials, inheritance rituals, marriage procedures, praying for rain and so on. If they attended funerals, for example, more than once, were the procedures exactly the same or did it depend on who was there, when it was held and whose funeral it was? Did the burial procedures for a rich person go the same way as for a poor person?
>
> Some participants recalled how they had observed the manipulation of traditional rituals – sometimes for the good but at times for the bad. For example, greed and power could inspire some members of the family to disempower bereaved women and children. But powerful elders could also use their influence to protect widows and orphans.

This can be demonstrated by looking at the concept of customary law, especially looking at the development of the concept of the chief in the context of labour migration, of the family and of the roles of men and women, the tribe or ethnic group, the nation and those of Africa or Africans themselves. It is most fascinating to analyze the development of the concept of pieces of land that are understood to be essentially belonging to specific ethnic groups such as Kikuyuland, Luoland, Matabeleland, Basutoland, Zululand and Mashonaland. These concepts appear to empower and yet disempower people.

Activities: African traditions and culture

There are many activities that can be carried out to demonstrate how the idea of 'African traditional society' is both an imperialist creation of European modernity and colonial engagement as well as the responses to that. European imperialism, colonialism and modernity in general do not operate in Africa as expected.

The problem for colonial discourse is that it wants to produce compliant subjects who reproduce its assumptions, habits and values – that is 'mimic' the colonizer. But instead it produces ambivalent subjects whose mimicry is never very far from mockery. Ambivalence describes this fluctuating relationship between mimicry and mockery, an ambivalence that is fundamentally unsettling to colonial dominance. In this respect, it is not necessarily disempowering for the colonial subject; but rather can be seen to be *ambi-valent* or 'two-powered'. The effect of this ambivalence (the simultaneous attraction and repulsion) is to produce a profound disturbance of the authority of colonial discourse (Ashcroft, Griffiths and Tiffin, 1998:13).

ACTIVITY

Identifying and owning or rejecting modernity

In groups, students identify modern skills, properties, activities and cultural practices which they disown because of pressures from their respective religions and cultures. Examples include the following:

1   An educated woman is made to feel that she has lost rather than gained something important in life. She is therefore forced to disown her education in the context of cultural and religious practices, for example, many African women have sacrificed their professions because of marriage and family expectations.

2   Being made to feel that to be rural is to be authentically African and to be urbanized is to take up foreign identities.

Today, people, especially men, are proud of their rural homes and see them as their true homes. They are proud of the identities and roles they are given in the context of the rural while urban and 'modern' Africa is presented as 'European'. Sometimes the pride of being 'African' amounts to a celebration of poverty. To explain the same point in another way, many people acquire certain practices, material goods, statuses and skills and abilities but refuse to accept them as part of their identities, for example, food, plants or even democracy and education.

...many people acquire certain practices, material goods, statuses and skills and abilities but refuse to accept them as part of their identities

From modernity to traditional societies

'Modernity' has come to mean more than the 'here and now'. It refers to modes of thought and social organization that emerged in Europe from about the sixteenth century and spread to other parts of the world through European imperialism and colonialism. Europe constructed itself as 'modern' (rational, dynamic, secular, scientific, dominated by urban life) and constructed the non-European as 'traditional' (static, primitive, emotional, religious, dominated by rural life).

Modernity is a discourse that enabled the large-scale regulation of human identity both within Europe and in its colonies. The emergence of modernity is coterminous with the emergence of Euro-centrism and the European dominance of the world effected through imperial expansion. Modernity emerged at the same time as European nations began to spread their rule. The European models of historical change became the tools by which those societies were denied any internal dynamic or capacity for development.

The European models of historical change became the tools by which those societies were denied any internal dynamic or capacity for development.

By the time the scramble for Africa took place, the turn from a civilizing mission to a law-and-order administration, from progress to power, was complete. In the quest to hold the line, Britain was the first to marshal authoritarian possibilities in native culture. In the process, it defined a world of the customary from which there was no escape (Mamdani, 1996:21).

The definition of the customary by the colonial powers meant the administration of the white settlers directly through the civil law of the state and non-settler Africa and indirectly through 'native authorities'. These channels were used to reinforce cultural practices and institutions in local communities which were compatible with the colonial powers and later with post-colonial authority; they were generally monarchical, patriarchal and authoritarian. For instance, they manipulated traditional religious myths about metaphysical connections between the land and indigenous rural communities. Hence, they talk about Mashonaland. Matebeleland, Manicaland, Kikuyuland, Zululand. And yet indigenous peoples had no title deeds to *their* land.

Customary law is state ordained and state enforced: it is not based on the needs and values of particular indigenous communities:

> 'The colonial government also asserted its right to depose and appoint chiefs…When government realized how important it was to have local people to exercise control over the rural areas on its behalf, it began to increase the powers of chiefs and to support cooperative chiefs economically… In the later years, the chiefship became associated with government power and government salaries' (Bourdillon, 1993:62).

It is therefore not surprising that Women and Law in Southern Africa concludes that 'the official customary law of southern Africa is a rigid, skewed and sometimes distorted version of the customary law at the time when it was collected, which often has little to do with the lives of the people in whose name it has been applied' (WLSA, 1997:5-6).

African identities are, in many ways, constructed by colonial and modernizing forces

In spite of appearance and general belief, therefore, African identities are, in many ways, constructed by colonial and modernizing forces. The idea of Africa itself is largely a European one (Mudimbe, 1988 and 1994). Chimhundu (1992) has demonstrated that the identity of the 'Shona' was largely created by colonial powers in collaboration with missionaries and élite Africans (also Vail, 1996:229-235).

Ranger has argued that most of the so-called African traditions are actually 'invented traditions'. He argues that 'tribes' were invented and reorganized to become the bearers of customary law. The favoured concept of the customary opposes the individual and the group, civil society and community, rights and tradition. This is called binarism – the cultural construction of reality which involves the suppression of ambiguities by postulating binary opposition of categories, black/white, man/woman and civilized/primitive. Binary oppositions usually establish relationships of dominance. The dominant concept of tradition or custom misses the liberatory possibilities in pre-colonial societies. It tells a one-sided closed story, which is difficult to believe.

We try… to recover categories, institutions and practices ignored by the dominant colonial discourse.

Our seminar tries to interrogate and open up the story by retelling it as more ambiguous and making more visible the predicament of women. We try, like Nzengwu, to recover categories, institutions and practices ignored by the dominant colonial discourse. Sometimes we demonstrate how Africans have appropriated colonial institutions, practices and strategies. It is exciting and challenging when we engage in some kind of archeology that demonstrates processes of appropriation and catachresis. These are processes in which the colonized, oppressed or marginalized empower themselves by appropriating some aspect of the dominant culture and claim that it also existed in their own prior to the domination. For example many Africans apply the terms 'nation', 'democracy' and 'religion' to groups, institutions and practices existing before colonialism.

It is even more exciting when these strategies are used to deconstruct patriarchal institutions in order to facilitate the construction of societies which are more just.

In the seminar we recognize the importance of acknowledging colonial domination and the responses of the African liberation struggles. As Mamdani points out:

> 'The form of (colonial) rule shaped the form of revolt against it. Indirect rule at once reinforced ethnically-bound institutions of control and led to their explosions from within. Ethnicity (tribalism) thus came to be simultaneously the form of colonial control over natives and the form of revolt against it. It defined the parameters of both the Native Authority in charge of the local state apparatus and of the resistance to it' (Mamdani, 1996:24).

Yet our seminar tries to widen the scope of the African social imaginary and go beyond the colonial discourse. Here, I use 'social imaginary' in Charles Taylor's sense of 'the ways people imagine their social existence, how they fit together with others, how things go on between them and their fellows, the expectations that are normally met, and the deeper normative notions and images that underlie these expectations' (Taylor, 2004:23). African people are more than mere victims and beneficiaries of colonialism, modernity, patriarchy and the liberation struggles. They are also active builders of and participants in these processes. We assume that people have more choices than they usually acknowledge. They make choices in constructing social identities and in building and responding to social realities. As Anthony Giddens points out:

> 'We begin from the premise that to be human is to know, virtually all of the time, in terms of some description or another, both what one is doing and why one is doing it...All human beings continuously monitor the circumstances of their activities as a feature of doing what they do and such monitoring always has discursive features (Giddens, 1991:35).

Human beings, therefore, are not passive objects of history, culture and traditions. This includes women. Bourdillon points out that there are social spaces and opportunities for individual human beings to contribute to the development of their cultures and traditions through the choices they make:

> 'We think of culture and tradition as coming from the past, something proven and stable on which we can rely. In fact, tradition and culture constantly change according to the choices we make. We choose things from the past that serve our present needs' (Bourdillon, 1993:9).

African people are more than mere victims and beneficiaries of colonialism, modernity, patriarchy and the liberation struggles

The oppressed, marginalized and exploited always have the power to contribute to their own liberation and to build their own identities.

Michel Foucault's work demonstrates that social power is not a zero-sum game. The oppressed, marginalized and exploited always have the power to contribute to their own liberation and to build their own identities. Human beings are not mere victims of cultures and religions, they also actively participate in their construction.

> 'Our culture gives us a framework within which we think and live. But we are not slaves to custom. We often cite culture and custom to support the actions which serve our interests. But, in fact, we often pick and choose from our culture those aspects which best help us to cope with our present circumstances' (Bourdillon, 1993:11).

Several concepts in post-colonial studies have been developed to deal with various processes and strategies used by African peoples to respond to colonialism. I have used the Routledge *Key concepts in post-colonial studies* by Bill Ashcroft, Gareth Griffiths and Helen Tiffin (1998) to discuss some of these strategies which are useful and relevant to the liberation of women and the struggle against monarchical, hierarchical, patriarchal and authoritarian contexts. We have in the past engaged in classroom activities that raise the issue of women's social *agency* in the contexts of African religions and traditions. The question of agency 'hinges on the question of whether individuals can freely and autonomously initiate action, or whether the things they do are in some sense determined by the ways in which their identity has been constructed' (Ashcroft, Griffiths and Tiffin, 1998:8) in their religions and traditions. In demonstrating the agency of women and the marginalized, the seminar encourages students to see the ambivalences, ambiguities, dislocations and points of abrogation in male-dominated societies. These are seen as opportunities to be taken advantage of through appropriation, deconstruction, catachresis and the development of a discourse of social justice, especially for women. As pointed out in *Key concepts in post-colonial studies*, '...both feminists and colonized peoples, like other subordinate groups, have also used *appropriation* to subvert and adapt dominant languages and signifying practices' (Ashcroft, Griffiths and Tiffin, 1998:102).

...the seminar encourages students to see the ambivalences, ambiguities, dislocations and points of abrogation in male-dominated societies

Conclusion

If Bourdillon is right, then we need to identify possibilities in our religions, traditions and cultures for the improvement of the lives of the disadvantaged of our societies, especially women. In Africa, it is critical to start with our ways of seeing, our philosophies and our religions. African philosophy, African religions and cultures have been historically used to undermine the welfare of women. Our seminar demonstrates that this does not mean they will always play that role. The seminar identifies and encourages the use of opportunities for women's liberation through analysis of African religions, traditions and cultures, emphasizing the historical and social nature of traditional religions and cultures.

Being on the SEARCWL programme and developing and conducting this seminar has challenged me in many ways. It has forced me to think more deeply about my own teaching and my own work at Arrupe Jesuit College which is male dominated. First, it has shown me how philosophy, as an historical and cultural tradition, has been male constructed and oriented. But it has given me opportunities to identify ways of turning philosophy into a liberating tool that can collaborate with other disciplines. As a philosopher, I have suffered my own humbling version of what Zygmunt Bauman (1987) called 'the fall of the legislator'. The seminar helped me to see how philosophy is not 'the queen of subjects' but one among equals. I have interacted with able, professional men and women who helped me to place philosophy in its academic context. Working with students trained in different disciplines and coming from various cultures of Africa has helped me to see more clearly the structures of power, control and authority and how philosophy and religion are implicated in them.

My work as the regional coordinator for eastern and southern Africa of the African Forum for Catholic Social Teaching (AFCAST) has benefited a lot from my experience of developing and conducting this seminar. My sense of the values of the church's social teaching has been deepened. For example, the moral challenges of respecting the dignity of every human person, especially that of women and the marginalized, have clearly been demonstrated to me.

It is easy to identify values and principles of social justice. It is more difficult to work concretely to realize those principles in the real world where philosophy is not the only discipline. In this real world, different religions, traditions and cultures do not only exist side by side, but they also interact with each other. The challenge that this programme has helped me to confront is how to mobilize, lobby and inspire people to work towards the liberation of every human being in a multi-cultural, multi-religious, inter-disciplinary context. Developing and conducting the seminar has made me appreciate more the need to inculturate Catholic social teaching. I am beginning to appreciate ways in which Catholic social teaching and indeed the church itself can grow by responding to the needs of the marginalized and by listening to the aspirations of women.

The seminar identifies and encourages the use of opportunities for women's liberation through analyses of African religions, traditions and cultures

The challenge that this programme has helped me to confront is how to mobilize, lobby and inspire people to work towards the liberation of every human being in a multi-cultural, multi-religious, inter-disciplinary context

Bibliography

Adorno T.W. and M. Horkheimer (1986) *Dialectic of the Enlightenment*, translated by John Cumming, Continuum, New York.

Adu Boahen A. (ed) (1990) *UNESCO General history of Africa, Volume VII: Africa under colonial domination 1880-1935*, abridged version, University of California Press, Berkeley.

Appiah K.A. (1992) *In my father's house: Africa in the philosophy of culture*, Oxford University Press, New York.

Ashcroft B., G. Griffiths and H. Tiffin (1998) *Key concepts in post-colonial studies*, Routledge, London and New York.

Babu A.M. (1981) *African socialism or socialist Africa?* Zimbabwe Publishing House, Harare.

Baker G.P. and P.M.S. Hacker (1984) *Scepticism, rules and language*, Basil Blackwell Publishers, Oxford.

Baker J., and T.A. Aina (eds) (1995) *The migration experience in Africa*, Nordiska Afrikainstitutet, Uppsala.

Bauman Z. (1987) *Legislators and interpreters*, Basil Blackwell Publishers, Oxford.

– (1992) *Intimations of postmodernity*, Routledge, London and New York.

– (1993) *Postmodern ethics*, Basil Blackwell Publishers, Oxford UK and Cambridge USA.

– (1995) *Life in fragments: Essays in postmodern morality*, Basil Blackwell Publishers, Oxford UK and Cambridge USA.

Beck U., A. Giddens and S. Lash (1994) *Reflexive modernization: politics, tradition and aesthetics in the modern social order*, Stanford University Press, Stanford.

Benhabib S. (1992) *Situating the self: gender, community and postmodernism in contemporary ethics*, Routledge, New York.

Bernstein R.J. (ed) (1985) *Habermas and modernity*, Polity Press, Cambridge.

– (1992) *The new constellation: the ethical-political horizons of modernity/postmodernity*, The MIT Press, Cambridge USA.

Bhabha H.K. (1994) *The location of culture*, Routledge, London and New York.

– (1983) 'Difference, discrimination and the discourse of colonialism', in F. Barker *et al.* (eds) *The politics of theory*, University of Essex, Colchester.

Biko S. (1978) *I write what I like*, a selection of his writings edited by Aelred Stubbs, Heinemann, London.

Bourdillon M.F.C. (1993) *Where are the ancestors? Changing culture in Zimbabwe*, University of Zimbabwe Publications, Harare.

Brubaker R. (1984) *The limits of rationality: an essay on the social and moral thoughts of Weber*, Routledge, London and New York.

Cesaire A. (1972) *Discourse on colonialism*, translated by J. Pinkham, Monthly Review Press, New York.

Clegg S. (1980) *Power, rule and domination: a critical and empirical understanding of power in sociological theory and organisational life*, Routledge and Kegan Paul, London.

Coetzee P.H. and A.P.J. Roux (eds) (1998) *The African philosophy reader*, Routledge, London and New York.

Eze E.C. (ed) (1997) *Postcolonial African philosophy: a critical reader*, Basil Blackwell Publishers, Oxford.

– (1997) *Race and the enlightenment: a reader*, Basil Blackwell Publishers, Cambridge, Massachusetts.

Fanon F. (1966) *The wretched of the earth*, Penguin, London.

Foucault M. (1970) *The order of things*, Tavistock Publications, London.

– (1977) *Discipline and punish*, translated by A. Sheridan, Pantheon, New York.

Galston W.A. (1991) *Liberal purposes: goods virtues, and diversity in the liberal state*, Cambridge University Press, Cambridge.

Giddens A. (1991) *Modernity and self identity: self and society in the late modern age*, Polity Press, Cambridge.

Graham G. (1990) *Living the good life: an introduction to moral philosophy*, Paragon House, New York.

Griaule M. (1975) *Conversations with Ogotemmeli: an introduction to Dogon religious ideas*, Oxford University Press for the International African Institute, New York.

Gyekye, K. (1997) *Tradition and modernity*, Oxford University Press, Oxford.

Habermas J. (1972) *Knowledge and human interests*, Heinemann, London.

Hall S. and B. Gieben (eds) (1992) *Formations of modernity*, Open University, Polity Press, Cambridge.

Hobsbawm E. and T. Ranger (1983) *The invention of tradition*, Cambridge University Press, Cambridge.

Hope A. and S. Timmel (1984 and 1995) *Training for transformation: a handbook for community workers, Volumes I –IV*, revised edition, Training for Transformation Institute, Kleinmond, South Africa.

Hountondji P. (1983) *African philosophy: myth and reality*, with an introduction by Abiola Irele, Hutchinson University Library for Africa, London.

Ingram D. (1990) *Critical theory and philosophy*, Paragon Issues in Philosophy, Paragon House, New York.

James G.M. (1954) *Stolen legacy: Greek philosophy is stolen Egyptian philosophy*, James C. Winston Publishing Co., Inc., Nashville, Tennessee.

MacIntyre A. (1981) *After virtue*, University of Notre Dame Press, Chicago.

Mamdani M. (1996) *Citizen and subject: contemporary Africa and the legacy of late colonialism,* Princeton University Press, Princeton.

Masolo D.A. (1995) *African philosophy in search of identity,* East African Educational Publishers, Nairobi.

Mbiti J.S. (1969) *African religions and philosophy,* 2nd edition, Heinemann, Portsmouth.

Miller D. (1976) *Social justice,* Clarendon Press, Oxford.

Mudimbe V.Y. (1988) *The invention of Africa: Gnosis, philosophy and the order of knowledge,* Indiana University Press, Bloomington and Indianapolis.

Nicholson L.J. (ed) (1990) *Feminism/postmodernism,* Routledge, New York and London.

Nkrumah K. (1964) *Consciencism: philosophy and ideology for decolonization,* Panaf Books, London.

Norman R. (1983) *The moral philosophers: an introduction to ethics,* Clarendon Press, Oxford.

Nussbaum M. and A. Glover (eds) (1995) *Women, culture and development: a study of human capabilities,* Clarendon Press, Oxford.

Nzegwu N. (1995) 'Recovering Igbo traditions: a case for indigenous women's organizations in development', in M. Nussbaum and J. Glover (eds), *Women, culture and development,* Clarendon Press, Oxford.

Oruka H.O. (1978) 'Four trends in current African philosophy', presented at the William Amo Symposium in Accra, Ghana, 24–29 July 1978, and quoted by P.O. Bodunrin, 'The question of African philosophy', in R.A. Wright *African philosophy: an introduction,* 3rd edition, University Press of America, Lanham, New York and London.

– (1990) *Trends in contemporary African philosophy,* Shirikon Publishers, Nairobi.

– (ed) (1991) *Sage Philosophy: indigenous thinkers and modern debate on African philosophy,* African Centre for Technology Studies, Nairobi.

Oruka H.O. and D.A. (eds) (1983) *Philosophy and cultures,* Bookwise Ltd, Nairobi.

Poole R. (1991) *Morality and modernity,* Routledge, London and New York.

Ranger T. (1985) *The invention of tribalism in Zimbabwe,* Mambo Occasional Papers – Socio-Economic Series No 19, Mambo Press, Gweru.

Rorty, R. (1980) *Philosophy and the mirror of nature,* Basil Blackwell Publishers, Oxford.

– (1989) *Contingency, irony and solidarity,* Cambridge University Press, Cambridge.

Said E. (1982) *Orientalism,* Routledge and Kegan Paul, London.

Sandel M. J. (1982) *Liberalism and the limits of justice,* Cambridge University Press, Cambridge.

Sandel M.J. (ed) (1984) *Liberalism and its critics,* Basil Blackwell Publishers, Oxford.

Schlag P. (1998) *The enchantment of reason,* Duke University Press, Durham and London.

Sen A. (2009) *The idea of justice,* Allen Lane, London.

– (1992) *Inequality re-examined,* Russell Sage Foundation/Harvard University Press, New York.

– (1987) *On ethics and economics,* Basil Blackwell Publishers, Oxford.

Serequeberhan T. (ed) (1991) *African philosophy: the essential readings,* Paragon Issues in Philosophy, Paragon House, New York.

Skillen A. (1977) *Ruling illusions: philosophy and the social order,* Harvester Press, Hassocks, Sussex.

Taylor C. (2004) *Modern social imaginaries,* Duke University Press, Durham.

Toulmin S. (1990) *Cosmopolis: the hidden agenda of modernity,* Free Press, New York.

Tempels P. (1959) *Bantu philosophy,* Presence Africaine, Paris.

Vail L. (1996) 'The creation of ethnicity in South Africa', in J. Hutchinson and A.D. Smith (eds), *Ethnicity,* Oxford Readers, Oxford University Press, Oxford.

Walzer M. (1983) *Spheres of justice: a defence of pluralism and equality,* Basil Blackwell Publishers, Oxford.

West C. (1993) *Beyond Eurocentrism and multiculturalism: prophetic thought in postmodern times, Volume 1,* Common Courage Press, Monroe.

– (1993) *Beyond Eurocentrism and multiculturalism. Prophetic reflections: notes on race and power in America, Volume 2,* Common Courage Press, Monroe.

Winch P. (1958) *The idea of a social science and its relation to philosophy,* Routledge, London.

Wiredu K. (1980) *Philosophy and an African culture,* Cambridge University Press, Cambridge.

– (1996) *Cultural universals and particulars,* Indiana University Press, Bloomington.

Wiredu K. and K. Gyekye (1992) *Person and community,* Ghanaian Philosophical Studies I, The Council for Research in Values and Philosophy, San Antonio.

Wittgenstein L. (1922) *Tractatus logico-philosophicus,* translated by C.K. Ogden with an introduction by B. Russell, Routledge, London.

– (1958) *Philosophical investigations,* translated by G.E.M. Anscombe, Basil Blackwell Publishers, Oxford.

Wright R. A. (ed) (1984) *African philosophy: an introduction,* 3rd edition, University Press of America, New York.

Do it, then do it again
The practical course and the dissertation

Julie Stewart

Africa needs highly skilled and competent researchers into law and legal issues. This is especially so with laws that affect women and girls and where there are intersections between formal state versions of law and adjudication and informal competing customary and religious adjudicating and reglementary[1] systems. More especially, there is a need for researchers from the continent in their own right, researching their own rites and the intersections between post-colonial state laws, received laws and religious and customary laws. One of the primary goals of the Masters in Women's Law is to turn out motivated, competent, independent local and national researchers in the field of women's law. Such researchers need to be able to empathise with the researched and provide insights into the issues to be researched from a personal perspective that gives an additional edge to the research. There is no intention to suggest that researchers from beyond the continent should not or cannot carry out relevant and important research but the time has come for 'home-grown' researchers to come to prominence on the continent. At a conference in Europe in 2009, I was chatting to a fellow conferee on the way to the tram who, on discovering where I came from, commented, 'There are more Africanists this time than ever before.' I retorted perhaps precipitously that 'I'm not an Africanist but a normalist'. Meaning that what I do is my daily work as a lawyer, lecturer and researcher interacting with all the systems that regulate and reglement lives – I did not discover whether he was offended by my response or not.

Legal research of the kind undertaken in women's law is not sex or gender neutral. It can never be strictly objective and disinterested but it can be methodologically transparent, sensitive and pertinent. Satisfying these criteria is one of the challenges to be grappled with as our masters students

One of the primary goals of the Masters in Women's Law is to turn out motivated, competent, independent local and national researchers in the field of women's law.

---

[1] 'Reglementary' being Falk Moore's useful term to describe non state recognized and enforced systems that regulate the lives of individuals.

tackle the two main research exercises carried out on the programme: the first semester field research, which is undertaken in the practical course, and the final semester dissertation.

In this chapter, I describe and discuss the research design and analysis processes that we use in these two courses. The chapter is broken down into two main sections: firstly the conceptualizing and designing phase of the research and secondly the analysis and writing up phases undertaken in each of these courses.

What takes place in the first semester field research in the practical course is replicated and extended for the dissertation field research and the analysis and write up phases. In the first semester, given the short timeframe for the field research and write up, students compile a short report which is more narrative in content than we expect in the much deeper and more analytical dissertation research and writing process. Thus, in reading the chapter, it will be apparent that the first semester practical course is intended to be an initial hands-on experience which prepares the students for the dissertation. Some students may also go through this process in one or more of the optional courses where they carry out a mini-research exercise.

The first semester practical course is a practical application of the theories and methodologies canvassed in the other three first semester courses – 'Theories and perspectives in women's law', 'Research methodologies' and 'Human rights and women'. At this point we are more concerned with the design process and a mini run-through than detailed research – it is about displaying the potential of research and how to accomplish it. The practical course assessment was 50 per cent for field research and write up and 50 per cent for a two-hour examination on designing a research proposal.[2]

One additional reason for the first semester field research is to demonstrate to students, before they begin the second semester optional courses, the importance of having a grounded understanding of issues that are canvassed and the potential significance of investigative research into issues that arise in those courses. Students are quite often inspired to take up issues that arise in their optional courses as topics for their dissertations.

One additional reason for the first semester field research is to demonstrate to students … the importance of having a grounded understanding of issues

One process, multiple outcomes

With up to 36 students on a programme,[3] it is imperative that we have a flexible but consistent approach to research design – an approach which can accommodate a multiplicity of different topics while at the same time enabling us to use a broadly cast uniform design template. This is not as difficult as it seems, providing that there is a broad guiding framework into which virtually

---

[2] Under the amended regulations: 75 per cent for the report, 25 per cent for the examination.

[3] There was an intake of 36 students in 2011.

any topic can be slotted.[4] The main challenge has been to design a standard set of problem identification and research design tools that are not confining in terms of conceptualizing issues – tools which demand rigour, keep the initial topic controlled but do not impede the development of new and emerging assumptions and the identification of critical intersections between areas and issues. I asked one of our current guest lecturers who had previously done the Diploma in Women's Law what the key was to her being able, as she had once told me, to quickly sort out her doctoral proposal at Stanford based on what she had done in the diploma. The question was difficult, in the sense of pinning it down to one specific element, but she thought it was because she was able to see how the pieces of the problem, however diverse, fitted together and also to identify potential sources of data and relevant materials.

I describe the methodologies, methods and analytical techniques we are currently using. As these are in a constant state of mutation, the process described at the time of publication will change, although not necessarily radically, with each new piece of work and certainly depending on grounded need with the next masters class.

Part I: First things first – choosing a topic

Normally the topic that a student chooses to research is influenced by concerns about women's needs, women's rights or women and the girl child's access to resources. However, choice of a topic to research can be influenced by many factors and students do not always readily articulate, even to themselves, why they have chosen a particular topic.

I deliberately added 'even to themselves' as often students cannot initially explain why they are interested in a particular topic. It is only when you probe more deeply into the topic and its connection to their lives that it becomes apparent. Not infrequently there is a surprise at the underlying reason that is evinced (see the example box on the next page).

the women's law approach… provides the framework to incorporate any appropriate theoretical and methodological approaches and methods that are pertinent and appropriate to the research being undertaken

The very nature of the masters programme means a women's law approach is paramount and this is true too for those who are not on the programme but seek us out as supervisors. So to that extent, perspectives and methodologies are largely predetermined. Yet at each point in the research a range of potential methodologies informs the way forward. This is because the women's law approach, as described earlier in this book, provides the framework to incorporate any theoretical and methodological approaches and methods that are pertinent and appropriate to the research being undertaken.

---

[4] This broad guiding framework is discussed in *Pursuing grounded theory in law* (Bentzon *et al.*,1998) and has been used by students, so we are informed, from disciplines other than law.

EXAMPLE

The topic formation process

An illustration of the dialogue that often takes place around the topic formulation process and the eventual revelation of why the research is being undertaken follows:

> One of our first diploma students undertook a study of how young girls, often below 12 years old, who were working as housemaids in Kampala were treated in arrangements made between their parents and the employer. A number of them had appeared before her as a magistrate, charged with theft from their employer. She had gone beyond her official remit and interviewed the girls and discovered that they had stolen because they received no personal reward for their work. Their earnings were paid direct to their parents. This helped inform her choice of topic. Some ten or so years later after a deeper study on these family arrangements for her MPhil, it emerged that she herself had been in a similar but fortunately more beneficial position in her aunt's home. Finally, in a human rights based article, the affinity that she felt with these young girls was revealed; an affinity that prompted her concern about their status and condition.

But it took a long while for it to be effectively articulated. We now try to get to this stage as early as possible. See Ssemanda Wolayo (2007) for a discussion of the cross fertilizations of personal and work experiences in formulating and conducting research. Suffice it to say that the key revelation may take place at any time in the research process and sometimes not until the point of a first draft and discussion of that draft.

Topic choice and the research cycle

Research at any level in university studies should not be done merely for the sake of compliance with degree regulations. The research should be undertaken to further knowledge and advance understanding in the relevant discipline. At this point it is often helpful to remind students of the research cycle, discussed in chapter 2, that shapes the research, theorizing, re-theorizing, research and analysis processes. This reminder places the students in the academic arena and demonstrates how they can make a contribution, small or large, to overall scholarship in a discipline.

Research is a serendipitous and uncertain process because what you research and how you research it will control what you find. What should emerge from research are new understandings of realities, evolution or adaptation of theories, new perspectives and critical insights. At SEARCWL, students are free to choose any topic to research for their dissertation, providing it is connected to women and the law.

ACTIVITY

Three moves to women and law game

Women's law as a focus gives a wide scope. More or less any issue can be rapidly connected to both women and to the law. I play an intellectual game, the 'three moves', when discussing topic selection. I state that any issue the audience cares to think of can be related to both women and law in less than three intellectual moves. I challenge the audience to come up with a topic in which this cannot be done. Over more than 20 years of playing it with classes and conference groups, I have never lost.

There is nothing magical or mystical in this, it is a simple case of sex and gender mainstreaming within law and legal issues, including human rights connections. All that is needed is to quickly unpack the issue and ask yourself how is it connected to human life and needs and from there to ask: How would it affect men or women?

No matter how esoteric and obscure the topic may seem, it is easy to make the connections to people, to women and then to law and also to human rights.

Remembering that women can be both included or excluded in relation to life issues, trade, science, even in the most esoteric of areas such as particle physics, is the key to the process. For example, issues you can pursue related to particle physics might be women's inclusion on research teams, women's education in the sciences and any sex-related special risks and dangers, if there are any, that women working in such a field need to address.

The first step[5] is to get the group or individual to identify their general areas of interest or their particular areas of interest within a prescribed topic, which will throw out useful perspectives and insights. In the masters dissertation supervision process, students are grouped according to countries, with Zimbabweans being allocated among all the SEARCWL based supervisors. The country basis of allocation facilitates field visits during data collection phases. These visits will be discussed in more detail later in this chapter – but we believe they are crucial to the efficacy of developing overall competence to conduct independent research. They also ensure that supervisors are familiar with the context and content of research and not least that the research is done.

Usually at this stage, even with prescribed topics, the ambit can be quite broad; after this initial phase, it has to be narrowed, usually considerably, and carefully focused.[6] The form we use to guide the process is shown opposite.[7]

---

[5] This is based on the in-house research design processes currently used at SEARCWL.

[6] Commissioned research also benefits greatly from this process as there are always nuances and hidden issues even in a relatively narrow research mandate.

[7] Obviously if it is for an individual the group references are removed but the exercise is identical in all other respects.

PRACTICAL COURSE: DEFINING AND DESIGNING RESEARCH TOPICS

Group name *(not compulsory but provides cohesion for the group)*

....

Group members

1..2...

3..4...

5..6...

A   Identified research problem – What needs to be researched? – Stage 1 in defining the topic

....

....

B   What are your/ the group's assumptions about the causes of the problem that you have decided to
       research. List your group's 4–6 main assumptions about the problem below:

●   ....

       ....

●   ....

       ....

●   ....

       ....

●   ....

       ....

●   ....

       ....

●   ....

       ....

Now for the next question! This is a critical question for women's law:

C   What is your objective in conducting this research?

....

....

Most students, whether as individuals or in groups, are able to come up with a general area of interest but effective research needs to be focused, controlled and manageable in relation to time, resources and geographical location. Our first instruction in formulating a topic is 'keep it narrow', yet many students even on the second time around in designing research still produce a wide, vague and a potentially time protracted research topic. Without fail, every student needs some guidance on how to focus on a much narrower issue within the broad general issue initially selected..

The dialogue shown in the box opposite is normal, in fact, expected. Most importantly it needs to be conducted with each student and with groups. Simply sending a student away and telling them to narrow their topic is rarely effective as grasping the notion of the breadth and potential depth of issues can only be informed by experience.

I will not elaborate the rest of the process, suffice it to say there is usually a realization based on having to unpack the emerging range of issues in detail that this is a broad area and that even a single aspect of it has many dimensions and ramifications.

Students are assisted in this process by filling in the relevant portion of the form after formulating (thinking about) their research assumptions (and articulating the nature of the problems or why they think there are problems). From these assumptions the research questions will be developed. Inevitably this process is interactive and somewhat repetitive, as each change requires reviewing the rest of the process. This review process continues throughout the life of the research. Once a clear and coherent set of assumptions is developed and their matching research questions generated, the various components of the research design can be considered and the methods to be used identified and developed. Rigorous attention to formulating the assumptions, using them as a way to probe the problem, also assists the potential researcher to see how complex and multi-faceted their chosen topic is.

Rigorous attention to formulating the assumptions, using them as a way to probe the problem, also assists the potential researcher to see how complex and multi-faceted their chosen topic is

At SEARCWL we use a standard approach to assist in the overall process. We proceed by stages with each stage building on the previous one. The second stage, after the initial broad area has been identified, pushes the student towards a much narrower topic. In a simultaneous process the research objectives and assumptions have to be identified and recorded – it is simultaneous as the one informs the other. The assumptions have to fit within the objectives but likewise the objectives have to be reflected in the assumptions. As the student formulates the assumptions it rapidly becomes obvious that there are many components to the broad topic they have identified. Usually at this point the general topic gets some degree of panel beating as well.[8] The process

---

[8] The topic is not the title of the research output document – that will almost invariably change as the work progresses – but it reflects the overarching interests and direction so even the term 'working title' is a little too defining.

EXAMPLE

Research topic dialogue with potential supervisor and supervisee

Supervisee:	Please will you supervise my dissertation? (Or – you are my assigned supervisor) I would like to write on 'women and human rights in Zimbabwe'. *(Sometimes it will be women in Africa[9] or comparing the rights of women in two, three or more countries and often internationally, 'to boot'!)*[10]
Supervisor:	Which women, which human rights are you interested in?
Supervisee:	Zimbabwean women and human rights. *(Looking at you askance and clearly doubting your capacity to understand even the simplest issue.)*
Supervisor:	*(Reaching for a thick book of human rights instruments.)* Well there are many different aspects to human rights. For example, and these are just a few potential areas, perhaps you want to look at those affecting health, application of the law, perhaps non-discrimination in a specific context ... *(flipping open the book to a strategic illustrative page).*
Supervisee:	Oh! But if I only do one I won't have enough to write!
Supervisor:	I can assure you that you will have more than enough to write. So think about whether you perhaps want to look at women and health. If you do then you would need to think about what aspects of women and health[11] are of special concern. You also need to consider which women, employed women, women in the informal sector, maternity issues? I can keep going! So what do you think you would like to research?
Supervisee	Ooh – yes, women's health, that is interesting.
Supervisor	So which aspects of women's health and which women would you like to research?
Supervisee:	All of them! *(Supervisee's face indicates that the potential supervisor seems intent on sabotaging their research plans and their life.).*
Supervisor:	How many words are you allowed to write; and when do you have to finish – or submit by?
Supervisee:	10–12,000 words and 6-9 months (plus other courses at undergraduate level) OR 18–25 000 words and 6-9 months (taught masters level).
Supervisor:	Well that is fairly short and a short timeframe. There are many aspects to women's health rights, any one of which would if thoroughly explored require examination of law, human rights, socio-economic constraints, geographical access, so you would need to decide on communities and areas. Ethnic and cultural considerations and restrictions will also probably be relevant. Is it to be about general issues of access to health care? If so, then which women would you research? Is it to be about access to reproductive health care and information for example? Which age groups? Urban or rural settings? Government obligations in health care provision, perhaps? If so, which groups of women will you focus on?
Supervisee:	Oh! I hadn't thought about all that! So I should choose another topic?
Supervisor:	No, it is a matter of focusing on a narrow issue as your entry point because it is bound to broaden from there, this is an explorative process. Why do you want to research in this area of the law and human rights?
Supervisee:	Well it *(whatever)* happened to X, or we struggle with it at work, *(perhaps some other insight filled comment)* *(Sometimes you get the answer – 'Because I am interested in women's issues. Then you have to probe until you get to the personal trigger.)*
Supervisor:	Ah! Well tell me about that problem and its various aspects ...

---

[9] This covers north, south, east and west Africa plus off-shore islands, a wide, complex group to tackle, even if you had time to master the whole arena of diverse religious, cultural and social patterns and of course legal systems.

[10] There are seldom resources for comparative studies and, even if there were, students often don't appreciate the need to fully understand the reality in other countries which may, on paper, appear progressive. In-depth research in each jurisdiction is needed to undertake effective and informed comparative research.

[11] It is the same regardless of topic, there are many potential aspects to every problem and even more to every area of the law.

is essentially the same for the first semester group research, the individual dissertation[12] and mini-researches within optional courses such as 'Women, commerce and law in Africa' and 'Women, law, family and social realities'.

Masters students are required to fill out the forms either as groups, in the first instance in the first semester, or as individuals in other courses and for the dissertation in the final semester.[13]

Formulating assumptions about the issues is the most critical part of the exercise

Formulating assumptions about the issues is the most critical part of the exercise and students are expected to inform this process from the work they have done on human rights and feminist theories and from cultural and religious insights generated in the first part of the first semester. For the dissertation, they can draw on all the first semester courses, especially the practical course, and from the optional courses they took in the second semester. In the case of undergraduates we expect them to go as far as possible with the process based on their other courses, in so far as they are relevant, and then we factor in human rights and other considerations as indicated by the research topic.

Formulating assumptions is a protracted process, especially the first time it is attempted. The exercise tends to wing back and forwards across the intra-net, between individuals or groups and supervisors, with comments and queries and at times impatience from the group or individual.

However, we persist in the detailing and refining exercise because once this is done fairly concisely and definitively, the process begins to flow. Paradoxically, despite the supervisors' rigour and 'pickiness', these assumptions are not to be treated as 'cast in stone'; they are malleable and constantly subject to modification in the field or as the research into the law or policy is pursued. Importantly the student has an early grasp of the ambit of the research and is able to cope with adversity in the field. After the first semester group experience the masters students are able to adjust their assumptions or at least articulate what seems to be skewed or problematic in relation to their assumptions by the time of their own field research.

The research to be undertaken is, with very few exceptions, qualitative

The research to be undertaken is, with very few exceptions, qualitative. There may be some minor statistical analysis, probably not even recognizable as such by statisticians. Some numbers may be tallied such as types and kinds of cases heard by fora, overviews of sentencing patterns and levels and other basic statistics but, realistically, apart from tallying respondent numbers, by

---

[12] At undergraduate level it is part of the final year of the degree programme and although some of the supervisees may have done women's law as an optional course, their experience of these approaches is varied. However, because of the rigour that is applied to the conceptualization of the problem and formulating the research most of the 'SEARCWL supervisees' seem to manage the dissertation quite competently.

[13] With undergraduate supervisees, we try if possible to convene them in a large group and introduce the process to them. This is however often difficult as undergraduates appear at different times seeking supervision – but that is another story.

EXERCISE
Teasing out the issues

Students begin by brainstorming and teasing out possible issues to research. Each person suggests a topic and then we link these and group them into around six broad areas. Students choose an overarching topic, then work together to formulate a broad research problem. If one or two areas arouse considerable interest, we refine the topics to enable complementary researches without much overlap. This multi-faceted nature of broad topics allowing two groups to work within their ambit also illustrates the unexpected depth and breadth of most potential topics.

Once the topics are roughly settled students can generate the assumptions. ('Roughly' is the best we can do at this stage as we will explore topics and issues more later.) Each student within a group takes up one assumption to develop and research.

This is hands-on learning so students will be familiar with the process when isolated in their home country for their dissertation research. They can draw on their recollections of processing data and shifting assumptions to determine what to do next or to solve a problem, even if communications with their supervisors are limited.

and large quantification is not used. The data collection process is grounded, every interview, observation or group discussion can and often does lead to reviewing and adjusting the assumptions and the research design.

Once the assumptions are honed to a reasonable level of relevance and precision, the next stage is to match these with research questions. Inevitably, producing the research questions requires revisiting the assumptions. Turning an assumption into a broad research question[14] raises aspects of the problem that might not have been adequately captured; if this is so, appropriate adjustments have to be made to the assumption and the question needs to be reconsidered, and so it goes back and forth. Once the topic and thus the territory of the research has been roughly settled (roughly because it will remain relatively malleable to the end of the writing up and editing stage), designing and planning the field research component commences. Although in this chapter what is discussed is predominantly field-based research, this design exercise can be used to map out what is needed, where to go and how to go about it for purely desk, internet and library based research.

Turning an assumption into a broad research question raises aspects of the problem that might not have been adequately captured

---

[14] To avoid confusion, these are not the questions to be put to respondents but the questions in the intellectual academic sense that the research needs or seeks to answer.

Theory, methodology and research design

Relatively early on in designing these research projects an interactive theory, methodology and methods choice has to be made. This choice will predetermine much of what is found and will shape what is sought to be uncovered in the research process. In the context of women's law, we need to consider the most effective ways to uncover the pertinent data and obtain a balanced and engendered perspective so that new insights and new theorizing can be undertaken.

Although this book describes methodologies and methods with a women's law bias, our suggested processes can be used to inform general approaches to determining the nature and form of research activities in other fields, in a less methodologically prescriptive way. Planning is all important so as to avoid rambling and potentially uncoordinated research processes.

At SEARCWL we try not to be constrained by theories, perspectives, methodologies or methods whilst at the same time we respect and use their conceptual significance, insights, direction and guidance.

Designing the actual field research requires the students to mentally map out the research arena geographically, predict probable data sources and assess the actors and structures they will need to engage with, who to interview and what to observe. Each research question (derived from an assumption) needs to be unpacked in terms of research needs and the logistics of undertaking the research need to be assessed in terms of person power and financial and other resources. Again, as at all other stages, students usually need to rethink the breadth of the research, often this point brings home the need to go narrow and deep.

Human rights, laws and the research design

Prior to departing for the field, comprehensive research plans are drawn up. This begins with a standard process. The first task is to link together assumptions and research questions with potentially relevant laws and human rights articles to build up an integrated research framework.

By listing potentially relevant national laws and policies in relation to the assumptions at the same time as listing the human rights articles that might be

> **NOTE**
>
> **The research budget**
>
> SEARCWL has a fixed budget for each student. For 2009/10 it was US$2,850 – we do not vary the amount between students and the research has to be tailored to fit the budget. Students usually complain that the small budget is unrealistic and the project unnecessarily complex. However, discussing the options produces a manageable and affordable research project.
>
> Some students still complain about the budget but, not surprisingly, these students often do the least actual field research. Other students obviously rustle up their own resources and treat their research costs contributions as their obligation to the programme and to women's rights. As you can imagine, a student who complains about the cost of secretarial and other unnecessary ancillary expenses gets very short shrift.

relevant, students can assess compliance with human rights imperatives at the formal level. Although, as those familiar with women's law approaches are aware, mere paper compliance is only the start of the compliance assessment process. The devil is in the implementation or non-implementation of the provisions in the legislation. Nor should we lose sight of the possibility that the issue under scrutiny may not have been expressly identified as a human rights or legal issue and that there may not even be any relevant law or even human rights directives on the matter (see box). The research may then become critical in identifying and recommending how the gap in the overall framework can be dealt with.

Likewise we encourage students to explore issues using the framework set out in chapter 2 that allows them to uncover pertinent local norms and customs. They need to assess such local norms and customs using the tools from the first semester and ascertain whether local practices satisfy basic human rights entitlements and how local norms and customs may violate human rights norms.[15] Human rights frameworks can be used to measure and assess local and national compliance

> **EXAMPLE**
> **Identifying gaps**
>
> One student, Fortune Chimbaru, herself a prosecutor and a mother, chose to research on the problems facing women with young children and babies who are subpoenaed as witnesses in criminal trials. Fortune initially, to her own surprise, found that the practice of barring children from the court while their mothers gave evidence had no legal sanction. Further, try as she might, she could not find a satisfactory human rights imperative that addressed the issue, even obliquely. This is the kind of situation that indicates a need to alert authorities and human rights bodies that they should consciously monitor and review sex and gender practices across the board. (See Chimbaru, 2008).

and even to inform the techniques recommended for negotiating greater human rights recognition and compliance at a local level. However, caution is required in using a human rights framework as human rights tend to dominate in terms of later analysis which may not always be what is required. At times we have to advise students to examine and assess national and local laws and customs more carefully before they plunge into a reformist human rights agenda.

Once this has been accomplished, the student has a rough working outline of the law (or absence of law), human rights and, probably, policy issues that are pertinent, well before the field research commences.

At the design stage it is important to determine where the relevant information to address the assumptions and answer the research questions can be obtained. This needs to be a flexible part of the design process, as information sources are in a constant state of flux and, especially using a grounded approach, they can change. Nonetheless a preliminary 'map' of where information is likely to be sought helps with overall organization of the research process and especially with logistics and deployment of resources. Not infrequently, at this

---

[15] For an example of such compliance see Hellum (2007).

stage it becomes apparent that resources are insufficient to encompass all the projected sources and thus some form of representative selection may need to be undertaken. Rigid sampling is not normally required as lawyers, legislators and courts are not necessarily moved by numbers but rather by issues and concerns – a discovery which sometimes causes initial consternation for social science based researchers who engage in research with lawyers. However, lawyers, especially those steeped in legal pluralism, will need to do careful sampling to establish the veracity of a claim. And this is especially so for claims regarding the nature and form of a customary or religious norm in substantiating that a custom or practice has transmuted, transformed or was originally mis-recorded or applied (see further on this in chapter 2).

Short-term research of this nature can be derailed by strikes, political unrest, wars, floods and other calamities. If the sources identification exercise has been carried out at the beginning of the research, it is easier to make adjustments while in the field and respond to any challenges presented – even if developments are totally unforeseen – because the notion of the research being disturbed in some way has been considered. In 2007, Fortune Chimbaru was faced with a protracted strike of prosecutors and magistrates in Zimbabwe during the most critical period of her research and court proceedings did not take place. Thus she was not able to interview more than two or three women who had come to court as witnesses. Of necessity, she had to transform the work into an analysis of how the prosecutors and judicial officers understood the issues. Although they were not presiding in court, she could access them in their offices and chambers.[16]

Researching what?

Precisely what is going to be researched in the narrower sense is the next step to tackle. Students have to be able to identify the arenas they want to examine. This varies from project to project and between individual projects even in the group research. If the research is a component of studies at SEARCWL, the subject matter must be connected to the law in some way but this includes all its pluralities and interrelated institutions.

The process requires going assumption by assumption and mapping the potential of each area to yield data and to assess the probable value of the data to be collected. The first table opposite is an example of what needs to be identified but obviously the categories vary by research project. Using this first table initially involves just ticking the boxes for each assumption. Then a second round takes place to identify more detailed issues in relation to each of the broad arenas. The second table deals with law but there is usually a wide

---

[16] See Chimbaru (2008). The research became an interesting exercise in gendered attitudes in the judicial system.

Table to identify the different arenas of the research

Assumption/ research question	law	custom	culture	economic issues	religion	government	other
1							
2							
3							
4							
5							
6							
7							

Table to unpack one arena of the research in more detail

Assumption/ research question	law	aspect1	aspect 2	aspect 3	aspect 4	aspect 5	aspect 6
1							
2							
3							
4							
5							
6							
7							

range of potential issues under each column so this would also be done for all the other major areas as well.

It is sometimes at this point that both supervisee and supervisor become acutely aware of the enormity of the topic, which might not be evident until all the potential aspects are unpacked. If this happens, there is a strategic opportunity to re-assess and consider whether a narrower entry point would be advisable. Once again, little is lost by such a decision, as in many instances the other aspects inform the research but they become ancillary rather than central. Of course if a significant monograph is being written or it is a multi-faceted research with numerous students as in the first semester, it is possible to maintain the wider ambit of the research.

Researching who?

When considering researching the law we emphasize that law in its written form is the product of institutions and the human mind; it does not exist without human intervention. Nor are the structures which represent the law actor neutral. This makes an actors and structures data collection framework appropriate for any grounded studies in law. Likewise an analysis of how actors shape and affect structures that determine the content and application of law has to be part of such empirical studies. Also we must explore how the 'inhabitants' of the structures are influenced by the forces within the structures (Bentzon *et al.*, 1998; Giddens, 1991). Thus we need to identify actors at all pertinent levels of structures so that as far as possible we obtain a holistic picture of influences and sources of influence. Chimbaru's research is again illustrative. There were different levels of awareness and approach and thus responses to the women's child care problems, from the guards at the gate of the court to the most senior judge in the court complex. The guards would respond that they are merely following what they assume to be the rules whereas the judge would respond, as was the case, with questions about the source of the rule, its authority and its content.

Identifying the potential respondents in advance and drawing up a projected respondents (actors) table alerts both supervisor and supervisee to the need for careful sampling. Asking why you've chosen that person or identified that post, for example, forces a careful consideration of the data to be sought and also the relevance of the selection to the overall research process. Thus, the supervisor needs to ensure that the supervisee has carefully and purposively selected who to interview as an overall group or individually. Merely collecting interviews on a random basis is rarely productive unless you need a general overall impression of the views of the public at large on a particular issue. If this needs to be undertaken then professional assistance from statisticians is invariably required.

...we need to identify actors at all pertinent levels of structures so that as far as possible we obtain a holistic picture of influences and sources of influence

Who are the actors you will target and why are they important to your research?

Assumption/ research question	Who will you research? Why?	Where will you research them?	How will you locate/sample them?
1			
2			
3			
4			
5			
6			
7			

In determining who to interview, a male/female balance, where both males and females are potential interviewees, is usually important. Even more important is the process of actively seeking out both male and female key informants, as well as male and female general respondents. Conscious efforts have to be made to locate the 'other' sex or gender. While concern about the paucity of female respondents among key informants is common, this can also affect the numbers of male respondents when the issue is perceived as being female in content and form (such as issues around female circumcision – see Ondieki, 2006). Men may be significant players in sustaining cultural practices, we may also assume they support particular practices. Thus, their assumed views direct women's thinking about matters. Yet men may be potential allies in reshaping practices. If they are not engaged, women with vested interests, such as traditional birth attendants and circumcisers, can hide behind men's assumed attitudes and control. Such women may then claim that such culture and attendant practices cannot be changed because of male resistance. Men may be unaware of or indifferent to the practices or deeply concerned about the need for change. But everyone is guessing or making unsupported assumptions about their views and attitudes (see Ondieki, 2006).

Conscious efforts have to be made to locate the 'other' sex or gender

At this stage it should be evident that even one assumption, thoroughly unpacked, its extent mapped, the actors and structures identified as well as the pertinent law and human rights analyzed and applied, could be the subject of a fruitful piece of research.

Bureaucracy and research

Students also need to assess how easy it will be to obtain the required data and what bureaucratic or other barriers are likely to hamper the research process. Thus a back up or alternative plan needs to be available or at least possible. By and large SEARCWL masters students, coming from work experience and from positions of professional authority, have an easier time obtaining access to key informants and research sites than undergraduate students but not always. Persistence is perhaps the best way forward but finding alternate routes to the data may be necessary. Sometimes officials deny students interviews but the same data may be available from official reports. While they may miss out on personal titbits and insider information, at least they can maintain progress.

The complexities of obtaining permission to research have to be examined on a country by country basis, as well as government department by government department and organization by organization. This can be tedious and delay progress but there is nothing to stop the student speculating on why permission is refused or delayed. Is there something to hide? It might even be a possible topic for research. Over the years a number of students at SEARCWL have speculated on why some non-governmental organizations may not want to be researched; their own experiential data may indicate that the organizations may not have been as scrupulous in conducting their activities as they ought to have been or as they have reported. Similarly, bans on conducting research in rural areas prior to elections point to the probability of improper practices in manipulating voters which incumbent governments might not want exposed to outside scrutiny.

Corroborating data from different sources is important so students must consider how to ensure the evidence they collect is not a one-off aberration.

Oh no, it's not going as expected!

No research is without problems and all too often a student abandons a viable topic early in the research because they encounter unexpected problems and barriers. Students in the field need to be able to begin the process of redirecting the topic and thus a short exercise in anticipating what to do in such cases is useful. Twice over the years SEARCWL students in countries other than Zimbabwe have abandoned a perfectly viable topic because of barriers they encountered. In both cases the decision was not transmitted to the supervisor in advance. In one case the student switched from looking at children and education to looking at adult education and in the other, it was a total change. Both of these episodes prompted a much more careful focus on managing problems and barriers in the design stage and facilitating an adjusted study, as Chimbaru did, rather than a change of topic. Thus addressing these issues as part of research design is important where there may be limited contact with students at critical points in the research.

Inevitably, the problems that occur are not those considered in advance. Nonetheless, having contemplated some problems should assist the student to take a proverbial deep breath and think the issue through before changing direction. Of course the best course of action is for the student to contact the supervisor and thoroughly discuss the matter. Although making contact is increasingly easier, even in an African rural context, it is not always possible.

What problems do you anticipate in carrying out your research? How will you deal with them?

Problem examples	Response/action examples
1 Permission to research denied – for example to prisons, child-related situations	Don't abandon – are there ways around the issue? The refusal itself is a major finding – why was it refused?
2 Prisons – constraints on inmates frankness	Perhaps look for ex-prisoners
3 Patriarchal controls – male chiefs who deny access to the researchers or try to control group discussions, and so on	Alternative venues?

A similar approach is needed when assumptions are not holding up, either totally or partially. At such a point it is vital for the student to pause and think about the implications of the challenge. It may be a positive finding in that changes have taken place and people know and assert their rights. Then the important question is why, then why again until an answer emerges and perhaps a new assumption will re-orient the research. The student has to anticipate possible challenges to assumptions in advance but this does not require adjusting the assumption until a sustained challenge to it occurs. One potential problem is students overreacting the first time an assumption is challenged. It is important that the assumption is further tested before adjustments are made. See the analysis section of this chapter for a fuller discussion of this.

The data collection process and research

I turn next to the field-based preliminary analysis of data. During the data collection process the methodological implications of what is taking place must be at the forefront of the student's mind. Students need to review what they are finding and revise their assumptions and research methods on a daily basis. As the field research and data collection proceeds, analysis is taking place. This is markedly different from research which is based on predetermined questions and rapidly compiled answers for later processing. Thus, at any stage in the data collection process, students should be able to reflect on the assumptions and how they are faring. They should be able to identify emerging issues, respond to external imperatives and have a sense of how the findings are generally shaping up.

Below: In the field: Women in an entrepreneurial saving scheme in Mwanza, Tanzania sharing out the annual profits

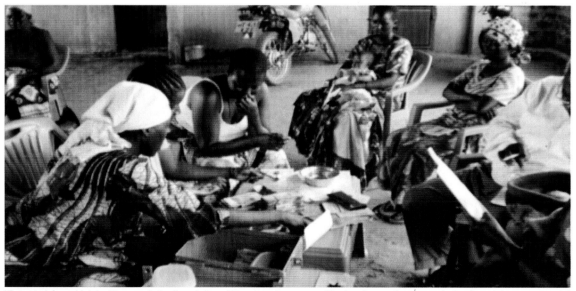

Extracted from Malula Nkanyemba's dissertation, 'Women entrepreneurship development: a case study of models assessment in facilitating women to generate social-financial capital in Mwanza City, Tanzania'.

In both the first semester and the final dissertation field research, supervisors[17] are present. The supervisor travels with the students to the research sites in the first semester field exercise and in the final semester they arrive to supervise during the field work. These interventions have their own specific agendas and are designed to enhance, troubleshoot and generally encourage and support the research process. As supervisors we find it instructive and informative to visit the research sites and discuss the research in depth. Although such visits may not be feasible on other programmes – they require funding and time – they should be seriously considered when and wherever possible.

To facilitate, monitor and gain significant insights from the research process, the significance of a meticulously maintained field diary cannot be overemphasized. This is a different kind of document from notes made in recording the collected data. It is a prompt to the researcher's mind about issues arising from the research. Again this is a flexible framework and many other categories can be added as required. Some useful issues to keep track of through the field diary are set out in a diary format below. If students maintain this and link the later research narratives as they compile them, the analysis process becomes much easier to manage.

Above: Dr Amy Tsanga in front of a greenhouse on a flower farm in Kenya – she was supervising a dissertation on conditions affecting women farm workers

---

FIELD DIARY

Date .... Place ....

Activity .... Interviewee.....................................

Observation ....

Notes

Observations

Notes of special Interest

Reminders – things to do, check up on necessary follow ups and verification

Daily review of assumptions and what is happening to them

Possible adjustments of assumptions?

Issues for discussion with supervisor.

---

[17] We do not have the luxury of visiting the research sites of the undergraduates we supervise but we do have mental maps of Zimbabwe in our heads and experience of research in the Zimbabwe context. On reflection these students may miss out to some extent on useful insights that we might be able to provide from the specific research context.

EXAMPLE

Cutting through the rhetoric

There have been countless times when just by visiting a remote, desolate or underdeveloped area, we gain insights that reshape emphasis and direction in work in progress. A trip to an outlying area of Zimbabwe with Tsitsi Mariwo, who was researching small-scale women vegetable growers and their marketing and developing options, evoked the query – *But are they small-scale?*

We become entrapped in nomenclatures and recycle development rhetoric and labels uncritically. The outcome of the research was that they are not small-scale and need to be considered as entrepreneurs in their own right – a critical shift in thinking about their development input needs as active farmers not those undertaking mini income-generating activities (Mariwo, 2008).

 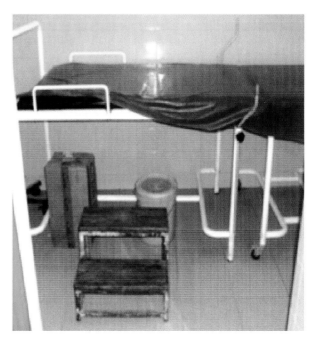

Above: In the field
Left: Disabled women leaving an interview near Dar es Salaam
Right: The labour ward bed that such women would have to climb onto, often with no assistance from nursing staff – an issue only evident during a field visit.

Extracted from Sakina Sinda's dissertation, 'A comparative study on the right to maternal health care of physically disabled women in three districts in Dar es Salaam, Tanzania (SEARCWL, 2010)

Part II: Analysis – getting a handle on the mass of data

All field work in the programme starting from the first semester to the dissertation involves collecting predominantly qualitative data. Usually this is in the form of interviews, group discussions, observations and distillations from records. Some quantitative data may also have been gathered. This is usually in the form of simple statistics about numbers of cases, incidences of phenomena, numbers of litigants, applicants, clients, patients, victims or other simple number compilations. Sometimes numbers of instances of particular forms of litigation, court decisions or administrative interventions are recorded. These are usually background materials rather than key to the overall research process but, as always, it depends on the work being undertaken. The discussion in this section of the chapter focuses primarily on analyzing qualitative data.

Analyzing qualitative data presents significant challenges. The sources of data, especially in grounded studies, are frequently diffuse. For example the researcher may have conducted group discussions or elicited open-ended information from varied respondents, observations, records and case law materials. Thus, appropriate ways of tackling the data in an integrated manner have to be devised. Once again there can be no rigid prescription of how to do it. Any advice given has to be seen simply as advice and not as a command.[18] What works for one set of data may be inappropriate for another set but we can offer general guidelines.

> ### NOTE
> #### 'Just think and add ink'
>
> Strangely, some students assume that books, journal articles, conference papers and the like somehow materialize instantly in final form direct from the author's brain onto paper or the computer. Convincing them of the agonizing process of analyzing, composing, editing, rewriting and rethinking is difficult. Somehow they feel deficient when we return their work with comments, queries and suggestions for improvement. Yet the work may be more than competent and progressing well. The expert's apparent process of 'just think and add ink' is not as easy as it seems from an outsider's perspective.

Doing it once and then again!

In the first semester, groups discuss the day's work with their supervisor every evening. This high level of contact continues to the end of the semester. After the field work and preliminary group analysis, we do a fairly intense one to one supervision of the analysis and write up stages. Each student has a period of one to one supervision in their home country during the dissertation field work and there is constant interaction with the supervisor during the final semester data analysis and write up.

---

[18] There are computer generated tools that search the narratives based on key words but we have not attempted to use these at SEARCWL although we believe it is a process that merits further investigation and assessment.

NOTE

This is harder than I thought!

Invariably some groups obtain a lot of data quite quickly but they need to carefully analyze what they have and look at emerging issues or reconsider their initial assumptions which might have been too simplistic. They have to be encouraged to critically review what they have found and consider other aspects they might pursue. Others will be tired, fraught and footsore, so supervision is a mixture of dishing out calming advice and encouragement in more or less equal doses.

I recall a number of groups and individuals over the years during this first semester exercise who revealed as the week proceeded, that it was all much harder than they envisaged. Some indicated that they thought they could go out for one day, collect the data and then spend the rest of the week relaxing at the hotel or shopping. Usually by the end of the week these same students are lamenting that they do not have enough time to follow up all the leads they have tracked down. Self evidently, this alerts them to the potential needs and perils when they are on their own in the final semester.

This amount of supervision may not be replicable in other programmes but in terms of research capacity development, the inputs bear fruit. As noted elsewhere, students from the programme seem to gain an advantage in formulating problems, writing proposals and using research techniques which they carry into further studies.[19]

During the first semester field research exercise every night each group has a one hour session with their supervisor. This means that the two supervisors spend two to three hours every evening going over the day's work with the students. Supervisors conduct less structured discussions and chats throughout the week, as and when the need arises. This is the start of the analysis process. At this point we do not inform them of this but wait until a couple of nights later on in the week when the realization seems to be literally popping out of their answers and further questions.

...students from the programme seem to gain an advantage in formulating problems, writing proposals and using research techniques which they carry into further studies

---

[19] Both Dr Tsanga and I have noticed when supervising some of our former diploma students on other masters programmes that, compared to the other students on those programmes who we either supervised or whose dissertations we examined, there was a markedly higher level of research competence amongst our own graduates. It might be that because they followed our processes we were more enthusiastic about their work. However, as far as we could be objective it seemed that their work was deeper, ultimately might be quite broad and yet remained more coherent and controlled.

First night jitters

The first night after the students have been in the field is invariably filled with questions about how their assumptions are holding up. It is unlikely that any group escapes without one or more assumptions being challenged to a greater or lesser extent. This is a critical time in the initial research process – it is filled with peril and opportunity. As discussed earlier in this chapter, research can be derailed if students don't respond to challenges to assumptions but it can also be enhanced as new insights are generated. To facilitate this process we ask questions along the following lines:

...research can be derailed if students don't respond to challenges to assumptions but it can also be enhanced as new insights are generated

1   *How are your assumptions holding up?*
    Each student responds with regard to their main assumption and sub-assumptions, in relation to their portion of the overall group research.

2   *What were your main findings today?*
    This flows logically from the assumptions question – because without findings there can be no challenges to the assumptions.

3   *What is the situation with your anticipated sources of data? Were they as expected? Did new sources emerge? Were some sources inadequate, non-existent?*
    Usually there are some surprises and more sources emerge than had been initially anticipated. Some assumptions are challenged. Both these outcomes are regarded as positive and the student is encouraged to explore why the research went the way it did.

Not infrequently when an assumption is challenged or even trounced, the student asks: 'Should I try another topic?' or 'Should I not mention this in my write up?' Our response is a definitive no in both cases. We then point out that this is a normal part of the process and that the correct response from the researcher is to analyze why and how the assumption has been challenged. Rarely, if the initial design process has been thorough and informed, is an assumption that meets such a fate totally inappropriate or without some substance. Often a challenged assumption may reflect, as discussed in the previous section and in chapter 2, a significant change in social or cultural attitudes. It may, given the kind of research that is being undertaken, be a view that has been distilled from previous work by other researchers which has not been re-explored through recent empirical research.

...a challenged assumption may reflect ...a significant change in social or cultural attitudes

Sometimes it is possible to rethink the issues from the perspective of why is something effective when it was assumed it would not be effective. Of course, after just one day in the field, there is a distinct possibility that the assumption was challenged in a relative way. Perhaps it was the socio-economic situation of the respondents that shaped the finding. So it is always important to consider whether the assumption in its initial form needs to remain on the agenda to be further tested. It is possible to have the initial assumption and an adjusted version running parallel to each other in the research process. From such a juxtaposition of assumptions, important findings about socio-economic or cultural situations of respondents may emerge. There are also likely to be insights into how social, cultural and economic situations are changing.

Through whose eyes? – questioning assumptions

Researching in groups, especially groups who come to the research from different professional backgrounds, different countries, differing cultures and religions, highlights how each of us views the world and other people's lives through our own personal lens. A classic example is assumptions about legal information dissemination and lack of awareness among rural communities of basic legal and human rights. Literacy and legal literacy levels differ greatly both intra-country and inter-country. A researcher or group often expresses surprise at the number of individuals in a rural area who know their rights. This might be turned into an adjusted or revisited assumption when it is uncovered, as happens, that the problem is not lack of knowledge of the law but issues of accessing the courts or administrative bodies. Some of these early challenges reflect how ingrained our views and attitudes are: they reflect how we replicate, often unquestioningly, standard opinions and prejudices.[20] Notions that rural women are illiterate or that they are amongst the poorest of the poor are sometimes profoundly challenged. As when we engage one on one with rural women and probe and discuss their lives from their perspectives, they become rounded and nuanced individuals. This provides better understanding as to how we should interact with them and assess their grounded needs.

Notions that rural women are illiterate or that they are amongst the poorest of the poor are sometimes profoundly challenged

As each day proceeds, individual research capacity is shaped in the research process. We inculcate the confidence to 'follow one's nose' within the overall guidance of the assumptions and the design.

Settling into the process

On the second night of the first semester field research process, the questions tend to refocus on assumptions. They then move onto the findings that are emerging and whether they are what we style emerging issues. Emerging issues are those issues that keep coming up but which lie outside the initial ambit of the assumptions. Dealing with emerging issues can be tricky because sometimes they are clearly new but related issues that are integral to the research. At other times they may be interesting but peripheral to the research being undertaken. In the former case, there is probably a need to incorporate

---

[20] Prejudice is used here in the sense of pre-judged – pre-formed views often with no critical awareness of the actual situation.

them into the research. Thus new assumptions and research questions have to be generated along with all the other tasks previously undertaken in the earlier stages of the research design. In the latter case the decision can be made to note the issue and even perhaps refer to it as one of those areas that might require consideration in later research.

The most difficult decisions to make are those concerning issues that are interesting, pertinent but not necessarily integral to the current thrust of the research. Yet, given sufficient time, they would probably merit incorporation. If limited time or resources are a factor, then the problem is self solving. In such a case the issues should be noted and the focus maintained on the original assumptions. If time or resources are flexible then it is probably worthwhile pursuing the matter. However, this of course begs the question, 'Is it integral to the research or peripheral?' A discussion with one's supervisor may assist but, if this is not possible, one approach is to ask the question 'Can I achieve my overall research objective without exploring this issue? If the answer is no, or it is unclear then it is probably better to include the issue, as it can always be 'discarded' at the time of writing up.

Making progress?

While still in the field, just by these simple questioning processes, students are analyzing and gaining understanding. Thus the meticulous processes demanded in designing the research, rather than being confining, become potentially liberating.

A major breakthrough comes when an individual student makes an informed decision in the field to respond to an emerging issue by generating a new assumption in response to key critical findings. This is the beginning of an incisive iterative analytical research process.

The very nature of the qualitative and grounded research process means that we have more problems maintaining the narrow focus of the research. Thus it is more likely that some issues will be sidelined than that new or peripheral, albeit interesting, issues included. Where the emerging issues are central to the topic or arise from more nuanced analysis of the data, the focus of the research needs deepening.

Usually such outcomes require a discussion between supervisor and supervisee. There is a further element and that is the assessed capacity of the student to juggle issues. A strong student can handle multiple perspectives and issues whereas a weaker student is usually best advised to stick to the straight and narrow. Such decisions are the supervisor's sorry lot in life.

Maintaining the momentum

On the third night of the first semester field work, questions are informed by what has transpired earlier in the week. Usually focus is on triangulating data, difficulties and gaps in the research data. How will they fill these gaps? Do they still need to find respondents? Are they sure they have sufficient data to answer the research questions? It may be important to remind groups about the various forms of records that they might be able to access. Perhaps they can deploy one or more of their number to seek them out. By this stage they only have one or two days left and the potential enormity of the overall research starts to 'sink in'. Which is precisely what we intend.

In the individual field research phase for the dissertation in the final semester, we employ more or less the same process. Intensity is greater and we put more emphasis on ensuring that the initial narrative account of the research is maintained and that the field diary is kept up to date. On average we spend two to three days with each student. This involves visits to field sites where this is possible and relevant. Over the years we have gained immensely from these visits in terms of understanding the countries in the region and their peoples. Where we go, who we go with and what we see and hear provides us with perspectives that are not usually available to others and certainly not to conventional tourists. One of my doctoral students, a Zimbabwean living in Arusha and working at the Rwanda tribunal, told people she was introducing me to that 'this is the only programme where the student decides what the supervisor does and sees'.

...'this is the only programme where the student decides what the supervisor does and sees'

Once the research has been recounted to the supervisor and the inevitable questions about assumptions are asked, a one to one dialogue between supervisor and supervisee begins. This dialogue continues to the completion of the work. Precisely how it is structured is determined by the topic, the perspectives and the methodologies employed. At a deeper level, the findings and how they are engaged with the assumptions, human rights, laws, customs and practices and other pertinent matters constitutes the analytical framework. These would be rambling and diffuse discussions to the outsider although they are conducted within the same framework as the first semester group discussions. Hopefully, data is aired and thought processes stimulated.

With a carefully monitored and grounded research process, by the time the formal data analysis process commences, a considerable amount of analysis has already been undertaken.

> **NOTE**
> ### Food for thoughts
>
> Supervision by motor vehicle is an interesting process as driving to and from the research site or sites, which may be some distance away and apart from each other, offers perfect opportunities to discuss the research.
>
> We usually do this along the lines of the first semester process, on a one to one basis and most importantly in a relaxed atmosphere. Feeding one's supervisees and having relaxed discussions over meals, gives time for reflection and is less intellectually threatening and thus usually more productive than formal sessions.

Formal data analysis – do it

In the first semester, data analysis continues on the return from the field. Formal data analysis exercises occupy a week. Students then prepare a disposition of their chapters. This is an elaborate table of contents that the supervisor reviews. As we have sat with them in the field and discussed their findings in evening sessions, the supervisors are able to direct pertinent questions as to why some data seems to have been excluded or de-emphasized and other data included. Theoretical perspectives that might be pertinent are discussed in the light of what the student has found. This is also the time to start probing about their findings and conclusions and whether they have documented the evidence to support them.

Once we have reviewed the disposition of chapters and asked the critical question as to whether there is any data that does not have 'a home' in the disposition, the student commences writing and writes for roughly ten days. The usual process is that the student fills in the disposition or framework with data, findings and conclusions but writing is a very individual activity. Supervisors consider and comment on the first drafts and then final editing and submission takes place. These are relatively short pieces of 5,000–6,000 words and we treat them like chapters in a book about the group research topic, although each student has to write up their methodology individually. So there has been a group supported first run through of the research process – it is short but shapes and informs the final semester individual process.

Then do it again

We set aside roughly twelve weeks for data collection in the final semester of the masters programme although we expect students to spend around four weeks of consolidated time. Then the data analysis and write up process takes seven weeks[21] at the end of which students submit their dissertations. We expect students to return with their research narratives complete and some preliminary classification of data already done. We actively discourage them from starting the formal writing process before they return. Those who do start often have a rude awakening when they find they made little of their data and they need to start afresh but, inevitably, some can do it and some cannot.

The way the human mind works through data collected and interposes it with theories and perspectives from multiple sources cannot be reduced to a series of exercises or formulae

The way the human mind works through data collected and interposes it with theories and perspectives from multiple sources cannot be reduced to a series of exercises or formulae. The best we can do is to suggest ways to enhance the process. Constructive critiques of students' work also improve analysis and writing and these are factored into the analysis process.

---

[21] In 2011 we extended this to a possible nine weeks for those who might need extra time. This was responding to those who may need extra language assistance before they can produce a final version of their work.

Getting down to basics

First and foremost in the analysis process is the task of preparing the research narrative. Just by doing this the data is cycled yet again through the researcher's mind and insights begin to emerge.

Insistence on the preparation of the full research narrative is a first requirement of the analysis process. This must be done by the students themselves. Although we treat it as mandatory for each student to prepare the entire narrative themselves, it is not always possible to ensure this. Some students, especially in the final semester, may use secretaries or field assistants of whom we are not aware (see box on the right).

As supervisors it is essential to impress on the students that they have much to gain by what should at this stage be a third traversing of the field data. First they record the data in its raw form in the field, second they write up the day's data in a more formal fashion and third they compile and write the narrative. Each one of these stages produces analytically important insights; the further the process proceeds, the greater the insights.

The next part of the process is designed to take the student from the level of a narrative, albeit in some cases a sifted and issue-integrated narrative, to a deeper level of analysis where they identify more crosscutting issues. Students sometimes perceive the preparation of the narrative as the end of the process. Sometimes they arrive for the data analysis seminar with a compiled narrative and literature and law review and assume that it is just a matter of a little editing and then they can submit (see box on the right). Suffice it to say, they initially quibble about needing to do anything more. Once they start to interrogate the data, however, they appreciate the need to comb through it in a variety of different ways and develop a more thorough and broadly engaged analytical structure.

NOTES
Making sure the students do the work themselves

With more mature students who have professional lives and ancillary services provided in the workplace, it is vital to stress the importance of doing the write up themselves. We have experienced those who obtain tape recordings of interviews or take along secretarial assistance and it is the secretary who transcribes the narrative and writes up the narrative from shorthand notes. This defeats the whole purpose of the exercise but it is usually the quality of the work that suffers as such work tends to be superficial. We frequently can tell when this has happened.

I'm finished mine already!

Some students say nothing to the supervisor but boast to fellow students that they're ready to submit. We discover this from occasional comments during the analysis process. Although we cannot generalize, in many instances such students produce the weakest final versions as they do no more than tinker with their previously prepared work.

Once the narrative is complete, it can be subject to a series of interrogations. One way to commence this process is to revisit the research design process and turn the elements of the design into interrogative tools, thereby stimulating analytical insights.

The simplest initial approach after the narrative is complete is to consider the fate of the original and field-informed assumptions. This is done in conjunction with the field diary which has hopefully been scrupulously maintained throughout the research process. The students need to use the comments in the field diary, especially those relating to assumptions and emerging issues, to re-address the wider and deeper implications of the data. From this point a more thorough engagement with the assumptions to see how they fared needs to be made. They will have done some of this in the field but they need to continue and repeat it where necessary as an integrated holistic process.

For some students the interrogation of the assumptions may present an ideal framework for the data analysis and write up of the work. But in other cases it may be clear that the research undertaken has pushed the boundaries and implications of the findings far beyond the assumptions. Thus, the basic framework needs to be shaped around emerging issues, human rights, law reform, gendered implications or some other imperative (see box below).

Precisely how the next stage of the process works in the mind of the student is difficult to discern. Individuals perceive the data through their personal lens. A supervisor or colleague who reads the narrative can make suggestions but the final distillation is multi-faceted and ought to be distinctly individual in orientation. Because we supervise in the field, it is possible to prompt recollections and push the teasing out of issues and categories based on our own recollections. This becomes especially pertinent at the formal data analysis session in the final semester.

Having interrogated the assumptions, the next goal in the process is to develop potential analytical categories. Each piece of work will require content-related specific categories. Some of these will be gender based, some socialization or religion based. Some may be sex based or related to administrative and governance issues. Some will be human rights and law based issues. Some may involve actively engaging with the plural dynamics of women and girls' lives. (For a fuller discussion of this see Hellum *et al*, 2007: xx–xxviii.) The crux of the process is prompting the students to categorize their data in a variety of different ways.

These first stages are designed to spark the analysis process and to facilitate the production of eclectic but controlled writing frameworks.

EXAMPLE

New rights or traditional entitlements?

Olivia Mchaju-Liwewe found herself confronted with theoretical questions about how to incorporate, address and defend women's land rights derived in a matriarchal society. How does one strategize in asserting such rights when they clash with externally-generated development programmes that take no account of women's prior customary rights? They insist that women's rights have to be created rather than that they are reversionary and arguably residual.

Her work finally emerged more as a methodological debate and a discourse on how to profile the seeming anomaly of women's superior land and other rights in the global development rhetoric. A rhetoric that assumes women's subordinate status and focuses on agendas and reforms directed at securing greater rights for women. Whereas the focus could be on, in such cases, securing and protecting the rights women already have (Mchaju-Liwewe, 2008).

There is no obvious standard starting place for categorizing qualitative data; this all depends on the data. However, one possible starting point, especially in work on plural systems of law, is to do some simple quantification of trends and phenomena.

Tables can be used to compile information gathered from records, judicial decisions, policy determinations – almost any pertinent form of data. Examining these compilations reveals similarities and inconsistencies as well as alerting the researcher to anomalies that may be significant.

Self evidently, the researchers need to adapt these processes for their own purposes but by the final semester and the data analysis process, all they need is a reminder of the process. Whether they want reinforcement or reassurance, invariably if I ask students: 'Can we skip the presentation and just get on with the process?', they insist that I 'do it again'.

A watershed point is when researchers can begin to revisit concepts and theories and assess their continued relevance, pertinence and validity. Theorizing and re-theorizing from a solid research base becomes feasible and do-able. Reminding students of the significance of the research cycle, discussed in chapter 2, is advisable at this point.

At this first level of cut through, in all probability, students will have had their assumptions tested and their theories may also have been challenged. They may find that data collected is inconsistent with that from other sources. These challenges and inconsistencies have to be explained; they cannot be ignored or avoided. It is important at this stage to affirm the student's credentials as a potential authoritative researcher and writer. This is what it is all about. This is why the course exists! It is also at this point that the theorizing, research and methodological choices diagram needs to be re-invoked – see chapter 2.

Making connections – linking data and theory

At this point, if the process has been thoroughly carried out, the student should have a reasonably comprehensive profile of the issues, the fate of their assumptions and challenges to existing theories if there are any. They should have mapped the interconnected law and reform issues, as well as the interrelated human rights implications. They should also have a sense of the wider implications of the research.

To round off the preliminary analysis process, the most important and revealing task is to revisit the assumptions and ask what happened to them in the research process. How were they adjusted and most importantly do they need to be more deeply interrogated in the light of an ever building 'pile' of findings. These interrogations of assumptions are directly linked to the process of challenging theories, thus one critical interrogation of the data is: What are the implications of what happened to your assumptions with regard

...the most important and revealing task is to revisit the assumptions and ask what happened to them in the research process

113

to theorizing and re-theorizing? Why were the assumptions challenged? Why were they upheld? The most important interrogation of the data being: Why? Why? Why? Simply put, the why question is the stimulus for theorizing.

The evidence to effect this challenge to theories should be in the hands of the researcher at this point. To avoid hasty or partially supported conclusions, it may be necessary to assess the strength of the data gathered by a process of triangulation. In the design stage anticipating sources of triangulation of data was recommended. At this point that table is turned around and used to provide evidence of triangulation. Not all data will require this approach. However, there are times when multiple interpretations and perspectives are evident and these different sources need to be drawn together to provide supporting evidence.

One example might be where a change in a customary practice has been identified. The questions that this poses are whether it is an isolated instance of change, whether it is manifest only in one area, whether it is only within one socio-economic group and whether it is embraced by traditional leaders, women, men, local administrators or others? (For a further discussion – see Stewart, 1998).

Human rights linkages

Revisiting human rights concepts and formulations may also be indicated by the findings as they emerge. Given that most students are working in evidently plural settings, they are most likely to undertake the analysis from a position within metaphorical crossroads between a multiplicity of perspectives and normative orders. These crossroads can be identified either singly or multiply and most frequently end up looking like complex flyovers. The interleading roads or sectors might be national legislation, customary or religious laws and practices, official policies and practices – whatever seems pertinent and fruitful. What ought then to be apparent is that the analysis is moving towards formulating crosscutting findings and integrating discussions of the findings with legal, human rights and existing theories.

The issues to be raised and interrogated in a human rights context are situation, region and country specific

The issues to be raised and interrogated in a human rights context are situation, region and country specific but we can usually ask some general questions about human rights compliance. Students will also be or ought to be familiar with the human rights exercises covered in the first semester and should be able to re-invoke these in the data analysis process.

A first level of assessment of compliance, which harks back to the research design stage, is assessing to what extent the domain is being researched. Does national legislation, administrative action and government policy comply with international human rights norms and to the national constitutional provisions?

This is a question that students will have preliminarily explored at the design stage but revisiting the question in the light of research findings advances their understanding of the areas under consideration.

As the linkages are made, the implications of those linkages and the nature of the data uncovered need to be engaged with each other. What can be facilitated, for example, are findings about whether the law has or lacks efficacy. About whether and how administrative processes facilitate or hinder access to rights. How interpreting legislation or applying case determinations affect the pursuit of rights and entitlements. Insight may also be gained about individuals' responses to law and legal process, including a comparative assessment between different levels of courts and different forms of law.

Research of the kind undertaken by SEARCWL students may reveal human rights violations. It may reveal partial human rights compliance on the part of the state and the need to raise human rights awareness among identified groups. It may indicate gaps in the legal framework, in the judicial process and in information dissemination or administrative responses to human rights entitlements. It is unlikely that the findings on human rights or the law will be one dimensional. Thus they will need to consider what is significant about the different facets of the findings.

Research of the kind undertaken by SEARCWL students may reveal human rights violations

Questions that arise from such an exercise might be: Is law reform required? Are the human rights instruments adequately framed? Is there a need to raise certain issues to be profiled in the guidelines for national reporting procedures? (for further on this, see Stewart, 2007) Is there a need for a national awareness campaign on women and girls' rights in a particular area of the law? Is there a need for community-based dialogue around cultural issues? The potential lists are, as always, extensive but if the student analyzes the findings and tackles them issue by issue the required insights and interventions emerge.

Methodology is critical

As discussed earlier the methodology or methodologies chosen, as well as the methods used significantly influence what is found during the research. Thus, it is also important to be able to assess the efficacy and impact of methodologies on the research. Students should make a final cast through the data by reconsidering the implications of the methodological approaches, methods and problem identifying techniques that they used to inform the research design. If they adopted a gender perspective in planning the research and paid careful attention to the views of women in all categories of potential respondents, there will probably be a distinct difference in relation to findings from research carried out in a general survey method. There may also be a distinct difference between findings from research that only engaged with key officials and from research that carefully targeted a wide range of actors in an administrative process.

Taking a grounded approach to determining who respondents should be and engaging in thorough open-ended interviewing and group discussion processes would have yielded more nuanced data than closed question processes. Thus, what was done, why it was done and how it was done have to be revealed and their impact assessed. In other words students need to explicitly and carefully describe the methodologies and methods employed and analyze their efficacy.

...students need to explicitly and carefully describe the methodologies and methods employed and analyze their efficacy

Despite our emphasis on methodologies and their significance in the overall research process, getting students to describe and discuss their methodologies and methods has been one of our most challenging tasks. However, in the past couple of years, there has been some improvement. Perhaps this is because we can now refer students to a collection of good examples from previous programmes. Perhaps as the research design process becomes more detailed there is a greater appreciation of the role of methodology and the link to theorizing. Dr Amy Tsanga observed on reading this section:

> 'I think also the weaknesses of previous students have been used
> as a backdrop for discussing how to engage more effectively with
> methodology vis à vis their assumptions and research questions.'

Nonetheless this is an aspect of the research process that requires more attention on all fronts, not least because methodologies are always mutating.

Going public

In the third week of the data analysis process in the final semester of the masters programme, students are required to present their key findings and overall research profile to their fellow students, supervisor, available guest lecturers[22] and other interested people. They are also urged to reveal any particular methodological challenges they encountered and any new methodological approaches or methods they used. A classic example of this would be where a student was initially reticent to engage in discussions in a taboo area around sexuality and then discovered that dialogue was possible if they handled the topic carefully and sensitively. Research experiences are grist to the mill of the SEARCWL research design development process. Prior to the presentation, they discuss what they are going to present in some detail with their supervisor.[23] The presentations are made to small audiences which

---

[22] Lecturers who undertake courses in the second semester are invited, as are lecturers who present on specialist areas in the first semester.

[23] This exercise is not carried out in the first semester, partly because of time constraints but also because the focus is on the hands on field experience and the benefit to be gained from group interactions and group analysis exercises.

include lecturers from the various optional courses on the programme. The discussions that follow each presentation are thorough and extremely helpful, not just to supervisor and supervisee but also to the lecturers, as they often see the work that has gone on in the classroom earlier informing the research process.

After the presentations, students draw up dispositions of their chapters, just as in the first semester, following exactly the same processes and, after comments have been made by supervisors, writing begins.

Writing – the lonely journey

Writing is an individual process and we encourage students to use their own personal style and shape the dissertation as they see fit, providing that all essential elements are present. The stronger the student, the greater their ability to structure the dissertation to convey the findings, engage with theory and follow the research cycle in an open, engaging and effective manner. The less confident the student, the greater the need to provide a standard template into which they can write – this will probably be:

...we encourage students to use their own personal style and shape the dissertation as they see fit

- Introduction – statement of the problem
- Literature and law and policy review
- Methodology chapter – research design, record of the research and the efficacy of the research process
- Findings chapters
- Discussion and conclusion

These sectors of the writing up process can be integrated if indicated by the analysis, so that literature and law are integrated with pertinent research findings; methodology can be handled in a similar way. The coherence of the process depends on the overall conceptualization of the research and the analysis process which should have been controlled, holistic and thoroughly grounded in the research data.

Writing is where the research process falters for some students. We are all aware of students who have not finished postgraduate degrees with significant research components because they have not been able to tackle and coordinate the research, analysis and writing phases to produce a workable integrated framework through which to present their work. So far on the masters programme, all students have been able to submit their completed dissertations within the required timeframes or within a reasonable additional period of time where there have been pregnancies, family problems, illnesses or other factors that interrupt the smooth completion of the writing process.

The orderly process of the research and the analysis undoubtedly helps; but part of the success in this last phase of the programme is the collegiate and supportive atmosphere among students. No one wants to be left behind. Also there is support from supervisors and from language experts as required. The presentation phase forces the pace and students have to make strategic decisions about what their most significant findings are and how they shape the outcomes of the research.

The presentation phase forces the pace and students have to make strategic decisions about what their most significant findings are

Conclusion

This chapter discussed, at some length, the logistics of identifying a research topic and designing the research process to effectively address the issues raised by the topic. At SEARCWL, we have found that by following these processes students are comfortable with undertaking research, they develop their proposals rapidly, especially their individual final dissertation research proposals, and they go to the field with a reasonable level of competence to make research decisions and manage the overall research process.

Although the research processes described focus on law, human rights and related issues, they can be used to inform other research areas. At SEARCWL, we would argue that even if no empirical research is contemplated, the processes can nonetheless be used to inform purely desk-based research, whether it has a legal or human rights content or not.

The first semester field research in the practical course consolidates the teaching in the first semester by focusing on applying the theories and methodologies gained in the other courses. The dissertation is the culmination of the masters programme. Through it we hope to provide the skilled researchers that the continent needs. It is a labour intensive but exciting period. As supervisors we are rewarded for our efforts and benefit immeasurably from the increase of useful, incisive and at times quite brilliant research that students carry out.

Bibliography

Bentzon A.W. *et al.* (1998) *Pursuing grounded theory in law, south–north experiences in developing women's law*, Tano-Aschehoug, Oslo, Mond Books, Harare.

Chimbaru F. (2008) 'The burdened witness: catering for the needs of mothers with small children required to give evidence in criminal trials in Zimbabwe', masters dissertation, SEARCWL, UZ, Harare.

Hellum A. *et al.* (2007) 'Paths are made by walking: introductory thoughts', in A. Hellum *et al.*(eds), *Human rights, plural legalities and gendered realities: Paths are made by walking*, Weaver Press, Harare.

Hellum A. *et al.* (2007) 'Human rights encountering gendered land and water uses. Family gardens and the right to water in Mhondoro communal land', in A. Hellum *et al.*(eds), *Human rights, plural legalities and gendered realities: Paths are made by walking*, Weaver Press, Harare.

Mariwo T. (2008) 'What are we doing to rural women's entrepreneurship? A case study of the non-recognition and diverted attention of women engaged in vegetable farming in Mutoko', masters dissertation, SEARCWL, UZ, Harare.

Moore S.F. (1978) *Law as a process, an anthropological approach*, Routledge and Kegan Paul, London.

Ondieki, E, (2006) 'Culture and traditions among the Abagusii community influence the practice of genital mutilation: grounded notions and perspectives about male and female attitudes on how to maintain cultural identity without a cut', masters dissertation, SEARCWL, UZ, Harare

Ssemmanda H. Wolayo (2007) 'Working with custom. Promoting children's rights to livelihood by making *de facto* guardians responsible' in A. Hellum *et al.*(eds), *Human rights, plural legalities and gendered realities: Paths are made by walking*, Weaver Press, Harare.

Stewart, J.E. (1998) 'Why I can't teach customary law', in J. Eekelaar and T. Nhlapo (eds) *The changing family: family forms and family law*, Hart Publishing, Oxford.

– (2007) 'I can't go to school today' in A. Hellum *et al.*(eds), *Human rights, plural legalities and gendered realities: Paths are made by walking*, Weaver Press, Harare.

5

And you expect me to do this myself?

Information and communication technologies: grappling with new skills

Sesedzai Munyaradzi, Thembani Malapela and Cecilie Mariri

When a new intake of masters students arrives not only are they expected to grapple with theories and methodologies but they are compelled, literally and unsympathetically, to use computers to submit all their work for assessment from the very first day. Many of their lectures are presented in Powerpoint, to which they can subsequently have access. They are expected to be able to access the internet, deal with their emails and become, very rapidly, fully computer literate. They are expected to be able to search library catalogues on line. SEARCWL is a tough task mistress when it comes to these issues and there is little sympathy for those who have been left behind by the computer revolution.

Consulting the shelves in the SEARCWL library

This chapter consists of three separate parts written by different members of our information and communication technologies team, and each part focuses on one component of the programme. In Part I, Sesedzai Munyaradzi describes her experiences, humorous and otherwise, of introducing the masters students (well some of them)[1] to that terrifying beast the computer. In Part II Cecilie Mariri outlines the library resources available, both at SEARCWL and from partner libraries, that are designed specifically to help students researching issues relating to women's law. Finally, Thembani Malapela outlines his approach to teaching legal information literacy skills in Part III.

---

[1] Some of the masters students come well equipped with computer skills and find that their knowledge is greatly valued by their computer-wary and unskilled classmates.

Part I: Teaching computer skills to adults – best methods for best results

Sesedzai Munyaradzi

Information and communication technologies (ICT) have ushered in a new era of knowledge and information delivery. Students on the programme as potential ICT users need to be properly oriented in terms of attitudes and skills to derive full benefit from them. SEARCWL makes sure that each graduate leaving the centre fully appreciates the benefits of these technologies Students who are wary about ICT when they arrive, leave the centre literally addicted to their laptops and internet access. Unfortunately they may struggle to function at the same levels when they return to work environments where access to ICT may be limited.

At work in the SEARCWL computer room

Being influential people like judges, magistrates, lawyers in private practice and senior government officials, our graduates should be positioned to promote ICT in the region when they complete the masters programme. Thus we hope they will force the pace in the acquisition of the necessary skills and equipment in their workplaces. In so doing they will spread competency in a critical area of regional development and thus enhance the capacity to engage with global agendas.

...we hope they will force the pace in the acquisition of the necessary skills and equipment in their workplaces.

We hope that after completing the programme they do not go back to their old ways of paper and pen, dictation or asking someone else to do their emails. It is important that they continue to build on the skills they have acquired and that we, initially, force on them.

The adult learner and acquiring computer skills

The average age of SEARCWL masters students is 35[2] with the age range falling between 26 and 55. They come from different backgrounds and cultures and it is interesting to observe their different responses and behaviours in ICT classes. According to Scheppegrell (1987), 'the greatest obstacle to older adult learning is the doubt – in the minds of both learner and teacher...'. Russel (2004) regards ageing as a process not a condition and certainly the SEARCWL masters students prove that new skills, even in an alien terrain, can be acquired with the right motivation and perhaps pressure.

Some students' responses to ICT instruction on day one, make me doubt that they will ever master computer skills. They make simple tasks seem

---

[2] This figure was calculated from two groups of qualifying applicants and sample size used was 75.

impossible but – *a luta continua* – we take up the struggle. Some students adapt slowly to basic aspects such as screen glare and mouse usage. Their earlier education was probably based on 'chalk and talk' and thus technology in the classroom presents a challenge. Many are aware that they work at a slower pace than their children or grandchildren on the computer and are amazed at how youngsters acquire the skills with no formal training. They feel slow and ponderous and probably embarrassed by their lack of computing skills.

Many mature students attempt to understand everything at once

Many mature students attempt to understand everything at once, leading to frustration. It would help if they could learn as children do with simple usage and surface level interfaces first. They want to know why it works the way it does instead of focusing on what is actually happening and accepting that answers to the why questions will arise later in the programme. Some students rapidly appreciate the value of the computer and just get on with using it.

It is clear from students on the programme that adults have more developed critical faculties and these can be a hindrance to learning computer use for the first time. The students' responses accord with the views of writers who suggest that adults relate new knowledge to previous experiences, although the nature of experiences differ: 'Adults adopt a deeper, comprehension-focused approach to learning as opposed to the surface-level assessment-focused approach of children'. Justice and Dorman (2001) confirm this in their findings on older students' life experiences in relation to their learning patterns.

Students should never be overloaded with skills they may not need at the point of entry

Experience on the programme indicates that effective ICT training for adults needs to be carefully paced and low in intensity. Students should never be overloaded with skills they may not need at the point of entry but rather be taught what they need to know to accomplish current tasks. In conventional ICT skills training students are often bombarded with too many new skills at once and have to try to keep up with the trainer. Meanwhile at the back of their minds they are asking: *Where on earth will I apply all this? Is this relevant?*

The theory portion of the training is the most problematic as it seems irrelevant to the students at first. Many of them are used to learning for the purposes of passing examinations after which the bulk of the knowledge can be discarded.[3] However, once a student has had time to question and explore for themselves how something can be done or after they have struggled to carry out a task, any solution finally presented to them usually 'sticks'.

Thus at SEARCWL computer usage training is limited to what really needs to be learnt at any particular time. As an ICT trainer I try to allow each student to follow their own route in class, at their own pace. Fortunately computer

---

[3] Section editor's comment – this is a common comment throughout the SEARCWL courses, as many students in the initial instance expect to learn by rote and are surprised that they are tackling issues by using different approaches, methodologies and skills.

instructions can be given with alternatives – two or three different ways of performing the same task (see box on the right).

We allow students to choose the set of instructions that best suits them or seems easier to follow. This means they explore the machine further on their own, which is the best way to master computers. The key to learning and effective usage is playing around with the machine as extensively as possible and that is what we encourage and support.

Given the opportunity, many of the students would probably choose to skip this training as they view it as an extra burden on top of their existing load of work. They sometimes arrive at the ICT class with this attitude too but we do not accept it. In a questionnaire given to a set of students in 2007 before the course commenced, 42 per cent indicated their discomfort at having to deal with computers and even do any typing at all. It might be viewed as a menial task or it could indicate a hidden fear of having no knowledge of how to go about it at all. It all boils down to having no appreciation of how ICT can be used as a tool to enhance the quality of their work. Thus it is important to reassure students as soon as possible that many of them are in the same situation, and that they will all eventually master the task.

> **EXAMPLE**
> **More than one way to do it!**
>
> There are always many ways to carry out the same task and students usually find one method more intuitive than another.
>
> For example, here are the different instructions for putting page numbers into a word document:
>
> 'On menu bar, click *File*, select *insert*, select *page number* – choose position and alignment and click OK.'
>
> *Alternatively*
>
> 'On menu bar, click *View*, select *header and footer*, position cursor on header if you want page numbers on top of page or on footer if you want them at bottom of page by using up and down arrows. On header/footer toolbar click on the *insert page numbers* (second icon), use the space bar to position page number at centre or to the right. Click on close to close header/footer toolbar.'

As adult learners, the students need to know that 'half the things a man knows at twenty are no longer true at forty – and half the things he knows at forty hadn't been discovered when he was twenty!' (Clarke, 1977). True but it is perhaps especially difficult to learn strange new skills which use no previous knowledge. At the same time, their old attitudes to learning and thinking are being profoundly challenged in the other courses. Thus students need to realize that such technology will involve continuous learning for the rest of their lives as the technology evolves.

To make their sense of dislocation worse, their own children seem to be miles ahead of them in the ICT field. Sometimes a student has confessed: 'I couldn't even ask them how to do this as they made me feel stupid and I don't like that.' No wonder they resist ICT if after all their previous learning and their hard-earned professional status, they suddenly feel ancient or dull. The only way forward is for them to catch up on the technology and talk the language of the age, as they say, 'If you can't beat them, join them'.

Probably because of these external stresses and internal lack of confidence they place high value on peer support. By the end of the first lecture those with previous experience and knowledge emerge and they immediately become class mentors and trainers – actually relieving the trainer's load. Even the peers with no knowledge become a source of encouragement, 'Oh so I'm not the only one needing attention here. Even Judge … doesn't know!'

Despite the emerging peer support, pedagogically, we still need to be aware of the needs of the adult learner, considering their personal issues, pressures and responsibilities. Unfortunately time is tight and the time available for ICT never allows for full consideration of all these factors.

Given the pressures on students to become ICT competent and the increasing pressures of their other work on the programme, the learning environment needs to be comfortable and informal. We create an atmosphere of fun and appreciate that no two learners have the same learning style, expectations or competence and we adapt our approach accordingly.

What goes on in there? The training sessions

Unlike in other courses where adults are self directed and have a clear idea of their purpose in undertaking training, in the ICT class we leave our students with no choice – they have to undertake it, willingly or otherwise. Classes are not compulsory. No registers are taken, the ICT course used to attract only a few marks, there are no examinations or assessment tests, yet we know students have no alternative: they will eventually embrace the technology. We wait for that 'aha' moment to arrive, as it signifies motivation to learn. Those who do not attend the introductory sessions, thinking them irrelevant or not important since not examined or believing they already know what they need to know, eventually crawl into class having realized they must master certain aspects of the training to achieve certain goals. In the very first week of the masters course, students must make short submissions online as part of the continuous assessment for the methods and methodologies course. They cannot submit the assignment in writing and the schedule means there is no time to get someone else to type, e-mail and submit a soft copy on the file server for them. Everyone else is busy with their own work and outsiders have no access to our file servers and mail boxes.

This automatically gives us the basis for the first lesson. Here are the questions they will need to be able to answer just to hand in the assignment:

1   What is a file server? How do I access it to submit my assignment?

2   What e-mail facility will I use? How do I compose an email and attach a file to it?

3   What about the typing? Where do I start? What about the document presentation and formatting?

4   How much time do I have? Will I be able to make it? (*Oh no – was coming here a wise decision?*)

At work in a training session

As students who avoided ICT classes start to visit the ICT office with such questions, they are told it was covered in the last session. They then start to feel that they are missing out on something. Many are surprised at the uncompromising insistence on ICT and at this early stage are unable to see its immediate relevance to their studies. The bottom line is that they have to acquire these skills to use in all aspects of the masters course. It is also impressed on them from day one, that *all* of the lecturing staff, including the director, do their own typing and ICT activities. Further, they rapidly discover that programme support staff are not interested in typing for them or doing their internet searches. Powerpoint presentations are devised, typed and graphics produced by the lecturers, no matter how doddery they might seem.

All this plus being in class with age mates makes the students feel less intimidated and forces them to acquire the necessary skills. *If my colleagues can sit there and listen, why can't I?* Seemingly, they begin to feel more comfortable as they confront the electronic beast. But, importantly, we ensure that every task they undertake has a discernible positive outcome. They need to feel in control of the technology to be able to manage it on their own.

After completing a task, such as successfully creating an automated table of contents in Microsoft Word, the students and trainer can write down the numbered instructions together and then go through them again. Students then learn how to write their own instructions clearly in future and refer back to them when they need to.

I also find it helpful to give learners alternative approaches, for example using the keyboard instead of the mouse (see box). If students face difficulties with tasks like using the mouse in highlighting text, open up the discussion so different students can explain how they overcame the problem. Japanese research (Umemuro and Shirokane) carried out in 2003 supports the confidence boosting approach. Explanations from peers as well as an appreciation that others have had a similar problem helps to build up confidence and enthusiasm and coincides with the researchers' views that these are important factors in improving computer skills.

However, some become frustrated at their failure to keep pace with the rest of the class. Sometimes there are sighs of relief but there is also occasional switching off of machines to start all over again when a student has got lost somewhere in what seems to be a maze. Also, screams of joy are heard as someone finds they are able to carry out a task as instructed. The machine is blamed a lot in the process.

EXAMPLE

Mouse or keyboard?

To highlight text you want to format, we use the drag facility of the mouse but here are some alternatives:

1   With cursor at beginning of text, put the shift key down, keep it down as you press the arrow keys.

OR

2   Click on *Edit* on menu bar, select *Select all* (this will highlight all the text in that document).

EXAMPLES

Accusations, excuses and complaints directed at the computer

This thing is dead!

I use computers every day but not this way

I can only use my laptop.

It's refusing!

This computer is different from the ones I know.

My work has all disappeared!

The usual complaint levelled at the lecturer is: *You are moving too fast!*

Some students do not complain but do not participate in discussions. They just sit and gaze at the screen or into space. If you ask them a question they just shrug their shoulders and yet they will write up their notes.

Despite all the complaints and frustrations it is gratifying to watch how adult learners start to bond and assist each other. Those who manage to successfully complete a task peep at their neighbour's screen and offer to render much needed help. An open lab setup is useful as students can sit and share things they have found useful. The exclamations and excitement at their achievements means that peers in the lab realize that someone has succeeded and this benefits all the others.

The computer as subject matter

Using computers means thought patterns have to change as well as class behaviour patterns. The subject is not neutral. It imposes its own discipline. Bernstein (1997) suggests that 'computing is more than a set of skills, it is a culture. It is full of concepts and jargon which are difficult to absorb.' Familiar words are found in the subject vocabulary but they bear new meaning, as with words like *File, Host, Application* or *Server*. New words are coined – *scrollbar, bandwidth, proxyserver* and the like. Coping mechanisms differ, some cope better with the new vocabulary while others want old manual writing, filing and typing terms. Thus, especially in the beginning, words must be thoroughly explained with examples they can relate to.

Many students lack confidence in the machine and even describe themselves as 'techno-phobic'. Another problem is that some students are constantly probing for the relevance of what they are being taught and if they cannot see it immediately, they become frustrated.

As they are already trying to remember how to carry out previously assigned tasks and more tasks and information are constantly being added, it helps to repeat task steps over and over and give slow, clear and explicit instructions.

The best way to learn about computers is through a form of apprenticeship says Agre (1994), who suggests that the learner works on some real tasks with someone who already has the skills. Many other authors agree and go on to stress that making mistakes is part of the process. Bean and Laven (2003) recommend numbered instructions. This definitely works because when a learner has a problem, you refer them back to the written instruction, ask them to follow each instruction explicitly as you watch and pay full attention and 'boom!' – the result is right on their screen. This is where you get comments like, 'It behaves when you are there (trainer). If you go away it will refuse.'[4]

Some learners are willing but have considerable difficulties in grasping and carrying out the instructions given. The trainer has to be careful not to disparage them or make them feel inadequate but to be as encouraging as possible. If such learners are mishandled, they may give up completely and claim to 'never want to deal with computers ever again in their lives!'

DeJoy (1991) says 'when learning is without precedent, individuals do not have personal images of themselves as successful learners.' It is thus important for the trainer to give relevant examples and models that students can relate to in order to achieve success (see box below).

The nature of computer skills can truly be termed inflexive because there can be no discussion about it, things are either done this way or that – nothing else works. So despite the alternatives available for instruction sets, computer packages are designed with specific sets of rules to use them. What works for one package may not work the same way for another package or even for the next version of the same package. The subject also requires a specific learning environment as much of the work is hands on – thus a computer lab, power, network and internet access are essential components of the learning experience. Practical application of skills as they are acquired is vital. Attempting to give even an introductory lecture in a lecture room is fruitless. One has to be sitting at the machine.

Having worked as a computer trainer for some time, I have grave doubts as to the value of giving the first-time user a book of instructions. It is unlikely to be positively used. Most likely it will be viewed as any other boring manual and left to accumulate dust somewhere in their room, although it very much depends on the learner. I would still rather have students write down instructions they themselves feel are important. Some tasks are much too simple to bother writing instructions for yet others can only be remembered after continual reference to instructions. Some instructions can be written and others are not even in a manual and for comprehensive training you cannot leave

> **EXAMPLE**
> **Starting with the 'known'**
>
> When teaching file organization, you can put it as follows for them to picture what is taking place:
>
> *'Picture the folder as a box file like you have in your office where you file documents. Now a 'document' in computer terms is a file. Therefore inside a folder you have files.*
>
> *'You can also subdivide your box file to categorize your documents by subject matter. In the same manner a folder can be further subdivided by creating subfolders within a folder for files to be saved by subject matter.'*

---

[4] Section editor's comment: This is absolutely correct. When Sesedzai advances on my office computer it immediately pulls itself together and behaves; having been on a wild frolic of its own prior to that moment!

out anything. My approach is that it should be the student's choice to make according to what they have grasped and what they have not as individual capacities differ. What is worth remembering for them is what should be worth writing down. The official manuals in the meantime grow thicker and unless the user is an enthusiast, they are probably ineffective. Computing is something you learn by doing,[5] just like driving.

The trainer

The trainer's prime focus must be the student and not the technology. After a general introduction to computer use and available software packages, students should be given future lesson times when they can develop computer skills of their own choosing. Each learner must be helped to successfully achieve her goal. Trainers need to be flexible, patient and open to questions and *must* treat learners with respect. They need to have the information at their fingertips. Alm, Gregor and Newell (2002) stress the value of a more mature instructor as a role model. It intimidates more mature learners when a disrespectful 20 year old teaches them unless the instructor can adjust their instructional style to suit the audience. Trainers must do what they can to lighten up the mood, for example by talking about embarrassing situations they or other staff members have encountered in the ICT learning process. There must be minimal use of jargon but students will have to be introduced to it gradually as ultimately they will have to grasp and use the jargon.

During training sessions, trainers should feel comfortable admitting when they have made a mistake in issuing instructions and also when they do not know the answer to a question. They can promise to try and find out and make sure they remember the promise by the time of the next session. Should one of the group members suggest something or an alternative method of carrying out a task, the trainer can admit to learning it for the first time themselves. Computers continue to present challenges for everyone and everyone is constantly learning. Such an approach helps students relax – not everything can be known and kept at one's fingertips. No matter how long you have worked with computers, you will discover that there is always something else you do not know. Software continues to develop; even a trainer cannot keep pace. It gives students a real boost to discover that they know something the trainer does not know and this helps create a learning from each other environment rather than the traditional set-up where only the teacher knows. This motivates even those who understand computers to come into class not only to learn but

---

5 Section editor – there was a time when constant manual reference was both necessary and inevitable and there was no embarrassment as the whole area was new. But in the twenty-first century there is an assumption that you know and are expected to know the mysteries of computing and computer technology.

to teach or to show off their knowledge. It motivates faster students to work harder to discover new things that they can come and share.

Research carried out in Australia came up with the following desirable characteristics for an ideal ICT trainer for adults:

- A high level of ICT skill and confidence
- Extensive literacy teaching/training experience
- A background in working with adult learners and an understanding of the principles of adult learning
- The ability to identify and understand the needs of the learners and to adapt sessions and courses to those needs.

An ICT trainer for a class of adults performs many roles and cannot simply rely on being an instructor or an expert. One trainer, Shneiderman (1988), says that his experience moved him to being a 'guide on the side' and believes this works as you guide different people doing totally different tasks.

What has worked for SEARCWL

The aim of training our students is to build their capacity through knowledge, skills and competences and each learner acquires these differently. Emphasis is on gaining skills rather than qualifications. We structure the course so that it focuses on essentials to achieve goals needed to pass other courses. Abandoning ICT classes would mean failure to achieve in all the other courses. So, it is a small course but a critical one that makes a world of difference to the students' potential success. Results from this course are reflected by performance in all other courses. Some consider it traumatic that they might fail to complete the masters course because they fail to master the technology. These fears are usually manifested as complaints. It is important to remember that we are often dealing with senior officials – 'I have a secretary back home who would do this for me. Why should I have to type anything?' But she is so far away and obviously she cannot be brought all the way here for purposes of your assignments. You can certainly empathise as a trainer but only for a short while. The lecturers will not be lenient if the reason for non or late submission of an assignment is attributed to lack of computer skills.

At SEARCWL the initial strategy is to give students a problem task to encourage learning ICT skills. They enter their very first lab session on the first Thursday or Friday of the course after having attended six lectures of a varied nature in the earlier part of the week. They bring with them an assignment from the methodology course which is already due on the following Monday by 4pm. This means they have the weekend and a few spare hours on Monday to complete the assignment and to comply with the instructions for submitting it. The assignment has to be submitted in three formats – a hard copy, a soft

...the initial strategy is to give students a problem task to encourage learning ICT skills

copy on a folder on the centre's file server and a soft copy that has to be emailed to the course lecturer as an attachment.

The worst case scenario is as follows for some of the students. They have just arrived in this country for the first time, they have not been to town. They have no knowledge of computers whatsoever and they don't even know the meaning of the words 'soft copy' or folder. The time within which to hand in the assignment is also too limited to go off looking for typing services. Even if typing services were available, what guarantee is there that one will get a soft copy for online submission or emailing? Most people offering typing services are wary of foreign disks collecting soft copies from their machines due to viruses so only provide hard copies. The email has to come from the student's new university email address, an intranet address that will function even without internet access. The only solution that remains for most is to attend the ICT class to obtain the instructions that will get this particular assignment out of the way. Of course there will be a group of locals with other alternatives who will go elsewhere but in the end they too will join in as systems differ with organizations.

The students' best continuous learning mechanism is active experimentation. They must be encouraged to keep experimenting, for example by exploring the desktop, opening and closing windows. If it gets all mixed up, they can go back to the desktop, back to the start button and proceed from there. They need to know that there is no harm in making mistakes as (almost) anything done can equally and easily be undone. For example, if page numbers have been inserted they can be removed. Both sets of instructions must be given – for doing and undoing – to encourage experimentation. Equally important is being able to communicate with them via email even within the same building. Students must be able to send an email to the trainer to ask questions like: *How can I apply line spacing to my document*? The trainer can then reply with a set of instructions that they can apply and get results from. This will make it easier in future when they want to obtain instructions from the internet as so much help is available, including from help menus on new applications.

The lab needs to be open to students all the time so that whenever they have any free time they are free to go there and work at their own pace.

The lab needs to be open to students all the time so that whenever they have any free time they are free to go there and work at their own pace.[6] Just the thought of being able to work alone later, undisturbed, takes away the desperation to learn and grasp everything immediately. An open lab also means students can just take instructions and watch visual aids during the training and then to go through exercises on their own at their own pace later. They achieve giant leaps alone, under no pressure, undisturbed and working at their own pace. If they learn what they need to learn at a particular time even

---

[6] The computer experience for the intake in 2011 was different because students were all using their own laptops which they were assisted to buy through their scholarships. These students will have plenty of time to 'play' and experiment and expand their computer knowledge.

if it is different from what the others are learning, this helps them grasp issues more quickly. As a trainer, I only plan carefully for maybe the first three or four sessions. In subsequent sessions, I am there to assist individuals with different issues, according to individual requests and needs. All work has to be typed and submitted electronically, and assignments are due on a regular basis. We teach how to create Powerpoint presentations when the new skill is needed. We meet to introduce the new ideas whilst old skills are being honed.

Why do we have to do it this way?

It is important to explain fully to students why they are learning each topic. For example, anyone who has either gone through the tedious process of typing out a table of contents themselves or waiting for someone else to do it so they can check it, immediately responds with enthusiasm: 'Really – is that actually possible?' Then they anxiously wait to see how that happens (see box below). When explaining longer processes such as the table of contents it is better for learners to initially concentrate on your visual aid as you go through the process demonstrating and explaining each step. Students should see and appreciate the result first as they are reassured that you can do it too. Then repeat the process with them working on their own computers. Give instructions step by step, slowly repeating each step. Agree together on a set of numbered instructions to achieving the task. Let them do the exercise alone as you move around to assist anyone lagging behind. They each work on their own documents, on a real task.

Knowles (2005) says that facilitators must help adults become aware of their 'need to know' – in this case the need is to be accurate, neat and fast. Stress the time saved. Stress that the computer will actually identify the correct page numbers, whereas you are bound to make a mistake. Most documents are changed as they are edited and proofread. After you finish editing the document, you can issue a command for the table of contents to self correct, that is, 'auto update'.

When dealing with examples, pick ones from their experiences. They themselves are resources for learning. Amongst the group we have directors of organizations, senior civil servants or programme managers and asking them for practical examples increases their participation. They might be able to suggest where the mail merge facility shown in the example box over the page would come in handy within their work environments. When they carry out the function on the computer each individual can work on their own example. They are then

---

> **EXAMPLE**
>
> **An automated table of contents**
>
> This is a valuable computer function. After you have finished typing your dissertation which could be 80 pages or more and have four major chapters and include subsections within the chapters, you need to draw up a table of contents.
>
> This function will assist you to pick up the various chapter headings and sub-headings and compile them for you neatly into a table of contents, with all the correct page numbers.
>
> No need to wade through it yourself to find the headings and page numbers and type them up into a list. The computer will, as it were, do the job for you but only and only if you follow the instructions ...

ready to learn since you will have created a 'need to know' in order to cope effectively with real life situations. Although our students are at SEARCWL, all the examples do not have to necessarily relate to women's law or the course – they can also come from the students' work environment. Everyone has experienced a salary rise and the excitement that comes with it. For greater interest in class use such examples to open up their minds. This helps build a positive attitude towards the computer. You can even use simple examples from their school or university careers (see examples box below).

It is important to also bear in mind that ICTs are not only for use in commercial circles but in the home environment as well. So give examples

EXAMPLES
Merge mail facility

In our next example imagine you want to type basically the same letter to all the 300 employees in your organization. But because you want it to have a personal touch and it must address the individual, we want each of the 300 letters to have a name, department and new salary according to the recent salary increase just announced.

What would be the content of such a letter? What are the variations required in the letter? Difficult? Well, this is how we can handle such a task. Bearing in mind it will save time and be more accurate. The facility is called Mail merge in Microsoft word…

Class positions

You remember that in primary education teachers would give you a class position based on your marks? Excel would be able to help a school teacher to come up with the class positions. The teacher types in pupils' names and marks in any order, highlights and selects the sort command and chooses to sort by marks in descending order. Look at that. How many seconds did that take? How can it be done without computer assistance? How long would it take? You can also sort the very same selection by name in alphabetic order. In the process of sorting the computer keeps the name and the mark together. Would a human being be able to achieve such accuracy?

Times tables

Your daughter or granddaughter needs to learn times tables. Microsoft Excel will assist you to create them within minutes, print them out and help her. Type in the first two consecutive number of the tables: 4 and 8 for the 4 times table. Block the numbers. Place your curser at the bottom right corner of the blocked data. Make sure the curser has turned black + hold the black + and drag going down. The computer uses the difference between the two numbers to put the rest in place. The same applies to days of the week and months of the year. For these just type Monday or January only and drag the black + either downwards or sideways.

that assist and create a necessity for a computer in a home environment (see times table example in the box opposite).

With creativity, even the most uninterested learner will join in. Adults want to learn what they can apply in the present. They are life, task and problem centred in orientation thus they want to learn what will help them perform tasks or deal with problems they confront in everyday situations and those presented in the context of real life, says Knowles (1984). Adults tend to respond to potent motivators such as self esteem. Trainers need to be wary of prescribing any standardized approach to facilitating learning. Each person learns in a different way.

The outline of the content of the whole computer training course we offer is shown over the page.

And in the end – from resistance to empowerment

The transformations that take place are best captured from students' comments as they leave the centre having completed their master's course and comments received long after they have left SEARCWL. The most interesting ones are especially from those who came in whining, complaining and resisting the whole idea of doing their own work. Excerpts have been taken from the external evaluations of the Masters in Women's Law course:

> 'I would say that over and above what students took away with them when they left SEARCWL, those who did not have any computer knowledge would like to say a heartfelt thank-you to SEARCWL for the life skill.'

They describe the new skill as empowerment.

We have had students at SEARCWL who have become so attached to the computer and who appreciated it so much as a tool that they have purchased laptops of their own – something they may never have dreamt of spending money on previously. They have ended up buying flash disks, external hard drives and other computer peripheral devices such as digital cameras and even LCD projectors. One comment from an ICT course survivor was:

> 'Now my secretary is really in trouble. She would delay documents knowing I was helpless in this area. Next time she does that she will find them all done and in an even better format. She will be shocked.'

ICT TRAINING CONTENT AT SEARCWL

Lesson 1

- Lab and computer use rules

- Logging on to a particular server or to a local machine

- Passwords and security

- The Desktop being the starting point. Desktop settings for your profile – Adding the most useful icons to your desktop which are *My computer, My network places, Internet Explorer* and *My documents*. It should be noted that these are the four essential icons needed for one to navigate the computer.

- Windows – what are they; parts of a window and uses; moving windows, minimizing and maximizing them.

- How to connect to a networked printer and how to access the Internet using internet settings that work in our environment. It should be emphasized how these settings differ from place to place.

- Accessing the *File server* – which will have been set up with course folders and password protected personal home folders. The course folders would contain any pertinent course material in soft copy with a folder for submitting assignments for that particular course. Home folders is where they should save their own work rather than use lab computer C drives. They must also be aware that they will not always maintain the use of the same machine but having their work saved on a file server will allow them to move from one lab machine to the next yet be able to retrieve their information.

- Within each student's home folder which would obviously be empty at the start, they have to learn to organize their own files by the creation of folders and should know how to create documents and save them in relevant folders with appropriate filenames. All this for purposes of being able to easily locate a document when you need it. Subfolders should be created within folders.

- Accessing their new university specific mail boxes and using them effectively – to compose mail, reply and attach files. Although they may have web-based email addresses such as yahoo and gmail, it is essential for them to use the institutional addresses. These are faster to access and work even with internet access problems. They then learn that it is more effective even within the same building to make a request through the email than by running up and down with verbal requests. Emails are definitely read and paid attention and can be referred to later.

- If they have documents they could be carrying on CD or flash disks or removable hard drives, we show them how to copy files across various storage media and across folders, for example from a flash drive to a home folder and vice versa.

- At this point emphasis has to be on the aspect of backup – that a document should not only sit on one media but must have a copy elsewhere, either on their laptop C drive or in their home folder. Any storage media is prone to damage and a loss of an 80 page document is virtually irretrievable. One should be able to go back to another media, pick up the document and continue to function. Drastic examples can be given such as: 'What if a bank were to lose all its client records?'

- Care for the various storage media like flash disks and CDs should be taught so as to minimize risks of loss of information.

- Creating documents using a word processor. Simple editing such as underline, bold, italicize, line space and so on. Saving the document as taught appropriately on various media and in folders.

- Submitting documents to lecturers as per the lecturer's instructions.

From this point, they then have time to type their assignments. For first timers it is one finger poking at the keyboard and looking for the letters of the alphabet on the keyboard which happens to have some odd organization of keys. It is definitely not in alphabetic order. *Where is the j, I can't find j!*

Lesson 2

Spreadsheets – when is it necessary to switch from Word to Excel? Graphic representation of data. Importing graphs created in Excel to Microsoft Word to be part of the main document.

Lesson 3

- MS-Powerpoint – visual aid for presentation. Slide creation, layout, backgrounds, animation. Printing slides – a number of them on a page, moving slide content to Microsoft Word and vice versa

- From here on, an appreciation of the computer is built in and any learning will be at their request. This is the stage where those who were not in the first set of tutorials come in to ask for help

Part II: SEARCWL library resources

Cecilie Butenschøn Mariri

When students have acquired the basic computer skills, it is time to introduce them to the library resources. Thus, they can use their computer skills to search in the library catalogues and find out where required literature is shelved. As most of the students are adults, with at least one bachelor's degree, they are expected to know how a library operates. Though quite a few have not been students for a while and are not used to computerized library systems.

The introduction to the SEARCWL library systems starts with a presentation of the University of Zimbabwe library in general, moving onto a special presentation of the women's law library and how to use it as a tool or a pool of resources for learning and reproducing knowledge.

> 'Legal studies are essentially a library-based exercise. Learn how to use the library wisely and effectively. It is a resource to be used properly. Inefficient use will result in you wasting valuable time and your academic work will suffer' (Thomas and Cope, 1996).

The introduction consists of the following components:

- The collections and how to search the Online Public Access Catalogue (OPAC)
- Internet resources relevant for the masters degree programme in women's law
- Evaluation of the quality of information
- Bibliographic references and citation

The following will thus describe both the contents and methods of what we teach and some useful advice related to what kind of literature a women's law library should hold.

Collections

The Women's Law library is a special collection situated outside the University of Zimbabwe Faculty of Law library. It is not only a collection of law books but also has a number of titles on women's situation in various parts of the world and in various environments. The emphasis, however, is on women in eastern and southern Africa.

One can replace 'women' with 'gender' in most of the listed topics. The collection also holds biographies, fiction and poetry describing women's situation.

Other topics include: feminist theory, human rights, governance, women's participation in politics, development economics and women's role in development, violence against women and children, children's rights, masculinity; religion – in short: all areas of life that are important in relation to women's rights and gender equality.

There is a small reference collection (dictionaries, bibliographies, encyclopedias and maps), a collection of relevant journals and collections of statutes and law reports.

Ideally, the women's law library should have statutes and law reports from all the countries our students come from. Unfortunately, that is not possible in reality. However, more and more can be downloaded from the internet and having a regional network is useful for requesting required Acts, Bills or cases from other countries, which can be sent as soft copies. The students themselves have their own networks and often supply soft copies of such material to the librarian. They also often leave behind pamphlets, reports, national gender policies and the like when they finish the programme.

> NOTE
> **Women *plus* collections!**
>
> There is a lot of literature on 'women and something' in general, such as:
>
> Environment
>
> Education
>
> Development
>
> Work
>
> Marriage/family/inheritance
>
> Conflicts/war
>
> Access to land/resources
>
> Sexuality
>
> Health; HIV/AIDS
>
> Reproductive rights
>
> Women as criminal victims
>
> – and as offenders

At the commencement of the masters programme students are advised to spend some time browsing the library shelves so they can get an idea of what is where. Some of the students actually do so and thus become more independent of the librarian in finding the literature they need.

...having a regional network is useful for requesting required Acts, Bills or cases from other countries

Searching the OPAC

The University of Zimbabwe has an Open Public Access Catalogue (OPAC) which can be approached via the university library homepage. A demonstration is given, showing how to search by author's name, title or subject and then how to interpret the list of results. Students are given a small test in searching for books and then have to locate them on the shelves.

Ideally, after having tried a couple of times by themselves, the students should be able to locate the books in the library for retrieval. However, students are often a lazy lot – and it is so much easier to ask the librarian for assistance!

The University of Zimbabwe law librarian, as discussed in the final part of this chapter, shows the students how to use the e-resources: electronic journals and institutional repository.

Searching the Internet

After the basic introduction to the internet by the ICT manager, the time has come to learn how to use the world's information and knowledge resources. I have observed that too many students just use ordinary Google, without realizing the possibility of conducting refined searches in 'Advanced search' or Google Scholar – or in other search engines.

Students need to be instructed in the basic principles of Boolean search (and - or - not) which is equivalent to the alternatives found for example in Google advanced search (see extract below). By defining exactly what one wants information about – and also defining what one does *not* want included – one may get references or links to the most relevant sources instead of a 'three million results' list.

A valuable tool that has been made for us by senior reference librarian Pamela Snyman at the University of Cape Town's Bram van Zyl Law Library, is a booklet which lists a lot of valuable and tested websites. For example, it lists general sites for: spelling; library catalogues; citation guides, including specifically for legal research; journals; legislation; international human rights instruments; and selected women's studies sites. This list is updated by SEARCWL for each new cohort of students.

Google Advanced Scholar Search   http://scholar.google.fr/advanced_scholar_search?hl=en&as_...

Web Images Videos Maps Shopping Books Gmail more ▼   Scholar Preferences | Sign in

Google scholar **Advanced Scholar Search**   Advanced Search Tips | About Google Scholar

Find articles with **all** of the words   Results per page: 10 ▲▼ Search Scholar

with the **exact phrase**

with **at least one** of the words

without the words

where my words occur   anywhere in the article ▼

Author Return articles written by

e.g., "PJ Hayes" or McCarthy

Publication Return articles published in

e.g., J Biol Chem or Nature

Date Return articles published between ___ — ___

e.g., 1996

Collections **Articles and patents**

◉ Search articles in all subject areas (☑ include patents).

○ Search only articles in the following subject areas:

☐ Biology, Life Sciences, and Environmental Science   ☐ Medicine, Pharmacology, and Veterinary Science
☐ Business, Administration, Finance, and Economics   ☐ Physics, Astronomy, and Planetary Science
☐ Chemistry and Materials Science   ☐ Social Sciences, Arts, and Humanities
☐ Engineering, Computer Science, and Mathematics

As many of the students are new to IT and online searching they are made aware of some online internet tutorials, for example 'Internet for lawyers' at the Virtual Training Institute (*http://www.vts. intute.ac.uk/tutorial/law/*). The opening page is shown on the right.

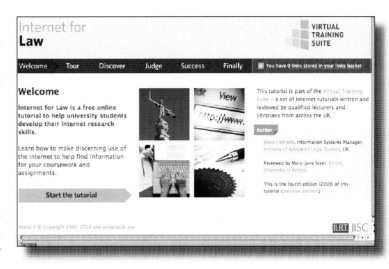

Evaluation of information quality

One expects academics to have learnt to be critical of *all* and *any* information sources, whether they are in print or electronic. Because our students are well past a basic degree, we assume they know this. But as some are new to using the internet, it is important to stress the importance of verifying the sources and their accuracy. Evaluating the quality of the information found on the internet is crucial for many reasons. The quantity of information is so vast and absolutely anyone can feed the world with articles and any other information and 'facts'. A good example is Wikipedia which is gaining popularity and students must be made aware that the information there may not always be accurate or reliable.

During the library orientation and at crucial points in the programme students are taught to look for a few critical factors in verifying the value and accuracy of the source:

- Who is the author?
- Which organization or institution published the information?
- When was it written or updated?

They are also strongly advised to note the URL and the date the information was accessed, unless they make a print copy.

Citations – bibliographic references

At the end of the masters degree programme, dissertations are typed – and a bibliography or list of references adds the finishing touch to the 'masterpiece'. Of the many activities we undertake in the programme, referencing and compiling bibliographies is one of the most difficult in which to obtain effective compliance. During the first semester, we introduce the students to making bibliographic references, with a small test to see if they have grasped the essence of the process. Some students do not keep a careful list of all their references and the complete citations as they research various topics. This leads to a last-minute panic as they try to find the source of a quotation.

Despite clear instructions, plus examples, as to the nature and form of referencing and compilation of bibliographies many students find this critical academic task difficult. There are several international standards and styles for citations and bibliographic references and students may be used to different forms but often there is no form followed, just a jumble of titles and occasional reference to publishers and years.

SEARCWL recommends the simple *Chicago* style. All this requires the student to do is put the authors and year of publication in brackets in the text and to create an alphabetical list of references at the end of the paper or dissertation. Students can use other styles but the style or standard they choose must be followed all the way through. *Be consistent*! is our main message. Generally it is recommended that footnotes are reserved for comments, explanations or digressions. We discourage complex footnoting with book titles and authors and *ibids*, *opcits* and other often baffling references backwards and forwards within the text. Yet they sometimes still appear and their use can flag copying from other texts. Students are also inclined to shift the order of joint authors or editors around especially where the lecturer they are submitting the work to is a joint author but not the listed first author or editor. Perhaps believing this will earn them kudos marks but not realizing the rules of author order in citations.

The librarian is obliged to look through all dissertation bibliographies to see whether the students have fully understood how to make a reference list. Surprisingly, few manage the task easily. Some students group their references under books, articles, internet sources and so on, some number their references which is not necessary if they are in alphabetical order by authors' surnames.[7] What is obviously the most problematic for students is citing chapters or essays from books and articles or reports found on the internet. Ordinary monographs and articles from journals seem relatively easy to get right.

Cases and statutes are useful listed in separate groups but books, chapters, articles, reports, unpublished material and dissertations need to all be in *one* alphabetical list, regardless of whether they are printed or electronic versions.

We discourage complex footnoting with book titles and authors and ibids, opcits and other often baffling references backwards and forwards within the text.

---

[7] Section editor: Part of the problem with author's names is that in some countries in the region people put their family or surname first and then given names. This can cause confusion especially when family and given names could be interchangeable – such as Samson Gideon.

Some problems, some possible solutions?

The information literacy skills search sessions are compulsory and we give students a small test on searching the catalogue, searching for literature using Google scholar or at least using advanced search in Google and making bibliographic references. The students' answers are marked and make up a small part of the total mark in the research methods and methodology course. One problem with this approach is that, true to the spirit in the ICT sessions, students help one other, so hand in identical answers – using the same fonts and even with the same spelling errors! Several different tests would probably make copying more difficult – students would have to locate the other students with the same set of questions.

The SEARCWL reading room: a quiet place to work

Many students still find it more convenient to ask the librarian for help than to try to locate books on the library shelves themselves. One solution to this lack of independence may be a not so helpful librarian!

Students often use simple Google to search the internet, resulting in an overflow of links, most of which are probably irrelevant. In future we plan to give the students more hands-on practice in using advanced search engines during the information literacy skills course.

Students often use simple Google to search the internet, resulting in an overflow of links, most of which are probably irrelevant.

Most students have problems making bibliographies for their dissertations. There are several programmes available that will automatically make bibliographic references for you and this would probably be a good investment, for both students and staff. Nevertheless, we recommend that students learn to do references themselves. They also need to appreciate the value of reading other authors' bibliographies to find information of interest.

'My book is overdue!'

On a more entertaining note: the library's alarm gate is triggered when a student enters the library with books that have not had their alarm strips de-activated (or the machine for de-activating the strips is working poorly). Many students look alarmed, and exclaim: 'Oops, my books are overdue...!'

Part III: 'Separating the wheat from the chaff' Experiences in teaching legal information literacy skills and approaches for women's law

Thembani Malapela

Library-based instruction for information literacy skills needs to be dynamic and this is reflected in the evolution of the courses run at SEARCWL. In the early stages of the Diploma in Women's Law, an 'induction tour' or 'library tour' was considered as the main essential for the students. Since the introduction of the Masters in Women's Law course, however, a much more proactive approach has been taken, especially with information literacy skills. Students face a daily explosion of information resources and the challenge of using these resources effectively and responsibly (Kasowitz-Scheer and Pasqualoni, 2003). In this section I discuss the teaching methodologies we employ in teaching of information literacy skills as a component of the research methodologies and methods course in the masters programme. The focus is mainly on retrieving information from electronic resources, legal databases and other internet-based databases and how to use that information for academic purposes. I also discuss the methodologies used in teaching access to electronic resources and consider my experiences in teaching that component in the programme. I also offer insights on possible advances and future prospects for the teaching of this component of the masters programme.

On the masters programme the focus is not just on information literacy skills but more particularly on legal information literacy skills which are generally defined as:

> '…the ability of legal researchers to *know* their legal information needs, to be able to *locate* that information and *sift* (or *evaluate*) that information to retain what is essential, *organize* that information and finally be able to *communicate* it to other people' (American Library Association, 1989).

The major aim of information literacy in the context of legal research is to ensure that a student can analyze a legal problem and offer a 'road map' of some sort for obtaining the correct information to provide an accurate legal answer. There are many subject-specific forms of information literacy, such as computer literacy, library literacy, legal literacy and financial literacy. Each one has its own particular techniques and search requirements embedded in the methodologies of the subject being researched.

Legal information literacy facilitates a deeper understanding of how and where to find legal information, the ability to judge whether that information is meaningful and, ultimately, how best that information can be packaged to address cases or issues at hand. It is more 'an analytical skills course' rather than merely a 'skill of comprehension course'. A successful legal information skills course should enable students to think critically and reason logically through the sources available on the internet when faced with a legal problem. It should provide a dynamic link between particular information needs and the sources and channels required to satisfy those needs (Darch *et al.*, 1997).

Objectives and learning outcomes

Information literacy is a compulsory component for all students on the Masters in Women's Law programme. It forms an important part of the first semester 'Methodologies and methods in women's law' course'. The syllabus for that course reads:

> 'To continuously evolve and develop the methodological tools and methods to *equip* candidates *to identify, critically analyze areas of law* that require reform,…to enhance the rights of women…To develop students IT skills so that they become computer literate and able to *use the internet* as a research tool, use and where necessary *instigate* the development of legal databases' (emphasis ours).

Content and objectives of the online resources sessions

The online resources sessions involve the student learning how to use the following networked databases available through the University of Zimbabwe network:

1 *The South Africa Law Reports* on JUTASTAT e-publications
2 *The Zimbabwe Law Reports* on Butterworths
3 *Eastern African Law Reports* on Butterworths
4 *Justis*, the online legal library of the United Kingdom, European Union and Irish law
5 SAFLII, judgments online for the SADC region
6 Electronic journals available via the International Network for the Availability of Scientific Publications (INASP)

In accessing these resources we try to cater for the needs of students from different common law systems since the masters programme draws students from different jurisdictions in southern and eastern Africa. These resources are useful in preparing their assignments and also for their dissertations in the third semester.

The specific objectives of the sessions are:

- To provide students with access to various primary legal materials available for their jurisdictions;

- To extract the essential materials from those legal sources, to answer questions posed in the course and in the future;

- To understand how legal information is organized on networked electronic resources and on the internet;

- To have a broad knowledge of women's law sources of information;

- To identify and find relevant legal sources and materials to address emerging issues in women's law;

- To conduct efficient searches on legal databases and websites and to locate relevant information, to hand in assignments online and to manage information exchanges by e-mail.

Teaching approaches at SEARCWL

The components of information literacy skills as indicated above are taught using the following approaches: computer lab sessions, library tours and the online approach. This combination creates the unique nature of information literacy skills training at SEARCWL.

Online research strategies and assessments

Before the instruction commences students are given a questionnaire to fill in to ascertain their computing and legal research skills level. This helps us decide on the different levels of instruction that will be needed. Inevitably there are different levels of existing competence, with some students already able to access materials electronically and others with virtually no knowledge at all. It is also important to realize that not all the students are lawyers.

Legal database training

Legal databases mimic the construction and layout of hard copy law reports and statutes thus as an introduction to legal databases students examine law reports and statutes from selected southern African countries. We review the different components of a report judgment and statute in preparation for introducing the networked databases such as the South African Law Reports and the All England Law Reports which are online and available on the SEARCWL network. This hard copy to electronic approach has proved effective as the lawyers are familiar with the hard copy resources already and it is user friendly to non-lawyers.

EXERCISE

From legal problem to search

Your lecturer has requested you to do a mini-research project which is to be presented in class. Amongst other things the assignment requires you 'to retrieve cases to do with genital mutilation of the girl child in sub-Saharan Africa'.

Using any of the legal databases available on the SEARCWL network:

Step 1

Generate key words

Step 2

Compose a search strategy:

- Use the search operators such as AND, OR and NOT as well as brackets to formulate your search
- Where possible use the wildcards and truncation to cater for the possibility of different word forms and spelling variations

Step 3

Send the search strategy by e-mail to the following address:

lawexams@law.uz.ac.zw

or deposit it into the assignments folder on the SEARCWL server.

To ensure there is no copying and to encourage individual initiatives, students are given different search topics – though all papers test the same skills.

Initially students focus on locating cases by name and standard legal citation modes. The next exercise is to search for appropriate cases or statutes by using key words. At this point students are taken through the features of the Folio Views software that runs the JUTAStat®, South African law reports and the Zimbabwean law reports. The emphasis is on how the students can convert a research question into key words. We focus on how to translate a general legal problem into a search query. An example exercise is shown in the box above.

Electronic journals

After instruction on accessing primary legal sources the students move on to searching for secondary sources online. When giving instructions on accessing e-journals I use the same approach as with the primary sources which makes the transition easy. We start with the print journals that they are familiar with and then proceed to the e-environment. Samples of print law journals are provided and students examine them, this is especially important for un-lawyers.

Students need to be aware of terms that are used in the e-environment. The following terms are explained: journal title, issue, volume and number, for example the components of the citation: *The International Journal of Comparative Law*, Volume 10 (2) are explained. One would expect postgraduate law students to be aware of this but some 40 per cent of the class do not know about these citation modes and locators. This is quite high since un-lawyers make up only about 20 per cent of the class. When we asked them about this gap in their knowledge, some of the lawyers commented that they used to 'take those things lightly'.[8]

Students are then introduced to the e-journals database available over the University of Zimbabwe network and also available free over the internet. The following electronic journal databases are used as classroom examples: EBSCOhost, JSTOR and Emerald. The stages in accessing these via the University of Zimbabwe network are given to students in detail. As some students check emails during lab sessions instead of paying attention we sometimes threaten them with a test at the end of the session.

During the classroom sessions, students are given time to go step by step through the process of accessing electronic journals. We show them how to browse through a journal by scanning the contents pages and the abstracts. Thereafter, they learn how to download the full article either as Word or pdf documents. They are surprised to see how convenient this is. Some students have had citations provided to them in the past by lecturers and have never had to actually access sources independently. Consequently citing online journals is a challenge for most students and we end the sessions by explaining how they should cite an online journal article (see Part II of this chapter for the citation methods).

Advances and future prospects

The online search section of this course has evolved over the years as the resources change. Legal research used to be based on books available in the law library, however, more and more publications are becoming digital. There is a new movement called the 'Free access to law movement', an open access initiative to ensure that primary legal materials are available over the internet for free. This is the umbrella name for the collective of legal projects across several common law countries that provide free online access to legal information such as case law and legislation (Wikipedia, 2008). It would be easier to have an online module for the course which focuses on such developments. The instructional method then will be purely an online mode.

---

[8] It should also be noted that the scarcity of library resources such as law reports, statutes and journals means that many students in the region literally do not get a chance to access even printed versions of these resources.

Bibliography

Part I

Agre P. (1994) 'How to help someone use a computer', *Network Observer Magazine*, 1 May, available online at: http://www.hawaii.edu/intlrellpols320/teachcomp.html

Barnes L. (undated) 'Achieving success with adult learners. As more mature adults pursue career changes, educators must be ready! Teaching tips from the Career Institute', available online at: http://emarketing.delmarlearning.com/milady/milady_news_fall05_classroom.asp,

Bean C. and M. Laven (2003) 'Adapting to seniors: computer training for older adults', *Florida Libraries Newsletter.*

Bernstein D.R. (1997) 'Is teaching computer science different from teaching other sciences?', paper presented at a computing conference in Eastern Small College in Pomona, October, available online at: http://www.keen.edu/~dbernste/Csdiff.html

Clarke A. (1977) 'The world of 2001', *Vogue* magazine.

DeJoy J. K. (1991) 'Incorporating microcomputer technology into adult learning environments', in R. Hiemstra (ed), *Creating environments for effective adult learning 50, Summer 1991, New directions for adult and continuing education*, Jossey-Bass Inc, San Francisco.

Geddes G. (undated) 'Old dogs and new tricks: teaching computer skills to adults', a paper, University of Strathclyde, available online at: http://www.ics.heacademy.ac.uk/italics/vol5iss4/geddes.pdf

Hazzlewood J. (2001) *TALANT: The third age learner accessing new technology*, Discussion paper D11/2001 Centre for Research and Learning in Regional Australia, available at: http://www.crlra.utas.edu.au/

Justice E. M. and T. Dorman (2001) 'Metacognitive differences between traditional-age and non traditional age students', *Adult Education Quarterly Newsletter*, available online at: http://www.eric.ed.gov/ERICWebPortal/search/detailmini.jsp?_nfpb=true&_&ERICExtSearch_SearchValue_0=EJ624288&ERICExtSearch_SearchType_0=no&accno=EJ624288

Knowles M.S., R.A.Swanson and E.F. Holton III (2005) *The adult learner: the definitive classic in adult education and human resource development*, 6th edition, Elsevier Science and Technology Books, California.

Knowles M. (1984) *The adult learner: a neglected species*, Gulf Publishing Co., Houston.

R.I.T Online Learning (2010) 'Adult learners', available online at: http://online.rit.edu/faculty/teaching_strategies/adult_learners.cfm

Russel H. (2004) 'Ageing well: older adult computer learners', available at:http://aare.edu.au/opap/rus04241.pdf

Schleppegrell M. (1987) 'The older language learner', the National Teaching and Learning Forum, ED287313 Sep 87, ERIC Clearinghouse on Languages and Linguistics, Washington DC, available online at: http://www.ntlf.com/html/lib/bib/87-9dig.htm

Schneiderman B. (1998) 'Relate-create-donate: a teaching/learning philosophy for the cyber generation', *Computers & Education* 31(1):25-39 Aug 1998.

Smith M.K. (2002) 'Malcolm Knowles, informal adult education, self-direction and anadragogy', *The encyclopedia of informal education*, available online at: http://www.infed.org/thinkers/et-knowl.htm

Part II

Bertnes, P.A. (2003) *Faglig informasjon på internett : kvalitet og kildekritikk*. Abstrakt forlag, Oslo.

Snyman, P. (2007), *Women and the law: a web research guide*, Brand van Zyl Law Library, University of Cape Town, Cape Town.

Thomas P.A. and C.Cope (eds) (1996) *How to use a law library: an introduction to legal skills*, 3rd edition, Sweet & Maxwell, London.

Virtual Training Institute (undated) *Internet for lawyers,* accessed online on 26 May 2010 at: http://www vts.intute.ac.uk/acl/tutorial/law

Part III

American Library Association Presidential Committee on Information Literacy (1989) *Final report*, ALA, Washington DC.

Darch C., C. Karelse and P. Underwood (1997) 'Alternative routes on the super highway', *Independent Online-Higher Education Review*, Independent Educational Media, accessed online on 10 July 2008 at: http://www.libraryinstruction.com/infolit.html

General Council of the Bar (2004) 'Bar vocational course', Centre for Legal Education, London, accessed online on 30 October 2008 at: http:www.ukcle.ac.ac.uk/resources/tlr/concept.html

Kasowitz-Scheer A. and M. Pasqualoni (2003) 'Information literacy instruction in higher education: trends and issues', accessed online on 16 September 2005 at: http://www.ericdigests.org/2003-1/information.htm

O'Brien J. (2000) *Managing business information systems*, Prentice Hall, New York.

Wikipedia (undated) *OPAC*, accessed online on 30 June 2008 at: http://en.wikipedia.org/wiki/OPAC.

THEME

TWO

Gender analysis
of legal frameworks

6

Women's rights are human rights: moving beyond the slogans

Elize Delport

Influences and approach

For more than 20 years, I have worked with the human rights of women at many levels – always keeping at least one toe in academia. Teaching the human rights component of the women's law programme has always been a highlight of my calendar for this is the only opportunity I am afforded to freely and extensively share knowledge and experience gleaned in many different ways.

As a young academic, I was willingly side-tracked by the exciting gender and human rights activism that marked the dying years of apartheid and South Africa's transition to democracy. It was a steep learning curve and it soon became clear that our sisters in Zimbabwe had a great deal of gender and human rights knowledge and experience to share. So it was that I pitched up (uninvited) at the offices of Julie Stewart where I have ever since received generous and wise counsel and support.[1] Women in Law and Development (WiLDAF) also stepped in to hone my lobbying and advocacy skills in those early days.

At home, in South Africa, serving on the Legal Committee of the Women's National Coalition[2] taught me the value of collaboration and consultation and

---

[1] I would like to acknowledge Professor Julie Stewart's input in this chapter, especially in the section on making the connections in relation to the right to education.

[2] During the transition to democracy, the Women's National Coalition (WNC) brought together South African women from across the political, ideological and socio-economic spectrum. Following a two-year long consultative process, the WNC compiled and adopted the Women's Charter for Effective Equality. To some extent, this charter influenced the drafting of some sections of South Africa's first democratic constitution and subsequently guided the adoption of various laws relevant to the human rights of women.

forever shaped my perception of law as a necessary but somewhat limited instrument for social change. Without activism, awareness-raising, political commitment, strategic and effective policy as well as sufficient budgetary allocation, law alone is not likely to bring about significant improvement in the lives of women in developing countries.

A term of office as a commissioner of the first constitutionally-established Commission on Gender Equality followed. It was an overwhelming and humbling experience that taught me that it was far easier to criticize other people's efforts to grapple with gender-related issues than to find workable solutions to many gender-related problems. As South African society voiced their needs and expectations, it became apparent that the ideals of non-discrimination and equality between men and women espoused by our constitution bore little resemblance to the daily reality of many of her citizens. Challenges such as gender-based violence, HIV and AIDS, pervasive patriarchy and widespread poverty often left me feeling like a fraud when I was preaching the gospel of human rights and gender equality.

...it became apparent that the ideals of non-discrimination and equality between men and women espoused by our constitution, bore little resemblance to the daily reality of many of her citizens...

Life after the Gender Commission has brought exciting opportunities for involvement at the United Nations level as well as at the level of the African Union. Assignments in many African countries as well as the Middle East, South East Asia, Latin America and China have afforded a wonderful opportunity to develop a comparative understanding of the human rights of women and to share emerging and best practices. Involvement with the United Nations mandated University of Peace and missions to post-conflict countries such as Sierra Leone and Liberia also convinced me of the need to include elements of humanitarian law, international criminal law as well as the basics of conflict-resolution and peace-building when teaching courses on the human rights of women in Africa.

All of these experiences have shaped my approach to developing the curriculum for and teaching the human rights component of the masters programme in women's law.

The format of the course has now changed as it has become a first semester compulsory course. However the observations about the course and its components remain relevant to the teaching of human rights courses however they may be constructed.

Semester 1

How to eat an elephant?[3]

The human rights component that I have been teaching is divided between the first and the second semester.[4] The first semester involves taking the whole masters class for basic human rights familiarization. Some of the students go on to take the second semester human rights elective course where issues are explored in much more depth. The first semester one week on human rights is designed to introduce the concept of human rights and provide a synopsis of the legal and policy frameworks at the United Nations level, the African Union level and the Southern African Development Community (SADC) level relevant to the human rights of women in Africa. The hope being that this paints a broad picture of challenges as well as opportunities and strategies that may prove useful in effectively pursuing and developing women's human rights.

By the end of the week, each student should have a general understanding of the range of instruments available and be able to identify the rights that have been created at the supra national level that they can draw on in their work in the future. At the very least, they should be able to recognize potential human rights issues and initiatives, know where to look them up, what merits further exploration and what has potential for action and activism.

Acknowledging that many students were not exposed to human rights at the undergraduate level, I often set a pre-course exercise that allows students to engage with human rights instruments in the context of their own countries. One strategy is to direct students to important websites and request them to collect relevant information. So, as many of the students test their new-found computer skills, they also have the opportunity to familiarize themselves with the basic human rights instruments and the performance of their countries with regard to these instruments.

The aim of such an exercise is to:

- Introduce students to important human rights related websites;
- Introduce students to a few of the key international instruments to be considered in this module;
- Encourage students to form an overview of the human rights situation in their countries by tracking ratification and reporting status;
- Enhance debate in the classroom.

---

[3] One bite at a time, of course!

[4] As mentioned, we have now changed the format of the human rights component but the spirit and thrust of the course will remain the same so I use the present tense throughout.

EXERCISE

General human rights country profile

United Nations system

1   Visit and explore the website of the United Nations High Commissioner for Human Rights (www.ohchr.org). Note any interesting features that you may wish to share with the class.

2   Read the text of the following international instruments:

●   Universal Declaration of Human Rights

●   International Covenant on Civil and Political Rights

●   International Covenant on Economic, Social and Cultural Rights

●   Convention on the Elimination of all forms of Discrimination Against Women (CEDAW)

3   Go to: http://www.ohchr.org/EN/countries/AfricaRegion/Pages/ZAIndex.aspx

Select your country.

4   Click on 'Status of ratification'. Note the instruments ratified by your country as well as any reservations that may have been entered.

5   Click on 'Reporting status'. Note the reporting status of your country.

6   Go to: 'UN treaty bodies most recent concluding observations'. Note and summarize the highlights of the most recent concluding observations with regard to your country.

7   Establish if your country has participated in the 'universal periodic review' (If so, read the country documentation at your leisure).

African regional system

8   Visit and explore the website of the African Commission on Human and Peoples' Rights (www.achpr.org). Note any interesting features you may wish to share with the class.

9   Read the text of the following instruments:

●   African Charter on Human and Peoples' Rights

●   Protocol to the African Charter on Human and Peoples' Rights on the Rights of Women

10   Note the status of periodic reports submitted by your country.

At the start of the week many students are unfamiliar with, and intimidated by the human rights terminology and concepts that they come across during the exercises.

Continuing the quest for active engagement with human rights instruments, I encourage students to make the link between their existing knowledge and experience and the substantive provisions of the instruments. The simple act of holding the text of a human rights instrument in your hands – touching it, turning the pages and coming across provisions you are able to relate to – often proves very empowering. A simple exercise is all it takes (see the exercise on the concept of human rights opposite).

One of the dilemmas faced by those new to the human rights field experience is how to deal with the multiple levels of the United Nations organs, as well as the multiple levels and 'legal' positioning of the human rights instruments, in particular the Convention on the Elimination of all forms of Discrimination Against Women (CEDAW) and the Protocol to the African Charter on Human and Peoples' Rights on the Rights of Women in Africa (the Women's Protocol).

It is common sense, really

I do not start with the technicalities of the instruments but rather with a way of raising their potential as instruments for reform, action and litigation. So, for instance, in progressing towards using CEDAW, the focus is on identifying and addressing discrimination against women. I suggest that they initially set aside the 'C' in CEDAW and focus on the essence: the elimination of all forms of discrimination against women.

But how then does one identify discrimination? Using personal experiential data has proved to be a good opening gambit. I do not start with the complex legal definition of the concept of discrimination but with students evoking home-based experiential data as an entry point into tackling human rights issues. It is also important for students to appreciate that human rights instruments can be used in multiple and different ways to stimulate development and inform law reform and activist agendas.

The '24 hour' exercise (see box on the next page) proves useful in this regard. This exercise has been around for many years in many guises and allows students to engage with a number of sensitive issues in a fun and non-threatening manner. Discussions and feedback from the various groups may provide the foundation for analysis of issues such as the distribution of labour between men and women.

EXERCISE

The concept of human rights

- List the basic needs of human beings
- Find the corresponding rights in the Universal Declaration of Human Rights

---

I suggest that they initially set aside the 'C' in CEDAW and focus on the essence: the elimination of all forms of discrimination against women.

EXERCISE

24 hours in the lives
of women and men

Whose lives are we looking at?

Group 1

A family living in an urban setting.
*(Describe the composition of the
family)*

Group 2

A family living in a rural setting.
*(Describe the composition of the
family)*

The task

- Draw a table to provide for the
  24 hours in a day.
- Draw a vertical line in the
  centre of the page.
- On the left side, record what the
  women in the family are doing
  at every hour of the day.
- On the right side, record what
  the men in the family are doing
  at every hour of the day.

The concept of discrimination arises naturally from this exercise as there is an automatic process of comparing women's position to that of men, or women in other countries and situations. In essence discrimination is perceived by reference to the situation of others. Following a brief presentation by each group, students are requested to reflect on various aspects emerging from the 24 hours exercise. So, for example, the following could be considered:

Effect and impact of division of labour:

- Is the division of labour equal?
- What does this mean for women and men:
  - in economic participation
  - in decision-making
  - in relation to education
  - in relation to health
  - with regard to other spheres of life?

Bringing international human rights law home

Another key approach in the first week is to dispel any notions that international human rights law is too specialized and arcane to have any impact at national or grassroots level. Introducing exercises that focus on the students' existing knowledge and experience and their capacity to determine what the pressing issues are for women in their home countries, forms the foundation of a process aimed at making human rights tools accessible. This is an approach students feel comfortable using and it does much to dispel concerns that they will not be able to get to grips with the intricacies of international human rights law.

I ask each class member to imagine that they are president of their country for a day and during those 24 hours they can change women's position forever and right all wrongs that women have suffered – well, prospectively obviously. I note the presidential 'to-do' list on a flipchart and later, when discussing CEDAW and the Women's Protocol, we revisit the list to tick off the items that are covered by the provisions of these two instruments.

After these exercises, I give a brief history of CEDAW and stress its importance in developing and addressing women-specific needs which are not expressly dealt with from a sex or gender based perspective in the United Nations Universal Declaration on Human Rights and other human rights instruments.

We then compare the country and social context based 'experiential' lists with what is covered in CEDAW by marking off what the class has identified as women's rights issues. This reveals, often to their surprise, that CEDAW is not as comprehensive as they might have previously imagined. Typical issues that remain unaddressed are widowhood, harmful traditional practices and skewed, purportedly religious, practices, all of which bedevil the lives of women in eastern and southern Africa. The table has now been set to illustrate the need for a home-grown human rights instrument that reflects those issues relevant to women in Africa. An introduction to the African Charter on Human and Peoples' Rights leads to the examination of the Protocol on Women and other interventions such as the SADC Protocol on Gender and Development, both of which capture and develop African or African regional-specific human rights needs of women, such as the problematic practices in relation to widowhood, mourning and inheritance practices as well as some religious or quasi-religious practices.

The combination of multiple instruments and levels of their application in different international, regional and national fora can be puzzling. I explain that some of these complexities arose because at the time some of the earlier United Nations instruments were drafted, Africa was not well represented and Africa-specific issues were not directly addressed. Thus post the formation of the African Union and its forebear the Organization of African Unity, there were initiatives to develop instruments centred in and focused on Africa.

...at the time some of the earlier United Nations instruments were drafted, Africa was not well represented and Africa-specific issues were not directly addressed

This is also an opportunity to raise the strategic value of the African instruments in dealing with women's rights and pursuing women's basic entitlements. These instruments cannot be labelled as 'foreign western influences and interferences' which is one of the stock-in-trade responses of some African leaders and decision-makers when challenged on the matter of granting women basic human rights and equality with men.

Thus all students should have basic knowledge of human rights and their potential by the end of the first semester. Although not part of what I tackle, the various ways in which students use human rights frameworks in other courses and especially in their first semester practical work, further enhance their knowledge of and capacity to use human rights in addressing issues that affect women.

Semester 2

An overview of course structure and content

When presenting the human rights course during the first semester, I engage students in discussions regarding their particular interests and topics that they wish to have included in the curriculum for the human rights elective course during the second semester. Whereas there are some non-negotiable elements to the curriculum for this elective, I allow a sufficient degree of flexibility to incorporate some of the specific wishes of the students and also to incorporate new developments relevant to the human rights of women in Africa.

The human rights elective course runs over a period of six weeks, of which one week is set aside for reading. Students who opt for the elective human rights course generally have a good recollection of the first semester and thus it is easy to build on concepts introduced earlier. Deepening the understanding of CEDAW and the African Women's Protocol were non-negotiable elements of the elective course curriculum.

The typical structure of the curriculum is shown on the page opposite.

Setting the stage
In order to enhance class discussions and encourage students to share useful comparative perspectives, I start off by requesting students to develop a gender profile of their countries.

Basic questions and guidelines are contained in the example exercise box on page 160, but one could also add questions with regard to the Beijing Platform for Action +15 Review, the Universal Periodic Review, and so on.

Developing synergies
During the second semester it becomes apparent that human rights as a touchstone or performance evaluation tool is central in other aspects of the programme and it was a key reference point in the students' work in the first semester group field research. This indicates that it will be equally if not more important during the third semester in their individual dissertations. The use of human rights articles, as I discovered when I attended the third semester data analysis sessions, is crucial in shaping their research designs. Using human rights articles aids students in narrowing and focusing their topics and in pointing to issues of compliance and possible strategic legal and policy interventions.

The second-semester programme

Week 1

Deepening students' understanding of United Nations legislative and policy frameworks relevant to the rights of women is the primary emphasis in the week. There is a strong focus on the substantive provisions as well as on monitoring and implementing CEDAW, including the reporting obligations. We introduce students to a CEDAW role play exercise (discussed later) which is sometimes scheduled for later in the course. We discuss the Beijing Platform for Action as a useful framework providing a blueprint for implementing CEDAW effectively. We also consider the mandate, functions and activities of the United Nations gender structures.

Week 2

The second week focuses on deepening understanding of African legislative policy and political frameworks relevant to the rights of women in Africa. We emphasize substantive issues as well as monitoring and implementing the African Women's Protocol. We consider the mandate and activities of the Special Rapporteur on Women in Africa and relevant developments at the level of the African Commission on Human and Peoples' Rights. The Solemn Declaration on Gender Equality was introduced as a political instrument that creates significant opportunities for monitoring, lobbying and advocacy. Students are introduced to the gender structures within the African Union and the United Nations Economic Commission for Africa. We also look at African Union policies on gender and reproductive health.

Week 3

This week is reserved for reading and preparing assignments.

Week 4

In this week we discuss the tools and strategies relevant to promoting, protecting and implementing women's human rights. We examine national machinery promoting gender equality and discuss its efficacy. Experts on particular topics are invited to make presentations during this week.

Test case litigation, gender mainstreaming, gender budgeting and monitoring from a gender perspective are some of the tools and strategies considered. Training on advocacy and lobbying within the African context also prove useful.

National human rights and women's rights machineries are considered from a comparative perspective. We also explore and discuss mandates, activities, challenges, opportunities and best practices.

Week 5

During the final week, we explore topics of current, crosscutting and/or special interest. This is also an opportunity to invite experts to come and share their knowledge and experience with the class. Topics covered include the gender dimensions of HIV and AIDS, the gender dimensions of poverty and the effectiveness of aid. We have been fortunate to have visiting experts make presentations on the gender considerations arising from the work of the International Criminal Court, Rwanda (Arusha tribunal), on gender and international criminal law and on the gender dimensions of humanitarian law. Students are introduced to the multi-sectoral and integrated approach to implementing CEDAW effectively as originally developed by UNIFEM, West Africa. The Zimbabwe Women Lawyers Association has also conducted a workshop on the preparation of CEDAW shadow reports.

Week 6

Finalizing assignments and the examination

EXERCISE
Country profile – human rights of women

In order to obtain a profile of the human rights situation of women in your country, please provide concise information on the following:

A   Country-specific information on gender issues

● Does the constitution of your country make any reference to equality between men and women and or the prohibition of discrimination on the grounds of sex and/or gender?

● Are any other constitutional provisions relevant to the promotion of gender equality and the elimination of discrimination on grounds sex and/or gender?

● Is there any legislation or are there any policies that you consider particularly useful in promoting gender equality and eliminating discrimination against women?

● Is there any legislation or are there any policies that you consider particularly problematic in promoting gender equality and eliminating discrimination against women?

● Describe your national machinery for the promotion of gender equality. So, for instance, does your country have a Gender Ministry, a Gender Commission, a Human Rights Commission with a gender mandate, gender focal points in government departments or a combination of the above?

B   The Convention on the Elimination of all forms of Discrimination Against Women (CEDAW)

● When did your country ratify CEDAW?

● Did your country enter any reservation(s) to CEDAW? If so, what is the nature of the reservation(s)?

● What is the reporting status of your country in respect of CEDAW?

● Is there anything arising from your country's CEDAW report or the concluding comments of the CEDAW committee that you wish to share with us?

● Are there any innovative strategies or best practices with regard to the implementation of CEDAW that you wish to share with us?

What makes this course exciting to teach is the rapidity with which these fundamentals are grasped, internalized and argued over from an activists' standpoint and I am sure the experience will be similar in the new format of the course, The potential of peer learning is greatly enhanced by the students' ability to provide instant comparative perspectives and share experiences and best practices

There is much debate about the efficacy of as well as the problems posed by a so-called '(human) rights based approach'; the course does not focus on this directly but rather provides a fuller understanding of human rights and their potential value and role in development and change initiatives. How students subsequently use the knowledge will need to be situation and context sensitive and appropriate and it is vital that they develop the empathy to do so.

Encouraging a critical and analytical approach

One vital point that students have to learn to appreciate is that in terms of international law the various instruments are documents of consensus. Thus they do not necessarily reflect the highest desirable standards. Rather they reflect the level at which consensus can be obtained or the level at which those who might object to certain clauses can register a minimal level of reservations. Unfortunately one has to acknowledge that the text of instruments such as the Protocol to the African Charter on Human and Peoples' Rights is not always as clear and unambiguous as may have been desired.

When engaging with the text of international human rights instruments, I encourage students to be critical, analytical and to identify challenges as well as opportunities. To encourage such an approach at a practical level, I often set the assignment on the Women's Protocol, shown in the box on the right. This assignment never fails to shed new light and reveal fresh perspectives on ambiguous aspects of the Women's Protocol.

ASSIGNMENT

Protocol to the African Charter on Human and Peoples' Rights on the Rights of Women in Africa – challenges and opportunities

As countries prepare to implement the Protocol to the African Charter on Human and Peoples' Rights on the Rights of Women in Africa (the Women's Protocol), apparent inconsistencies and ambiguities in the text deserve attention. Focusing on these inconsistencies and ambiguities:

1   Discuss any *one* provision in the Women's Protocol that may pose a *challenge* to effective implementation. Explain your concerns. Propose an amendment or interpretation of this provision that may better support the promotion of gender equality. (For example, article 6 c)

OR

2   Discuss any *one* provision in the Women's Protocol that may provide an *opportunity* to follow an even more progressive approach to the promotion of gender equality. (For example, article 4.2a)

*Where appropriate, please refer to other relevant international, regional and sub-regional instruments and policies.

Making the connections

It is also important for students to appreciate that rights are linked and that one cannot consider one right in isolation from other human rights. For example, taking article 10 of CEDAW on education which provides:

> 'States Parties shall take all appropriate measures to eliminate discrimination against women in order to ensure them equal rights with men in the field of education'

There are eight sub-articles. To make article 10 effective it is necessary to look at the sub-articles as critically interlinked elements of the quest to eliminate or at the very least reduce discrimination against women in education. One might take sub-article (d) which provides for 'the same opportunities to benefit from scholarships and other study grants' and challenge the students to unpack the prerequisites for this sub-article to be effective.

Responses are usually quick, and there is an appreciation that making scholarships and grants available will not assist many girls or women as they may not have even the basic minimum educational qualifications to benefit from such opportunities. Given their individual backgrounds and their personal experiences, the students are able to provide a rich pastiche of the obstacles, no matter how clear the human right might be, that will preclude women from benefiting from its provisions. If there has not been compliance with sub-article (a) which mandates the same conditions for career and vocational guidance as their male counterparts, they will not have taken the appropriate subjects or will have been discouraged from thinking about higher education. So sub-article (d) remains essentially aspirational.

The urban/rural divide at government school level reveals disparities in funding and in the availability and quality of teachers

Pushing the class to then unpack other aspects of sub-article (a) reveals the dichotomy that particularly bedevils education in many African countries. The urban/rural divide at government school level reveals disparities in funding and in the availability and quality of teachers. Rural schools, government schools in particular,[5] have great difficulty attracting and retaining staff, they frequently depend on temporary teachers and school leavers waiting to enter tertiary education or obtain a better paying position. Again, experiential data from the students fleshes out this debate. Following on from their experiential exercises in the methodologies and the theories courses, they rapidly interrogate the educational system in terms of not just gender but also budget allocations, teachers' salaries and availability of resources for schools.

The next obvious link is for a class member to hone in on sub-article 10(b) which mandates that there should be:

---

[5] Some privately-run rural schools are well endowed and are not faced with such problems but rural schools in general are the most under-resourced and unattractive teaching positions.

'...access to the same curricula, the same examinations, teaching staff with qualifications of the same standard and school premises and equipment of the same quality.'

Manifestly this is not the case between urban and rural schools. Facilities will vary significantly, the subjects on offer will depend on staffing and the availability of the appropriate textbooks and equipment. Many rural schools do not have science laboratories, nor do they have suitably qualified science teachers so inequality between urban and rural learners, let alone across the gender divide, is profound.

Discussions about eliminating gender stereotyping are often conducted in the world at large in a vacuum of unreality. Pupils, parents and teachers come from deeply traditional and religious backgrounds where stereotyping is the norm, yet it is not seen as being problematic as this is the way things are and have to be. The fact that students have imbibed the skills to interrogate gendered patterns of social organization in the first semester courses assists them in identifying the need to tackle discrimination in education in a holistic manner and especially to appreciate that to move forward in terms of one specific human right, requires support in the form of implementing interconnected rights. For example, the right to education for the girl child cannot be separated from protection against early marriage and from differentiation in household chores and family responsibilities between the girl child and the boy child. Parents who cannot perceive a life path for a girl other than marriage present an obstacle to her continuance in school that no amount of curriculum revision can by itself overcome.

...the right to education for the girl child cannot be separated from protection against early marriage and from differentiation in household chores and family responsibilities...

Power relations within the school and how they influence the girl child's self perception frequently surface during such debates. Female members of the class often have graphic examples of how their own schools were structured, how the power lay with the male teachers. The head teacher is usually male, those who teach the more senior classes are frequently male, while those teaching the junior classes are usually female. So girls learn from home and school, without necessarily being told as such, that they occupy subordinate positions. Girls' sports teams, despite sub-article (g) which mandates the same opportunities in sports and physical education, are unlikely to be as well equipped as boys' teams in coeducational schools. Boys' teams also receive more attention and public accolades than the girls' teams. Certainly in an African context all this leads to questioning the injunction in sub-article (c) that coeducation should be encouraged.

A conclusion that we inevitably reach, through these interrogations and through the various exercises in the first and second semester courses, is that there is an insidious process that leads to the institutionalized exclusion of the girl child from many aspects of a beneficial curriculum and thus from taking up career options that are more readily available to the male child. Girls may

be subtly or not so subtly excluded from science classes and from technical classes thus closing down avenues into engineering and related careers which are more lucrative than more traditionally female, support-oriented careers such as secretarial, nursing and junior school teaching. Conversely, boys may find themselves discouraged from taking home economics, even if they desperately want to, and from fashion and related courses – stereotypes rule the way in which schools are run and children's lives are ordered.

A similar approach can be taken to any of the rights in CEDAW or in the Women's Protocol. One can use experiential data to develop a critique of the possibilities they offer and of the direct and perhaps more importantly the indirect discrimination that takes place leading ultimately to a sense that the normal is that girls and women are not as successful and do not take up educational opportunities, so that is that! An appreciation of the social and economic parameters in which education takes place ought to inform the kinds of interventions and measures that are needed to tackle the root causes of discrimination and girls and women's lack of capacity to effectively compete with men.

The students themselves, being already university graduates, established in their careers ...are evidence of how the barriers can be broken

The students themselves, being already university graduates, established in their careers, often on a clearly successful upward career trajectory, are evidence of how the barriers can be broken and of how family attitudes shape girls and women's lives both positively and negatively.

At the cutting edge

I use assignments to introduce a practical element and provide the opportunity to actively participate in new debates or activities that may shape the women's human rights agenda.

I use a tried and trusted CEDAW role play to introduce students to the practicalities of reporting under CEDAW. The role play was originally developed by Professor Goran Mellander of the Raoul Wallenberg Institute for Human Rights and Humanitarian Law of Sweden and formerly a CEDAW committee member. The role play focuses on the presentation and consideration of the fictitious periodic report that has been submitted by the rather gender insensitive country of Bananistan. Students are divided into four groups: the committee, the government delegation, civil society and the media. Within these confines, the provisions of CEDAW and its reporting guidelines, students are encouraged to give their imagination free reign. The results are invariably amusing and students seem to enjoy participating in the role play as much as lecturers enjoy observing it.

As part of an assignment, students were once asked to comment on the 'Draft reporting guidelines for the Solemn Declaration on Gender Equality in Africa'. Their comments were forwarded to a colleague who was at that stage tasked with finalizing these guidelines. This provided a good opportunity to participate in an activity that in some way shaped the human rights of women agenda. Hopefully this encouraged students to actively participate in such activities as they may arise in future.

Prostitution and the human rights responses to it is always a hotly-debated topic. Recently, the call by the South African Law Reform Commission for comment on its discussion paper on adult prostitution provided an ideal topic for an interesting and practical assignment. Submissions by our students were forwarded to the commission and are now being considered as part of the 3,000 and more such submissions received. Hopefully this experience will encourage students to regularly take the opportunity of commenting on such discussion papers or draft legislation.

A picture paints a thousand words

When it comes to examining particularly sensitive issues, I often use an appropriate film to introduce the topic and generate debate. As I initially ask students to share their observations with regard to the film, a comfortable distance is created that encourages open and honest debate without the need to be defensive:

- The film, *Monday's girls*, was particularly useful for opening up discussions about potentially striking some balance between custom, culture and the human rights of women.

- *Water* starkly illustrates human rights violations flowing from the status of widowhood in India and makes for interesting comparisons.

- *A woman's place* is useful in illustrating the universal nature of discrimination against women but also tells inspiring stories of initiatives aimed at promoting and attaining gender equality.

- A range of films introduce the issue of gender-based violence. I have found the South African-produced film, *Soul City*, particularly appropriate and powerful within the context of gender-based violence in southern and eastern Africa.

ASSIGNMENT

Comment on the discussion paper on adult prostitution*

The South African Law Reform Commission (SALRC) has developed a discussion paper on adult prostitution and is calling for comment on it. The paper is featured on their gender CD and is also available on the website of the SALRC.

With reference to CEDAW, the Protocol to the African Charter on Human and Peoples' Rights on the Rights of Women and drawing on relevant comparative perspectives and best practices, comment on this discussion paper.

Complete the SALRC worksheet for the discussion paper on adult prostitution and submit this with your assignment.

* Detailed knowledge of the South African legal system is not required for purposes of answering this assignment.

'Monday's girls'
A film produced by Lloyd Gardner and directed by Ngozi Onwurah, 1993, United Kingdom / Nigeria

- *One hit is never enough* is particularly useful in providing a comparative perspective of gender-based violence, how it manifests itself and how it is dealt with in three different countries.

Following general class discussions regarding issued raised by a particular film, I usually move to more structured group discussions. Below is an example of questions developed for group discussions following a film focusing on gender-based violence.

EXERCISE
Gender-based violence group discussions

Discussion 1

- How does your society view or perceive gender-based violence?
- What message is conveyed by government officials, the judiciary, the media, and so on?
- What are the root causes of gender-based violence in your society?
- Is reliable data available?
- What exacerbates gender-based violence in your society?

Discussion 2

- Has your country put in place laws and policies to address gender-based violence? Discuss.
- Describe the processes that contributed to the introduction of such laws and policies (if any).
- Who are the main stakeholders involved in implementing gender-based violence laws and policies?

Discussion 3

- Focus on the following intervention points during your discussions:
  a   Prevention
  b   Protection
  c   Support to victims or survivors.
- Has your country encountered any challenges in implementing gender-based violence laws and policy? Explain.
- Has your country developed best practices and innovative strategies in dealing with gender-based violence? Please share.

To round off the course a programme officer from Zimbabwe Women Lawyer's Association (ZWLA) has run a workshop on shadow reporting on CEDAW. ZWLA has in the past coordinated shadow reporting by non-governmental organizations in Zimbabwe and thus senior staff members are well placed to discuss, describe and give advice on how this can be carried out. In conducting these workshops ZWLA drew on the work of the International Women's Rights Action Watch Asia Pacific (IWRAW Asia Pacific) which produced a comprehensive set of guidelines and templates for shadow reporting – these can be found at: htttp://www.iwraw-ap.org/using_cedaw/sr_guidelines.htm. The guidelines can be adapted for shadow reporting under other treaties and conventions by proceeding article by article to obtain the thematic framework.

Conclusion

I try to make this a hands-on practical course while at the same time introducing the theoretical aspects of the human rights debates. Now that the course is becoming a compulsory course it should enrich the students' capacity to apply a human rights lens to all the courses they take. Fitting in as it did with the other first semester courses and now tying in as a compulsory course, students gain the capacity to link theory, human rights and research methodologies to create a launch pad for the rest of the programme and especially for the third semester dissertations.

Human rights … become integrated tools in the pursuit, identification and implementation of women's rights

Human rights through these processes become integrated tools in the pursuit, identification and implementation of women's rights, not as exotic elements but as baseline markers for what must be delivered and what must be provided for women to attain meaningful equality both with men and among women.

Bibliography

Beyani C. (1994) 'Towards a more effective guarantee of women's rights in the African human rights system', in R. Cook (ed) *Human rights of women. national and international perspectives*, University of Pennsylvania Press, Philadelphia.

Byrnes A. (1998) 'The Convention on the Elimination of all forms of Discrimination Against Women', in W. Benedek, E.M. Kisaakye and G. Oberleitner (eds), *The human rights of women: international instruments and African experiences*, Zed Books, London.

An- Na'im A.A. (1990) 'Problems of universal cultural legitimacy for human rights', in A.A. An-Na'im and F.M. Deng (eds) *Human rights in Africa: cross-cultural perspectives*, Brookings Institution Press, Washington.

Cook R. (1994) 'Women's international human rights law: the way forward', in R. Cook (ed), *Human rights of women: national and international perspectives*, University of Pennsylvania Press, Philadelphia.

Charlesworth H. and C. Chinkin (2000) *The boundaries of international law: a feminist analysis*, Manchester University Press, Manchester.

Charlesworth H. (1994) 'What are women's international human rights?', in R. Cook (ed), *Human rights of women: national and international perspectives*, University of Pennsylvania Press, Philadelphia.

FEMNET (2003) *From OAU to AU and NEPAD: strategies for African women*, FEMNET, Nairobi.

– (2004) *Advocacy around African women's human rights within the AU and its specialized mechanisms*, FEMNET, Nairobi.

Fraser A.S. (1999) 'Becoming human: the origins and development of women's human rights', *Women's Rights: A Human Rights Quarterly Reader* 21(4):3-56.

Frostell K. and M. Scheinen (2001) 'Women' in A. Eide, C. Krause and A. Rosas (eds) *Economic, social and cultural rights. A textbook*, 2nd revised edition, Kluwer International, The Hague.

Leary V.A. (1990) 'The effect of western perspectives on international human rights', in A.A. An-Na'im and F.M. Deng (eds) *Human rights in Africa*, Brookings Institution Press, Washington.

Nowak M. (2003) *Introduction to the international human rights regime*, Martinus Nijhoff Publishers, Dordrecht.

Murray R. (2001) 'A feminist perspective on reform of the African human rights system', *African Human Rights Law Journal* 1(2):205–24.

Liebenberg S. (1997) 'A theoretical overview of the UN Convention on the Elimination of all forms of Discrimination Against Women (CEDAW)', *Southern African Feminist Review* 2 (2): 27–35.

Steiner H.J. (2003) 'International protection of human rights', pages 757–88 in M.D. Evans (ed), *International law*, Oxford University Press, Oxford.

Tomasevski K. (1993) *Women and human rights*, Zed Books, London and New York.

7

Women, crime and criminology
Reflections on the law from a transnational perspective

Lillian Tibatemwa-Ekirikubinza

Part I: Focus, aims and methodologies

This course is about women as offenders, women as victims of crime and thus women as witnesses in court processes. We focus on the responses of criminal law and the criminal justice system and its agents to women who appear in the criminal justice system. Throughout the course we discuss how gender inequality creates and perpetuates crime by and against women and how this inequality is expressed and embodied in the criminal justice system. By analyzing statutory and judge made law, we expose the extent to which the legal framework (criminal law and criminal justice) serves patriarchal interests. We answer the question: to what extent do societal, cultural and customary norms, values and practices which lead to injustice and discrimination against women continue to inform statutory law and judicial decision making? And if they do, what should be done to correct the situation – judicial activism, legislative reform, public interest litigation?

Throughout the course we discuss how gender inequality creates and perpetuates crime by and against women and how the inequality is expressed and embodied in the criminal justice system

In discussing criminal law and the criminal justice systems of various countries, the course identifies best practices of law reform through judicial activism, public interest litigation and legislative processes in different countries.

The course also deals with criminology as the study of causes of crime and, from a gender perspective, concedes that in some specific ways, crimes by and against women are a function of social structure and power relations.

Teaching a transnational class is made easy by the fact that over the years the course consistently receives students from the same countries – Kenya, Malawi, Tanzania, Uganda, Zimbabwe and Zambia. These Commonwealth countries[1] share common legal traditions, arising out of a common history

---

[1] Zimbabwe is no longer part of the Commonwealth. Also its legal system is mainly Roman Dutch although it has strong Common law influences.

of British colonialism. The codes of criminal law and procedure operating in the said states were inherited from the colonial period and were based closely on nineteenth-century English criminal law and principles of criminal liability, the definition of offences, and so on. In the light of this background the course makes use of case law from as many of these jurisdictions as are available in bringing out the gendered assumptions underlying case law as well as cases of judicial activism as a viable tool for facilitating social change or transformation.

Expected outcomes of the course

The course encourages students to think critically about criminal law and its underlying values and to consider the relationships between criminal law (legal rules) and the social context. Furthermore we expect the course to equip students with a critical understanding of the operations of the criminal justice system and of the social, political and cultural context in which criminal law operates. This enables them to think about how (if at all) criminal law can be used to change social institutions, identities and practices.

By exposing students to the influence of criminology (theories of crime) on how women are treated by the criminal law and criminal justice systems, we encourage them to reflect on practical ways of improving the treatment of women

In line with the need for law reform, we hope that students will appreciate the value of judicial activism and public interest litigation in the realization of women's human rights.

By exposing students to the influence of criminology (theories of crime) on how women are treated by the criminal law and criminal justice systems, we encourage them to reflect on practical ways of improving the treatment of women – as perpetrators of crime, as victims of crime and as witnesses in courts of law. Students are enabled to question the validity of so-called 'scientific' theories of crime.

Teaching methodology

In teaching a transnational course, I adopt a variety of approaches which in combination provide an innovative way of teaching a transnational class. I use the *lecture method* to introduce theories and principles underlying criminal law, criminal procedure and criminology. The lectures are supported by scholarly articles from feminist and other scholars of crime. This helps the class relate general theories of crime to women and analyze the extent to which theories of crime impact on the way the criminal justice system handles crimes by and against women.

Using the *case study method*, students are provided with court cases and statutory provisions from different jurisdictions (usually represented in class) and are asked to analyze the gender implications of court decisions and legislative provisions. Such exercises help individuals understand the influence gender has on the application of criminal law by agents of the criminal justice system. We thereby enable students to appreciate the gendered nature of both legal reasoning and the operation of criminal law in action. The analysis exposes gendered assumptions and inequalities that underlie both statutory and judge made law.

The class is also called upon to apply human rights instruments at international and regional level as well as national constitutions to critique the legitimacy of particular statutory provisions and case law and answer the question: to what extent can such instruments be the basis for law reform? Students are requested to use particular human rights instruments as a tool for advancing law reform.

Analysis of statutory provisions and court cases may be done at individual level or through group exercises. The groups may be based on country of origin or discipline-specific divisions.

We ... enable students to appreciate the gendered nature of both legal reasoning and the operation of criminal law in action

Overview of the chapter

This chapter is divided into four main parts. In the first part I give an overview of the general thrust of the course. In the second part I examine more closely some of my entry points in teaching and interrogating key concepts in criminology. The major examples I draw from are menstruation and infanticide. In the third part I single out the sexual offences of adultery and rape to illustrate how I tackle the gendered nature of the law in this field. I also give an overview of some of the class exercises that I give to students to interrogate problematic provisions using their own national constitutions and human rights instruments. Finally, in the fourth part I examine violence against women and by women and the approaches that I adopt in looking at the key issues that emerge for legal analysis.

Part II: Entry points into women, crime and criminology

The importance of criminology in understanding women's experiences in the criminal justice system

Noting that African sources on crime and criminology are sparse and criminology as an academic discipline is still in relative infancy, I find it necessary to begin with a selective review of western theories concerning women and crime as well as women and the criminal justice system. Apart from noting that traditional criminology is either gender blind or sexist, I note that the existing criminology theories were developed in and validated on western societies yet the people of Africa differ culturally and sociologically from people in western societies. We thus need to undertake criminology research in Africa. Although the methods and tools of investigation used in the west may be used in Africa, the content of criminology may be conditioned by the diversity of the socio-economic and cultural factors in different societies.

DISCUSSION & ANALYSIS
Criminology

The discussion and analysis of criminology deals with the following questions:

- To what extent are theories of crime gendered and how do they influence the response of the agents of the criminal justice system to crime and to the treatment of women as offenders and as victims of crime?

- To what extent does gender (societal expectations, roles, and so on) push an individual into criminal behaviour?

- To what extent does gender affect what are perceived as causes of crime?

- To what extent does the societal definition of what is criminal depend on whether the actor is male or female?

- In which ways is the treatment of an offender (by the criminal justice agents) dependent on whether such an individual is a woman or a man?

- In which ways is the treatment a victim of crime impacted upon by the fact that the individual is a woman?

- In which ways is the treatment of a witness impacted upon by the fact of being a woman?

'Traditional' criminology and the case for feminist criminology

I take the students through the journey of criminology – from traditional theories of crime to feminist criminologies (see box). It is noted that, in general, classical or traditional criminology largely ignored and was silent on female criminality. Crime was perceived as an essentially male activity. Criminological theories were rarely concerned with analyses of female criminality and criminologists seemed to have been content with either subsuming the discussion of women offenders under 'general' theories – in other words they implicitly assumed women were dealt with in discussing men – or they dealt with women exceptionally briefly. The reason for the neglect of women offenders was that within the population of known offenders, women constitute a statistically marginal group in comparison to men (Smart, 1977). Developing theories based on male-focused research is in itself not a problem. What however is unacceptable is that theories developed on male subjects and validated on male subjects have been generalized as applicable to all criminals, women inclusive.

It is imperative that students realize that gender must be given a central place in understanding female criminality because:

> '...gender appears to be the single most crucial variable associated with criminality [since] the crime statistics of all countries, despite considerable legal and cultural variations, tell the same story; that women have lower crime rates than men' (Heidensohn, 1987:22).

Feminists have noted that this trend is not just a contemporary phenomenon because 'over long

periods of time and in many differing judicial systems, women have consistently lower rates of officially recorded crimes than men' (Heidensohn, 1985:2).

In the few instances where women were mentioned in traditional theories of crime, women offenders were considered abnormal. In the nineteenth century women were regarded as innately angelic and by the natural order incapable of violence. A violent woman was considered unnatural and looked at as insane – 'mad' but not 'bad'. The attribution of madness to women was due to a construct that women who conform are pure, obedient and benefit society. On the other hand women who dared to not conform – going against their 'natural' biological trait of passivity and compliance – must be mentally ill. A woman's insanity was linked to the menstrual cycle since a woman's personality was believed to be directed by hormones. It was believed that a woman's temperament was a direct product of her female physiology.

...in traditional theories of crime, women offenders were considered abnormal

For example, Lombroso and Ferrero (1895) considered women to be congenitally less inclined to crime than men. These scholars contended that the few women who are criminal are abnormal; they are genetically more male than female. The scholars insisted that the true, biologically-determined nature of women is antithetical to crime and if a woman is a 'true criminal type' she is biologically like a man.

Later, Otto Pollak (1950) claimed that it was not true that women were less offending than men. He contended that the presence of few women in the criminal justice system was due to the fact that men (who happened to be in charge of the system) were socialized to treat women in a protective manner. Female offenders were like their mothers and wives and thus the male police and judiciary could not imagine a woman engaging in crime. As a consequence, women's criminal activity was less likely to be detected, reported, prosecuted or sentenced harshly – so masking female crime is a consequence of chivalrous criminal justice agents.

I however also note that in addition to alleging a chivalrous criminal justice system, Pollak also contended that the low representation of women in the criminal justice system is due to women's ability to hide their illegal behaviour.

Pollak's contention is that females are inherently manipulative and deceitful, characteristics derived from a number of their physiological and social attributes. According to Pollak, characteristics which prove women's deceit are their passive roles during sexual intercourse and their ability to feign arousal and fake orgasm, as well as social norms requiring women to hide menstruation. Such deceit, according to Pollak, allows females to conceal their crimes which, if detected, would be similar in frequency to that of males.

Pollak's contention is that females are inherently manipulative and deceitful

In discussing this contention I generally get the students to do a number of exercises as highlighted in the box on the next page. Discussing their views on menstruation and women's reactions during sex in a context of socialization and cultural norms, before I present them with interpretations of women's behaviour by scholars, enables the class to objectively critique the validity of opinions presented as 'scientific theories of crime'.

In relation to their spouses (see exercise 1), it is common for male participants to state that they know of their wives' menses when they attempt to have sexual intercourse and the wives tell them of their condition. Some men reveal that during dating, their girlfriends do not reveal that they are menstruating but in marriage, women often reveal their condition. Over the years, I have noted that men who have stayed in marital relationships for a considerable number of years tend to reveal that their wives tell them of their menses in direct ways whereas those who are relatively new in marriage indicate that their wives communicate their condition in more indirect ways.

Asked about their mothers, all men have said that such information had never been communicated to them. Several of them contended that anything to do with sex and sexuality was never a subject of discussion between them and their mothers, it is 'too private' or 'too personal', they said.

Over the years, I have been informed by several women that as teenagers they would tell others that they were 'feeling unwell' and thus were unable to either go to school or participate in particular activities (see exercise 2). Quite often, women tell me that they would inform others that they had a headache or were suffering from malaria.

Asked why it was rare that they truthfully revealed the source of discomfort, the answer often was: 'When I started menses as a young girl, one thing I was told by my mother was never to let anyone know that I was menstruating' or 'As a young girl I was told in no uncertain terms that it was a shame, embarrassing for anybody to know you were menstruating.' Although a few women have said that they reveal their condition to colleagues and sometimes to female bosses, I have not come across a woman who reported that she was able to tell a male boss that she was menstruating.

Other exercises I take the students through are shown in the box on the right. In exercise 3, many women admit to having praised their sexual partners after a sexual encounter that the woman had not enjoyed. Asked to explain the 'lie', the most common

EXERCISE 1

Menstruation: men only

Men in the class form groups and discuss the questions below and then come back to report.

- Are you ever aware that your wife – partner/sister/mother/ office colleague/class mate is menstruating?
- If so how or what brings this fact to your knowledge?

EXERCISE 2

Period pains: women only

If you were suffering from dysmenorrhea and couldn't go to school as a teenager, what would you tell:

a   your colleagues?
b   your teacher?

As an adult, if you are unable to come to work due to discomfort as a result of menses what would you tell:

a   a male/female colleague
b   a male boss
c   a female boss?

answer was that it was to massage their male partner's ego. Many have said that they consider it a form of affirmation. I opine that this pattern points to society's criteria of individual self-worth, the way in which males are conditioned to value themselves as people. In patriarchal society, sexual prowess is central to the concept of masculinity and many people believe that a woman's primary concern about a male partner is his sexual prowess. It is thus a blow to the male ego for his sexual prowess to be in question.

In exercise 4, most men confess that they would be wary of a woman who initiates sex with them, especially if it is not within marriage, 'Such a woman would be too fast for me' was a common reaction.

In answer to the question in exercise 5 as to why they hide sexual feelings, some women said that it was because they had been socialized to believe that a woman who initiates sex is one of loose morals.

Both the answers from the men and the women are evidence that patriarchal society makes women feel guilty about sexual desire and that it is for this reason, not because women are inherently deceitful, that females take on passive roles in sexual activity. On the other hand, patriarchy demands that men retain dominance over women and it is for this reason that a man states that a woman who initiates sex with him is 'too fast'.

Sigmund Freud's theory of women's behaviour: women as 'castrated men' and as a 'lack'

I introduce Sigmund Freud who at the beginning of the twentieth century came up with some theories to explain women's behaviour. We do some exercises to raise the issues (see exercises 6 and 7 on the next page). Freud defined women as 'castrated men' and as a 'lack' since they do not possess the male sex organ (Mitchell and Rose, 1984). He theorized that all women experience penis envy and seek to compensate for this inferiority complex by being exhibitionistic and narcissistic. Freud contended that due to penis envy women are pushed into fabricating false accusations against men.

EXERCISE 3
Sexual intercourse: women only
In pairs discuss the following questions:
- Have you ever, after sexual intercourse, communicated to your partner in the act (husband or friend) that the sexual encounter had been great, when in fact you had not enjoyed it?
- If the answer is 'Yes', what is the reason for this conduct?
- Have you ever felt like having sexual intercourse but kept it to yourself although in the company of your husband or partner? Why?

EXERCISE 4
Sexual intercourse: men only
In your love relationships has a female partner ever initiated sexual intercourse with you – especially during the early period of your association?
If yes – what was your initial reaction?
If it has never happened, how do you think you would react if it occurred?
If it has never happened, what could be the reason?

EXERCISE 5
Sexual intercourse: women only
In your love relationships, have you ever initiated sex with your male partner? If not, why not?

EXERCISE 6

Wishing to be men: women only

● Have you ever wished you were a man?

● If the answer is yes, what was or is the basis of your wish or preference?

The common answers for women who state that they sometimes wish they were men were:

− 'Growing up as a girl with male siblings, I often felt that my parents gave much more freedom to my brothers than they did to me ...'

− 'My brothers seemed to have more time to play than us the girls; we seemed to be more involved in house chores than my brothers were ...'

− 'Men seem to have it so easy ...'

EXERCISE 7

Wishing to be women: men only

● Do you at times wish you were a woman?

● If, yes, what are the reasons for this?

It is pertinent to note that when men are asked whether there are moments in their lives where they wished they were women, the answer is almost always an emphatic NO!

It is noted that in all the years I have taught the course, no woman has reported being envious of men because of their possession of a penis. The question therefore is, how valid is Freud's 'theory'? My interaction with women, who 'confess' a desire to be men, indicates that the wish is rooted in the fact that men in patriarchal societies have and are entitled to more privileges than women are, just because they are male. None of the women have indicated a longing to have a penis.

The course later looks at the question: in which ways do theories such as these impact on the treatment of female victims of sexual abuse? This is answered through analysis of the evidential rule of corroboration which inter-alia provides that it is dangerous for a court of law to convict a person accused of a sexual offence on the basis of a female's complaint without independent evidence that supports her testimony. The need for independent confirmation is said to be essential because:

> 'Human experience has shown that in these cases girls and women do sometimes tell an entirely false story which is very easy to fabricate, but extremely difficult to refute. Such stories are fabricated for all sorts of reasons, which I need not enumerate, and sometimes for no reason at all' (Lord Justice Salmon in *R v Henry & Manning*).[2]

A result of the rule is that where a court convicts an accused in the absence of corroborative evidence and it is not manifested in the judgment that the court has directed itself to the question of corroboration and warned itself of the 'danger' of acting on uncorroborated evidence of the complainant, the conviction will normally be set aside by an appellate court.

The various exercises help us question the validity of 'theories of crime' and unpack the root basis of so-called scientific explanations of behaviour because they impact on the way the criminal justice system treats women.

Pollak (1961) also fundamentally stressed biological and physiological factors, albeit in association with social factors, in order to explain female

---

[2] All case details are included in the index of legislation and cases at the end of the book.

criminality – he concedes that sociological factors play some role but crime is primarily linked to biological and psychological factors. He asserted that there is some biological, psychological or social imbalance which induces women to commit criminal offences. He contended that the 'generative' phases in a woman's life such as menstruation, pregnancy and menopause are frequently accompanied by psychological disturbances which may upset the balance of the individual or weaken her internal inhibitions and thus become causative factors in female crime.

The premenstrual syndrome as a defence

As recently as the 1980s, biological explanations for women's criminal behaviour were still being encouraged with the resurfacing of the premenstrual syndrome as a defence to a charge. Again, I discuss these theories against a backdrop of exercises (see box on the right).

Some women, but not all, cite physical discomfort and pain as a consequence of menstruation. It is also common for women to state that they tend to be short tempered and irritable. Men also sometimes state that women associates and family members are sometimes touchy during their menstruation. Some women also confess that they do not engage in sports and limit social interaction.

Some of the questions I put to the class after they have done the exercises are:

- Is it possible that the short temper arises out of the fact that a woman's freedom is restricted rather than that there is a hormonal imbalance in her body during either menstruation or pregnancy?

- Is it possible that women who have been brought up to believe that a pregnant woman is short tempered play the part in order to release pent up anger not tolerated under other circumstances?

These questions are meant to make us reflect on the extent to which socialization rather than hormonal imbalance (biological determinism) may make women behave violently with the attendant conclusion: it is the stifling social conditions and oppressive constraints of traditional female roles that contribute to women's criminal acts.

It may be the way society rejects a menstruating woman that makes her irritable rather than hormonal imbalance.

EXERCISE 8
Menstruation: women only

- Apart from blood flow, does your life change in any way during your menstruation?

- If the answer is yes – has anything become easier as you have grown older?

EXERCISE 9
On pregnancy

Women:

Apart from the physical changes in your body, can you recall any other changes about yourself during pregnancy?

Do your life activities change in any particular way?

Men:

Apart from the physical changes in your wife or any other female associate's body – what would you say you have noticed about women during pregnancy?

The danger inherent in biological determinism is that these explanations diminish women's ability to make rational decisions.

The danger inherent in biological determinism is that these explanations diminish women's ability to make rational decisions. Biological explanations of crime imply that female crime is a product of individual rather than social forces and influence. Such explanations seem to suggest that the solution to female crime lies in treating individual cases rather than overhauling the social order which perpetuates the social imbalances of power that generate crime. The theories isolate the crime from the social context and help maintain the existing social order.

Contrary to the treatment of women by criminologists, male criminality is often understood to be a consequence of socio-economic factors. Consequently, scholars call for improvement of economic factors, for example, a reduction in unemployment levels if young males are to be kept out of property related crime. We use the sex-specific defences of premenstrual syndrome and infanticide to explain ways in which biological determinism may negatively impact on women's status in society by allowing policy makers to ignore women's lived realities. As examples of premenstrual syndrome in action we examine the cases of *R v Craddock* and *R v English*.

In interrogating the validity of premenstrual syndrome, I question students' perceptions towards menstruation. This is through the exercises on menstruation set out earlier. We have also had discussions which reveal that in many communities a menstruating woman is perceived as unclean and is prohibited from engaging in activities normally availed to her. For example, many women have been told not to receive 'Holy' Communion during menstruation. In some societies, a menstruating woman should not prepare meals. It is perhaps due to this that women state that one of their worst nightmares is to be told (even by a female colleague) that their dress is stained with menstrual blood. No woman wants her 'unclean' status to be exposed to the public.

...menstruation related taboos have significant implications for women and gender relations that ramify throughout society

In deconstructing premenstrual syndrome it is noted that within the wider society the fact that women menstruate is clouded with taboos and is treated with a lot of suspicion and sometimes awe. Patricia Weiser Eastel notes that cross-culturally, menstruation has been the object of fear and derision. In many tribes and religions, taboos are enacted at menses with women being kept secluded from the group. This biological fact is used to exclude women from accessing authoritative positions and from arenas of explicit formal power. As Deidre Helen Crumbley (2006) observes, menstrual taboos are often associated with low social status and in religion, menstruating women are prohibited from sacred space and ritual acts. What we must note is that menstruation-related taboos have significant implications for women and gender relations that ramify throughout society. In many societies there is a belief that menstruation empowers women to cause harm as they choose. Thus Semonides, a Greek philosopher, warned of the moody nature of women:

> 'One day she is all smiles and gladness. A stranger in the house seeing her will sing her praise ... But the next day she is dangerous to look at or approach. She is in a wild frenzy ... savage to all alike friend or foe.'[3]

Infanticide as a defence

We also note the statutory creation of infanticide as a sex-specific offence and defence in the criminal codes of many nations of the world. In discussing the ingredients of infanticide and the premenstrual syndrome, we expose the dangers inherent in biological determinism and reveal that theories of crime impact on the criminal justice system's treatment of women.

In many jurisdictions statutory law recognizes post-natal depression and presumes that a woman who kills her child of less than 12 months does so due to mental instability arising out of hormonal imbalances caused by the birth of her child. The woman's criminal responsibility is thus mitigated.

Using research based on interrogation of women who have been processed through the criminal justice system for infanticide, we explore the question: to what extent is the killing of a young child by its mother a result of socio-economic and cultural pressures rather than hormonal imbalance? We use the research by Stewart, Sithole and Gwaunza *et al.* (2001) on Zimbabwe and by Tibatemwa-Ekirikubinza (1999) on Uganda which locates infanticide, concealment of birth, unlawful termination of pregnancy and abandonment of young children within the framework of uneven power relations, lack of economic power and discriminatory laws. The discussions expose the 'fact' that criminal law is more ready to portray women as ill than it is to expose the stifling social conditions and oppressive constraints of traditional female roles that contribute to women's criminal acts.

...criminal law is more ready to portray women as ill than it is to expose the stifling social conditions and oppressive constraints of traditional female roles

We expose the fact that society and the law are more willing to cure women's diseases than to change women's social circumstances. These conclusions arise out of a critical reflection on what kind of women kill their young offspring, and the socio-economic and cultural factors that 'drive' a woman to kill her own offspring. Is the predominant cause of child killing, puerperal mental disturbance (as assumed by the law) or is it socio-economic and cultural forces in a patriarchal society – such as an attempt to save the honour and reputation of an unmarried girl in a society that stigmatizes pre-marital pregnancy or an unmarried or divorced mother's realization of her financial inability to cater for the child's needs?

---

[3] Cited in Patricia Weiser Eastel, 'Women and crime: premenstrual issues', in *Trends and Issues in Crime and Criminal Justice 31*, Australian Institute of Criminology.

Part III: Analyzing statutory and judge made law

In analyzing statutory and judge made law, I use particular offences to expose the extent to which the legal framework (criminal law and criminal justice) serve patriarchal interests. These include sexual offences, in particular the offences of criminal adultery and rape.

Sexual offences – criminal adultery and rape

The course exposes the fact that sexual offences are highly gendered and contribute to the disempowerment of women. Society's control of women in a patriarchal society is perhaps more in the area of sex and sexuality than in any other area. One of the tools for controlling women is the law and more specifically criminal law. The law more severely sanctions female behaviour which falls within sexual behaviour than it does other deviant conduct. On the other hand the law actively sexualizes female offences and places specific violations within the context of sex-roles or sexual offences. To what extent are these realities a result of traditional theories of crime?

The law more severely sanctions female behaviour which falls within sexual behaviour than it does other deviant conduct

The course deals with the following questions: to what extent and in which ways is criminal law employed to control women's sexuality? And to what extent is society's conceptualization of crime a reflection of gender as a constitutive feature of hierarchical social power? In which ways is criminal law an expression of society's expectations of women's sexual behaviour on the one hand and men's behaviour on the other hand? In this I use Uganda's criminal law of adultery prior to 2007 as a case study and raise a number of issues (see question box on the left).

The criminal law of adultery prior to April 2007

Section 154 of the Penal Code provided that:

| 'Any man who has sexual intercourse with any married woman not being his wife commits adultery and is liable to imprisonment for a term not exceeding twelve months or to a fine not exceeding two hundred shillings; and in addition, the court shall order any such man on first conviction to pay the aggrieved party compensation of six hundred shillings as may be ordered.'

QUESTIONS
Discrimination and law reform

- In which ways is substantive criminal law used to discriminate against women?
- What are the possible agents of and tools for law reform – civil society (human rights non-governmental organizations), the court and judicial activism or lawyers in private practice?
- Could the legislature and the executive play a more meaningful role?
- Beyond legal reform – how to deal with societal reaction?

2   'Any married woman who has sexual intercourse with any man not being her husband commits adultery and is liable on first conviction to a caution by the court, and on the subsequent conviction to imprisonment for a term not exceeding six months.'

Students do an exercise in analyzing the implications of the provisions of Section 154 of Uganda's Penal Code from a gender perspective. The case studies on the next page are used as a backdrop for this analysis.

Public interest litigation at work:
Constitutional Court Petition 13 of 2005[4]

I share with the class for individual study, the Uganda Constitutional Court Petition reproduced below:

'Law and Advocacy for Women in Uganda[5] brought a petition challenging the constitutionality of section 154 of the Penal Code Act. This was under article 137 (3) of the Constitution which provides that a person who alleges that an Act of Parliament or any other law is inconsistent with or in contravention of a provision of this Constitution, may petition the constitutional court for a declaration to that effect. The petitioner alleged that the above provision is contrary to articles 20, 21 24, 31, 33, and 44 of the Constitution[6] and infringes fundamental human rights enshrined

EXERCISE 10

Challenging Section 154 of the Penal Code

Use your own national constitutions and/ or relevant human rights instruments to challenge Section 154 of the Penal Code Act.

The group will need to imagine that a provision identical to Section 154 (as cited in the main text) is on their country law books.

From the perspective of the right to equality, what specific human rights instruments would such a law contravene?

The class can also be divided into appropriate groups composed of individuals from different countries, to analyze the punishments under Section 154 from a gender perspective.

---

[4] *Law and Advocacy for Women in Uganda v Attorney General of Uganda*

[5] An association that advocates for women's rights

[6] The relevant provisions are as follows:

Article 20 (1) provides that fundamental rights and freedoms of the individual are inherent and not granted by the State; (2) The rights and freedoms of the individual and groups enshrined in (the Bill of Rights) shall be respected, upheld and promoted by all organs and agencies of Government and by all persons.

Article 21 (1): All persons are equal before and under the law in all spheres of political, economic, social and cultural life and in every other respect and shall enjoy equal protection of the law. (2): A person shall not be discriminated against on the ground of sex … (3): For the purpose of this article, 'discriminate' means to give different treatment to different persons attributable only or mainly to their respective descriptions by sex, …

Article 31 (1): A man and woman are entitled to equal rights at and in marriage, during marriage and at its dissolution

Article 33 (1) Women shall be accorded full and equal dignity of the person with men.

Article 43 (1) provides that in the enjoyment of rights and freedoms prescribed in the Bill of Rights, no person shall prejudice the fundamental or other human rights and freedoms of others or the public interest.

HYPOTHETICAL CASE 1
Uganda v Mukasa

On the 1 October, 2004 Mukasa, a male aged 20 years is brought before a Grade 1 magistrate. He is charged with having committed 'criminal adultery' under section 154 of the Penal Code Act. According to the facts, Mukasa is married. On 20 September, 2004, following a tip off from Mukasa' wife, the police arrested him having sexual intercourse with an *unmarried* woman aged 20 years. The police arrested Mukasa at a hotel where he had spent a night with the young woman. The two were caught red-handed having sexual intercourse.

Issues

The issues which the prosecution would have to prove would be:

1   That Mukasa had sexual intercourse with a woman
2   That the woman in question was married to another man at the time of sexual intercourse with Mukasa

Holding

Since the woman with whom Mukasa had sexual intercourse was unmarried at the time, Mukasa cannot be convicted under Section 154.

Note

Although Mukasa is married, his marital status is not of essence in determining his guilt. It is the marital status of the woman he had sexual intercourse with that is an issue. Convicting Mukasa would violate article 28(7) of the Constitution which provides that no person shall be charged with or convicted of a criminal offence which is founded on an act or omission that did not at the time it took place constitute a criminal offence.

HYPOTHETICAL CASE 2
Uganda v Babirye

On 1 October 2004, Babirye, a female aged 20 years is brought before a Grade I magistrate. Babirye is charged under Section 154 of the Penal Code Act.

According to the facts, Babirye is married to one Opio. For months, Opio suspected that his wife was having a love affair with a young man, Pinto. Pinto is *unmarried*. On 20 September 2004, Babirye was seen entering a hotel with Pinto. An hour later, the police 'raided' the hotel and Babirye and Pinto were caught red-handed having sexual intercourse.

Issues

The issues which the prosecution had to prove were:

1   That Babirye had sexual intercourse with a man other than Opio.
2   That Babirye was, at the time of the sexual intercourse, married to Opio.

Holding

Babirye is guilty of adultery. She is married to Opio but had sexual intercourse with a man other than Opio.

Note

The fact that Pinto is unmarried does not affect the legal outcome. It is Babirye's marital status that is of essence.

It is clear that the ingredients which constituted criminal adultery differed on the basis of whether the accused was male or female.

in International Conventions that Uganda is signatory to. The sum effect of the provisions is recognition by the law that men and women are equal before the law in all spheres of life (including marriage) and that discrimination on the basis of sex is prohibited by the law.

'The respondent filed answers opposing the petitions wherein it was contended that the section is not unconstitutional and does not discriminate against anyone on the grounds of sex or marriage within the context of the Constitution. He averred that the impugned section is acceptable and demonstrably justifiable in a free and democratic society and fosters the sanctity of marriage which is within public interest limitation as prescribed by article 43 of the Constitution.

'He further averred that the section does not go against the principles enshrined in the Constitution and striking it out would encourage immorality and promiscuity which are contrary to public policy and the letter and spirit of the Constitution, particularly article 126(1) of the Constitution.[7]

'The court agreed with the petitioner that the section is inconsistent with all articles which provide for equality before the law and prohibits discrimination on grounds of sex and 31(1)(b) which gives equal rights between married couples at and in marriage and at its dissolution.'

The court agreed with the petitioner that the section is inconsistent with all articles which provide for equality before the law

The court declared the penal law of adultery unconstitutional.

Media (societal) reaction to the court ruling

I share with the class societal reaction to the court ruling as represented in various media fora.

- 'Adultery no longer a crime!'– headline of both the *New Vision* and *Daily Monitor* newspapers of April 6th 2007.

- 'Decriminalization of adultery will lead to break down of marriage, to spread of AIDS', stated another headline (*New Vision*, Monday 9 April 2007)

- 'The ruling stirred plenty of outcry in this largely Christian East African nation. Many church-based groups argued that it promoted immorality, promiscuity and Western decadence' (Anna Sussman, *Women's e News* at http:www.womensnews.org/article.cfm/dyn/aid/3215/context/cover/

---

[7] 126 (1): 'Judicial power is derived from the people and shall be exercised by the courts ... in the name of the people and in conformity with law and with the values, norms and aspirations of the people.'

Societal attitudes to men and women's behaviour with regard to their sexuality is persistently unequal and legislation has historically supported this inequality

The question is: is it only when women's sexual conduct is restricted and not that of men that society will be saved from the negative consequences of the decriminalization of adultery?

The ruling was also later on linked with domestic violence thus:

— The *Daily Monitor*'s 'Lizard', 16 April 2007 was entitled: 'It's now jungle law at work'. This was in reference to its story entitled 'Man loses arm over adultery' wherein it was reported that after the constitutional court scrapped the law on adultery, some people have started taking the law into their hands.

— The *Daily Monitor*'s editorial on 17 April 2007 insinuated that two reported cases of husbands taking the law into their hands resulted from the decriminalization of adultery.

The insinuations were that decriminalization of adultery has left 'injured' husbands with no option but to attack their wives or the wives' lovers.

Lessons learnt from the case study

● There is a relationship between criminal law and the social or cultural context.

● Criminal law is often a reflection of society's underlying values.

● Society's expectations of women's sexual behaviour vary from what is expected of men.

● Society's conceptualization or definition of crime is a reflection of gender as a feature of hierarchical social power.

● It is imperative that we use the concept of gender to unearth the violation of women's rights in criminal law and criminal justice.

● Gender inequality is expressed and embedded in criminal law.

● Public interest litigation is a powerful tool of legal reform. It can be used effectively by civil society.

The gendered nature of rape and the cautionary rule of corroboration in assaults of a sexual nature

Through use of case law from different countries, we analyze judicial interpretation of the definition of rape: What (according to case law) constitutes rape in the various jurisdictions represented in the class?

Comparison of legislation from different countries leads to the issues of the role of parliament in ensuring gender equity. The discussions answer the question: how can human rights activists in countries with provisions which violate women's rights use the more gender sensitive laws of other countries (within Africa) to move their national legislative bodies to amend the law from a women's rights perspective? Examples of such comparison is between Uganda, Kenya and Zimbabwe's provision on the definition of rape as indicated in the exercise (see box) and the extracts from the laws that follow.

Uganda

Section 123 Uganda Penal Code:

> 'Any person who has unlawful carnal knowledge of a woman or girl, without her consent, or with her consent, if the consent is obtained by force or by means of threats or intimidation of any kind, or by fear of bodily harm, or by means of false representation as to the nature of the act, or in the case of a married woman, by personating her husband, is guilty of the felony termed rape.'

Kenya

Section 3 (1) of the Kenyan Sexual Offences Act (No 3 of 2006):

> 'A person commits the offence termed rape if
> (a) he or she intentionally and unlawfully
> commits an act which causes penetration with his or her genital organs; (b) the other person does not consent to the penetration; or (c) the consent is obtained by force or by means of threats or intimidation of any kind.'

Zimbabwe

Section 65 of the Zimbabwean Criminal Law (Codification and Reform) Act:

> '(1) If a male person knowingly has sexual intercourse or anal sexual intercourse with a female person and, at the time of the intercourse (a) the female person has not consented to it; and (b) he knows that she has not consented to it or realizes that there is a real risk or possibility that she may not have consented to it; he shall be guilty of rape and liable to imprisonment for life or any shorter period.'

EXERCISE 11
Statutory provisions on rape

The class works in country groups and writes down their country's statutory provision on rape. We compare the different legal provisions and consider the following questions:

1. To what extent or in which ways does gender guide the definition of rape in each country's legislation?

2. To what extent is the definition of the offence of rape a reflection of societal expectations of
   a   Men
   b   Women in a particular country?

3. To what extent is the definition of rape a reflection of the concerns of
   a   Men
   b   Women in a patriarchal society?

MORE QUESTIONS

Comparing laws on sexual assault

Using the information about the laws in Uganda, Kenya and Zimbabwe, students also discuss the following questions:

- What potential is inherent in Kenya's amended law (and lacking in Uganda's law) for assuring justice to victims of sexual assaults, the majority of whom are women?

- What can Uganda learn from Kenya?

- Looking at Zimbabwe's provision, is there need for further amendment of Kenya's amended law?

- In which ways can we use the Kenyan law to improve Zimbabwe's provision?

The rape trial and proof of rape: Penetration of the vagina by the penis

I introduce this topic by the following question:

> 'Your six year old daughter comes running to you. She lifts her dress and pointing to her groin says: what is this mummy/daddy? What would your answer be?'

The students react with shock and disbelief but in no class has anybody's answer to the question been: 'vagina'. The answers have always been couched in euphemisms such as 'wee wee', 'georgina', and so on. In no case has a parent in my class said he or she would tell a little boy that the name of the male organ is penis. Rather it has been 'animal', 'stick', 'georgee' and so on. So we move on to the next question:

> 'What did your mother give you as the name of the vagina?'

The reaction is generally something like:

> 'What? What have you said?'

> 'My mother? We never talked to her about such big words.'

It is clear that both the men and women in class are uneasy about the questions put to them and often hope that they have misheard what I have just said. I develop this discussion with exercise 13 for the women (see box on next page).

Analysis of case law is also a good way of getting students to gain insights into the challenges of handling rape cases, especially within particular cultural contexts where it is not easy for people to talk about their private parts. As an example I have given students the facts about the case that follows and asked how they would handle the case if they were judges presiding over such a rape trial. I point out that each ingredient constituting the offence must be proved beyond reasonable doubt if a conviction is to be entered.

Uganda v Tumuhirwe Criminal Session Case No 296/93

The accused was indicted for statutory rape of an underage girl. The girl testified that on the relevant day, she was sleeping and woke up to find the accused on top of her. In the words of the complainant the accused had entered his *omukira* (tail) into her vagina.

Would they on the face of it accept that penetration with a penis had taken place?

When each group has discussed the issue for a few minutes, I give them the arguments of the counsel of the defendant in that particular case as below:

'Counsel for the accused argued *inter alia* that the complainant did not know what was inserted into her vagina. There was thus doubt whether she had been defiled. She kept telling the court about '*omukira*' which literally means 'tail' and yet human beings do not have tails.'

What would your verdict be?

Where a group is in agreement with the counsel's argument that in such a case, the prosecution would have failed to prove the case beyond reasonable doubt as is the cardinal principle in criminal prosecutions, I remind them that many of them had said to me that the words 'penis' and 'vagina' are too big to be mentioned, especially by a young girl.

I then share with the class the holding of the court:

'It is true the complainant in her testimony informed the court that the man who defiled her used his tail but in the course of her testimony she clarified that by tail she meant that part of the body used by a man when urinating. That explanation left no doubt that she was sexually violated by a man using his penis. We all know what she meant by her use of euphemism.'

Examining law reform through judicial activism in African courts

Under English common law, the evidence of a complainant in a sexual offence had to be corroborated with either direct or indirect circumstantial evidence. All judges were obliged to warn themselves and the assessors of the danger of convicting an accused person on the uncorroborated evidence of the complainant in a sexual offence. This rule was taken up by many of the former colonies of Britain. The value of international human rights instruments on discrimination against women and the right to equal protection by the law as

EXERCISE 12
Drafting an ideal provision

In groups, the class is requested to draft a provision which solves the weaknesses in the various jurisdictions and to come up with an ideal provision.

EXERCISE 13
Talking about it: women only

- If you had an infection and presented yourself to a doctor, what word would you use to explain that you had an infection in the vagina?

  Responses:

  '*I have a problem down there.*'

  '*In my womanhood.*'

  '*The birth canal.*'

  '*Private parts.*'

- Would you ever use the word 'vagina?'

  Responses:

  '*Definitely not!*'

  '*Not a black woman!*'

  '*Perhaps a white woman would.*'

  '*One knows the exact word, but never mentions it.*'

  '*Those words are never mentioned. It is vulgar, immoral. Never used.*'

  '*Vagina and penis? Those are big words.*'

well as the value of national constitutions has been reflected in the fact that judges have started questioning the desirability of the rule on corroboration. In this regard we examine various cases that have come before the courts and in which judges have questioned the rule of corroboration.

Examples include *Uganda v Peter Matovu* where Justice E.S. Lugayizi did not hesitate to condemn the rule as unconstitutional and discriminating against women. The accused was indicted for defilement of a girl under the age of 18 years.

In South Africa, in the Supreme Court of Appeal in *S v Jackson*, Oliver JA said of the cautionary rule in sexual assault cases:

> 'It is based on irrational and outdated perceptions. It unjustly stereotypes complainants in sexual assault cases (overwhelmingly, women) as particularly unreliable ... the evidence in a particular case may call for a cautionary approach, but that is a far cry from the application of a general cautionary rule.'

We also look at *S v D and Another* in which the rule was abolished in Namibia. Reference is also made to the article by Hatchard (1993) 'Abolishing the cautionary rule in sexual cases in Namibia'.

Part IV: Domestic violence

Why domestic violence?

In addition to sexual offences, the course involves a discussion of domestic violence, its consequences and how domestic violence is handled by legislative pronouncements as well as by courts of law. The course answers the question: how does gender inequality lead to the perpetuation of violence by husbands against their wives? In doing this we look at domestic violence not just at the global level but more specifically from the perspective of African experience. I use examples of empirical research on African communities to reveal the gendered nature of domestic violence.[8]

The case studies are used to elucidate the social, economic and cultural factors that may precipitate a man's violence towards his wife. The studies reveal that society attributes a higher status and gives more power to men than it does to women merely on the basis of sex. Within patriarchy men use violence as a tool to retain their power, domination and control over women.

---

[8] For example: Tibatemwa-Ekirikubinza (2007) *Men's violent crime against wives in Uganda* and Vetten (2005) *Addressing domestic violence in South Africa: reflections on strategy and practice*

Most of the explanations given by husbands as reasons or causes of their violent actions against their wives can be interpreted as an attempt by the men to reassert their societal given authority over their wives. The binary logic of gender (masculine/active versus feminine/passive) is inherently violent in the way that it creates social hierarchies and legitimizes inequalities in power. 'Gender roles powerfully influence other kinds of social roles, and such roles are policed by violence' (Greig, 2001:10).

A common finding of studies on domestic violence is that a woman's adultery is often a cause of men's violence against wives. The course consequently analyzes the law's interface with women's adultery. I contend that by recognizing a wife's adultery as adequate provocation for a fatal assault, judge made law has given legitimacy to particular assumptions about femininity and masculinity.

...by recognizing a wife's adultery as adequate provocation for a fatal assault, judge made law has given legitimacy to particular assumptions about femininity and masculinity

What Jones (1980:310-1) said about homicides in American society is also true of the African situation: '...standards of justifiable homicide have been based on male models and expectations'.

Domestic violence is discussed within the context of gender-based violence and within the discourse of patriarchy. The course calls for analyses of international, regional and national pieces of legislation:

- The United Nations Declaration on the Elimination of Violence against Women
- The African Platform for Action (Dakar Declaration) of 1994
- The Protocol to the African Charter on Human and Peoples' Rights on the Rights of Women in Africa

We assess the value of international human rights instruments on gender-based violence as well as national constitutions in the fight against domestic violence. We also examine the impact of attempts to address the problem by legal means:

- How does criminal law and the criminal justice system react towards violence against women?
- To what extent is the law's reaction a reflection of society's perception towards the status of women in patriarchal society?

Following Takyiwaa Manuh's analysis in her article, 'African women and domestic violence' (2007), I ask the following questions:

- What are the similarities and differences in the experiences of African countries that have attempted to pass domestic violence legislation?
- What lessons can be learnt in the process?
- How do attempts to pass such laws connect to the lived realities of ordinary women?

We discuss examples of law reform through statute in Africa – Malawi, South Africa and Zimbabwe. We analyze the strengths and weaknesses within the already existing pieces of legislation. We also discuss how African jurisdictions with no specific legislation on domestic violence can use judicial activism to ensure protection of women as a group most vulnerable to domestic violence in the 'African' family.

Violence by women within the domestic arena

The course also discusses women's violent crime and answers the question: how does gender inequality lead women into violent criminality? In answer to Dorothy Roberts' (1994) call I analyze women's violence within the context of patriarchal power. More specifically, I examine the interface between African patriarchy, the law and women's violent criminality within the family. We answer the question: what socio-cultural values and norms within patriarchy increase the chances that a woman will resort to violence against: her husband, her own child and her co-wife or the husband's other woman?

...a significant number of women are processed through the criminal justice system for violence against those they are supposed to love

To reveal the lived realities of women who resort to violence as a means of conflict resolution, I use case studies of empirical research on African communities.[9] The case studies reveal that society's horror or shock that a significant number of women are processed through the criminal justice system for violence against those they are supposed to love (family members) is no solution; society must alter the socio-economic, cultural and legal arrangements that deprive women of more humane ways of conflict resolution.

The gendered nature of criminal defences: self-defence and provocation

The course brings out the importance of appreciating the gendered nature of the crime of homicide and thus the application of defences commonly put forward by perpetrators of homicide. We analyze case law, looking at the responses of criminal law and the agents of the criminal justice system to:

● violence against women
● violence by women in the domestic setting.

I analyze the defences of self-defence and provocation and how they are interpreted by case law. How do gender inequality and gendered assumptions affect the courts' interpretation of self-defence and provocation?[10]

---

[9] For example: Lillian Tibatemwa-Ekirikubinza (1999) *Women's violent crime in Uganda: more sinned against than sinning* and Matovu Vero (1995) *Effects of polygamy on women: a case study of Bulenga sub-county, Masaka district, Uganda.*

[10] See *R v Thornton* No.2 (1996) 2 AER 1023; *R v Ahluwalia* (1992) 4 AER 889.

Self-defence

The defence of self-defence permits the use of *reasonable* force against another person when one (A) *reasonably believes* that person (B) is threatening her or him with *imminent* and unlawful bodily harm and that the force used is necessary to *prevent* the threatened harm.

A person is entitled to use deadly force *only* in the reasonable belief that the other is threatening him or her with imminent death or serious body injury and that the deadly force is necessary to avert the harm.

We tackle the question: what do the courts consider to be serious enough injury to warrant a fatal attack? I divide the class into groups and distribute different case studies to each group.

The case of *State v Wanrow*[16] from America is also used as a case study.

Provocation

In several African jurisdictions, when a person intentionally kills another but successfully pleads that his or her violent act was a consequence of a provocative act by the deceased, such an offender will be guilty of the lesser offence of manslaughter and not murder.[11] Although the killing is unlawful and is accompanied by ill intent, the law takes cognizance of human frailty and treats the offender with some degree of leniency.

In order to successfully plead provocation, the offender must prove the following:

- The offender (A) acted in the heat of passion arising from loss of self-control.
- The loss of self-control (by the offender) must be a direct result of an *unlawful* act committed by the victim (B).
- The offender must have reacted immediately after the provocation (without having had time to cool from the passion caused by the provocation).

What the offender (A) is saying is: Yes – I killed B. I killed B because he or she committed a wrong towards me. B's wrongful act led me lose control and to therefore attack him.

In considering the question of provocation, courts apply both a subjective and objective test. The court considers the question: did the unlawful act of

EXERCISE 14

Provocation and relevance of cultural background of accused

- Analyze from a gender perspective, the court's pronouncement on the relevance of culture in a finding of provocation.
- What could be the danger of such a pronouncement?

---

[11] Country groups are asked to present their statutory provisions on provocation as a defence or a mitigating factor in a murder case.

...the courts' interpretation of the questions related to objectivity often deny women's perceptions of provocation

the deceased as a matter of fact lead the accused to lose self control? (the subjective test). But also answers the following question: would any other reasonable person have lost his power of self control and acted as the accused did? (the objective test). Although statutory laws which create the defence in many of the jurisdictions we deal with in class do not limit the use of the defence to male offenders, the courts' interpretation of the questions related to objectivity often deny women's perceptions of provocation. I use court cases (case studies) of women's failure to successfully plead provocation.

CASE STUDY 1

Uganda v Margaret Kazigat H.C.C.S.C. NO. 116/75

The accused and her friend sold a local brew in the accused's house. The deceased and another man had a drink in the house of the accused. When the accused asked them to leave, the men said they wanted to drink more. The accused left the men drinking and went to her bedroom to sleep. She switched off the light and closed the door. Some time later she felt someone holding her by the throat. She tried to free herself. The accused struggled with the stranger in the course of which she got a knife and stabbed him. After the deceased had been injured he revealed he was the accused's brother-in-law. The accused stopped but the deceased had been fatally injured and he died later.

Question

If you were a trial judge and the accused pleaded self-defence, what would your verdict be?

After the group has answered the question and shared its opinion with the class, I hand over to them the judgment that follows:

In discussing the applicability of self-defence Lord Justice Ssekandi said:

> 'This appears to be a borderline case. On the facts, the accused could have been entitled to self-defence... It may very

well be that she went far to use a knife on a person whose designs in advancing towards her were very clear. The intruder quite obviously was not a robber or killer. It appears he was seeking to assault the accused sexually. The use of a knife would have been the last resort but not an immediate alternative. In any case, the accused was trying to protect her womanhood and ... the case is really borderline. The accused could not be acquitted on the basis of self-defence.'

The class is invited to critically analyze Ssekandi's judgment from a gender perspective.

Pertinent questions for analysis

- Is sexual assault or rape not as serious, or perhaps even more serious an injury than robbery?

- Is property more important than one's womanhood or bodily integrity?

- Is rape not an inherently violent act, an assault?

- Why should a man's anger which causes him to kill his adulterous wife or her lover be understood more than a woman's anger towards her rapist?

These validate Naffine's (1987:3) observation that:

'Law's reasonable man … represents the male point of view. That is to say, the mythical man of law is intended to be ungendered, an objective standard of human conduct, and yet the characters are invariably men. And of course, they are deemed to be reasonable men. In [the law's] search for a perfectly impartial standard of reasonable human behaviour, [courts] have retained in their mind's eye an image of a man, not a woman.'

CASE STUDY 2
Rex v Nana Jabu Lukhele High Court of Swaziland

The accused who worked as a gardener left work with a friend and went to a drinking place. When the two left the drinking place, they were joined by the deceased. The deceased stood in front of the accused and told her that he wanted to have sexual intercourse with her. She resisted but he continued to harass her. In the process she fell or he pushed her down and pressed her on the ground. The accused's face was, as a result, bruised. The accused got up and ran away. The deceased went after her, caught up with her and blocked her way, insisting that he wanted to have sexual intercourse with her by force. The accused produced a knife and stabbed him. The accused was charged with murder.

Question

If you were a trial judge and the accused pleaded self-defence, what would your verdict be?

After the group has answered the question and shared its opinion with the class, I hand over to them the judgment that follows:

Lord Thwala held:

'He wanted to have sexual intercourse with her by force. Then the accused at a later stage produced a knife and stabbed him. Was she not acting in self-defence? Rape is like any other property or life. To be raped you have to protect or defend yourself … There was a reasonable explanation as to how the knife was in her dustcoat pocket. It is a tool of her employment, she cuts vegetables with the knife in the garden … I do not think that her action exceeded the legal bounds of self-defence. I find that her actions were justifiable in the circumstances. I come to the conclusion that she acted in self-defence; I therefore acquit her.'

Discussion

Students are asked to discuss the judgment from a gender perspective.

On the other hand men's interpretations of acts of others are more likely to be accepted as indeed provocation by courts as indicated in case study 3 below.

CASE STUDY 3

Rex v HUSSEIN S/o MOHAMED 9 East African Court of Appeal 52

The accused alleged that his father in-law was planning to move to Nairobi and to take his daughter, the accused's wife, with him. The accused finally forbade his wife to go. The wife replied:

'Go away, sala, budmash, harami'

(These are terms of abuse which literally mean brother in-law, vagabond, scoundrel).

She spat at him and said:

' I have seen many males like you and I shall see more in the future. You are not the only man in the world … open the door for me, I want to go to my father just now. I do not want to live with you.'

The accused seized a dagger and stabbed his wife many times and she died.

Question to the class

Would the accused successfully plead provocation?

I then share the following judgment with the class.

Judgment

The East African Court of Appeal returned a verdict of manslaughter on the basis of provocation. The court agreed with the two assessors' opinion that if a wife utters those particular words to her husband, 'words so bad and with deep hidden meaning' the man would naturally lose the power of self control.

Questions

● What is it in the words that would make a reasonable man (in patriarchal society) lose self-control?

● Would any other man not only lose self-control but also stab his wife?

Conclusion

The value of the course to students: some students' voices

After a class on the rape trial one of the students, a female law judicial officer, stated:

> 'In all my 22 years as a judicial officer it had never hit me that corroboration in sexual offences has such damning inferences on women. I religiously looked for it … (now I realize) to the detriment of complainants. I have no doubt that there are a lot of judicial officers who fall in the same category and fail to recognize corroboration for what it is … resulting in injustice within the justice system.'

Another much younger judicial officer wrote to me three years after going through the course and said:

> 'Prior to the course my approach to criminal cases was that the law had to be applied "dryly" as it appears in statutes. … For example, in rape trials I used to narrowly interpret the facts and assess the evidence without understanding how the so-called legal principles came to be coined. Having gone through the course and interrogated the bulk of the legal provisions … I was transformed and I now appreciate that there is more to the law than is seen on paper. The study on the development of some principles and theories alerted me to go beyond the rules as they appear … I had hitherto always doubted the evidence of rape victims because I had been trained to believe that there is need to warn myself… I had been guided by the opinion that women frame men as a result of flopped relationships, believed that since women never say yes to sex … But I now think seriously about the other side – how many women have the courage to stand in court and talk about sex?'

After our interrogation of the defence of provocation, another judicial officer said that the course had helped her appreciate particular ways in which gender inequality and gendered assumptions affect the courts' interpretation of self-defence and provocation. She exclaimed:

> 'Oh my God, it is clear there are women I convicted of crime who I now know I should have acquitted if I had meaningfully interpreted the defence of self-defence.'

Personal reflections: the teacher's voice

It is humbling to note that I share some of the reflections of my students. One of the lessons I have learnt as I teach the course is that in my earlier days as a teacher of criminal law on the undergraduate course at Makerere University, I had for years contributed to producing law practitioners who hardly ever interrogate legal provisions from a gender perspective. I had passed on my knowledge of legal principles without 'lifting the veil' to reveal the assumptions underlying legal provisions. I can thus say:

> 'Oh my God! There are women who my students convicted of crime who should have been acquitted if I had more meaningfully taught my students – trained them to interrogate the bulk of legal provisions and more specifically the defences of self-defence and provocation. There are women who have been denied justice as victims of sexual assault just because as a teacher, I failed to help students appreciate judicial activism as an invaluable tool of justice delivery.'

In other words the course has helped me subscribe to a feminist vision of criminal justice.

Bibliography

Brownmiller S. (1975) *Against our will: men, women and rape*, Simon & Schuster, New York.

Bull S. (2003) 'Violence against women: media (mis) representation of femicide', paper presented at Women Working to Make a Difference, Seventh International Women's Policy Research Conference, June 2003, accessed 13 May 2009 online at: http://www.iwpr.org/pdf/ Bull_Sabrina Denney.pdf.

Campbell D.W., P.W. Sharps, F. Gary *et al.* (31 January, 2002) 'Intimate partner violence in African American women', *Online Journal of Issues in Nursing* 7(1):4, available online at: http://www.nursingworld.org/ojin/topic17/ tpc17_4.htm

Chakwana Deliwe C. (2004) 'Domestic violence', chapter 15 in *Malawi: DHS, 2004 – final report (English)*, available online at: http://www.measuredhs.com/pubs/pub_details. cfm?ID=575&ctry_id=24&SrchTp=country

Crumbley D.H. (2006) 'Power in the blood: menstrual taboos and women's power in an African instituted church', in R.M. Griffith and B.D. Savage (eds) *Women and religion in the African diaspora: knowledge, power and performance*, Johns Hopkins University Press, Baltimore.

Dobash E. and R. Dobash (1979) *Violence against wives*, The Free Press, New York.

Easteal P.W. (1991) 'Women and crime: premenstrual issues', *Trends and Issues in Crime and Criminal Justice*, Australian Institute of Criminology, Canberra, available online at: http://www.aic.gov.au/documents/2/4/7/ {24751E93-85A8-4533-AE23-5C769034917E}7Dti31.pdf

Freud S. cited in J. Mitchell and J. Rose (eds) (1984) *Feminine sexuality: Jacques Lacan and the ecole freudienne*, Macmillan, Norton and Pantheon Books, London and New York.

Gelsthorpe L. and A. Morris (1988) 'Feminism and criminology in Britain', *British Journal of Criminology* 28: 223-240.

Williams G.L. (1969) *Learning the law*, 8th edition, revised, Sweet & Maxwell Ltd, London.

Gonzalez-Brenes M. (2003) 'Domestic violence, bargaining and fertility in rural Tanzania', Department of Economics, University of California, Berkeley, available online at: http://www.sscnet.edu/polisci/wgape/papers/4-Gonzalez. pdf

– (2004) 'Domestic violence and household decision-making: evidence from East Africa', Department of Economics, University of California, Berkeley, available online at: http://www.sscnet.ucla.edu/polisci/wgape/ papers/7-Gonzalez.pdf

Greig A. (2001) 'Racism, class and masculinity: the global dimensions of gender-based violence', panel paper prepared for an INSTRAW/UNICEF conference, accessed 2009 online at: http://un-instraw.org/en/special-collections/ violence-against-women-racism-class-and-masculinity/ view.html

Heidensohn F. (1987) 'Women and crime: questions for criminology', in P. Carlen and A. Worral (eds) (1987) *Gender, crime and justice*, Open University Press, London.

– (1987) *Women and crime: the life of the female offender*, New York University Press, New York.

– (1985) *Women and crime*, Macmillan, London.

Henderson L. (1991) 'Law's patriarchy', *Law and Society Review* 25(2)411-444.

Fechner H. (1994) 'Three stories of prostitution in the West: prostitutes, groups, law and feminist truth', *Columbia Journal of Gender and Law* 4(26):47–53.

Jones A. (1980) *Women who kill*, Holt, Rinehart & Winston, New York.

Kendall K. (1991) 'The politics of premenstrual syndrome: implications for feminist justice', *Critical Criminology* 2(2):77–98.

Lombrosso C. and W. Ferrero (1895) *The female offender*, Fisher Unwin, London.

Ludsin H. (2003a) *South African criminal law and battered women who kill: Discussion document 1*, Centre for the Study of Violence and Reconciliation, Johannesburg, available online at: www.csvr.org.za/wits/papers/papluds1. htm

– (2003b) *South African criminal law and battered women who kill: Discussion document 2*, Centre for the Study of Violence and Reconciliation, Johannesburg, available online at: www.csvr.org.za/wits/papers/papexec2.htm

MacFarlane B.A. (1993) 'The historical development of the offence of rape', originally in Wood and Peck (eds), *100 years of the criminal code in Canada; essays commemorating the centenary of the Canadian criminal code*, Canadian Bar Association, Ottawa, available online at: http://www.canadiancriminallaw.com/articles.

Manuh T. (2007) 'African women and domestic violence', *World Changing Team* (online journal), available at: http:// www.worldchanging.com/archives/007653.html

Matovu V. (1995) 'Effects of polygamy on women: a case study of Bulenga subcounty, Masaka district, Uganda', masters thesis, Arts faculty, Makerere University, Kampala (unpublished).

Mitchell J. and J. Rose (eds) (1984) *Feminine sexuality: Jacques Lacan and the ecole freudienne*, Macmillan, Norton and Pantheon Books, London and New York.

Morris A. (1987) *Women, crime and criminal justice*, Basil Blackwell, Oxford.

Naffin N. and F. Gale (1989) 'Testing the nexus: crime, gender and unemployment', *British Journal of Criminology*, 29(2): 144–156.

Pollak O. (1950) *The criminality of women,* University of Pennsylvania Press, Philadelphia.

Radford J. and D. Russell (1992) *Femicide: the politics of woman killing*, Open University Press, Buckingham.

Roberts D. (1994) 'The meaning of gender equity in criminal law', *The Journal of Criminal Law and Criminology* (1973) 85(1): 1-14.

Schneider E.M. and S. Jordan (1978) 'Representation of women who defend themselves in response to physical or sexual assault', 2 Am. J. Trial Adv. 19 (1978), reprinted in E. Bochank and E. Krauss, *Women's self-defense cases: theory and practice* (1981), Lexis Law Publisher, Charlottesville.

Smart C. (1977a) *Women, crime and criminology: a feminist critique*, Routledge & Kegan Paul, London and Boston.

– (1977b) 'Criminological theory: its ideology and implications concerning women', *British Journal of Sociology* 28(1):89–100.

Spelman E. (1988) *Inessential women: problems of exclusion in feminist thought*, Beacon Press, Boston.

Stewart J., E. Sithole, E. Gwaunza *et al.* (2001)*: Joy or despair? Women and gender-generated reproductive crimes of violence,* WLSA, Harare.

Tamale S. (2005) 'Gendered bodies, sexualities and negotiating power in Uganda', paper presented at the conference, Negotiating Gender Justice in Göteborg, 2005, Working paper No. 10, CGGS, Göteborg University.

Tanner R.E. (1970) *Homicide in Uganda,* Scandinavian Institute of African Studies, Uppsala.

Thompson R.B. and D. Erez (1994) 'Wife abuse in Sierra Leone: polygamous marriages in a dual legal system', *International Journal of Comparative and Applied Justice* 18(1 & 2): 27–37 (Spring/Fall 1994).

Tibatemwa-Ekirikubinza L. (1999) *Women's violent crime in Uganda: more sinned against than sinning,* Fountain Publishers, Kampala.

– (2005) *Homicides and non-fatal assaults in Uganda,* Fountain Publishers, Kampala.

– (2005) *Criminal law in Uganda: sexual assaults and offences against morality*, Fountain Publishers. Kampala.

– (2007) *Men's violent crime against wives in Uganda: an affirmation of skewed masculinity?*, Women's Law working paper No.2, Faculty of Law, Makerere University, Kampala.

Vetten L. (2005) 'Addressing domestic violence in South Africa: reflections on strategy and practice', United Nations Division for the Advancement of Women, South

8

Teaching women, law reform and social justice strategies
through dialogic and hands-on learning

Amy S. Tsanga

In this chapter, I seek to describe how I have developed and used my course on women, law reform and social justice strategies[1] to get students to examine the challenges and explore appropriate ways of grappling with the transformative potential of legal services. These include interventionist strategies such as lobbying for law reform, legal and human rights advocacy on individual and group rights, as well as empowerment initiatives through a variety of education programmes.

The underlying theme that informs this course is to what extent law can be used as a tool for social justice for women. The aim is to get students to understand and appreciate some of the key entry points that they can use in this endeavour. This involves breaking down the legal system into its substantive, structural and cultural components to understand the broad areas of concern as far as the legal system goes. Women's inferior legal status may emanate from the fact that the laws are unjust or discriminatory; the cause on the other hand may lie in the application of the law which may be prejudicial or arbitrary towards women; women may also be unaware of their rights. At a basic level, if the problem is centred on the substantive component then *law reform* may be the most appropriate strategy. Lobbying aimed at influencing public officials, especially parliamentarians, to secure passage of legislation is a key strategy. Where the problem lies with the structural component then *advocacy* may be more effective. Where culture is the problem then *education*, encompassing media campaigns, legal awareness, training of lawyers and legal personnel as well as paralegals may all be appropriate strategies (Schuler, 1986:4). This

The underlying theme that informs this course is to what extent law can be used as a tool for social justice for women.

---

[1] I use the term 'social' to relate to society and the welfare of human beings as members of that society. The term 'justice' on the other hand relates to the quality of being just and fair particularly as regards conflicting claims. The collective term 'social justice' therefore relates to specific issues affecting human society that raise concerns of just and fair treatment.

basic understanding of the components of the legal system lays the foundation for a more detailed engagement of where to lay the emphasis in our activism. It also makes it easier to understand power dynamics at each of these levels.

The inspiration for crafting a course of this nature emanates from my field experiences working as a lawyer with grassroots communities before joining the reflective field of academia. Key to this experience was unearthing some of the urgent analytical and practical gaps in training the lawyers and non-lawyers who increasingly find themselves working with disadvantaged groups, in particular women, in a variety of settings. Essentially, as explained below, the challenges that bedevil knowledge and activism for transformation are intricately linked to the overlap of issues of concept, content and methodology.

...the challenges that bedevil knowledge and activism for transformation are intricately linked to the overlap of issues of concept, content and methodology

All too often activist interventions spend too little time conceptualizing the settings and context where the problems that they seek to address are located. Human rights for instance, provide a core conceptual framework within which today's social justice activism takes place. A key argument is that the concept of human rights itself, if not located within the political and historical experiences of the target groups, can simply scratch the surface and stall rather than promote the dismantling of unequal relations, while hiding behind rhetoric and slogans (Shijvi, 1989:80; An-Na'im, 1994). From a women's human rights perspective, we explore the dilemma for women that emanates from cultural identity on the one hand and human rights on the other. Of concern are also conceptual challenges centred on engagement with religious and customary laws. We examine the question of human rights priorities – what are they and who decides? What are the implications for women?

Similarly, shifts in development perspectives also illustrate how activism, in terms of content and methodology, is highly influenced by the dominant developmental paradigms of the day (Hyden, 1993).

Much of the activism around women's rights in Africa takes place through non-governmental organizations. The role of the non-governmental sector as a provider of services and an important change agent is therefore also significant to analyze conceptually. This is particularly so in light of the romanticized purity that has indeed often accompanied our perception of this sector when compared to the state on the African continent (Carson, 2001; Tripp, 2001; Onyango, 2002).

Much of the activism around women's rights in Africa takes place through non-governmental organizations

The role of lawyers as change agents is yet another fertile terrain for conceptual introspection from a social justice perspective. The last two decades in particular have witnessed discernible shifts in the focus of lawyers in the developing world. This is especially so with the growth of non-governmental organizations and also the emphasis of the global human rights agenda. While not detracting from the major inroads lawyers have made in working with disadvantaged communities, still key questions arise as to the efficacy of that engagement. In what ways, for instance, has work with grassroots levels strengthened interventionist strategies such as mediation and settlement since women are often not looking for strictly legal remedies? What has this meant in terms of working with other disciplines? Is feminist and human rights jurisprudence filtering through to judges and magistrates in their interpretation of legislation? Is there a shift in black letter lawyering that reflects the impact of strands of feminist jurisprudence that call for bringing on board women's lived realities in dealing with the law? How is the need for continuing education being addressed for judicial officers and with what results? In the various countries that students come from, has the women's agenda for equality and justice benefited at all from having lawyers in public policy?

The content of what is focused on has significant bearings on whether social justice will be achieved for the intended beneficiaries – at least from their viewpoint. In reality, this means unearthing and understanding some of the critical concerns that affect the lives of our people on the continent. Does aid, for instance, compromise the issues that we prioritize in our social justice struggles on the continent? What could be different in our prioritization if current struggles did not go with the flow of donor money? Lawyers in the third world have, for example, been criticised for helping to create and maintain political economies which produce international dependency, skewed distribution of wealth and power, as well as persistent and growing inequality (Dias *et al.*, 1981).

Thus for instance, some of the urgent concerns include access to health, education, housing and food to mention a few. Peace and security are another real concern on the continent to date. Their absence fundamentally affects the realization of important civil as well as social and economic rights. Grasping how these issues impact on women is crucial. Yet despite such issues being significant from a legal and social justice perspective, they have not until recently emerged as core issues of concern for activism at the grassroots level. Also, with the growing emphasis on social and economic rights, how do we engage with such issues in a manner that does not make them the exclusive engagement of professionals who are able to interpret the complexities of human rights law?

Understanding what issues are vital for social justice and why those issues are critical is therefore a key aspect of the conceptual dialogue. How best to go about addressing the identified concerns is the other side of the coin. Consequently, the two threads that tie this course together are theory and method: the theoretical considerations that emanate from our social, economic and political realities within a local and global context and, secondly, the challenges of practical application in changing some of these realities. My course is therefore aimed at students who are interested in sharpening their

Some children, like those in the photo above in Ethiopia, end up doing chores like collecting water and child minding which prevents them from going to school

perspectives in engaging with the conceptual and methodological realities of social justice activism. They include lawyers and non-lawyers as multi-disciplinarity is key to effective interventions.

The course is divided into two parts. The first part addresses a range of issues from a conceptual and analytical perspective. As an entry point, students are required to read selected texts and we use these as a backdrop for constructing dialogue and developing exercises on selected themes as will be illustrated throughout the chapter. The second part of the course is devoted to a practical exercise on aspects of the course, which the students choose, design and undertake themselves.

In light of the thrust of the course as described above, in this chapter I essentially draw on selected themes to illustrate how I engage both the dialogic and hands on approach to enhance students' skills in social justice activism.

Part I: The dialogic approach to selected social justice concerns

1 Law reform and activist challenges

In examining the potential of law reform in contributing to changes in women's lives on the continent, an entry point is the acknowledgment that different bodies of law underlie Africa's legal development. These include received western laws, customary laws and religious laws. From a law reform perspective, the existence of these multiple sources of law essentially means that the reformer is not starting from a clean slate. Right at the outset this legal landscape may pose difficulties for law reform in terms of the likelihood of resistance such as when legislative reforms grounded in received laws encounter competing legal norms embedded in any society (Falk Moore, 1973; Allot, 1980; Tsanga, 2003). Given that customary law is most preserved in many countries in matters of personal law, substantive equality for women may be slow in coming due to cultural resistance and protectionism. This may be especially so where reformed laws have not effectively tapped into existing legal forms that people are already familiar with but have sought to replace them. We also explore the range of normative orders that impact on women's lives and the ways that we can make use of these in shaping gender-sensitive societies.

Given that the students who take up this optional course come from different legal jurisdictions, I have sought to develop dialogue using questions which enable us to appreciate the nuanced realities in each context, as indicated in the exercise box on the next page.

Religion has a strong influence on many women's lives throughout Africa

The reliance on the west for models of law reform continues to be a reality in Africa due to the influence that colonialism had on the legal system. However, customary and religious laws have continued to affect the lives of many. Thus the important question in reforming laws today is how we can harness this for legal development in meaningful ways. Engaging students in a discussion of *how* rather than *whether* religious and customary laws can be used for development is essential to the appreciation of the challenges that any law reform process on the African continent ought to grapple with. Generally, we reflect on how customary and religious laws have been approached in the law reform process and the extent to which custom and religion have been used, if at all, as building blocks in effecting change that addresses power relations.

Engaging students in a discussion of how rather than whether religious and customary laws can be used for development is essential

Other key issues also arise when it comes to law reform, for example: the question of priorities; who is behind the reform; the speed with which the reform is undertaken; or whether the reform is preceded by a careful needs assessment (Faundez, 2000: 30-48). We analyze the concrete ways in which law reform has been used as a strategy to equalize the playing field for women in particular in each of the countries represented by the student body taking this course. If law reform is to be useful and effective, understanding how needs assessment can be carried out is vital. Indeed, selected case studies confirm how law reform on the continent has not often been preceded by a careful needs assessment or careful consultation or participation of the groups to be affected by the reforms. In this regard we examine, for instance, Zimbabwe's experiences with the Legal Age of Majority Act passed in 1981 (Tsanga, 2003: 52-92).

I therefore analyze with the students how needs assessment for law reform could be carried out on specific issues. Even though neglected in the past, there are some efforts at participatory law reform that are worth examining and that we can draw from in terms of needs assessment and participatory law reform, such as the constitutional making process in South Africa and the Domestic Violence Acts in Malawi and Zimbabwe. The

EXERCISE
Presentations: dialoguing Africa's legal development

For the questions that follow students are often divided into country clusters. They prepare in advance and are asked to make a presentation to the rest of the class. This also makes it easier to see areas of similarity and difference in the countries represented.

- What are the key bodies of law that exist in each of our countries?
- What is the status of women as compared to men under each of these bodies of law?
- What influences have been particularly significant in shaping the legal system in our countries?
- How is customary law generally regarded as a source of law?
- What models have been adopted in the development of customary law?
- What have been the challenges?
- How has Islamic law influenced development of the legal system in any of the countries?
- Should African modernity come out of African tradition in as much as western modernization came out of western tradition?

aim of participation in law reform is not so much that the tensions and points of contention will be eliminated but that areas needing attention in any awareness exercise will be apparent right from the start as opposed to being discovered only as an awareness programme unfolds (see exercise box below).

We also explore some of the guidelines for influencing policy and reform, such as, research and analysis, understanding the political and economic situation, and whether it is the right time to carry out the reform. In this regard, Zimbabwe's efforts at marriage law reform as undertaken by the Zimbabwe Women Lawyers Association (ZWLA) is used as a case study.[2] We also look at the issue of how people can best participate in the process. How to build allies in government and other structures of power is also key to grasp. Clarity on why the reform is necessary as well as strategies for persuading different target groups are examined. We also look at the use of the media, in terms of how it can be harnessed effectively for the agenda in question.

I dialogue with the students regarding the institutions that exist in their countries that have a bearing on the efficacy of law reform so that they understand how they can hamper the efficacy of laws. Using law reforms affecting women as a backdrop for discussion we examine how weak institutions have impacted on those initiatives. Domestic violence legislation is often a good example as it requires strong institutional support in the form of accessible courts and police stations. South Africa's experience with domestic violence legislation in this regard as well as Malawi and, more recently, Zimbabwe provide useful reflections (Artz and Moult, 2001; Saur *et al.*, 2005).

Another exercise that students do on law reform is shown on the next page.

EXERCISE
Analysis: some key questions for understanding the nature of law reforms

● What are the experiences generally in each country represented as regards law reform processes?

● Has gender been a priority? If not what have been the priority areas for law reform?

● Has having women in parliament had an impact on law reform processes? If so how? If not, why not?

● What has been the pace of law reform initiatives, especially those affecting women?

● Do you agree that too much reform at once can be detrimental to the reform process? If so, how? [3]

● To what extent have the law reform initiatives been preceded by needs assessments?

● What form have these needs assessments taken?

---

[2] We rely on Anna Rueben's study of the ZWLA's law reform which she undertook as part of her master's dissertation on the women's law programme. See Rueben (2004).

[3] The example I often examine here are a series of inheritance cases that came before the Zimbabwean courts between 1987 and 1999 following the Legal Age of Majority Act. For a detailed analysis of these cases see Stewart and Tsanga (2007). The question for analysis is what can we learn from this experience about law reform and the role of the courts?

EXERCISE

Taking law reform through its various stages

Select an area that affects women and that has attracted law reform in your country.

- Describe and analyze what the law was in a particular country prior to the reform.
- Examine and analyze the processes that were involved in bringing about the law reform in question.
- Analyze the factors that have a bearing on the efficacy of the law in question.
- What examples are there that impact on women where reform has taken place but application has been a problem?
- Training and changing the culture of bureaucracies is considered as important as law reform. What examples can you give, particularly drawing on women's experiences where training and changing bureaucratic culture has been a key issue?

2   Dialoguing women, culture, constitutionalism and human rights

Given the primacy accorded to culture and traditions in most of our African countries, the primary concern is how to address tensions that often arise between the observance of culture and the adherence to human rights. How, for instance, should activists go about getting people to abandon practices that are clearly at variance with women's human rights, in a way that is non-defensive and non-offensive to the holders of such traditions?

In examining possible strategies, I use as a backdrop the arguments and propositions made by Maboreke (2000) on the one hand and An-Na'im (1994: 167-188) on the other. I examine each in turn and the dialogue and exercises that emanate from their suggestions. In essence, Maboreke asks whether women should continue to rely on the law to question the entrapment of law and tradition. Her illustration is the practice of pledging young girls as compensation, usually for a murder committed by a person in her family. A girl is generally given to the family of the deceased to avenge his spirit and is expected to have children for this family at some point. She notes that there is no shortage of laws dealing with this matter. The law is unequivocal in its condemnation. It forbids pledging, it criminalizes sex with a minor; laws also exist to remove a child from a harmful environment. Yet despite the existence of such laws, pledging of girls takes

By examining articles like the one below, the students gain an insight into the current tensions between tradition and human rights and can debate the arguments for and against retaining these practices

Exorbitant bride price cause for concern

By Phyllis Kachere

Roora (lobola), the bringing together of two families yesteryear, has today turned commercial with some in-laws asking for over $300 000, making the would-be bridegrooms have second thoughts.

Feminists have blamed this whole aspect of commercialisation as it puts price tags on women

Extract only from The Herald (Harare)

205

DISCUSSION

Key questions for discussing women, human rights, culture and law reform

- What are some of the problematic customs and cultures that impact on women that continue to exist in our countries amidst the existence of human rights instruments that discourage these practices?

- Has state law been used to try and change some of these practices? If so, with what success?

- What is your response to the argument that the legal rights argument is bankrupt for women in our contexts?

- Do you subscribe to the notion that culture can be an empowering framework for women with which to engage men? If so, how?

- Are women short changing themselves when they take part in cultural nationalism?

- In practice, how do women deal with the tensions that often exist between human rights, cultural identity and gender identity?

place even if it is not as common an occurrence. It is in the light of these realities that she argues that instead of working with laws, women are better off exploring ways of working with culture. According to her, although culture prejudices women it can still be an empowering framework for them. It is against these arguments that we dialogue on the issues listed in the box on the left.

Interestingly, once we try to unearth examples of how we could use culture from within, students recognize that it is not so easy. We have discussed, for example, whether women would increase their leverage if they found ways of contributing to their own *lobola* payments. This is one cultural practice that is not dying away even among educated women in those countries that have it. As expected, the views are mixed. Some opine that far from gaining any leverage, women would lose power as a man may feel no obligations towards a woman for whom he has not paid *lobola*. The jury is still out. However, looking at living customary law in the area of inheritance, one could argue that women's ability to slowly assert their rights is a good example of working within culture to change culture.

An-Na'im in a similar vein argues that one way of addressing the culture/ human rights dichotomy is by engaging methodologically in two processes. The first is to have internal discourse drawing on internal experiences and achievements of the cultures in question. He also believes that any efforts for change must draw on the same source that the original practice was founded on. The second stage of the process is to engage in cross-cultural dialogue to enhance understanding of human rights and commitment to such values and norms by other cultures. The argument here is a straightforward one. For people to be persuaded to change, it is often useful to point out what others in a similar situation have done. The closer they are to our reality, the more likely the efficacy of the persuasive argument.

I have often asked students to examine the practical implications of An-Na'im's suggested methodological approach of anchoring the norms of international systems within their own cultural traditions. His suggestion of using 'internal discourse' within the framework of each country and 'cross-cultural dialogue' among the various traditions of the world is discussed from the viewpoint of what this would actually mean in practical terms using key problems in a particular country.

An example that students have chosen to dialogue on in the past is early marriage as this is fairly common in many African societies. As they have noted, the reasons can often be economic and stem from extreme poverty. Marrying off a young girl brings in bride-price which can alleviate poverty. Students examine the range of applicable human rights instruments to assess the violations at hand and to craft appropriate arguments.[4] Issues for internal discourse include: health implications for girl children that might arise from early marriage; the need for education and the long-term benefits that may accrue to the family from having an educated girl child; the need to experience childhood; and the possibility of government loans and subsidies to combat poverty.

From a cross-cultural perspective they state that they would focus on campaigns about early marriage in other countries and especially on implications for human rights. Methods such as posters, role plays, radio and television are seen as useful in this regard. Given that formal and informal education are also regarded as key tools for changing attitudes and practices, we discuss how these can be used in practice. Garnering support for reforms that impact on customs and traditions can also be more effectively done by engaging with traditional leaders. Consequently, examining the role of traditional leaders in different settings and the strategies being used to bring them on board can provide useful insights for exchange among the students.

EXERCISE
Cross-cultural dialogue

Select an example of your choice affecting women where you see a conflict between human rights, as stated in the instrument that your government has signed, and religious or customary laws. Discuss how you would persuade people to begin to look at the issue differently by using:

a   internal discourse and

b   cross-cultural dialogue

3   Interrogating gendered inequalities through gender training

In recognition of the significance of the work being carried out by women's organizations in which training clearly emerges as an important strategy, a key issue I get students to focus on is how to address the realities of patriarchal gender dynamics and the impact that these have on the possibility of change.

As a backdrop for analysis, we examine the arguments made by Josephine Ahikire (2007) who raises questions about the type of gender training that is being engaged in by the feminist movement. Her core argument is that gender

---

[4]   These include, for example, the Convention on the Rights of the Child, articles 24, 28 and 29 in particular and article 6(b) of the Protocol to the African Charter on the Rights of Women.

training has taken a more technical approach. Its original mission, to question and find tools to explain and address male dominance, is neglected. As she sees it, politics and feminism need to be brought back to the gender agenda. She isolates three types of training: women-focused training based on capacity building for women in specific areas such as politics and decision making; train the trainer type training that focuses on gender analysis; and the third type which focuses on increasing self awareness, especially among women, so they can identify sources, manifestations and consequences of gender inequality in their lives and institutions. Her argument is that the third type is hardly ever used and that the first two types constitute the mainstream.

...politics and feminism need to be brought back to the gender agenda

Some of the students have engaged in gender training and shared their experiences with the rest of the class which illustrated the prevalence of the first two types of training:

> 'I started off by studying a course on gender and politics in Africa at the university. As part of the assignment for my studies, I carried out a workshop on gender-based violence for an aid agency and its workers. I focused on basic concepts such as looking at gender, sex roles, gender mainstreaming and handling matters relating to gender. After I graduated, I also worked with gender mainstreaming as a programme specialist for UNDP in northern Tanzania. I was managing three programmes and concentrated on mainstreaming gender in all activities. Mostly I would have a session on gender within a wider training programme. The session would be anything from 40 minutes to one hour.'[5]

Another's experience was as follows:

> 'I worked on a sexual and gender based violence project for an international non-governmental organization. I was responsible for the database. Our organization generally carried out one week training programmes which touched on psychological issues, data management, demographic characteristics of clients – men, women and children – nature of cases, where violence occurred, action taken, referred to who and so on. We generally targeted entry points where all gender-based violence would be reported, for example the police, clerks of court, health sector, clinics. We also targeted data managers. It was not easy however to get the police for instance to change their system and structures. Our programme differed according to who was being trained.'[6]

We explore how best issues of power and gender can be approached in a manner that speaks to African realities. Students do a group activity that

---

[5] Malula Nkayemka from Tanzania, social justice student, 2009.
[6] Shadreck Banda, 2009 class. Zambian who worked for CARE International.

allows them to interrogate and engage with the above perspectives and to analyze the implications of bringing back feminism into the gender agenda (see exercise box on the right).

I have also looked at the issue of gender training to combat gender bias in the courts. Since legal justice for women is dependent on a number of core factors, such as the legal framework, legal literacy, access to courts and in particular fair treatment in the courts, I zero in on gender training as this has become an important area of focus with social justice activists. The core characteristics of gender bias are said to include stereotypical attitudes about the roles of men and women, cultural views about relative worth and myths and misconceptions about social and economic realities of both sexes (Wikler, 1993: 98). As such, apart from the ability to access the courts, fair treatment in the court is therefore vital in the realization of justice.

As part of the larger practical exercise in the second part of the course, students have also in a previous class engaged with the issue of gender training as discussed more fully later.

EXERCISE
Gender, power and control

Using critical feminist lenses of power, transformation and change, discuss the sources and manifestations of inequality in each of the following problems that affect women:

- Divorce
- Custody
- Child and spousal support
- Domestic violence
- Sexual assault

How do you think the underlying issues of inequality can be addressed as part of tackling power and contributing to social transformation?

4   Dialoguing priorities for human rights activism

Combining civil and political, as well as social and economic rights, is now generally deemed in human rights analyses as the more holistic and preferred approach to their realization as opposed to one which is largely one or the other. While embracing the value and inevitability of such an approach, the continent's plethora of problems makes it unavoidable to engage in a discussion of what should be the areas of emphasis within this holistic framework. It is in this light that I have found it useful for social justice students to understand the complex nature of human rights issues on the continent beyond universal approaches. Of central concern are the implications for women.

In terms of what should be our human rights priorities on the African continent, Shivji (1989: 80), for example, has argued that we need to forefront concerns such as the right to self-determination and the right to organize. Core elements of his right to self-determination include rights such as formation of independent states, secession, enjoyment of culture, tradition, religion and language, freedom from domination and exploitation and the right to determine freely the economic and political systems of our countries. While significant within the African context, arguments for self-determination have notoriously sidelined women's issues as have those for the protection of tradition and culture, among others. Yet at the same time because women have often become victims of sexual violence and plunder in the struggles for self-determination within African countries, addressing the issue has a certain urgency for women's peace and security.

Odinkalu (2003: 1–37) has opined that concerns such as state building and citizenship, education and health care, as well as streamlining human rights monitoring bodies so as to direct more resources towards building stronger institutions for human rights monitoring, need to be given centre stage. The essence of his argument is that the human rights project in Africa is about eliminating poverty and disease, and freeing citizens and inhabitants to realize and enjoy their full potential. As far as state and citizenship goes, the concern is with unconstitutional changes of government that have bedevilled the continent and the exclusion of presidential candidates with foreign parentage. As regards mainstreaming human rights institutions, the core concern is that there is currently an inflationary tendency in setting up bodies when those that exist do not function well and are poorly funded. An example of a poorly supported human rights body being the African Commission on Human and People's Rights. Women also seem to have become caught up in an endless quest for guiding principles instead of consolidating the ones that we have gained (see discussion box).

There is general acknowledgement that the issues identified by authors such as Shivji and Odinkalu do indeed take their cue from realities across the continent. The perception however is that within this matrix, social and economic rights have a tremendous impact on women's lives and their quest for empowerment. This is more so given that not all countries are in conflict but virtually all of them in sub-Saharan African could improve their record on the delivery of social and economic rights. It is for this reason that the course veers towards strengthening our understanding of concerns such as the right to education, health and housing. These have over recent years become the focus of emerging human rights jurisprudence which has also provided indicators as to how activist issues can be fashioned. Space does not allow me to grapple

DISCUSSION

Prioritizing human rights concerns

We frame our discussion around the following questions:

- What are your views on the nature of problems put forward as priorities in Africa by the different authors?

- How are these significant to women when examined with feminist lenses?

- For women in particular, what are the key issues?

- How do these issues tie in, if at all, with what is currently being addressed on the ground?

- Why do you think it has been so difficult to realize social and economic rights on the continent?

- What implications do these difficulties have in terms of action that needs to be taken?

with how the dialogue on each of these is shaped in class. So for illustrative purposes, I zero in on the right to health to illustrate how we address the conceptual issues and also how students later use these issues in developing an activist project on the right to health.

Our entry point in dialoguing the right to health is framed on an understanding of observed realities in our countries. An exercise on contextual realities shapes this dialogue (see box opposite).

My 2009 class, for example, comprised students from Zambia, Malawi and Zimbabwe. The Zambians identified their core health issues as HIV/AIDS and related diseases, malaria, maternal and infant mortality, and sexual and gender based violence. The core challenges centred on human and financial resources for health care and access to adequate health services. One of their concerns was the country's overdependence on donors whom they said determine the direction of health care. They also lamented the general absence of a model that draws on local resources for the realization of health. The unstable economy was also singled out as a challenge as far as generating resources for social needs is concerned.

EXERCISE

Introducing the right to health

- What do you consider to be the priority issues on the right to health in your country?
- What are the issues for women?
- What do you consider to be the core challenges facing your government in addressing these issues?
- What do you think your government can do differently in addressing the right to health care?
- How can individuals and civil society ensure that their governments take the necessary legal or non-legal measures to address these issues?
- What does your constitution say on the right to health?
- What remedies are available in your country for those whose right to health is violated?

The Tanzanians identified similar problems and added access to clean water and a clean environment as being major challenges for health. Lack of safe food and safe medication was also seen as problematic, especially with the growing use of fake drugs. The limited population covered by health institutions was also seen as a problem. Failure of the state to address these challenges was seen as stemming from the fact that politicians themselves do not use local hospitals. They often prefer to go overseas for medical treatment. Corruption and bribery is also endemic. People are also poor and cannot afford health care services. To this overview Zimbabwe added the problems of the massive brain drain and limited outside assistance in the face of sanctions, compounding the problem of access to health care. Malawi zeroed in on the problem of poor planning as the majority of the population in the rural areas are not within reach of health care services.

It is against the backdrop of these practical realities that the core provisions impacting on the right to health in the various instruments are analyzed.[7] In terms of the scope of the right to health, we discuss the elements that make up the right to health care including those relating to preventative health care. We examine elements relating to preconditions for health care such as safe drinking water, adequate sanitation, nutrition and health-related information. Having already isolated some of these themselves, makes it that much easier for students to grasp the meaning of the right to health and its scope. Zimbabwe's 'Operation Murambatsvina' and the impact it had on women and children's lives is also used as a concrete example to discuss preventative health care. Most people who were displaced found themselves without access to safe drinking water or adequate sanitation, let alone health services in general.

The core content on the right to health care, which consists of elements that the state must guarantee regardless of resources, is examined using the World Health Organization's guidelines. We unpack the fact that the minimum content has significant bearing on the rights of women since it lays emphasis on: maternal and child health care including family planning; immunization

On health issues, the local newspapers are a rich resource for the students – highlighting the main health concerns of the day and people's attitudes to them. Below is a selection of headlines of such articles from The Herald (Harare, 2001–2006)

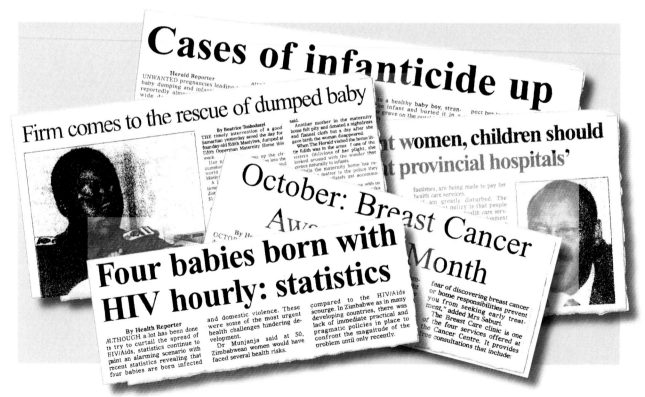

Cases of infanticide up

Herald Reporter
UNWANTED pregnancies leading ...
baby dumping and infan...
reportedly alme...
wide ...

to a healthy baby boy, stran...
infant and buried it in ...
grave on the ou... pect her...

Firm comes to the rescue of dumped baby

By Beatrice Tonbodzayi
THE timely intervention of a good Samaritan yesterday saved the day for four-day-old Edith Mastyiwa, dumped at Edith Oonperman Maternity Home this wreck.

said.
Another mother in the maternity home felt pity and donated a nightdress and flannel cloth but a day after she gave birth the woman disappeared.
When The Herald visited the home little Edith was in the arms f one of the sisters Oblivious of her plight, she looked around with the wonder that comes naturally to infants.
while the maternity home has re... matter to the police have... diately get accommo...

...t women, children should ...t provincial hospitals'

facilities, are being made to pay for health care services.
...am greatly disturbed. The ... policy is that people ...ealth care serv... ...ionment'

October: Breast Cancer Month

OCTOB...
By H...
Aw...
OCTOB...

fear of discovering breast cancer or home responsibilities prevent you from seeking early treatment," added Mrs Saburi.
The Breast Care clinic is one of the four services offered at the Cancer Centre. It provides free consultations that include:

Four babies born with HIV hourly: statistics

By Health Reporter
ALTHOUGH a lot has been done to try to curtail the spread of HIV/Aids, statistics continue to paint an alarming scenario with recent statistics revealing that four babies are born infected

and domestic violence. These were some of the most urgent health challenges hindering development.
Dr Munjanja said at 50, Zimbabwean women would have faced several health risks.

compared to the HIV/Aids scourge. In Zimbabwe as in many developing countries, there was lack of immediate practical and pragmatic policies in place to confront the magnitude of the problem until only recently.

---

[7] These include article 25 of the Universal Declaration of Human Rights; article 12 of the International Covenant on Economic, Social and Cultural Rights; article 12 of Convention on the Elimination of all forms of Discrimination Against Women; article 24 of the Convention on the Rights of the Child; article 16 of the African Charter; and article 14 of the Protocol to the African Charter on Women's Rights.

against major diseases; appropriate treatment of common diseases and injuries; and provision of essential drugs. Also as regards the underlying conditions for health care, it is the state's duty to ensure: education concerning prevailing health problems; promotion of food supply and nutrition; and adequate supply of safe water and sanitation.

Guiding principles that have been developed for the state, such as ensuring *availability, accessibility, quality* and *equality* in access to health services are analyzed in terms of what they mean in the context of each country. The state's obligation to *respect, protect* and *fulfil* is also discussed in terms of its meaning for the right to health.

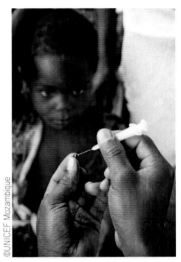

Are our governments spending enough on primary health care in the region?

In the spirit of adopting a multi-disciplinary understanding of the issue, in terms of benchmarks as outlined by the Committee on Social and Economic Rights, we also, where possible, look up issues such as expenditure on health care as a percentage of gross national product in the countries represented in the class. It is also often useful from a women's perspective to compare with expenditures spent on the army and security, for example. The amount spent on primary health care is also important as are statistics on the percentage of population that has access to trained medical personnel and to drugs.

Part II: Linking theory and practice

1 Dealing with gender bias among judicial officers: workshop on wilful transmission of HIV/AIDS and marital rape

In order to appreciate the challenges that emanate from biased judicial officers, in 2005 we decided to hone in on the opportunity to train judicial trainees using the sexual offences as outlined in the Criminal Law Code of Zimbabwe[8] as the backdrop for the exercise. The two aspects of interest in this Act that were regarded as important to engage with included the criminalization of the wilful transmission of HIV and marital rape. The aim was for students to understand how gender bias on the part of judicial officers on issues of sex and sexuality may lead to unfair treatment for women seeking relief in such cases. The target groups in terms of judicial officers were trainee magistrates and prosecutors at the Judicial College in Zimbabwe. The institution trains judicial officers at all levels and is also key in training non-degreed prosecutors and magistrates for the lower courts. Working with these trainees on a specific area of the law such as the then Sexual Offences Act[8] was regarded as an opportunity for social justice students to engage with the legal system in its various facets – the law's substance (content), the structure (the courts,

---

[8] The Sexual Offences Act has since been consolidated into the Criminal Law (Codification and Reform) Act Chapter 9:23.

GENDER TRAINING WORKSHOP

Objectives

- Participants should be able to share knowledge and experiences on the provisions of the Sexual Offences Act in respect of prevention of the spread of HIV.

- Participants should be able to identify the gender dimensions of the Sexual Offences Act in relation to the prevention of the spread of HIV.

- Participants should not be influenced by traditional values and gender stereotypes in the exercise of their discretion.

- Participants should be able to identify limitations in the Sexual Offences Act for possible law reform.

- Participants should be able to acquire critical consciousness on the Sexual Offences Act so that they are gender alert and sensitive in exercising their discretion.

enforcement agencies) and culture (the shared social attitudes) especially given our class discussion on how each of these presents challenges for women. The overall aim of the exercise was to develop the participants' critical consciousness of gender and its application to the law. Four students, three lawyers and one police officer, were assigned the exercise. Given the size of the judicial class (50 trainees) they were divided into two groups of 25. Two students were assigned to work with each group. The students planned two parallel morning workshops and drew up the objectives, as listed in the box on the left.

In creating critical dialogue on how women in marriage are often exposed to HIV/AIDS, one of the teams used a real-life based testimonial video produced by a local women's legal organization, Zimbabwe Women Lawyers Association, to further discuss aspects such as testing, disclosure, burden of proof and the difficulty in prosecuting wilful transmission.

They also developed a case study for small group discussion based on the video testimonial. The case study tasked the groups to:

1 Identify the stereotypes in the case study and explain their origins and consequences.

2 Discuss whether courts are immune from social prejudices.

3 Advise the woman, using the Sexual Offences Act.

4 Identify any shortcomings in the law and make recommendations for reform.

The law was interrogated from the perspective of power dynamics, especially in placing the burden of proof on wilful transmission on complainants who turn out to be mostly women. They often come to know of their status when they present themselves for antenatal care. For some, their dependence on men for money for medical care also means that they generally come out much earlier regarding their status.

The students also developed a questionnaire which yielded useful views on the workshop's value in terms of exposing judicial officers to facets of gender dynamics.

For example one trainee noted that:

> 'The sessions were very relevant and useful to me and I gained new ideas which include the fact that as a legal officer you should be able to identify stereotypes and distance yourself from them so as to apply the law effectively and fairly.'

Another stated that they had 'gained insight on the relationship between sexual offences and HIV'. Others appreciated grasping the differences between gender and sex and the importance of the difference. Another commented that the 'video clip made me understand the difficulties victims are facing'.

The students carrying out the exercise also gain useful insights into the challenges of 'transformation activism'. For example, they recognize that change cannot be brought about through one session only. In fact, in this instance, the half day which had been slotted in for the exercise was clearly not adequate in terms of time, with trainees expressing a preference for workshop lengths which ranged from as short as one day to as long as one week on this particular topic.[9] In this exercise students also got to grips with the difficulties of changing attitudes especially when it came to discussing the issue of marital rape.

One student noted in her critical write up as follows:

> 'While lauding the success of the workshop, it is worthwhile to note from the recommendations on the sentencing of marital rape offenders, how influences of culture and religion impact on reasoning. In as much as the concepts of gender stereotypes were understood by the participants, when it came to giving recommendations on sentencing, they had this to say:
>
> – 'Sentence for marital rape is too harsh and will end up breaking up families.'
> – 'Sentence is not corrective or rehabilitative.'
> – 'Victims should be given a chance in determining what type of sentence is to be handed over to their husbands.'
> – 'Will cause shortage of food supply if husband is incarcerated.'
> – 'Non-custodial sentence like caution and community service.'
> – 'Factors surrounding the offence and the state of the marriage should be taken into consideration, for example, separation.'[10]

---

[9] They do however, receive input on gender as part of the overall course module so this particular session sought to build on to an existing initiative.

[10] Millicent Odeny, Kenya 2005 class.

When analyzing these recommendations, the student noted that despite being composed of both men and women, it was surprising that no group came up with a radical approach to sentencing, either by supporting or suggesting stiffer penalties. To her, this showed that people in general and women in particular are still entrapped between tradition and the law in making their choices.

2 'The naked reality':
A video production on women's right to maternal health

The second example I discuss in relation to engaging students in a practical exercise to address gendered power balances is the production of a video entitled 'The naked reality' which examines women's right to maternal health care. This was done by the 2007 class. Five students were responsible for producing this 20 minute video. Students were responsible for assessing needs, drawing up the objectives, creating a storyline and the overall planning and design of the video.

I must emphasize that the exercise was not about testing students' expertise in video production but about testing their ability to communicate and conceptualize key concerns on important social justice issues such as health in this particular case. The shooting of the video was done with the help of technical experts. Also, I brought in a development theatre specialist to assist with comments on conceptualization who also came in later to assess the value of the end product as a communication tool. He was particularly valuable in getting the students to narrow down their audience in terms of message delivery and on the need to have a clear theme running through the storyline. Largely aimed at policy makers and legislators, the group was particularly concerned with the need to domesticate the right to health and ensure the state's allocation of adequate resources for maternal health as part of its obligations. At the core of their concern were poor rural women who often do not have *available, accessible, acceptable* and *quality* maternal health services.

The main challenges for poor rural women in accessing health care include transportation difficulties, poverty, lack of access to health care information and lack of access to health care in relation to HIV/AIDS. The choice of a video as a tool for communication with policy makers and legislators was influenced by the perception that a video would allow them 'to see women's lived realities and listen to their stories as told by them in their social settings'. An earlier first semester research study, as part of exposure to research methods, provided valuable background information and alerted them to the grave difficulties women encounter in accessing proper maternal health care in the Zimbabwean context.

Findings from this research provided useful data in terms of women's needs in maternal health care given the limited time available to students in carrying out this practical exercise. In some cases, the research revealed that women even have to produce their own kits if they are to give birth in the hospitals. The booklet on pregnancy and childbirth in Mali produced by the Centre for Reproductive Rights also provided useful data about lived realities in African settings and a good exposé of the human rights considerations (Centre for Reproductive Rights, 2003). Students drew on important concepts on health in international human rights instruments such as the International Covenant

EXERCISE
A video on the right to health

The storyline

The gist of the storyline centred on a rural woman, Tambudzai, who finds herself pregnant for the ninth time and recalls her not so pleasant experiences with her eighth pregnancy in which she lost her baby on delivery. One of her experiences during that pregnancy, was her husband's refusal to let her be tested for HIV/AIDS. He also refused for her to attend antenatal lessons.

Further, he had misused the money she kept for the baby and as a result she had been unable to purchase the necessary kit required by the hospital for the birth of the baby, which included plastic sheeting, plastic gloves, two packets of pads or cotton wool, razor blade and a cord clamp. (In light of Zimbabwe's economic meltdown then, some hospitals required patients to bring their own kit.) In her case, because she had gone to the hospital without the kit, the nurse had refused to assist her. She gave birth in the bathroom and lost her baby. The video envisions a scene in the rural areas. In it Tambudzai basically relives the above experiences as she realizes that she is pregnant again.

The objectives

The specific objectives of producing a video on maternal health care were stated by the students as follows:

1   To appreciate the challenges that women in rural areas experience in decision making over issues that affect their own health.

2   To identify the barriers that limit access to health information by women and men.

3   To identify patterns of poverty, power relations in the family, social exclusion and discrimination which is usually sustained by gender inequalities, social cultural factors and a government policy framework which is far removed from reality.

on Economic, Social and Cultural Rights (ICESCR), the Convention on the Elimination of All Forms of Discrimination Against Women (CEDAW) and the Protocol to the African Charter on Human and Peoples' Rights on the Rights of Women, as well as the Convention on the Rights of the Child. The Constitution of Zimbabwe, as well as documents such as the National Health Strategy for Zimbabwe (1997-2007) provided valuable background information in terms of government policy.

The value of bringing together a panel of experts for the final assessment of the student initiative is that they bring in insights that have a bearing on how change can be facilitated for the problem in question. For example, with this particular exercise, apart from the theatre and communications expert, my colleague and myself who acted as gender and human rights commentators, on the panel of assessors we also included a female gynaecologist. One of the latter's observations was that men could have been engaged more positively in the storyline by having a scene, for example, where men talked to each other about the challenges women face in attaining their right to maternal health care. She also stated that it has become increasingly important to examine ways in which men can be harnessed by using positive role models of men who have been of assistance. Such 'man to man' programmes, she argued, have significant potential in changing power relations.

While the theatre and communications expert applauded the storyline and deemed the end result of the production very good, his perception was that more could have been done in speaking to how the video was to be used practically as a communication tool. While the group did produce a manual, they tended to neglect it in the actual presentation. Students were also made to realize the importance of bolstering information with the written word, for example by producing pamphlets and brochures to consolidate key messages, especially around health as a human right in this particular case.

This approach to learning which combines the theoretical and the practical is something that the students appreciate. As one student noted in her self evaluation of the exercise:

> 'The practical exercise component of the course work is a very vital learning experience for law reform and social justice work in our different countries such that it needed more time than was given. It demands not just the conceptual understanding that can be communicated to the audience but creativity too which reflects lived realities…'

The video was in English but students also realized that in order to communicate effectively it would also be useful to produce such materials in the local language.

Activist projects over the years have also included consciousness raising sessions with trainee teachers on topics such as sexual harassment, corporal punishment and statutory rape involving girls under the age of 16, and HIV/AIDS and the law. For example, recognizing the importance of education for women, we have examined the manner in which sexual harassment within educational institutions can stand in the path of women's enjoyment of the right to education. The choice of topics however also has to take into account the interests of the target groups. For example, the teacher's college personnel have been keen that we address the topic of sexual harassment within educational institutions – whether in terms of their female students being harassed or male teachers doing the harassing. I have also had to choose activist projects that allow all students to participate regardless of language barriers, given that students come from different countries in the region. The teacher's college is particularly good for this exercise because English can be used as a medium by all students. Video productions and educational brochures have also been produced on various topics. In addition students have engaged with theatre as a form of communicating legal messages and have produced a play on access to housing.

Women need to be able to claim their right to education at every level in the system

Conclusion

The combination of law and lived realities helps to ensure that we are producing graduates who are able to make the linkages between theory and practice in very practical ways. A key challenge of teaching the course in this way, though, is always the timeframe within which all this has to be achieved. With four contact weeks, we basically devote two weeks to the conceptual part and another two weeks to the practical and its concepts. However, as the aim is to provide reflective fields for analysis from both angles, the intensity is well worth it as the students themselves always acknowledge at the end of it all. An additional bonus to crafting a course of this nature, is the number of students who increasingly choose to focus on social justice related issues in their detailed dissertations. By doing so they are undoubtedly contributing to a groundswell of knowledge based on women's lived realities in the field of access to justice.

From law reform to understanding the role of critical institutions, to grappling with very real social justice concerns for women, students have bravely taken on the challenge of moving beyond the orthodox approach to access to justice that in the past narrowly focused on legal aid. I also use the word 'bravely' deliberately because in some cases the topics require robust and persistent engagement with state authorities and actors in order to understand their omissions. In our African contexts, being granted an audience by state authorities to do research on public institutions cannot be taken for granted.

This is despite the value that such research can hold in bringing about policy changes.

Examples of student topics in the field of law reform include analyzing efforts at lobbying for marriage law reform in Zimbabwe (Rueben, 2004) and examining the factors that delayed the passing of the Domestic Violence Act in Malawi (Fletcher, 2006). Studies have also been carried out on the critical role of state institutions in accessing justice for women. An example in this regard is the analysis of the role of the Ministry of Women's Affairs in Zimbabwe (Matizha, 2006). The role of the Ministry of Justice's Legal Aid Department has equally been put under scrutiny (Murinda, 2008). Others have examined the role of non-governmental organizations in making justice accessible to women (Siveregi, 2006). Focus on specific social and economic concerns affecting women have included an exploration of the impact of Zimbabwe's economic melt-down on access to maternal health care (Mapepa, 2008) and the gendered impact of access to land, water, food and shelter among squatters in Kenya (Nyongesa, 2008).

The course is also an excellent example of how realities on the ground that are aimed at improving women's access to justice have helped to shape a whole new area of what I would call aca-activism – an infusion of academia with activism. While student dissertations obviously differ in quality depending on the abilities of the students, still what we have in our arsenal are clear efforts by students to engage with the different components and aspects of the justice system that have a bearing on women's access to justice.

In terms of forward projection, because this course is essentially founded on conceptualizing grounded practices in relation to the legal system, there is no doubt that its shape and character will continue to be infused by the ever changing advances in our quest for justice for groups such as women. However, a more immediate and urgent concern that emerges from teaching this course, and in particular its impact on student dissertations, is how best we can ensure that the research that has emerged is used by relevant players. While we place all dissertations on the Centre's website, it goes without saying that in the African context, the use of the web is still far from being touch of the button for the majority of people. In the immediate term, a strategy may be to distil like-minded topics into digestible booklets and to circulate them widely and use them as a basis for engagement with relevant bodies. Former students might also want to explore having relevant seminars at country level as part of alumni contributions to the quest for substantive justice for women.

Bibliography

An-Na'im A.A. (1994) 'State responsibility under international human rights law to change religious and customary laws' in R. Cook (ed) *Human rights of women: national and international perspectives*, University of Pennsylvania Press, Philadelphia.

Allot A. (1980) *The limits of law,* Butterworths, London.

Carson E. (2001) 'The seven deadly myths of the US non profit sector: implications for promoting social justice worldwide', in C.V. Hamilton *et al.* (eds) *Beyond racism: race and inequality in Brazil, South Africa and the United States,* Lynne Rienner Publishers, Boulder, Colorado.

Centre for Reproductive Rights and Associations des Juristes Maliennes (2003) *Claiming our rights: surviving pregnancy and childbirth in Mali*, Centre for Reproductive Rights, available online at http://reproductiverights.org/en/document/claiming-our-rights-surviving-pregnancy-and-childbirth-in-mali

Dias C.J., R. Luckham, D.O. Lynch and J.C.N. Paul (eds) (1981) *Lawyers in the third world. Comparative and developmental perspectives*, Nordiska Afrikainstitute and International Centre for Law and Development, Uppsala.

Falk Moore S. (1973) 'Law and social change: the semi-autonomous social field as an appropriate field of study', *Law and Society Review* 7(4)719-746.

Faundez J. (2000) 'Law reform in developing and transition countries: making haste slowly', in Faundez *et al.* (eds) *Law in its social setting: governance development and globalization*, Blackstone Press, London.

Fletcher R.M. (2006) 'Addressing gender-based violence in Malawi: an analysis of the factors delaying the passing of the proposed Prevention of Domestic Violence Bill', masters dissertation, SEARCWL, University of Zimbabwe, Harare.

Hellum A., J. Stewart, S.S. Ali and A.S. Tsanga (eds) (2007) *Human rights, plural legalities and gendered realities: paths are made by walking*, Weaver Press, Harare.

Hyden G., (1993) 'Shifting perspectives on development: implications for research', in M. Maast *et al.* (eds) *State and locality: proceedings of the NFU annual conference 1993*, University of Oslo Centre for Development and the Environment, Oslo.

Maboreke M. (2000) 'Understanding law in Zimbabwe', in A. Stewart (ed) *Gender, law and social justice*, Blackstone Press, London.

Mapepa P. (2008) 'The implications of the current economic crisis on pregnant women's right to maternal health in Zimbabwe: a case study of Harare Hospital', masters dissertation, SEARCWL, University of Zimbabwe, Harare.

Matizha C. (2006) 'A stumbling block or foundation builder: an assessment of the Ministry of Women Affairs in promoting women's rights in Zimbabwe', masters dissertation, SEARCWL, University of Zimbabwe, Harare.

Moser C. (1993) 'Training strategies for gender planning: from sensitization to skills techniques', in *Gender planning and development: theory, practice and training,* Routledge, London.

Murinda P. (2008) 'Access to legal aid for indigent women: an analysis of the services offered by the Legal Aid Directorate in Harare', masters dissertation, SEARCWL, University of Zimbabwe, Harare.

Nherere P. (1993) 'The limits of litigation in human rights enforcement', pages 117-136 in P. Nherere and M. d' Éngelbronner-Kolff (eds), *The institutionalization of human rights in southern Africa*, Nordic Human Rights Publications, Oslo.

Nyongesa G.C. (2008) 'Right to land, clean water, food and shelter: a case study of the gendered effects on squatters of the Constitution's failure to address these rights in Mogoto, Kenya', masters dissertation, SEARCWL, University of Zimbabwe, Harare.

Odinkalu C. A. (2003) 'Back to the future: the imperative of prioritising for the protection of human rights in Africa ', *Journal of African Law* 47: 1–37.

Oloka Onyango J. (2002) 'Modern day missionaries or misguided miscreants? NGOs, the women's movement and the promotion of human rights in Africa', in B. Wolfgang *et al.* (eds) *Human rights of women: international instruments and African experiences,* ZED Books, London.

Parenzee P., L. Artz and K. Moutl (2001) *Monitoring the implementation of the Domestic Violence Act: first research report 2000-2001*, University of Cape Town Institute of Criminology, Cape Town.

Rueben A. (2004) 'Law reform strategies : a critical analysis of the ZWLA lobbying and advocacy programme for marriage law reform', masters dissertation, SEARCWL, University of Zimbabwe, Harare.

Saur M., L. Semu and S. Hauya Ndau (2000) *Nkhanza: Listening to people's voices: a study of gender-based violence in three districts of Malawi*, Kachere Series, Zomba, Malawi.

Schuler M. (1986) 'Conceptualizing and exploring issues and strategies', in M. Schuler (ed), *Empowerment and the law: strategies of third world women*, OEF International, Washington.

Shivji I. (1989) *The concept of human rights in Africa*, Codesria Book Series, London.

Siveregi J. (2006) 'A critical analysis of the pursuit of the feminist agenda through the experience of women's legal rights organizations in Zimbabwe', masters dissertation, SEARCWL, University of Zimbabwe, Harare.

Squires J. (2000) *Gender in political theory*, Polity Press, Cambridge.

Stewart A. (2000) 'The contribution of feminist legal scholarship to the rights approach to development', pages 3-18 in A. Stewart (ed), *Gender, law and social justice*, Blackstone Press, London.

– (2000) 'Implementing gender justice through the judiciary: a case study of judicial training in India', in J. Faundez *et al.* (eds) *Law in its social setting: governance development and globalization*, Blackstone Press, London.

Tong R.M. (1994) 'Introduction', in *Feminist thought: a comprehensive guide*, Routledge, London.

Tripp A.M. (2001) 'Women's movements and challenges to neo patrimonial rule: preliminary observations from Africa', *Development and Change* 32 (2001) 33-54.

Tsanga A.S. (2003) *Taking law to the people: gender, law reform and community legal education in Zimbabwe*, Weaver Press, Harare.

– (2007) 'Reconceptualizing the role of legal information dissemination in the context of legal pluralism in African settings', in A. Hellum, J. Stewart, S.S. Ali and A.S. Tsanga (eds) *Human rights, plural legalities and gendered realities: paths are made by walking*, Weaver Press, Harare.

Wilker. (1993) 'Exclusion of women from justice: emerging strategies for reform', in K. Mahoney and P. Mahoney (eds) *Human rights in the twenty-first century: a global challenge*, Martinus Nijhoff Publishers, Dordrecht.

Teaching women, social realities, family and the law

in African legal systems

Chuma Himonga and Julie Stewart

This chapter describes the methods we have used in teaching two components of the course on 'Women, social realities, family and the law' in the masters programme at SEARCWL since 2003.[1] The first part of the chapter gives a general overview of the objectives of the whole course and then focuses on the introductory component which deals with the general legal framework governing the family.

Drawing on grounded research experiences, the second part of the chapter examines the processes and rationale involved in getting students to unearth key areas of concern within the family arena for their possible future research.

Part I: Engaging with the general legal framework

Chuma Himonga

The course on 'Women, social realities, family and the law' uses various concepts of family law – marriage, divorce, custody and guardianship of children, maintenance and matrimonial property, among others – to explore and analyze the role of family law (customary and general law) and human rights in women's lives in the family, in the social, cultural and economic contexts and realities of African countries.

---

[1] The course is taught in three parts. The first part on the general legal framework is taught by Professor Chuma Himonga. The second part, led by Professor Julie Stewart, builds on the first part to pull out specific themes for research. Professor Anne Griffiths took the third part, on research design but has now joined the 'Women, commerce and law in Africa' course.

Designed within the whole programme's transformative approach, the course seeks to develop students' 'critical abilities, as well as transform their conceptual abilities and self-awareness'. Critical abilities involve students challenging their own preconceptions and those of their peers and teachers and the society at large. This approach, evidently, requires a method of 'teaching and learning that goes beyond requiring students to learn a body of knowledge [in this case the law] and then be able to apply it [to a set of facts] analytically' (Wiggins in Harvey and Green, 1993:16). In the context of the course concerned, this in turn requires that the teaching of family law transcends the theoretical to include relevant practical issues. Among these are issues of the pluralities of law and the consequent legal conceptual mixes and muddles by which women are expected to regulate their family relations, the implementation of the law and the social and cultural factors that have a bearing on this implementation process and on women's experiences with the law, and research. Thus both theoretical and socio-legal perspectives and research are important areas of focus for the course as a whole.

Objectives

The objectives of the course are:

- To set out the broad legal framework for considering the interplay between the family and the law, and social factors and their impact on the lives of women and the girl child;

- To look at responses to the rights of women and the girl child within the family that are shaped by factors that include but go beyond law;

- To develop, from the skills acquired in the theoretical and methodological courses in the first semester and from the relevant factors identified by the course, activist strategies for change to the benefit of women in a multiplicity of ways;

- To translate theory into methodological practice through a concrete research project that deals with women and the girl child's lived experiences on the ground;

- To foster an interdisciplinary approach to and understanding of the intersections of women and the girl child's experiences and law in its pluralities; and

- To build on students' diverse forms of knowledge and skills in constructing an understanding of the opportunities, challenges, problems and barriers in using law.

Methods of delivery

The method employed in teaching the first component, if not the whole course, is evolutionary and exploratory in the sense, firstly, that the fine-tuning of the teaching method is an ongoing process. It seeks to incorporate pedagogical needs and classroom diversity as they emerge over time, as well as to accommodate changes in the substance of what is taught. With regard to the latter, family law and related legal fields are among the fastest changing areas of law, due mainly to the influence of human rights at national and international levels.

...family law and related legal fields are among the fastest changing areas of law, due mainly to the influence of human rights at national and international levels

The methods employed in teaching the first component of the course take into account and use the diverse backgrounds of the students who take the course. The students come from different African countries, from both legal and non-legal disciplines and with different working experiences. The class of 2005, for example, had the following profile: a nurse with a sociology background; a lawyer working in the Attorney General's office; a lawyer working with the United Nations Children's Fund (UNICEF); three lawyers working as magistrates; two lawyers in private practice; and one gender project officer with a teaching background. These men and women came from at least four different African countries in eastern and southern Africa. It was this kind of diversity that enriched the course and the delivery methods.

As developed over the two programmes in which the course has been taught,[2] the teaching methods combine lecturing and seminar presentations with two goals in mind. The first goal is to give students a theoretical understanding of the legal and conceptual framework that impacts the situation of women and the girl child in the family in the African context. The second is to enable students to appreciate the socio-legal perspective of the course using the challenges of implementing the law as a focus. In order to achieve the first goal, lectures are delivered on five topics discussed in the next section. The second goal is achieved through seminar presentation by students, while both these goals are reinforced by essay and examination as forms of assessment. The methods of delivery are discussed under the relevant headings below.

Lectures

At the general level the lectures focus on how the regulation of various aspects of family law under domestic law (customary, general and constitutional law) and international law (human rights instruments) affects the situation of women and the girl child in the family, as opposed to on the rules or legal doctrine per se. For example, I examined the constitutional provisions of countries like Zambia and Zimbabwe that protect some areas of family law,

---

[2] For the sake of convenience we use the present tense in describing the teaching methods .

including customary family law, from the application of the Bill of Rights and how these provisions impact on women and girl children's social realities. In their effect, these provisions ensure that statutory laws, customs and practices that discriminate against women in marriage and, in turn, deny married women the legal capacities necessary to participate independently in the economic, business and public life of their societies, are validated. They also place beyond challenge marriage laws that set different marriage requirements for boys and girls, for example, the minimum age for marriage is usually lower for girls than for boys. These legal differentiations result in different social experiences for boys and girls in relation to schooling, for example.

This approach to teaching does not only give students an understanding of the aspects of the law dealt with and how they affect the lived realities of women but it also has the benefit of enabling students without legal academic backgrounds to deal with the subject matter of the course. With regard to the latter, all students, with or without a legal training background, can relate to the social effects of law in the lives of women (and men) in families.

This approach to teaching ... also has the benefit of enabling students without legal academic backgrounds to deal with the subject matter of the course

Taking account of the diversity of the class and the regional nature of the programme, the laws of selected countries are used as specific examples. Students are encouraged to reflect on the differences between the laws in these examples and the laws of their own countries in relation to the topic and to their compliance with human rights. In other words, students are required to reflect on the differences in the laws of the various countries, using compliance or non-compliance with human rights as the chief comparator. Using this comparator is not only interesting but also more feasible than direct comparison. Moreover, using human rights as the comparator allows for an understanding of local factors and issues.

Thus, at another level, the lecturing method fosters a 'grounded' comparative approach to understanding the legal framework in the sense that students draw from the laws in operation on their own familiar ground (countries) to understand the implications of human rights for family law and family issues and the subject matter of the course generally.

It is important to mention that students are required to read set materials relevant to the lecture topics (subject to the methodology challenges mentioned in this chapter). These materials are compiled into reading packs and distributed to the students before the start of the course. This is to facilitate student learning and coverage of the topics in lectures at a relatively fast rate, given the limited timeframe for the course. Preparatory reading is another way of bridging the legal knowledge gap for students with little or no law background.

As the method of teaching only comes to life in the light of the content, a sketch of the five topics covered follows.

1   The pluralistic nature of family law in African legal systems

This session highlights the different systems of law that have a bearing on family relationships in African countries – received law, customary law, religious systems of personal law and human rights. It also includes the idea of deep legal pluralism as this is critical to understanding the operation of law on the ground (the socio-legal perspective). Students are challenged to think about how this plurality of law might impact on women's legal status or their use (or non-use) of law in family matters. One example is how the plurality of law affects the social realities of women who marry under general law – according to the Marriage Acts, as described below.

In most cases the parties to these 'double-decker' marriages also conclude customary marriages even though this is not a legal requirement for a valid civil marriage. There are various reasons for doing this, the most important is to ensure that the marriage is recognized by the (extended) families of the parties; marriages entered into without the customary law requirement are often not recognized. This can mean that the widow is not 'purified' or 'cleansed' through the performance of appropriate rituals by the late husband's family upon his death; these rituals are performed only if the families of the parties considered them to have been married. This situation has both social and legal consequences for the widow.

The social consequences are that the lack of ritual purification reduces the widow's remarriage prospects, as people consider that such widows carry the (evil) spirit of their deceased husbands, which can in turn bring misfortune to the future suitor or husband. My research in Zambia (Himonga, 1995, 265–277) forms a basis for the class discussion of these social implications.

The legal consequence of the marriage not being recognized by the deceased husband's family is that the widow cannot inherit her husband's estate. She may be entitled to inherit under state law but the opposition of the deceased's family, which is sometimes accompanied with threats of witchcraft or other forms of intimidation, forces widows to give up their entitlements (Himonga, 1995: 170–173).

In other instances, the impact of the plurality of law in respect of the 'double decker' marriages is that it constrains women's freedom and capacity to take action to dissolve a problematic marriage. A case I use to illustrate this problem is that of a woman who wanted to divorce her husband in the High Court as required by general law. However, her husband frustrated her intention on several occasions by insisting that her family repay the *lobola* he had paid on the marriage before she could divorce him. But the repayment of *lobola* required the cooperation of her own family since the obligation to repay the *lobola* rested on them.

...the impact of the plurality of law ...is that it constrains women's freedom and capacity to take action to dissolve a problematic marriage

When she could not get her family to pay back the *lobola*, she hired a truck from Lusaka (in the central province) and went to her uncle's village in the southern province to collect the *lobola* cattle. In the uncle's absence she went into his kraal and loaded the number of cattle the husband alleged to have paid as *lobola*. She then took the cattle back to Lusaka to the informal settlement where her mother-in-law lived and left them in an enclosed structure in her back yard! Shortly after that she lodged her application for divorce in the High Court and her marriage was dissolved.

This woman was fortunate in that she had the courage to do what most women in her position would not do – to drive the cattle from her uncle's kraal and take them back to her husband's family. She also knew who had received the *lobola* cattle. In most cases the *lobola* is distributed among different relatives and the women on whose behalf it was paid do not know who took a share of it.

Another serious impact of the plurality of family law is that most women do not know what system of law they married under. Some go through forms of marriage in church ('white' weddings) thinking that they have concluded a civil marriage which provides a measure of security in terms of property and maintenance rights. Only upon the dissolution of the marriage by death or divorce do they discover that their 'white' marriage was either merely a church blessing, conferring no legal status, or was a customary marriage (if they had met the customary law requirements), giving them different rights from those expected.

...women ... are often caught at the intersections of law, practice and even the supernatural world

These scenarios clearly illustrate the impact of legal plurality on women who are often caught at the intersections of law, practice and even the supernatural world.

2 The conceptualization of African customary law

The conceptualization of customary law as living and official customary law is the focus of this session, along with the implications of this dichotomy for understanding women's grounded realities and protecting their human rights. The readings for this component include Martin Chanock (1985) *Law, custom and social order. The colonial experience in Malawi and Zambia* and Alice Armstrong *et al.* (1993) 'Uncovering reality: excavating women's rights in African family law'. I also draw students' attention to cases that clearly show the implications of the two forms of customary law for women's rights, such as *Bhe v Magistrate Khayelitsha*[3] (see Himonga, 2005), *Magaya v Magaya* and *Mabena v Letsoalo*.[4]

---

[3] See index of cases at the back of the book for details of all cases referred to.

[4] While the first two cases show how official customary law denies women's inheritance rights, the last case, although it has been criticised in some respects, shows how living customary law recognizes the right of women to negotiate their children's marriages, a capacity official customary law reserves for men.

3 Human rights

In addition to a low-level discussion of the universal/cultural relativism debate, this session draws students' attention to major international and regional human rights instruments as well as constitutional provisions that have a bearing on family law. The international and regional human rights instruments discussed include the Convention on the Elimination of all forms of Discrimination Against Women (CEDAW) and the African Charter on Human and Peoples' Rights respectively. At the national level, we discuss different models of national constitutional provisions. Examples include the newer constitutions of South Africa, Malawi, Uganda and Namibia, on one hand, and the older constitutions of Zambia and Zimbabwe, on the other. The latter were of particular interest because of their infamous provisions shielding family and customary law from the respective Bills of Rights. Although students have been introduced to human rights in the first semester, it is necessary to outline the human rights framework specific to family law and family relationships.

4 General law and customary law concepts of marriage, divorce, custody, guardianship and maintenance and matrimonial property during and after the dissolution of marriage

This session gives a brief overview of the content of the general law and customary law with regard to family law concepts listed above. This overview takes a comparative approach that focuses on two types of family law models prevalent in eastern and southern African countries (hereafter referred to as the region), using human rights as the chief comparator. The two models are Roman-Dutch law and English common law. While the experience of British colonialism left a common legal heritage in family law in most countries in the region, the Roman-Dutch law influence is very strong in some countries, such as South Africa and Zimbabwe, especially in the area of matrimonial property.

The main difference between these systems lies in the area of matrimonial property under the general law. Roman-Dutch law allows a great measure of freedom for the parties to determine the variable proprietary consequences of their marriage before they enter into the marriage. With the help of antenuptial contracts, which they have the capacity to enter into, the parties intending to marry may choose between state predetermined matrimonial property regimes. These include marriage in community of property and of profit and loss, marriage out of community of property and of profit and loss and marriage out of community but with the accrual system. Should the parties not choose, the law provides a default system, for example, this would be marriage in community of property in South Africa. On divorce, property distribution happens according to the rules governing the property regime the parties chose. These regimes are virtually unknown to common law in which the married parties generally own their property separately throughout the marriage. On divorce, the courts play a big role in property redistribution using statutory guidelines.

In comparison to common law, Roman-Dutch law matrimonial regimes provide some measure of certainty and security regarding the parties' property rights from the start of the marriage. More importantly, some regimes, such as marriage in community and marriage out of community of property, the accrual system, incorporate principles of equality and notions of fairness respectively, both of which are compatible with human rights.

Thus a comparative approach using human rights as a major comparator is essential to give a complete picture of the legal framework regulating various areas of the family.

As evident from the above examples, the idea of this session is not to give students a detailed body of rules that govern each of the various concepts under study. Rather, it is to present, in broad terms, the major features of the law in each of the two model legal system and to show how they affect the situation of women and girl children in family relationships.

5 Family law reform

This session introduces students to the importance of legal reform and law generally to the protection of women's rights and interests in families, on one hand, and the limitations of law reform in this respect, on the other. The theory of the law and the socio-legal perspective are brought into sharp focus, using the challenges connected with implementing new laws as a specific example. The latter is discussed later .

At another level, the session explores four dimensions of law reform:

- the need to reform areas of family law, especially customary family law;
- the importance of designing new laws that are sensitive to the prevailing social conditions in African countries;
- the limitations, ineffectiveness and dangers of ill-conceived or unrealistic law reform measures and the vulnerability of women and girl children;
- the role of the courts in law reform (judicial activism and the interpretation of the law).

We take the example of the reform of the customary law of marriage by legislation in a specific country as a medium for exploring the various dimensions. The legislation used as an example is the Recognition of Customary Marriages Act in South Africa (Act 120 of 1998). This Act is used to explore and discuss the need to reform customary family law to align it with human rights principles, such as the right to equality, as opposed to abolishing this system of law altogether. The main consideration in this assessment is the relevance and importance of customary law to the majority of people in African countries (the importance of the social context). The Act is also used to discuss realistic and contextual law making and the challenges of reforming customary law in African countries seeking to implement human rights. The focus of discussion is on the provisions of the Act to be discussed shortly.

With regard to judicial activism, *Bhe v Magistrate Khayelitsha* is used to discuss the issue of judicial boldness in challenging entrenched principles of (official) customary law, on one hand, and the challenges of enforcing such a decision with the likelihood of opposition from sections of society with vested interests, such as men, on the other hand.

Coming back to the challenges of implementing new laws, hypothetical (theoretical) situations and actual court decisions are used to demonstrate the effectiveness or otherwise of the law. In addition, attempts are made to assist students to visualise the 'grounded' realities of implementing the new laws through constructed images. One example I use is the implementation of section 7(6) of the Recognition of Customary Marriages Act.

Section 7(6) is one of the most important yet problematical provisions of the Act. It is important because it is designed to protect the matrimonial property rights of the spouses, especially women, in polygamous marriages through (a) the intervention of the court in the approval of the contract to regulate the polygynous family's matrimonial property system and (b) a fair distribution of the existing matrimonial property between the existing spouses prior to the conclusion of the next polygynous marriage.

Related sub-sections are also worthy of note. According to section 7(7), when considering the application for the approval of the contract in respect of a marriage in community of property or a marriage out of community of property but subject to the accrual system, the court must:

(a) terminate the marriage in community or the marriage out of community but subject to the accrual system and effect a division of the matrimonial property;

(b) ensure an equitable distribution of the property;

(c) take into account all the relevant circumstances of the family groups which would be affected if the application for the approval of the contract were granted.

In terms of section 7(8) all persons having sufficient interest and in particular the applicant's existing spouse or spouses must join in the proceedings for the approval of the contract.

Although subsections (7) and (8) do not mention prospective wives explicitly, it is arguable that they contemplate this class of women as being among interested parties who must join in the proceedings and as part of the family groups whose circumstances would be taken into account when the court considers the contract to govern the future matrimonial system. In any case, for the present purposes, I assume this interpretation to be correct.

Section 7(6) and the related subsections raise two problems. The first is the practical application of the provision. Every time a man wishes to marry a new wife, he and his existing wives and prospective wives, all of whom must join in the proceedings, must traverse the complex court procedures and incur the necessary legal costs, as well as travel costs to the relevant courts. This is not to mention the great distances some of them, especially those in rural areas, might have to cover to reach the nearest court with relevant jurisdiction (Himonga, 2004:269). The second problem is that the section creates the basis for women involved in the polygynous or anticipated polygynous marriage to compete for both the marital legal status and access to matrimonial property.

In order to assist students to translate these problems into grounded realities, I share my visual images of the practical implementation of section 7(6). I explain that these images come from my own experience of having lived in a rural area in Zambia for most of my childhood years but the situations and logistical problems described in this account are common to other African countries, especially in their rural areas.

In the rural area I grew up in, most men, including my close relatives, were married to up to three women at a time. The only mode of transport a few people could afford was a bicycle. I visualize the situation (see box) based on the assumption that the application for the approval of the contract by the court is heard in open court as opposed to a hearing by a judge in Chambers (behind closed doors in the office of the judge).

What legislators may have considered simple and reasonable requirements on paper can become a logistical and economic challenge in many parts of Africa where bus services are infrequent and expensive

© Joseline Kabasiime Musigye and EQUINET

SCENARIO

Polygyny and on the road to court

I see a man calling all his three wives the night before and telling them:

'I am aware that it is the rainy season and that you are busy preparing your groundnut and sweet potato fields for planting. I am also aware that there is little time left for you to plant the seeds before the planting season (determined by the weather pattern) is over. However, tomorrow you will not go to your fields. As you all know, I am getting married to Noxie. The law requires the approval of the contract to regulate our future matrimonial property system by the court and you are all required to be present in court when this contract is discussed and approved. The appropriate court is 20 kilometres away from here. On our way to the court, we must deviate from the route for five kilometres to pick up Noxie, as her attendance appears to be necessary.'

One of the wives protests:

'How can this be, did we ever have to go to court to get married to you? Don't these people [the law makers] know that, according to our traditions, the products (groundnuts and sweet potatoes) from our fields are the only property we will take with us if you divorced us tomorrow or if you died?'

The other wives join in and grumble and complain about the need to waste their whole day at the court instead of working in their fields.

The husband shrugs his shoulders, and retorts, 'Well, that is the law.' But he promises them that he will do his best to get them to court and bring them back to their fields as quickly as possible.

The next day the husband gets on his bicycle, with two of the women on the elongated back carrier of his bicycle (he spent the whole night extending the carrier to be able to carry two big women on it) and one on the cross bar. Then he stops over to pick up his prospective bride, Noxie, but he does not have enough space to accommodate her on his bicycle. So they continue the remaining 15 kilometres to the court on foot. They arrive at the court just before it closes and although they missed their time for the hearing, a few hours before they arrived, the clerk of court is sympathetic and gets their matter back on to the court case list. Fortunately, the husband gets his contract approved the same day, so they do not have to come to the court several times as most people have done in the past due to the court adjourning their cases.

Two months later, the man wants to marry again and the procedure is repeated!

A glance at the procedural complexity shows how unrealistic, if not unreasonable, the demands of section 7(6) are for people in rural areas

The broad issue embedded in the scenario is people's access to the facility for the execution of polygynous marriage property contracts. The implication of the practical problems and realities of obtaining the approval of the contract is obvious. The objectives of the provisions of the Recognition of Customary Marriages Act under discussion are good for the women but they are self-restricting by their procedural complexity and insensitivity to the social realities of the communities they are intended to serve. A glance at the procedural complexity shows how unrealistic, if not unreasonable, the demands of section 7(6) are for people in rural areas, for example.

Firstly, the very requirement that the contract be approved by a court of the ranks of the High Court and magistrate's court means that ordinary citizens require legal advice to understand and navigate the procedure for lodging the application and to actually lodge the application in the court with appropriate jurisdiction. Secondly, if the matter is heard in open court like any other ordinary application, then the parties would require legal representation. Thirdly, the parties will in any case require the services of a lawyer to draw up the contract. Fourthly, because the approved contract is required to be registered in the Deeds Registry,[5] it would have to be notarised by a notary.

It is important to stress that the complexity of the court contract approval procedure makes it unlikely that men will bother to conclude these contracts and anecdotal evidence suggests that only about two such contracts have so far been registered! The consequence is that women in polygynous relationships without the approved contract will continue to lose out when their marriages are invalidated as shown in the case discussed below.

Thus the imagery is intended to challenge the students to: (a) think about issues of law reform critically, (b) contextualize law reform within social realities and (c) view practical issues and strategies or steps necessary to make the law effective and beneficial to women and girl children on the ground to be as important as the content of the reformed law.

The session ends with a brief overview of the major approaches to the reform of customary family law by both legislation and the courts in the region, in order to make students aware of how different countries that have ventured to reform their family law have done it. The prominent legislation models are 'unification' and parallel systems. In the 'unification' model (or what others call 'integration'), all recognized systems of law in the country – customary law, religious personal law and general law (civil law) regulating the area of law concerned are incorporated into one statute, which creates minimum legal requirements for all marriages and applies to the whole country.[6] The parallel

---

[5] This is the implication of section 7(9) of the Act which provides that the clerk of court must send a copy of the approved contract to each registrar of deeds of the area in which the court is situated.

[6] An example is the Tanzanian Law of Marriage of 1971.

system model is where the general and customary law continue to operate side by side but customary law is reformed by legislation to create a new 'statutory customary law' system applicable to people who were governed by customary law before it was reformed. The variation in the new 'statutory customary laws' in different countries relates to the degree to which the reform statute substitutes customary law with civil law.

The 'reform' of customary law by the courts model is when courts are mandated by the constitution to develop all law that is fully recognized as part of the national legal system – legislation, common law and customary law – and through this development to align it with human rights in the constitution (the Bill of Rights).[7]

In concluding the lecture sessions, I return to the evolutionary and exploratory nature of the methods of teaching. Taking the example of section 7(6) again, lectures incorporate any cases decided under this section. Analyzing these concrete cases reveals the practical impact of the provision in question on women and how women experience the law in the context of their social realities. In other words, if I am teaching the course in 2011, I include an analysis of cases decided under section 7(6) in 2010 and incorporate them in the teaching and learning process. Fortuitously, there was such a case in 2010, *Mayelane v Ngwenyama and Another*, which was the first to interpret section 7(6) and for the sake of completeness, I describe it briefly.

The case concerned the competing rights of Mdjadji Mayelane and Maria Ngwenyama in a polygynous marriage. Mdjadji Mayelane married the now deceased Hlengani Dyson Moyana in 1984 and was unaware of his second marriage to Maria Ngwenyama in 2008. However, there was no approved contract for regulating the matrimonial property. The competition only related to the validity of the marriage but it had implications for the women's property rights in inheritance as well (see box on the next page).

Upon hearing the case, the court decided that Maria Ngwenyama's marriage was null and void . The drastic consequences of a void marriage are, inter alia, that the children of the couple are not legitimate and that parties do not inherit intestate from each other. The court advanced three reasons for this decision, one of which may be mentioned. It reasoned that the nullity followed from the fact that the court had not consented to the second marriage contrary to section 7(6).

---

[7] An example of this is section 39(2) of the South African Constitution, which states that 'When interpreting any legislation, and when developing the common law or customary law, every court, tribunal or forum must promote the spirit, purport and objects of the Bill of Rights.'

CASE

Mayelane v Ngwenyama and Another

The applicant, Mdjadji Mayelane and the first respondent, Maria Ngwenyama, resided in the same district in Limpopo but in different villages. Mdjadji had married her deceased husband in accordance with customary law in 1984. Her husband passed away in February 2009. The marriage was not registered, contrary to the Recognition of Customary Marriages Act, but this alone did not affect the validity of the marriage.[8]

The deceased man is alleged to have married Maria in accordance with customary law in January 2008. This marriage was confirmed by the headman of Maria's village. Mdjaji was unaware of the fact that her husband had entered into another marriage according to customary law until after his death. There was agreement by all the parties that no section 7(6) contract was approved by the court to regulate the future matrimonial property of the two marriages prior to Maria's marriage.

Mdjaji contended that the second marriage was void because of the failure to obtain the section 7(6) order. Maria countered this contention by arguing that her marriage was unassailable because it was properly and publicly performed in accordance with customary law (section 3 of the Act sets out the requirements for a valid marriage, including that the both parties consented to be married to each other under customary law, and that the marriage must be negotiated and entered into or celebrated in accordance with customary law).

In the light of the women's competing claims regarding the status of their marriages, the second respondent, the Minister of Home Affairs, refused to register Mdjaji's marriage. The Recognition of Customary Marriages Act provides for the possibility of registration in these circumstances as follows: If for any reason the marriage is not registered, any interested party who is deemed by the registering officer to have sufficient interest in the registration of the marriage may apply to the officer to enquire into the existence of the marriage. If the registration officer is satisfied that a valid marriage exists, he must register it [see section 4(5)(a) and (b)].

---

[8] See section 4 of the Recognition of Customary Marriages Act.

In this respect it stated:

> 'It is clear that this section is aimed at protecting both the existing spouse and the new intended spouse by ensuring that the husband must obtain the court's consent to a further customary marriage, albeit that such consent is expressed in proprietary terms. Both the existing spouse and the intending further spouse have a vital interest in having their relative proprietary positions safeguarded by the procedure that is laid down in sub-section (6). Most customary marriages are concluded by persons whose access to worldly goods is limited[9] and whose financial security may be severely prejudiced by an earlier or the conclusion of another marriage if such fact is not disclosed to the spouses and dealt with by the contract and the court's approval. The failure to comply with the mandatory provisions of this subsection cannot but lead to the invalidation of a subsequent customary marriage....'[10]

The court cited, with approval, the view held by Cronje and Heaton that an interpretation of the subsection 'which does not make the husband's capacity to enter in a further customary marriage dependent on the court's approval of his proposed matrimonial property contract would imply that the court approval is unnecessary'. The authors go on to say that the requirement for the court's approval would be a waste of time and money, 'and would leave the interests of the customary wives and their family groups unprotected. This would surely not have been the legislator's intention' (see box on page 236).

The analysis of this decision would include the following issues:

- The protection it accords to women (and which women);
- Its bias towards monogamous marriage women;
- Its drastic consequence for many women living under customary law – all marriages in which the requirements of section 7(6) were not met are now void;
- The further consequences of nullity in terms of the legal status of the children of the women whose marriages have been nullified, as well as in terms of the women's property rights;
- The lack of information and women's relative powerlessness to push for the registration of the contract even if they are aware of the law;

---

[9] This is of course, a very simplistic view as there are many wealthy polygynists. Although in some of these cases the women ought to know the consequences of being married without the necessary property contract, they nevertheless seem to take the risk.

[10] *Mayelane v Ngwenyama and Another* Judgment at page 7.

- The constitutionality of section 7(6) and related provisions, based on discrimination against people using customary law vis à vis those using civil law. In respect of this issue, it should be noted that matrimonial property regimes are not a requirement for the validity of a civil marriage. However, by declaring the marriage without the contract in question to be void, the court is adding compliance with a matrimonial property matter as an additional requirement for a valid customary law marriage which is not required by section 3 of the Act. This smacks of discrimination, as already intimated.

Seminars and assessment

The second goal of the teaching method in the first part of the course, the practical element, which enables students to appreciate the practical challenges and problems of implementing the law, is achieved mainly through students' presentations to the class in a seminar (see box). They each do a written presentation on a chosen or assigned family law topic (for example, custody, guardianship, divorce or distribution of matrimonial assets upon divorce) to be dealt with, if possible, under the law of their own country or under the law of any other African country they choose to research. Students are encouraged to choose a topic that enables them to draw from their work experience. The presentation is followed by a class discussion encouraging students to draw on their own or their country's experiences of the situation of women in relation to the topic under discussion.

The assessment exercises (essay and examination) reinforce the theoretical and practical goals of the teaching by requiring students to deal with legal and institutional/structural, social or cultural problems affecting women in their use of the law or to make recommendations for reforms to improve the situation of women. In dealing with these exercises, students are required, where appropriate, to draw from their

ASSIGNMENT
Seminar presentation

The assignment for the seminar presentation requires the students:

- to analytically discuss how the law on the chosen topic (general, customary or religious law) affects the situation of women and girls;
- to highlight particular problems encountered by women in the use of the law;
- to discuss the non-legal factors (cultural, social and economic) that impinge/impact on the practical operations of the law to the advantage/disadvantage of women;
- to include, as much as possible, concrete examples of cases or scenarios gathered from their own work experiences or countries relating to the difficulties women experience in using the law;
- to identify specific human rights instruments that they would use to interrogate the identified problematic areas of the law and non-legal factors to change/improve the position of women;
- to suggest legal reforms and/or non-legal remedies to improve the situation of women; and
- to include, where appropriate, specific examples of their experiences in their work or country in using human rights instruments to deal with problematic laws and non-legal factors to the benefit of women.

own experiential knowledge, observations and experiences of law in its pluralities in relation to families and communities in their own countries or in other African countries.

Methodological challenges

There are three major challenges regarding the methods employed to teach the legal framework component of the course. The first challenge is that of time. The two weeks allocated to this component put a lot of pressure on students to assimilate large amounts of information from their own reading and the lectures with little time for meaningful reflection on the material. The pressure extends to the students' reading in preparation for participation in class generally and to their class presentations.

Secondly, the dearth of relevant materials, especially legislation and court cases from countries in the region other than Zimbabwe and South Africa, makes it difficult to fully incorporate the element of student diversity in the delivery methodology.

Thirdly, the course has had a chequered history and has not been offered since 2005. There are a number of reasons for this – the lecturer was not available in 2007 and in 2009 only two students opted for the course making it non viable. However, the reason a number of students did not take it up related to their perceived need to have the 'Women, human rights and constitutions in Africa course' on their CVs. This desire seemed particularly strong for students who were not lawyers who thought that the human rights nomenclature would give them extra credentials when job seeking. No amount of discussion or rationalizing would get them to see that this was a spurious argument and that all the courses have a substantial human rights component. The pull of the job market was too strong for them to resist. This perception on the part of students has eventually led to a change of regulations with the human rights course moving to the first semester as a compulsory course and a potential cap on optional courses. This cap is not only in response to the family course but reflects the importance of second semester courses being effective seminar based courses and ones that build on a sound understanding of human rights..

In conclusion I would like to highlight the innovative aspect of the teaching of the general legal framework component of the course, which I would call 'experiential and participatory teaching and learning'. Teaching the course to mature students with diverse national and disciplinary experiences and perspectives resulted in a process in which students learnt from the lecturer, taught each other and taught the lecturer at the same time. Thus students not only learn from the lecturer but also enrich the subject content and learning process by their participation and shared 'grounded' experiences and reflection.

...students not only learn from the lecturer but also enrich the subject content and learning process by their participation and shared 'grounded' experiences and reflection

Part II: Plumbing the depths – or trying to!

Julie Stewart [11,12]

My own route into the field of women's law could best be described as a sideways process. I had never formally studied it as a legal discipline but had an instinctive affinity with it once I began to grasp its principles. The sideways process commenced with my first teaching course, 'Law of succession'. From the outset I was aware that there was far more to such a course than just the black letter law. The realities of death, dying and the needs of those affected by a death drove my conceptualizing of the framework of the course. So there was a little reality beyond the formal law in that course.

My serious engagement with the lived realities of individuals' lives was through the Women and Law in Southern Africa Research Trust (WLSA) where as a part-time research associate I worked with a mixed group of lawyers and social scientists. Suddenly I was part of an interdisciplinary team and learnt social science research methodologies and methods painlessly. As the only *murungu* (white) on the team, my absence of a deeply-rooted familiarity with local customs and practices meant that I was constantly questioning and interrogating the significance of what to my research colleagues seemed to be normal, unremarkable or obvious social responses. Also, along with my lawyer colleagues, my role was to supply legal detail, my un-lawyer[13] research colleagues reciprocated by exposing me to the lived realities of the remnant 'families' of deceased persons. I was in a very special and privileged situation. I penetrated social arenas seeing things through their eyes and benefiting from their social acceptance which would not, I believe, have been possible on my own. At the regional level I had the most profound eye-opening exposure to the broader nuances of families and family life and the differences that social situations, religion and other factors had on individuals and what I will for the moment term families.

Now, thinking about what I envisaged for the 'Women, family, social realities and the law' course, I realize that I was trying to provide students with the same investigative thrill. I sought to develop a capacity in the students

I had the most profound eye-opening exposure to the broader nuances of families and family life and the differences that social situations, religion and other factors had on individuals and what I will for the moment term families.

---

[11] Even the casual reader of this book will immediately spot that I turn up in many courses – probably too many, something of a poobah – but as the director of the centre I find that where is a gap it is incumbent on me to step in and try and keep courses going.

[12] I did much of the development and finalization of this section of the chapter while I was a Bram Fischer Visiting Scholar at the Law School, University of the Witwatersrand in South Africa. I would like to thank Wits Law School for their hospitality and intellectual stimulation but most especially for the opportunity to evade administrative duties and to think and write about matters legal and especially matters in women's law.

[13] For an explanation of un-lawyer see the research methodology chapter 2.

to identify research and law reform needs along with the skills needed to implement new and existing laws. I also sought to assist students to challenge the conventional thinking on matters related to families, domestic relationships and the law. One of the significant benefits of the WLSA research was that it provided the opportunity for a solid, professional, thorough re-analysis of the functioning of the law in its pluralities, from the perspective of the woman and the man, whom it affected in so many diverse ways. There was also a power to challenge conventional legal wisdom which was bolstered by the number of researchers working on a topic in a regional research collective.

There was ... a power to challenge conventional legal wisdom which was bolstered by the number of researchers working on a topic in a regional research collective

The biggest challenge, and it remains one of the major challenges for the women's law researcher even now, was how to effectively engage the outcomes of the research with the formalized versions of the law, be it general (received) law, revisiting of customary law, religious laws and other normative orders for the purposes of re-interpreting the law, driving law reform processes or implementing beneficial laws (see chapter 2 for further detail on this). It requires rigorous analytical frameworks and considerable intellectual effort to find the routes back into the more formal legal arena (Stewart, 1997, 1998).

The masters programme is regional so the investigative frameworks and tools have to be malleable, adaptable and not country specific. I have, in writing for this book, had to examine the process I use to transfer the insights gained from my experiences to the students so that they experience the re-thinking and reconceptualizing processes for themselves. It must become a process of self-informing discovery for the student. Added to this is an awareness that there is always a need to embark on yet another quest to unpack reality and law and actively engage them in 'dialogue'. How have I tackled this and how might I tackle it in future?

After the completion of the first two weeks of the course, discussed above, I run a week of student-driven seminars. In these seminars, they explore from their own grounded social and professional realities the factors that affect families and social realities in the domestic arena. We try to focus on factors that affect, positively or negatively, women and girls' capacity to use and benefit from human rights based interventions that increasingly influence and shape family-related laws in the region.

Writing this portion, it is an automatic reflex to use the word 'family' when describing relationships, no doubt because we cohere intellectually and emotionally around the term even when it may distort our need to deconstruct and unpack the meaning of terms. So an internal quest in writing this chapter is to address the impact of the language we use on how we think about, respond to and describe such relationships.

The first session involves the class individually and collectively brainstorming issues of critical concern. This can be an erratic process but

COURSE OUTLINE
Women, family, social realities and law (Section 2)

Focal points

- The realities of legal pluralism.

- Women and girls' lived realities in family and marital relationships. Women and access to and control over resources within marriage and relationships.

- Defining families and family obligations – expanding and contracting families, cycles of obligations and women's focus in accessing resources. Emotional resources versus material resources.

- Marital regimes and controlling women's rights and status in registered marriages, unregistered marriages, cohabitation and other partnership regimes. Who is a wife? Social realities of wife status

- The realities of relationships. Women are 'cattle in the kraal', 'cheap labour', 'the mother of my children', 'my old bag'.

- Women as access points to men's rights.

The realities

- Cultural and religious perspectives on marriage and family, cultural and religious duties and obligations that impact on women's lived realities. Births, puberty, weddings, funerals and associated activities; family ceremonies. Widows and women's experiences in relation to death – mourning practices – impact of mourning practices on women's inheritance rights and entitlements.

- Monogamy, polygyny, mix and can't match marriage regimes. Coping with the realities of polygyny and access to resources. Women as links, bonds, conduits for resource distribution within families.

- Women and gendered roles within and as determined by the family. The women's multiple burdens. Women as family resources.

- Women and status within families – women's power bases as a barrier to using family law reforms. Women competing for resources.

- Wives, mothers, grandmothers, daughters, daughters-in-law, sisters, aunts: conflicting duties and obligations. Generational conflicts between women in families: the control, economics and knowledge crisis.

- Women's access to and control of resources within families, women's capacity to use resources created by their own labour or from their own resources

- An assessment of realities – extra-legal/customary mediation of contribution and division of matrimonial assets on divorce, separation or death.

- Who can divorce whom culturally? – the clash between legal rights and lived realities. Naming and blaming.

- Who is a widow? Playing the inheritance game. Relationships of convenience and strategic alliances.

- Custody battles – children versus resources. Children as a legal battleground – the non consent/consent paper. Cultural pressures over children – best interests of the child in reality.

All sections of this part of the course are conducted on a seminar basis with active participation from students as a necessary component.

thinking back it is also a reflection of our WLSA processes. Some will focus on rights, others on realities, the task is then to marry[14] these up into coherent and deconstructible units. The issues canvassed represent only a small proportion of what could be investigated but the skills to be imparted are the real focus and providing there is a connection to women (girls), family, social realities and the law (in its pluralities) a few topics will suffice.

During these seminars, the focus is on the ever-present legal and social pluralities that mediate women and girls' life choices and opportunities for self actualization. Pointers to the kinds of issues to be covered are outlined below although each student is free (and encouraged) to raise new issues and direct the rest of the class and the lecturer to new perspectives to be explored.

What needs to be covered? What can be covered?

This course explicitly recognizes that women and girls' lived social realities need to be thoroughly understood and explored. Especially considering how, despite changes in women's legal status and changes in matrimonial and domestic property rights in some countries, women struggle to obtain and maintain beneficial access to and control over resources.

This course explicitly recognizes that women and girls' lived social realities need to be thoroughly understood and explored.

The course is relatively short and there is no time to cover all the laws that affect families, relationships, children's associations with parents, the complex issues and legal 'game playing' around divorce, separation, maintenance and other claims. Nor is it the mandate of the course to cover such content.

COMMENT

A word of caution

There is a tendency to regard women and girls' experiences within families as negative and portray them as used by and exploited by families and excluded from family decision making processes. Whilst I would not dispute that this may be the case in some families, there are a wide range of experiences of family – both negative and positive – that need to be mapped and analyzed.

Thus students need to constantly avoid generalizing from cases, which may be numerous in some areas, of girls not attending school to a general statement that girls do not attend school. Drawing on personal insights may assist in ascertaining the factors that promote the education of girls in some families and communities and uncovering factors that militate against the education of girls. Students need to see how they can explore their own realities in their own wider family-based groupings or those of women and girls in the wider communities from which the students come.

---

[14] The word 'marry' is pervasive and putting things and concepts together ends up as being described as 'marrying'. Can I escape the concept?

The lecturer's mandate is to assist students to identify, conceptualize and begin processes of addressing legal problems or those that are seen as social problems by those involved, which may have a solution or resolution lodged in the realm of law. The course is not about legal content but about developing critical analytical skills and evolving methodological approaches to improving the situation of women through the use of law.

The course is not about legal content but about developing critical analytical skills and evolving methodological approaches to improving the situation of women through the use of law.

Looking back at the course outline I generated for this second part of the course (see page 242), I note I tried to highlight a broad swathe of issues in the intersections between laws in all their pluralities and realities that might affect how women might choose to use law, avoid law or be deterred from using laws in resolving problems. Within such an intersection it is vital to recognize that women might be constrained in exercising their legal options by the consideration of their position in both maternal and paternal families as well as in marital families. What this presages is the need to locate women's position within relationships and in relation to how resource access affects their choices and options in life. Without wishing to constrain students in generating issues in the seminars, I have a list of focal points to use in the event of a hiatus in the issue generation process – perhaps better described as 'provocations' to start the process. An outcome of this process is for students to come to the realization that what for convenience we style family law is part of a rapidly changing legal arena.

For example, exploring how to respond to the 'best interests of the child' and how the gendered dimensions of parental care and custody entitlements affect our understanding of the best interests, is problematic in social situations where children are described as 'owned' and rights with regard to children are socially located firmly in the male parent in matters of guardianship. Many women are unaware of their rights in matters of guardianship and custody because of the dominance of the perception that males control children and children's welfare at the level of laws, even though the day to day realities of their lives are in the hands of women.

One issue the course will have to tackle in the future is child-headed families. These are becoming more and more common in the region and we need to consider how to confer appropriate rights upon them. We need to consider practical alternatives for their welfare rather than take a custodial welfarist approach which would lead to their being taken into care (Bonthuys, 2010). Customary and informal adoption arrangements are common in the eastern and southern African region and formal legal regularization of such arrangements is frequently not undertaken. Consequently rights conferred under general or received law on adopted children may not be realized by children in informal adoptions. Conversely, there are problems in formal adoptions where parents do not fully appreciate the implications of the adoption and believe that a child will be able to obtain educational or other opportunities. So students need to appreciate how to delicately probe for motives and also misconceptions in the actions of parents and other family members in relation to children.

What must be covered

The importance of probing what constitutes families and family obligations, especially expanding and contracting families, depending on individual or collective need, is an important arena for research (Ncube and Stewart, 1997). It is no longer possible to centre our conceptualization of human nurturing and social responsibility for children around a husband and wife or wives in registered marriages. There is need for a much wider formal legal conceptualization of family and inter-human responsibilities. State laws may have a relatively narrow recognition of who is responsible for maintaining a child or other family members which is at odds with what actually takes place. Women, often as sisters, aunts, grandmothers, daughters, cousins and beyond, are deeply embedded in these contexts and it is critical that students in this course appreciate the constant mutation of norms and values within the social arena (Hellum *et al.*, 2007).

It is no longer possible to centre our conceptualization of human nurturing and social responsibility for children around a husband and wife or wives in registered marriages

Mapping reciprocities: how individuals strategize

The levels of individual resource-based dependence or independence from traditional blood, kin and marital relationships affects how and with what strategic purposes in mind a woman or a girl will engage with or avoid family mediation in relation to her personal life and access to resources.

The WLSA research in the 1990s demonstrated that within broad family-based groupings, reciprocal obligations exist or are developed and we need to assess the impact that such obligations have on women's strategies in accessing resources (Ncube and Stewart, 1997b). Flowing from women's strategies in accessing resources there is a need to consider when and how women exploit emotional and material resources.[15] Women also need to be considered in their roles as links, bonds and conduits for resource distribution within families. Women and their gendered roles within and as determined by the family create multiple burdens and opportunities for women as they try to achieve self actualization and, most importantly, balance family relationships.

Women and women's work and contribution to the joint welfare of what, for want of an alternative term, I will continue to call the family, are severely

---

[15] The initial draft of this sentence included 'whether' but on reflection I decided that whether is not at issue, it will happen under various guises, the real questions are when and how.

under-rewarded when marital or social reproductive relationships break down. Women's work is often hidden, assumed to be the price for her social security within the family, so at dissolution of relationships she may go away empty handed. A significant component of the second part of the course is to unpack the way in which women experience the reality of the breakdown of relationships and the division of assets as opposed to the formal legal rules that ought to govern such dissolutions. Enabling students to develop the tools to make an assessment of such lived realities and how extra-legal negotiations and pressures mediate the outcome of division of matrimonial assets on divorce, separation or death, is an important part of the course.

There is a need for research in countries in the eastern and southern African regions on women's access to and control of resources within relationships. We also need to understand how women's capacity to use resources created by their own labour or from their own resources changes their status, position and power in families and especially in female hierarchies.

We ... need to understand how women's capacity to use resources created by their own labour or from their own resources changes their status, position and power in families and especially in female hierarchies.

Marriage: one, two, three or more?

The realities of women's experiences need to be considered in the context of the various marital regimes that both formally and informally control women's rights and their perceived status. Students are encouraged to use a comparative approach in assessing the impact of registered marriages, unregistered marriages, cohabitation and other partnership regimes on women's status and the status of children in relation to both parents. The consequences for women and children where men mix marital regimes, sometimes conscious of the formal legal barriers but at times in ignorance, need to be charted and assessed.

One issue that needs to be considered in such investigations is: how do women cope with the realities of polygyny? How does polygyny affect access to resources where there are multiple wives and dependants? A strategic and apposite question is 'who is a wife?' Students need also to be able to map the social realities of wife status. What is its significance? What are the obligations that being a wife create for her in her marital family? What are the benefits that she obtains or perceives she obtains from her status as a wife?

Valuing women: recognition by diminution

The realities in relationships and how they are regarded by the parties themselves and by those they associate with give clues to women's value in and to families. Getting students to describe how women are described often shows, despite their apparent demeaning form, the significance of women in resource and labour terms. Some references to girls and women are that they are 'cattle in the kraal',[16] 'cheap labour' or 'the mother of my children'. At one level these are pejorative comments which point to how women are regarded by their partners or spouses. In some instances they may be jocular but still retain a demeaning connotation. Yet, hidden within them is implicit recognition of the women's contributions and particularly their reproductive capacity. A counter and quite dismissive statement with regard to a man is: 'he is a good provider'[17] which often conceals a lack of continued emotional involvement but carries the recognition that he is adequate for some purposes, namely access to and provision of financial or material resources. Conversely there is growing frustration with the failure of many men to provide adequately or contribute to the maintenance of the family even during the subsistence of a relationship. Many women are the major contributors towards the maintenance of the family but this is inadequately reflected in the division of matrimonial assets at divorce.

Students are also alerted to the need to consider the role of women as access points and conduits, required by men to acquire rights or status. One notable southern and eastern African phenomenon is that to access land within ethnic groupings, a man needs to be married. Perceiving the significance of women in such situations becomes important in reconceptualizing women's access to rights and entitlements.[18] Thus whenever men's rights and entitlements are being probed, a complementary investigation into how women may effect the creation and transfer of such rights and entitlements should be undertaken (Stewart, 1998). In grasping the nature and significance of these issues we need to understand the plural forces that shape rights, duties and obligations within families.

> NOTE
> **Conditional rights to land?**
>
> In concentrating on the constraints that many women face in accessing resources, it is easy to overlook some of the restrictions that men might face.
>
> For example, if you ask the simple question: 'What qualifies a man to acquire land within family structures and entitlements? The typical response is: he needs to be married!'

---

[16] This is a reference to *lobola* payments where for the girl or woman's family bridewealth nominally in the form of cattle in some groupings within the regions will be transferred from her marital family to her natal family as compensation for the loss of her services and their projected reproductive and productive labour value to her marital family.

[17] The editor made the very pertinent comment that perhaps this is not widely applicable, I must confess that it is a *murungu* statement and one that dates from the 1970s and 1980s when I was engaging with mothers of small children who were not employed outside the home at that time. I was employed at the time and family expenses were shared between my husband and I. Whereas the women I refer to were not employed and were dependent on their husbands for their own and their children's support.

[18] This links back to the explorations and discussions on research methodologies in chapter 2.

Harking back to the first assignment in the methodology course, students are urged to consider practices and rituals – and especially sexed and gendered differentials between males and females – at births, puberty, weddings, funerals and associated activities and other family ceremonies (see chapter 2).

The importance of capturing and analyzing widows and women's experiences in relation to death, such as mourning practices and the impact of mourning practices on women's inheritance rights and entitlements, is emphasized. There are social realities that form no part of formal state laws which nonetheless deeply influence social outcomes. See Stewart and Ncube (1995) for a general elaboration on this.

Which women? Where?

We often overlook the reality that women may compete with each other for access to resources through men or even through other women. Women are wives, mothers, grandmothers, daughters, daughters-in-law, sisters and aunts and, for women, these roles may create conflicting duties and obligations. What a woman thinks and does from the perspective of a sister protecting her brother's interests may be very different from how she thinks and acts as a wife or mother, mother-in-law or sister-in-law.

EXAMPLE
Family hierarchies

When family ceremonies such as weddings and funerals are conducted in Shona society, a daughter-in-law (*muroora*) is expected to provide labour in cooking, serving and generally taking care of the needs of guests, especially men.

In a strictly traditional setting, a *muroora* is expected to cook and clean for her mother-in-law, as part of her induction into the marital family (Stewart and Ncube, 1997a). Each new daughter-in-law takes on the role in turn but these hierarchies would once have determined a woman's status with regard to her sisters-in-law and especially her mother-in-law.

Where families lived in close proximity to each other across generations in an agricultural setting, a woman's status and position was largely dictated by the age and status of her husband.

One is inclined, from a western perspective, to assume that female relationships are not mediated in the same way. A little introspection and personal experiential recall reveals that there are similar hierarchies that mediate the lives of women wherever they are situated. As Tove Bolstad shows in her research on wives on Norwegian farms, women are frequently the source of fulfillment for male contracts to which they are not direct parties (Bolstad, 2007).

Changes in power structures within families and the impact of changes in economic opportunities between different classes of women in the same family can create or fuel generational conflicts between women. Younger, educated women and those who have new economic opportunities can be seen as a threat to older women whose status and power depended on their building up social capital in their families – both marital and natal. Our students are especially well placed to undertake such analysis as they are able to exploit their skills and knowledge to improve their position and status in a family.

Changes in social, economic and professional status of women in recent years has created a situation where a woman with financial independence can reduce the amount of physical labour she needs to contribute at family gatherings, such as weddings and funerals, through her monetary and other contributions. Students who are asked to invoke experiential data from their own lives begin to appreciate that professional and financially independent women can assert power within families regardless of social, cultural or ethnic origins.

Discussions with students in class reveal the extent to which many of them have already exploited their financial power and their status outside the family to re-negotiate what is expected of them as a woman within the family. One approach that might be taken by those with financial capacity is to engage the services of other women, such as catering groups, to undertake the preparation and serving of food. However, she will still need to perform some of the functions from the past such as serving food. Employing other women to perform household activities, such as cooking and cleaning, providing child care and care of the elderly, is another way in which women are able to use their access to resources and employment skills to change the pattern of traditional expectations of women. Examining how women are translating and adapting older practices to meet their current situations is an interesting investigation into how practices evolve within families and communities.

Such women may find that disapproving attitudes towards their in-dependence and 'flouting' of women's traditional subservient roles are bolstered by actors beyond the family. Women's social situations and status are areas that are strongly contested within various religious groupings. Women who have independent financial means and status in employment are often exhorted to leave such power at the door of the matrimonial home (Mate, 2002). The church officials may also try to get them to subdue their often assertive behaviour so as to maintain the image of the good and submissive woman, especially within their marital families.

> **EXAMPLE**
> **Challenging power**
>
> One female student of Shona origin related how, having paid for the food provided at a funeral and helping to cook it with other women, she then told them that the women would eat before the men. The older women protested that the men should be served first. She insisted they eat and the men barely noticed. She had decided to defy so-called tradition as an experiment.

Examining how women are translating and adapting older practices to meet their current situations is an interesting investigation into how practices evolve within families and communities

Finding assessment criteria and tools

Women in the African context are routinely portrayed as oppressed and the poorest of the poor and most marginalized but this is not universally so. There are many women who have remoulded and reshaped their lives within traditional social contexts so that they meet both external demands and internal family criteria for acceptance. It is often these women and how they have managed their lives, regardless of where they are situated, that we need to study. Studying them helps to reveal the strategies they use to alter the trajectory of their lives but the tendency is to study sites of deprivation and marginalization. Rather, both should be considered appropriate for study.

Using a sex and gender aware filter to identify a focal area to which the interrogations can be directed is the next step. As the exercise for the seminars and submission indicates, the interrogations to be carried out cover more or less the same affective factors (details about this exercise process are given in the next section of this chapter). Overarching topics that groups have in the past chosen include, 'Girls and access to education' (CEDAW, article 10; Protocol, article 12) and 'Women and access to health' (CEDAW article 12; Protocol, article 14).

The number of topics depends on the size of the class. The topics above would probably yield around five to six deep sub-issues. These would then become the entrance points through which the role of the family, social realities and law can be explored. Hopefully, they will enable determinations of how the family and other family-like social relations affect women and girls' capacities to access and use rights and entitlements. Using a human rights based comparator allows for strategic comparisons to be made between countries in the region on human rights compliance and also to assess the steps that need to be taken at national level to ensure compliance with human rights imperatives. Significantly, in conducting such analysis students are quick to note the inter-relatedness and indivisibility of rights in general and how one cannot isolate rights from each

---

EXAMPLE

Education and health issues and cut-throughs

- **Political will**: Is there will within the parliament to pass or implement legislation giving women rights in the field under discussion?

- **Family attitudes**: Is the family prepared and willing to facilitate women accessing the rights being discussed?

- **National gender budgeting**: Is their awareness of the need to provide the resources to carry out whatever is required to improve girls and women's access to education or to health facilities nationwide?

- **Benefiting from rights and entitlements**: Are service providers aware of the time and other constraints on the lives of women and girls which may adversely affect their capacity to beneficially access rights and entitlements?

- **Religious constraints**: Is there collusion between families and religion that result in denying girls the right to assert their legal entitlements to attend or to continue in school or to access health services?

other when investigating and analyzing entitlements, compliance and access to resources.

Interesting cut-throughs, which could equally apply to both education and health, become the basis of individual presentations regardless of topic (see box on page 250).

Yes, this is still about families and women's experiences in families and other social relationships. Legal, economic and policy change does not take place within a vacuum; there is little point in arguing for a dramatic improvement in women and girls' access to education or legislating to create equal opportunity for girls and boys in school if there is lack of awareness of the need to educate girls and lack of commitment from families for girls to be educated. On a supervision visit to Uganda in 2009 Dr Amy Tsanga noted that a number of girls in rural areas had never attended school. This surprised her given the general appreciation of the value of educating girls in Zimbabwe.[19] Further, even where there is awareness of such need it may be frustrated if the national budgets are not sensitive to what has to be undertaken to realize such objectives.

EXAMPLE
Clinic attendance

The times for clinic attendance for pregnant women to receive antenatal check-ups are usually designed to facilitate the clinic or clinic personnel's needs rather than those of the women. While this might not pose problems for an urban woman who has physical mobility and relatively short commuting distances, it is likely to present problems for rural women who have long distances to travel and many family chores and responsibilities.

At one clinic in a rural area in Zambia, where women's commutes were long and arduous, the clinic imposed a punishment on women who missed antenatal clinics. Such clinics commenced around nine o'clock in the morning. Women who failed to attend, if they later reappeared, were expected to sweep and clean the yard and premises of the clinic. The clinic manager thought this a fair 'punishment' but was somewhat puzzled that women's attendance was steadily declining – the reason seemed obvious. Why one might ask were such women being punished?

The underlying problem was his failure to grasp the complexities of women's lives and the multiple tasks they needed to complete for and within the family before departing for the clinic. Imposing a punishment that would take up even more of their time seemed to be especially counter-productive.

---

[19] Although there are still instances where girls do not attend school or are withdrawn from school after grade 7.

Families, despite enabling legal provisions, may not have the resources to educate all family members. Absence of schools in close proximity to where the family is situated may adversely affect their position on sending girls to school. Not because they are resistant to girls' education but because they feel a need to balance issues of her safety against sending her a long distance to school in what they consider risky circumstances for her sexual integrity. Such concerns about her sexual integrity may not be altruistic but predicated on her value as a virgin at the time of her marriage.

Similarly, cultural and religious views may militate against women obtaining antenatal medical care. Women's medical needs may not be prioritized within the family or a woman may dismiss her own need for medical treatment, prioritizing the needs of other family members.

Students cull issues largely from their own experiences either within family, social and religious settings or from what they have observed or been involved in at the workplace.

Families and social realities always change – de-centring marriage

Families are mutating, perhaps dissolving and dissipating and thus family law as it once was may no longer be a core subject of concern in some countries. However, a course such as this, especially where the family itself is a key resource base, belies this approach. Where there is no welfare state, where individuals literally sink or swim on their own or can only rely on support within their social networks, the family – both nuclear and extended – remains at the centre of support and resource-based relationships.

Recognizing the shifting nature of relationships, whatever their connectors, informs the need to de-centre marriage as the legal basis of individual support obligations and entitlements. Whereas the right to marry is captured in the regional instruments, the right to found a family and the way in which law and society respond to the family, need to be re-assessed. Is marriage the basis on which this should be done?

Marriage is privileged, when in reality in legal terms it is merely contractual proof… of the obligations in most of our countries between a male and a female or a male and females

Much of what we do in the legal realm in supporting individuals is predicated on or privileges marriage relationships. We tend to mimic marriage in assigning responsibilities or assess entitlement by comparison with marriage. We measure responsibilities between men and women on the obligations created by marriage. Marriage is privileged, when in reality in legal terms it is merely contractual proof, established by the production of a marriage certificate, of the obligations in most of our countries between a male and a female or a male and females. This approach to the non-formal recognition of purely customary law (unregistered) marriages is juxtaposed with an ascertainment process as to what the emerging customary law norms are that would enable an appropriate ascertainment process. However, using an alternative approach of ascertaining the local recognition of the marriage or providing evidence of a socially recognized relationship may expose some women to internal family strategizing to exclude a claim, especially on the death of a family member.

Students are often shocked when marriage is described in such basic terms and delinked from the religious and emotional elements. Marriage can also be characterized as a means for the state or the community to assign care and support functions, imposing the burden of care on readily identifiable others – parents, spouses and other relatives. The existence of a marriage certificate linking the parties makes it easier to transfer and impose such obligations.

The existence of a marriage certificate … makes it easier to transfer and impose …obligations

Social recognition of marriage is an accepted route to establishing a relationship and is common in the regions our students come from. However, invoking social recognition may have different outcomes for women and men. Thus it is important to encourage students to draw distinctions between different recognition criteria and to consider what this means for men and women. For a woman, a marriage certificate is proof of obligations owed to her and a significant resource allocation and access route; for a man it is proof of obligations owed by him and there may be reluctance on the part of men to marry and take on such clear evidence of obligations he owes. Women will frequently complain that moving the relationship from one that might be described as customary or social to a registered marriage can be difficult or impossible as the man sees no need to do so. There is disparity between women and men's views of a formalized state marriage certificate and the benefits it brings.

This then raises significant issues for rights campaigners who understand the legal benefit to women of a registered marriage but meet with male resistance. Realistically it is not women who determine whether there will be a marriage but men. Women are often bereft of bargaining power in such situations and remain in tenuous relationships even where there are multiple wives because of their proximity to and access to resources otherwise not obtainable or so they may perceive it.

There is also a need to examine the clash between legal rights and women's lived realities as to what they can pursue in matters of divorce, custody and guardianship of children. Issues such as who can divorce whom culturally mediate women's courses of action. Put differently: what is socially acceptable? Women may also feel the need to strategize around matters of custody and sharing of assets. Abandoning some claims so as to create a better climate for negotiating custody rights over children may favour women who are challenging social preference for males to be given custody. One might put this crudely as children versus resources.

EXERCISE

Brainstorming session and seminars: Women, family, social realities and the law

Stage 1

The issue generation and consideration process is operationalized by the following classroom exercise:

1   We will start outside the law in our own understandings (assumptions) of women's lived realities and try to identify, through a morning-long brainstorming session, social realities that seem to affect women's use of human rights initiatives and formal legal remedies.

2   We will also explore ways of identifying and unpacking the form and content of customary value systems and customary laws. In particular we will seek to identify cultural, customary law, economic and social factors which indicate that human rights can be reconceptualized for women and the girl child within the overall social, economic and political structure of eastern and southern African nations.

3   We will conclude the morning exercise by parcelling out topics which can then be cut through on the basis of the issues identified as follows for group seminar presentations.

Stage 2

Each of the identified groups (4–5 people) will organize and conduct a morning seminar in which each member of the group presents and leads a part of the discussion.

We will try and identify these key sections of the discussion in class. However, they will probably cover the following issues, among others:

●   **A description** of the perceived factor/s, across a number of eastern and southern African countries;

●   **Assumptions** about its/their impact on women and the girl child's engagement with human rights and state law;

●   **Assumptions** about how the identified factors can be unpacked, analyzed and used as the basis for engagement with law reformers, ordinary individuals, social entities and society at large – so a holistic approach to the whole process is required;

●   **Tentative suggestions** about actual law and policy reforms, re-engagement with human rights bodies on redesign/reform of international instruments;

●   **Ideas** about developing national awareness and rights promotion campaigns to counteract the problems that have been identified and to promote new measures and laws.

Assessment is out of 15 for each participant – you will submit your facilitation materials for evaluation. You may use Powerpoint overheads, flipcharts, printed summaries, posters, stick-up cards – whatever you need to facilitate your part of the sessions. Creativity and innovation and engaging methods are especially welcome.

Children can become a legal battleground where the best interests of the child are subverted in the battle between the parents. There is always a need to ensure that students are aware of the risks of the non consent or consent paper in a divorce. Many students on the course have been magistrates or worked in legal advice roles in non-governmental organizations or government agencies and thus it is important they appreciate the need to deal with each case in a non-formulaic manner and use the full scope of the law when dealing with such matters. One has to constantly warn against the risk of taking the view that this is a standard approach and that therefore it must be 'okay'.

Women may also find that they experience significant cultural pressures over children and it is not unknown for threats of spirit-based revenge to be raised against their attempts to obtain custody or guardianship of children. At all levels of the judiciary, unless there has been awareness training and dialogue about women and children's rights, the best interests of the child might not be realized.

The course is as much about the social arena, perhaps more so, than it is about the law and rights. An understanding of the social arena is important for implementation and individual use of laws and to inform law reform and the strategies for its implementation (see chapter 2 – last page). That is the background against which students are asked to consider the situations in which women find themselves within the ambit of family, marriage, mimicked marriage or other determinative social settings. As will be seen from the final exercise, in this course students are required to go beyond the identification process and try and provide a holistic research and action plan to tackle the problems woman and girls face in relation to the social realities canvassed. The programme is nothing if not ambitious.

The course is as much about the social arena, perhaps more so, than it is about the law and rights.

Brainstorming sessions raise a variety of cut-through issues which are then divided into group work to be presented later in the week. Each student is expected to present a specialist component of the overall topic decided upon, although discussions normally precede this on a group basis (see exercise box on page 254).

The last bit – research design

The final part of this course is similar to that undertaken in the 'Women, commerce and law in Africa' course where students set about doing a research design or research proposal on a specific topic usually derived from their part of the group presentation. The design template is the same as that used in the research exercise undertaken at the end of the first semester (see chapter 4 on the practical course).[20]

For each student the emphasis becomes how they would tackle this in their home countries, although postulating and addressing a regional comparative research would not be ruled out. It must be remembered that this is not research to be carried out but a way of helping the students appreciate the research needs that are there and how to formulate an appropriate design. An assessment of existing laws, in all their pluralities, as well as relevant human rights provisions is also required. It is not beyond the bounds of possibility that some students might take up the challenge their research design presents and undertake it for their dissertation. If they do so, far greater refinement of the design and its ambit would usually be required.

Underlying this exercise is building the students' capacity to identify an area of research that needs to be undertaken, to consider the various components of such research and to produce an effective and implementable research design.

Initially Professor Anne Griffiths from the University of Edinburgh undertook this component of the course but when it was mothballed for various reasons she transferred to the 'Women, commerce and law in Africa' course, carrying out a similar exercise. If the course is resurrected in the 2011/12 programme as hoped, I will do these last two weeks of the course, a prospect that I relish. It takes me back to the heady days of the Women and Law in Southern Africa Research Trust research where I gained and honed so many of my own research skills.

---

[20] It should be noted that normally these two courses are taken in the first block of the second semester courses so always clash.

Bibliography

Armstrong A. *et al.* (1993) 'Uncovering reality: excavating women's rights in African family law', *International Journal of Law and the Family* 7(1993): 314-369.

Bonthuys E. (2010) 'Legal capacity and family status in child-headed households: challenges to legal paradigms and concepts', *International Journal of Law in Context* 6:45–62, available online at http://journals.cambridge.org/action/displayFulltext?type=1&fid=7282684&jid=IJC&volumeId=6&issueId=01&aid=7282676.

Bolstad T. (2007) 'Kår contracts in Norway: agreements made by men concerning women's work, ownership and lives' in A. Hellum *et al.*(eds), *Human rights, plural legalities and gendered realities: paths are made by walking*, Weaver Press, Harare.

Chanock, M. (1985) *Law, custom and social order. The colonial experience in Malawi and Zambia*, Cambridge University Press, Cambridge.

Hellum A. *et al.* (2007) 'Introduction' in A. Hellum *et al.* (eds), *Human rights, plural legalities and gendered realities: paths are made by walking*, Weaver Press, Harare.

Himonga C. (1995) *Family and succession laws in Zambia: development since independence*, Lit Verlag, Münster.

– (2004) Transforming customary law of marriage in South Africa and the challenge of its implementation with specific reference to matrimonial property', *International Journal of Legal Information* 32(2):260–270, official publication of the International Association of Law Libraries.

– (2010) 'State and individual perspectives of a mixed legal system in Southern African contexts with special reference to personal law', *Tulane European and Civil Law Forum* (2010) 25: 23-36.

Mate R. (2002) 'Wombs as God's laboratories: Pentecostal discourses of femininity in Zimbabwe', *Africa* 72 (4) 2002:449–567.

Ncube W. and J. Stewart *et al.* (1997a) *Continuity and change. The family in Zimbabwe*, WLSA, Harare.

– (1997b) *Paradigms of exclusion: women's access to resources in Zimbabwe*, WLSA, Harare.

Stewart J.E. and W. Ncube (eds) (1995) *Widowhood, inheritance laws, customs and practices in southern Africa*, WLSA, Harare.

Stewart J.E. (1998) 'Rights, rights, rights: women's rights', in P. Blume and K. Ketscher (eds) *Ret og skonsomhed i en overgangstid*, Akademisk Forlag, Copenhagen.

Wiggins cited by L. Harvey and D. Green (1993) 'Defining quality', *Assessment and Evaluation in Higher Education* 18(1): 9-34.

THEME

THREE

Power relations and transformation

10

Men, gender and law

Investigating the links between masculinity, gender and power

Victor Nkiwane

'The very processes that confer privilege to one group and not another are often invisible to those upon whom that privilege is conferred... men have come to think of themselves as genderless, in part because they can afford the luxury of ignoring the centrality of gender... Invisibility reproduces inequality. And invisibility of gender to those privileged by it reproduces the inequalities that are circumscribed by gender.'

Kimmel, 1993:30

'It is generally the case that the powerful have little reason to reflect on their position in society, for the most part tending to treat their position as normal, just or inevitable. This is true whether we are thinking of class, race, ethnicity or gender.'

Morgan, 1992:3

This chapter draws on experiences of teaching the course on masculinities and the law, to investigate the links between masculinity, gender and power relations. Before outlining these experiences, I highlight, albeit briefly, some of the realities that have given rise to contemporary concerns about masculinity.

As the two quotes above suggest, struggles for equality between women and men remain an area of continuing and critical relevance to any quest for a holistic understanding of economics, society, culture, politics and law in the contemporary world. However, a persistent and general assumption remains, even in otherwise knowledgeable sections of society, that any reference to gender is merely a code word for concerns that are specific to the interests of women. An inevitable consequence of such thinking is that gender is therefore unimportant or irrelevant to men. For example, I witnessed this attitude vividly on one occasion on 9 August, Women's Day in South Africa, in the small town of Ladybrand. Several people, mostly men, attempted to enter Standard Bank only to realize that it was closed. Most looked puzzled and some looked at their watches and mumbled in annoyance. Out of concern, I informed a group of four men that the bank was closed because it was Women's Day and a public holiday. One of them then shouted to some men across the street in *Sesotho*.[1] 'He says it is closed because it is a holiday for women!' The rest of the men then laughed, in a manner which suggested that they found it funny that there was such a holiday at all.

Jeff Hearn observes that:

> 'For many centuries, men, masculinity and men's powers and practices were generally taken for granted; gender was largely seen as a matter of and for women; men were generally seen as ungendered, "natural" or naturalized' (Hearn, 2007:13).

Given the above conceptions about men, women and gender, it is not surprising that until recently (in the 1970s in the west and as late as the 1990s in southern Africa) men have not been a subject of serious inquiry. The tendency has been to isolate specific aspects of masculinity and present them as common and universal (Morrell, 2001). This view, which has been dominant until recently, tended to obscure the reality that there is diversity within and among men. Instead, we have been made to believe and accept that certain forms of behaviour are essentially for men (and women) and that this distinction must be kept, pure and simple. We have seen, for example, the constructions of maleness that tend to put a premium on men's ostentatious heterosexuality, virility and promiscuity, their control of emotions and their acquisition and exercise of power (Epprecht, 1998:119).[2] Men who fail to meet these ideals are seen as feminine and weak, and are called all sorts of derogatory names.

...we have been made to believe and accept that certain forms of behaviour are essentially for men (and women) and that this distinction must be kept pure and simple

While there are clearly variations in dealing with the question of men in feminist discourses and standpoints, some, such as radical feminism, have tended to lump all men in one basket – seeing them all as oppressive (Reid and Walker, 2005:7).[3] The limitations of such views on and about men have become evident. This course seeks to show that there is diversity rather than homogeneity among men and that there is no typical man. Further, the course emphasizes that masculinity is not fixed for all time but is subject to changes as society changes. This has naturally led us to focus on masculinities in the study of gender relations.

Morrell has identified two fundamental reasons why we should study masculinity. First, we need to identify and explore the different forms in which masculinity, as a collective social form, is expressed in our society. This

---

[1] This is one of the languages spoken in South Africa and also in Lesotho.

[2] Nowhere is this more evident than in how the media depicts particular forms of masculinity.

[3] Men were situated as part of the problem – the abuser, the oppressor, the patriarch

enables us to investigate how masculinity is implicated in gender inequalities and how masculinities change. The second reason '… is to widen debates about gender and to promote a rethinking of masculinity which offers new ways of imagining masculinity and, for men, suggests new ways of being a man' (Morrell, 2001: xiv).

The call by Morrell places masculinity on the agenda in the study of law and gender relations. It is only when we understand how different masculinities are formed and how they change over time that we can effectively influence changes towards equal relations between men and women.

Part I: Contextualizing the course and its objectives

This course was initially entitled 'Men, gender and law: a masculinity perspective' and has since been shortened to 'Masculinities, gender and the law'. Regardless of the old or new title, it is not surprising to see eyebrows raised when such a course title is pitted against the other courses in the women's law programme. However, there are many good reasons why such a course is both necessary and complementary to the broad women's law objectives.

It is now generally accepted within feminist scholarship that emphasis on women's legal rights and the gap between rights and reality in women's lives is a skewed approach to women's legal needs. Also, many African women's rights activists discovered in the 1980s that at the grassroots level, male involvement was pertinent if women were to truly ever enjoy their legal rights (Tsanga, 2003).

In order to understand women's legal position, there is a need to examine male paradigms and male attitudes and explore effective ways in which to develop balanced sex and gender paradigms. For this reason the course seeks to develop analytical and research tools to explore the impact of male attitudes and male paradigms in the quest for equality between women and men.

In order to understand women's legal position, there is a need to examine male paradigms and male attitudes and explore effective ways in which to develop balanced sex and gender paradigms

While emphasis in the past has been put on the legal rights of women as enshrined in the international, regional and, in some cases, national human rights instruments, little has been achieved in realizing women's legal rights as men have maintained their dominance over women. This is because 'the relationships between men and women and society are not simply ones of difference (in which case one might expect two different parallel histories) but of inequalities in terms of power' (Morgan, 1992:29). The power difference is caused by several factors among which the major one is the social construction whereby men are socialized to dominate over women. 'All individuals who are identified as "men" are assumed to have some essential set of characteristics which are in some ways profoundly anchored to that title' (Morgan, 1992:41). Such an essentialist approach has led to a process of developing men with traits/

attributes that enhance and sustain patriarchy. For a long time this hegemonic[4] masculinity has been accepted as the norm, not only by men but by women as well, to the extent that a man who displays contrary traits is termed a 'woman'. Conversely a woman who displays male attributes in terms of providing financial and material support to her family attracts some admiration and is often referred to as a man. Acceptance of hegemonic masculinity 'means that over a large number of areas, men are taken as the norm, from which women are seen to deviate' (Morgan, 1992:29).

Since masculinity has found its way into all spheres of life – legal, religious, economic, social, political and cultural – we also need to focus on men in addressing gender issues. To achieve equality between women and men, a holistic and multisectoral approach is needed. The theory of different masculinities developed in Connell's (1995) seminal work and other authorities, provides entry points in deconstructing dominant masculinities and institutions of patriarchy and re-orienting them to embrace, accept, integrate and enhance rights of women, children and other groups 'subordinate' to men.

OBJECTIVES

The objectives of the course are as follows:

- To show the connection between studying and understanding issues of masculinity and those of gender and law;

- To identify important areas where masculinity is constructed and gender power exercised;

- To understand, through the lens of masculinity, how gender inequalities develop and are sustained, and how power is exercised by men over women;

- To understand that masculinity is not a fixed essential identity which all men have;

- To examine the role of law and other non-formal regulatory systems (custom, convention, tradition, social practice) in creating and maintaining 'desirable' masculinities and the suppression of 'undesirable' ones. Further, to understand how law and these non-formal systems can be used to effect changes in masculinities and gender relations;

- To articulate the significance of heteronormativity in the construction and maintenance of particular hegemonic masculinities;

- To explain why issues of masculinity need to be taken seriously in the quest for gender equality and how men can be incorporated in such endeavours in a positive way.

---

[4] The concept of hegemonic masculinity is addressed in the next section of this chapter.

This process may make the emergence of a 'new man'[5] possible – one who believes and embraces principles of equality, non-discrimination, fairness and human dignity of the sexes and other gender groups.

For the above reasons, the course is predicated on gender as a relationship and it sets out to examine constructions of masculinity and their impact on gender relationships. It explores the role of law and other social regulatory mechanisms (custom, convention, family, tradition, and so on) in shaping and maintaining particular gender relationships that are based on masculine constructions. The course further seeks to explore how an understanding of masculinity can contribute to addressing gender inequalities.

To facilitate a more 'advanced' take-off for the masculinities course as an optional elective in the second semester, an introductory four-hour session (spread over two days) is now a compulsory element of the first semester.

The course ... seeks to explore how an understanding of masculinity can contribute to addressing gender inequalities

Teaching method and methodology

In this context, the term 'methodology' is used to refer to 'the actual logic of social inquiry within particular paradigms', for example, positivism, marxism, and the various feminist theories. On the other hand, 'method' refers to the ways in which knowledge is gathered, imparted or shared.

Although the course is about men and masculinities, a deliberately pro-feminist approach is taken and no apology is made for that. This is because the course does not advocate for 'men's studies' as a counterpart to feminism.[6] Our contention is that a focus on masculinity is a logical and necessary next step in advancing feminist scholarship (Epprecht, 1998:135).[7] Such an approach helps us understand why patriarchy and other hierarchies that oppress women are so resilient and continue to be produced at all levels of gender relations from generation to generation.

In line with the established SEARCWL tradition, classes are interactive and the conventional lecturing method is deliberately avoided. Students are assigned and required to read a 'course pack' in advance and discuss the materials in class. In addition, we conduct exercises where students discuss issues in groups and report back in class, as illustrated later in this chapter.

---

[5] Debates about the 'new men' are fascinating and controversial. We address them later.

[6] 'Men's studies' is a diverse field and within it there are pro-feminist and anti-sexist scholars and advocates but there are also within it movements which feel threatened by the current worldwide movements and policies towards gender equality and have positioned themselves to counter developments either as individuals or as groups.

[7] Early feminist work was overwhelmingly concerned with women's experiences and history and how patriarchy maintained men's dominance over women. However, later feminist analyses have raised new questions about men as bearers of privilege in gender relations and how masculinities sustained this (Shefer, Ratele and Strebel, 2007: vii). It is precisely because of the success of feminism in this regard that theories of masculinities have developed.

Case studies based on current and topical issues and personalities have also proved useful. For example, the Zuma rape trial[8] provided sufficient material to expose how masculinity, especially the 'big man factor', can be used to the advantage of powerful men at the expense of women who dare to challenge them. In this case in particular, we had both men and women demonstrating daily outside the court during the trial baying for the complainant's blood for daring to take Zuma (seen as the future president of the African National Congress and the country) to court for the alleged rape. At the end of the trial, in which Zuma was controversially acquitted, some would argue, the complainant had to be placed under the state witness protection programme and sent overseas for her safety. Zuma went on to become the president of his party and country despite being tainted by such serious allegations.

However, subsequent to the acquittal, Julius Malema, the president of the African National Congress Youth League, another powerful figure in South African politics, took centre stage on the case when he made a public statement to the effect that the complainant had not been raped but instead had enjoyed a night of sex with Zuma because a woman who has been raped does not ask for breakfast and money for transport in the morning. He has since been dragged before the Equality Court by Sonke Gender Justice Links[9] and found guilty of making statements that were discriminatory and that denigrated women: it was considered hate speech which violated the constitution. He was fined R50,000 but he is currently appealing the decision. The Zuma rape trial case is thus a classic example of how dangerous it can be for a woman to challenge the 'big man'.

An important and critical method we have used successfully is 'life histories'. Students explore their personal histories and experiences and how masculinity has affected their lives. My colleague Robert Morrell[10] has had a huge impact on the students in dealing with masculinity and fatherhood using this method. This is a sensitive and sometimes emotional topic for most of the students as it challenges issues which they have taken for granted and considered 'natural' in the way in which fathers relate to families. I call it the 'crying session' because many students tend to break down when they talk about their fathers! More importantly, we examine how the law constructs fatherhood and the role of fathers in the family.

SEMINAR TOPIC
Exploring fatherhood

- *'The problem with the modern constructions of fatherhood and parental masculinity is that they are still rooted in the public/ private dichotomy. A full understanding of fatherhood is not possible without breaking down this public/ private divide'* (adapted from Collier, 1995).

Critically examine the above assertions in the light of how the law has constructed fatherhood.

---

[8] *S v Zuma* 2006(2)SACR191(W)
[9] Sonke Gender Justice Links is a South African organization of men that advocates for equality, focusing mainly on gender violence.
[10] Formerly Senior Professor in the Faculty of Education, University of Kwa-Zulu Natal. Robert has been a friend, mentor and co-lecturer on the course.

Another useful and effective teaching method is giving students seminar topics to research and present and then they critique each other. Marks are awarded for class participation and seminar presentations in addition to the long essay (5,000 words) they write. Each student generally makes one oral and one written seminar presentation. It is interesting to find the students honestly evaluating each other's performances during presentations.

A positive aspect about class participation is that it allows students to bring in their work and personal experiences and to relate them to the theories under discussion. The discussions are exciting, heated at times, but relevant. It is obvious that students learn better if there is more interaction among them.

Part II: Theoretical framework: understanding masculinity and its place in gender relations

In this section of the course, we spend time unpacking and addressing the concept of masculinity or masculinities as this forms a critical foundation to the course. The term masculinity is not easy to define as it varies in history, time and space. However, as a working definition, we define masculinity as:

> '...the ideals and codes of behaviours by which men define themselves as men. Masculinity is what makes men socially (as opposed to biologically) distinguishable from boys and women. It sets out for mature male-bodied people what their proper relations with other people should be, including what they may or may not say, feel, wear, and do, when they may appropriately laugh, cry, propose love and so on' (Epprecht, 1998:118-9).

From the definition it is clear that masculinity is socially constructed and as such, dynamic.[11]

The most coherent and consistent account of masculinity is found in the work of the Australian sociologist, Connell. She demonstrated that gender is a concept of power and as such 'being a man conferred power' which has been used to subordinate women (Connell, 1987). Individual men each enjoyed the 'patriarchal dividend', the advantage men in general gain from the overall subordination of women (Connell, 1995:79). From this point, power inequalities between men and women can be noted. In addition, based on the sex/gender differences, there is a division of labour where certain roles have been ascribed and associated with women and others with men. However, Connell went further and showed that although being a man conferred power, not all men shared this power equally and not all men were individually exploitative (Morrell, 2001:7).

...as a working definition, we define masculinity as: '...the ideals and codes of behaviours by which men define themselves as men...

---

[11] However, this is still an issue of intense debate and the influence of socio-biological theories is strong. For a summary and critique of socio-biological theories, see Connell (2002:ch 3).

In *Masculinities*, Connell developed the theory of different masculinities where she argued that while men oppressed and exploited women, some men dominated and subordinated other men. Under this theory, Connell observed four different categories of masculinities. First, there is hegemonic masculinity, which refers 'to the cultural dynamic by which a group claims and sustains a leading position in social life' (Connell, 1995). Hegemonic masculinity is regarded as the norm and it allows for men's dominance over women and considers women, as well as men falling below the standards set by hegemonic masculinity, as the 'other'. Morrell points out that:

Hegemonic masculinity is regarded as the norm and it allows for men's dominance over women

> 'Hegemonic masculinity does not rely on brute force for its efficiency, but on a range of mechanisms which create a gender consensus that legitimizes the power of men' (Morrell, 2001:9).[12]

Secondly, Connell also identified three categories of non-hegemonic masculinities:

● *Subordinate* masculinities, which entail specific gender relations of dominance and subordination between groups of men within the overall framework of society. One significant group of men subject to subordination is that of homosexuals who are dominated by heterosexuals.

  In 1995, President Mugabe of Zimbabwe described homosexuals as 'behaving worse than dogs and pigs' (*The Herald*, 12 August 1995).[13]

● *Complicit* masculinities which refer to 'masculinities constructed in ways that realize the patriarchal dividend without the tensions or risks of being the frontline troops of patriarchy' (Connell, 1995).

● *Marginalized* masculinities which come in as a factor of the interplay between gender and other factors such as race, class and ethnicity. This is where certain attributes, activities and behaviours are associated with certain groups based on race and class, and in such situations, one race or ethnic group may see itself as dominant over and superior to the other.

Morrell (2001:7) states that subordinate, complicit and marginalized masculinities are those developed outside the corridors of power.

From the theory of masculinities developed by Connell and others after her, we are able to draw up some salient features about the nature and role of masculinities in gender relations, as follows:

---

[12] However hegemonic masculinity will not shy away from brute force to suppress deviant masculinities or crude laws and legislation, for example, prosecuting homosexuals, when threatened.

[13] Quoted in Phillips (1997). Even women who fall below the standards of hegemonic masculinity, such as lesbians, have not been spared. In South Africa, for example, there have been a number of reports of rape of lesbian women, purportedly to make them 'straight'.

1   Masculinities are socially constructed:
    'Masculinity is not inherited nor is it acquired in a one-off way. It is constructed in the context of class, race and other factors which are interpreted through the prism of age' (Morrell, 2001:8).

2   Masculinities are dynamic, changing based on context. They are fluid and constantly produced and reproduced within gender relations.

3   Not all men have the same masculinities; they vary from one individual to another. There is no one essential masculinity so current debates talk of a plurality of masculinities rather than a particular masculinity.[14]

    Connell (1995) cynically suggests that 'if we are to unproblematically take "all men" as an object of study perhaps the only thing they have in common is their penises.' However, in rejecting universalism in masculinity we need to guard against over-individualizing men. It would be an over-simplification to move from a rejection of universalism to the other extreme of saying 'men are all different or that all men are individuals' because we then lose sight of the fundamental point made by Connell that all men benefit from the 'patriarchal dividend' by virtue of being men.

ACTIVITY

Understanding masculinities in gender relations

Students have 20 minutes to identify key aspects of masculinity – what they understand by the question 'What should men be and do?' They each write their own list of attributes.

The class then compiles a joint list and divides into groups of three to discuss the attributes, focusing on differences within the group about what are and are not appropriate attributes of masculinity and, more importantly, why they are inappropriate.

A number of issues should be kept in mind: the place of sexuality, work, family, body, race, class, age, leisure time use, health, friends, organizational affiliation, and relationship with women.

Careful attention should be given to:

–   Different understandings of appropriate forms of masculinity

–   How the behaviour and actions described would be viewed if women were responsible for them.

---

[14] Analyzing the men's different responses to the challenges to hegemonic masculinity is an important part of class discussions because it addresses crucial questions, for example, can men change? Can men be genuine partners in the fight for gender equality?

4   There are crisis tendencies in power relations and these tend to threaten hegemonic masculinities directly and this brings out multiple reactions. Morrell (2001) has identified three categories of these reactions: reactive or defensive, accommodating and responsive or progressive.

5   Emotional relations focus on the heterosexual:
    '…in the established gender order, the investment in emotional relations is organized through the heterosexual couple. This is the taken for granted meaning of "love" in popular culture and it has massive institutional support' (Connell, 1995:90).

Men who enter into gay relationships are seen as deviants who undermine genuine masculinity. Over and above this, feminism and 'gayism' are seen as waging war on traditional masculinity.

6   Masculinity is associated with providing financial security, as Connell explains, 'in relation to production, masculinity has come to be associated with being the bread-winner' (1995:90). This understanding of masculinity has far-reaching implications in constructing gender relations. It brings pressure and challenges to men who are unable to meet the requirements of a 'bread-winner masculinity'. The emergence of women in the workplace and as heads of households and bread-winners puts into question the whole concept of traditional masculinity (see Silberschmidt, 2005).

7   Inequalities exist between men and women and between men and other men in all spheres of life; there are power imbalances in who has access, control and ownership over resources and benefits and there is discrimination against women and non-hegemonic masculinities.

These salient points about the nature of masculinities must be kept in mind as we attempt to theorize about the relationship between masculinity, law and gender in the next section.

KEY POINTS
Discussing masculinity and gender relations

In theorizing the relationship between masculinity, law and gender we pay attention to the following:

● Different categories of masculinities

● Nature and role of masculinities
  – Their social construction
  – Their dynamic nature
  – The crisis in power relations that threatens masculinities
  – The dominance of traditional masculinities in gender relations
  – The association of masculinities with bread-winning
  – Inequalities between men and women and between men and men

Part III: Masculinity and law

It is now impossible to keep pace with books and articles that are being produced on men and masculinities. However, law has been notable in its reluctance to contribute to studies on men and masculinities. As Richard Collier points out, amongst this proliferating literature addressing masculinity '…it is curious that there are few texts which take as the specific object of study the relationship between masculinity and the law' (Collier, 1995).[15] This gap is unfortunate because law is an absolutely fundamental aspect of gender relations and gendering of men and masculinities.

It is necessary to explain the absence of men (or the nature of the masculine presence) in legal discourse. In addressing this issue, we need to take note of the feminist caution that 'masculinity is everywhere – so how can it be absent?' (Collier, 1995:5). Dyer's (1985) answer is that 'it is like the air – you breathe it all the time but you aren't aware of it much.'

To begin to understand this paradox, we must address the dominant forms of legal scholarship in teaching and research in law. In the curricular of many law schools in the north and south, questions of masculinity and power are notable by their absence. Thus a student of criminal law, constitutional law, or family law, among others, will study such courses and graduate without knowing that these subjects are constructed from a masculinist standpoint. This may be so even where the student has been exposed to issues of gender and law. However, the treatment of gender and law in such instances invariably follows the time-honoured tradition of focusing on women. Thus, issues such as discrimination in the law, equality between men and women, the low numbers of women in the legal profession, unfair maternity leave provisions, and so on, will be routinely covered to show unfairness in the law in its treatment of men and women. 'Certain judicial statements may be highlighted by the lecturer perhaps to provoke outrage or humour (or both) amongst law students' (Collier, 1995:30).

In the curricular of many law schools in the north and south, questions of masculinity and power are notable by their absence

In the Zimbabwean context, the *Magaya v Magaya* case is a favourite amongst academics seeking to illustrate how interpretation of law and the constitution by Muchechetere JA (incorrectly one has to say) discriminated against women in intestate succession (see box on page 272). However, masculinity, which is at the heart of such judicial interpretation is usually either absent or at best only implicit in critiques of this unfortunate decision.

---

[15] This is probably the most comprehensive treatment of the relationship between masculinity, law and the family, a most critical institution in understanding the linkages between gender and masculinity.

CASE NOTES
Magaya v Magaya and succession

This is a case where Zimbabwe's highest court, the Supreme Court, reversed an earlier decision, *Chihowa v Mangwende*, where it had ruled that because of the enactment of the Legal Age of Majority Act, which made every child a major at the age of 18, the primogeniture rule which excluded female children from intestate succession was unconstitutional.

It followed that the oldest child, whether male or female, was the heir.

In the Magaya case, the same court made a u-turn and said its earlier decision was wrong as it undermined the very essence of customary inheritance – that property devolved through the male line.

Fortunately this decision was subsequently changed by legislation which now treats all children, whether male or female, equally in intestate succession

It is obvious from the foregoing that there is a fundamental problem. A pertinent reason for this is identified by Collier:

> '… in turning to theorize the relationship between masculinity and law one comes against an immediate problem – the widely held belief in the legal academy that masculinity and "law" are somehow incompatible subjects' (Collier, 1995:30).

The reason for this is that positivism still reigns supreme in legal scholarship and education. Any serious attempt to challenge this 'truth' about law carries a serious risk of excommunication from legal academia. The pervasive ideology is that attempts to include such issues as masculinity are incompatible with serious legal scholarship.

This attitude persists in spite of the generally accepted view by legal academics of all ideological persuasions that law is not a politically neutral institution.[16] A counterpart to this view has been the purported rejection of the 'black-letter' approach to legal education in most law schools. It is quite fashionable these days for law schools to claim that they teach law in its 'social context', whatever that means. We even have a series of legal publications called *Law in context*. However, the impact of such scholarship has remained limited as positivism somehow still holds a sway.[17]

Radical feminism has been prominent in this charge. In general, the argument put forward is that the law and state are inherently male, oppressive and embody a masculine 'world view' (Collier, 1995:21). The most vocal figure in this tradition is Catharine MacKinnon (1983: 635-644) who argues that 'the state is male in the feminist sense. The law sees and treats women the way men see and treat women'. She challenges the purported neutrality of the law and rejects the use of liberal law and institutions by women. She writes that:

---

[16] This rather sweeping claim is based on the fact that even doctrines like positivism, at least the modernized versions, accept this. See for example, Dworkin (1978).

[17] Rejection of positivism is only a first step. Unless one is able to see the gendered dimensions of the institutions of law, legal methods and practice, the enterprise is bound to fail.

'Once masculinity appears as a specific position, not just the way things are, its judgment will be revealed in process and procedure, as well as adjudication and legislation' (1983: 658).

She argues further that male dominance:

'...is perhaps the most pervasive and tenacious system of power in history...it is metaphysically nearly perfect. Its point of view is the standard for point-of-view-viewlessness, its particularity the means of universality.' (1983: 638-9).

MacKinnon has a significant following within feminist legal scholarship. There is no doubt that her views are crucial in helping us to understand the link between gender, law and masculinity. However, seeing all men as a homogeneous group and law as the embodiment of power of all men is problematic. This flies in the face of our earlier arguments that there are differences in masculinities. To see the state as simply male in terms of the form and content of its laws is rather simplistic. If this were true, how do we explain the many successes achieved by women, through the use of law and state institutions, in securing many of the rights they have been previously denied? MacKinnon herself achieved major success in spear-heading the development of laws against sexual harassment.

What conclusion can we draw from all this about law and masculinity? First, we must reject the traditional legal method and scholarship that seeks to silence and exclude gender from legal discourse. Secondly, we must seek alternative discourses, drawn from feminism. Thirdly, while recognizing the link between men, law and social power we must reject essentialism by seeing all men as the embodiment of law and state power.

Linking theory and practice

The most important objective of this course is to show the connection between studying and understanding issues of masculinity and those of gender and law and to show that the study of men and masculinity could be complementary to feminism and open new frontiers for the advancement of equality. It is intended to show that masculinity needs to be taken seriously in order to take the cause for gender equality a step further.

...the study of men and masculinity could be complementary to feminism and open new frontiers for the advancement of equality

Beyond theorizing about law and masculinity in the teaching of this course, we try to see how these theories are at play in practice. In particular, we analyze how specific laws give expression to particular masculinities.

In this part of the course we draw examples from different legal fields ranging from family law, criminal law, labour law and customary law and customs, to mention just a few. For example, in family law, the law's approach to custody and guardianship issues in many countries remains deeply gendered. The law may create interim custody arrangements favouring the mother on the separation of the parents but there are gendered preferences that may emerge at the time that formal divorce proceedings are heard. Mothers may be discouraged from pursuing custody rights over their children because of the inadequacy of maintenance provided for in the consent paper between the parties. A father's guardianship rights over children, even if he has proved to be a relatively ineffectual or non-supportive father are rarely curtailed or denied. Mothers are frequently confined to custody only which is a replication of the gendered conceptions of parenthood that mothers have daily care obligations but limited rights with regard to the overall management of children's futures.

Gendered awards of custody persist in relation to older children with mothers receiving custody of female children and fathers of male children. In situations where judicial officers' thinking is influenced by religious or cultural tenets even young children may be awarded to the father based on the notion that children 'belong' to the father.

Custody of teenage boys may be varied from mother to father based on the notion that a boy needs a male figure and a disciplinarian. A typical example of this approach was the South African case of *McCall v McCall* involving the variation of custody of a twelve year old boy from the mother to the father. In granting the order the judge boldly stated that boys as they grow older should be with their fathers – 'a well-established proposition'.[18] He went on to state that the boy in question was now 'ripe for his father' and that he needed the 'masculine environment, including the discipline that his father will provide'.

In cases involving allocation of property at divorce, in jurisdictions where courts have a discretion to re-allocate according to the contributions of the spouses, there has been a general reluctance to give adequate recognition to the contribution of the spouse who is the homemaker, usually the wife. Rarely will the courts award a half share to a spouse who was not economically active, regardless of the length of the marriage.

In criminal law, we see masculinity at play in the way in which rape is treated

In criminal law, we see masculinity at play in the way in which rape is treated and in the continued existence of the marital rape exemption in some jurisdictions in eastern and southern Africa. In spite of progressive legislation on the definition of rape and rape trials, the practice is that the woman who alleges rape is always viewed with suspicion. This goes a long way to explain the high attrition and low conviction rates in rape cases.

Other examples are drawn from customary law and customs and practices. Students are asked to give examples of specific customs that are masculine or undermine the rights of women. Common examples suggested by students are

---

[18] See at page 200

the practice of female circumcision in some parts of Africa, attitudes towards wife-beating and the treatment of male and female children within the African family setting.

Students should develop a critical appreciation of the importance of masculinity in analyzing gender relations. By the end of the course, all the students tend to appreciate this and report that they are better placed to use the knowledge gained in their workplaces and personal lives. For some, the course is a journey of personal discovery.

A great strength of this course is the students' ability to apply the theories and perspectives from the course to reality. Most draw this from both their personal and professional experiences. Part of this can be attributed to Robert Morrell's session on life histories. Another area of strength is the students' ability to offer possible and practical approaches to solving problems arising from the different expressions of masculinity. At the same time they are realistic enough to appreciate the difficulties of changing established behaviour based on patriarchy, custom, masculinity, and so on, as well as the limits of law.

For example, in one year, two male students felt that the course had 'changed' their lives and perceptions and they had become 'new men'. They left the course convinced that men, subject to various constraints and conditions, could play a significant role in addressing inequalities and that knowledge of masculinity was critical. One of these two students was so patriarchal in outlook at first that he would quote extensively from the Bible to support the view that men were superior to women. By the end of the course he was quoting the very same Bible to support the argument for equality.

However, the issue of the changing men is both tantalizing and challenging. One has to distinguish between change at the individual, personal level and change at the wider, social level. While some men may change the way they live their private lives, for example, by contributing equally to housework and child care and treating their wives as equals, they may still want to be seen as patriarchs and display their masculinities in the presence of relatives and friends. For example, in the two-day session I had on masculinities with the whole of the 2011 intake (36 students) all of the eight male students admitted that while they did assist with housework, they did not do so in the presence of friends or relatives as they risked being laughed at or ridiculed. On the other hand, there are men who are prepared to put their masculinity on the line by openly and publicly playing roles and participating in activities that support gender equality regardless of the consequences.

SEMINAR
The 'new man'

Critically evaluate the assertions below drawing from your own country experience:

> '*There is a belief by some commentators that there is an emergent new man in Africa who is in favour of women's liberation, looks after children, supports women in their desire to develop careers and is sensitive and introspective. However, a closer examination would suggest that this is a simplistic view*'

...the issue of the changing men is both tantalizing and challenging

Part IV: Challenges of teaching masculinities

The first major challenge of teaching the course is a personal one. Being a man teaching a course about men in a programme whose focus is on women and women's advancement is a challenge. Given that women have, over the centuries, suffered oppression at the hands of men puts any man who pronounces himself as an advocate for gender equality in a dilemma because women have every reason to be suspicious. Indeed women have the right to ask why now? However, my experience with both colleagues and students at SEARCWL show that issues of legitimacy have been overcome and that masculinities have become an integral part of women's law teaching and research. Mapping out how the course fits in with the broader aims and objectives of the programme has been a fascinating journey into the unknown as there are not many legal scholars in the eastern and southern African region with an interest in law and masculinity. I have relied on western scholars in addressing some of the issues on law and masculinities.

...masculinities have become an integral part of women's law teaching and research

While western theories and paradigms are useful tools of analysis, there is need to guard against lifting them wholesale and applying them to different conditions and situations of eastern and southern Africa. We need to examine constructions of masculinity at the local level rather than 'force our understanding through universalizing theoretical models that posit "manhood" as some timeless, transcendent essence' (Kimmel, 2001:338). From this cue the course thrust advocates a grounded approach that looks at the lived realities of men and women in the region. The grounded approach enables us to take the lives and realities of the men and women students in the class in order to understand how masculinity affects gender relations in their own lives, communities and countries. The SEARCWL library has over the years been actively expanding its African collection on masculinities and this should aid in strengthening and developing this critical course from an African perspective.

ACTIVITY

Why work with men?

The following questions form the basis of our discussion.

- Should those involved in the fight for gender equality work with men?
- What are the advantages?
- What are the possible pitfalls?
- Are there any success stories we can cite to show the benefits of working with men?

Although the course is multi-disciplinary and requires and encourages students to draw from other disciplines, in analyzing some of the student's written assignments it is clear that in some cases not enough attention is given to law. As such, in strengthening the teaching of such a course, one of the areas I am looking at is giving greater attention to examples that show the connection between law, gender and masculinity. This is critical in order to show the students that questioning the legitimacy of certain laws that undermine gender equality or discriminate against women is not inconsistent with being a good lawyer. In other words, it is possible to be both a good lawyer and a good feminist activist.

...it is possible to be both a good lawyer and a good feminist activist

By way of expanding the course content, it seems worthwhile not only to strengthen its legal elements but to also bring in issues of social psychology in order to arrive at a better understanding of men and their behaviour. There is some overlap between aspects of this course and the course on 'Gender, law and sexuality'. The desirability or otherwise of this overlap needs to be explored as we also need to guard against trying to do everything.

Bibliography

Beauvoir S. de (1949/1984) *The second sex*, translated by H. M. Parshley, Penguin Modern Classics, Harmondsworth.

Collier R. (1995) *Masculinity, law and the family*, Routledge, London.

Chanock M. (1985) *Law, custom and social order. The colonial experience in Malawi and Zambia*, Polity Press, Cambridge.

Connell R.W. (1987) *Gender and power: society, the person and sexual politics*, Stanford University Press, Stanford.

– (1995) *Masculinities*, Polity Press, Cambridge.

– (2002) *Gender,* Polity Press, Cambridge and Malden MA.

Dworkin R. (1978) *Taking rights seriously*, Harvard University Press, Cambridge MA.

Epprecht M. (1998) 'Uncovering masculinity in southern African history', *Review of Southern African Studies* 2(1):117-142.

Hearn J. (2007) 'The problems boys and men create, the problems boys and men experience', in T. Shefer, K. Ratele and A. Strebel (eds), *From boys to men: social constructions of masculinity in contemporary society*, University of Cape Town Press, Cape Town.

Jeater D. (1993) *Marriage, perversion and power: the construction of moral discourse in Southern Rhodesia*, Clarendon Press, Oxford.

Kimmel M. (1993) 'Invisible masculinity', *Society* 30(6): 28-35.

MacKinnon C. (1983) 'Feminism, Marxism, methods and state: towards feminist jurisprudence', *Signs* 8(2):635–644.

Miescher S.F. and L.A. Lindsay (eds) (2003) *Men and masculinities in modern Africa*, Heinemann, Portsmouth.

Morgan D. (1992) *Discovering men: critical studies on men and masculinities*, Routledge, London.

Morrell R. (2001) 'The times of change: men and masculinity in South Africa', in R. Morrell (ed), *Changing men in Southern Africa*, University of Natal Press and Zed Books, Pietermaritzburg and London.

– (2001) (ed), *Changing men in Southern Africa*, University of Natal Press and Zed Books, Pietermaritzburg and London.

Ouzgane L. and R. Morrell (2005) *African masculinities: men in Africa from the late 19th century to the present*, Palgrave Macmillan, London.

Phillips O.C. (1997) 'Zimbabwean law and the production of the white man's disease', *Social and Legal Studies* 6(4):471-492 December.

– (2001) 'Myths and realities of African sexuality', *African Studies Review* 44(2):195-201.

Reid G. and L. Walker (eds) (2005) *Men behaving differently: South African men since 1994*, Double Storey/Juta Academic, Cape Town.

Richter L. and R. Morrell (eds) (2006) *Baba: men and fatherhood in South Africa*, HSRC Press, Cape Town.

Shefer T., K. Ratele and A. Strebel (eds) (2007) *From boys to men: social constructions of masculinity in contemporary society*, University of Cape Town Press, Cape Town.

Shire C. (1994) 'Language, space and masculinities in Zimbabwe', in A. Cornwall and N. Lindistarne (eds) *Dislocating masculinities: comparative ethnographies*, Routledge, London.

Silberschmidt M. (2005) 'Poverty, male disempowerment and male sexuality: rethinking men and masculinities in rural and urban East Africa', in L. Ouzgane and R. Morrell, *African masculinities: men in Africa from the late 19th century to the present*, Palgrave Macmillan, London.

Tsanga A. (2003) *Taking law to the people: gender, law reform and community education in Zimbabwe*, Weaver Press, Harare.

11

Teaching sexuality and law in southern Africa

Locating historical narratives and adopting appropriate conceptual frameworks

Oliver Phillips

Part I: Setting the stage
The challenge of studying sex

Public discussion of sexuality is invariably challenging as it automatically offers our intimate relations for public scrutiny; but public discussion of sexuality is even more challenging in those societies with institutional structures (linguistic, spatial, and so on) that specifically preclude references to sex when both men and women are present: Zimbabwe has gender-specific cultures of sex (Shire, 1994: 147-158). Rules strictly regulating the discussion of sex in mixed company have produced sexual vocabularies and lexicons specific to each gender and sexual topics that are reserved for discussion exclusively within same-sex spaces or other specifically gendered relationships. So it should be no surprise that the offer of a module entitled 'Gender, law and sexuality', with the novelty of free-flowing discussion of sexuality, presents a challenge for many students from the region. But this

[1] As author, I am responsible for any flaws in this chapter but neither the chapter nor the module would exist without many other people to whom I owe much gratitude, not least the students who registered for the class and then participated so enthusiastically. They contributed their time, energy and ideas with good humour, courage and commitment even in the face of bafflement, hunger and far too many power-cuts. Similarly, Julie Stewart and Amy Tsanga understood the need for the module and supported its presence with the same steady resolve that keeps SEARCWL so productive. Sylvia Tamale's stimulating intelligence, heartfelt laughter and disarming candour have made working together on this module a source of great joy for me. Ali Miller, Gayle Rubin, Carole Vance and Mikki Van Zyl have my enduring gratitude for the inspiration that came through participating in their classes, their sage guidance on what I might do with that enthusiasm, and for their ideas and concepts that I use so readily in this chapter.

trepidation is not exclusive to classrooms in the southern African region, as its prevalence throughout the world directly reflects the challenge that open discussion of sexuality presents in any location. Across the world, sexuality is ordinarily subjected to extensive regulation so that its mere discussion is patrolled by prohibition, taboo, discretion and licence, the strength and parameters of which vary according to social context, cultural scenario[2] and the gendered identity of the discussants. But one constant of this extensive regulation is its ubiquity, best reflected in the fact that we take the operation of such prohibitions, 'taboos' and discretionary licensing for granted in so many different countries and across such divergent cultural contexts.

For this reason, the deliberate discussion of sexuality immediately becomes disruptive, as its naked articulation and conscious examination automatically exposes the patterns and structures that underlie conventional assumptions about sexual propriety and gendered performativity. This word, 'performativity', is suggested by Judith Butler to represent a relational embodied practice whereby 'identity is performatively constituted by the very "expressions" that are said to be its results' (1990:25). In other words, our active performance of gender means we participate in the construction of identities which are not fixed but fluid in their response to the prevailing discourse of power; our dynamic embodiment of normativities reflects our reproduction of or resistance to hegemonic gender identities (hence Butler's subversive call for 'gender trouble'). Refusing the essentialist presumption that would reduce gender to a single biological foundation, this approach maps the constitution of identity and normativity through the contextual multiplicity of power relations, and thereby offers a platform for both theoretical development and political action. Speaking about sex might be seen as a step onto this platform, as it obliges us to articulate ideas, processes and conceptions that otherwise remain assumed, and their explicit articulation implicitly invokes their analysis and deconstruction. So speaking about sex inevitably renders visible relations of power that are otherwise concealed in discretion and protected by silence, making them vulnerable to critique and transformation. This is a process that is invariably challenging for students and scholars alike, to the extent that sexuality research and pedagogy have battled for space and credibility in defensive academies the world over. Thus, sexuality is a relatively new (albeit considerably grown and growing ever faster)[3] area of serious scholarship in legal academies around the world.

...speaking about sex inevitably renders visible relations of power that are otherwise concealed in discretion and protected by silence

---

[2] For more on the shaping of 'sexual scripts' including the importance of 'cultural scenario', see discussion later in the chapter, and refer to Simon and Gagnon (2007: 31–40).

[3] Scholarship of sexuality has developed into a body of work far too large to begin detailing here but for an example of recent work specifically discussing the interface of academic research, pedagogy and sexualities, see the recent edition of the journal *Sexualities* 12(5) October 2009 which is dedicated to issues related to teaching sexuality and sexuality research.

In addition to the broader objective of mapping, critiquing and possibly contributing to this global growth, a key purpose of this module, 'Gender, law and sexuality', is to explore the conjoined issues of sexuality's location in southern and eastern African scholarship and its significance in local contexts beyond the classroom. This course therefore reflects a need and simultaneously represents an opportunity for local scholars to contribute to developing a framework appropriate for studying sexualities in a regional context. This is a process that can only be achieved through building a body of local research and critically appraising how the personal, the political, the theoretical and the empirical might all be effectively joined to better understand the history of sexuality's local regulation, the significance of its proclaimed silences, the nuance of its licensed discretion and the potential impact of challenging these structures. Addressing these questions will inevitably render the local relevance of sexuality scholarship (and hence of this module) self-evident, both in relation to the law and more broadly.

The module is taught in two separate but connected blocks: the first by myself (Oliver Phillips) and the second by Sylvia Tamale. They share the overall objective of uncovering the multiple ways in which sexuality is regulated and the extent to which that regulation is also instrumental in constructing gendered relations of power. This entails situating the relationships of gender, sexuality, law and custom within a local and regional historical context. This chapter discusses the first part of the module (the part that I teach), which has three primary aims:

...the overall objective ... [is] uncovering the multiple ways in which sexuality is regulated and the extent to which that regulation is also instrumental in constructing gendered relations of power.

- to critically examine some theoretical and conceptual approaches that have elsewhere been central in analyzing the social and legal construction of sexuality and its relationship to the construction of gender;
- to understand the way these have been critiqued and adapted in other post-colonial contexts and to assess how they might be shaped by local post-colonial critiques of law and custom;
- to build on these appraisals to consider critically the extent to which these theoretical and conceptual approaches might be adapted in students' own local contexts, if at all.

For this analysis to have any real purchase in developing knowledge and creating platforms for further research and policy, it is important that the discussions of these theoretical constructs and concepts are rooted in a reality that students recognize and that engages rigorously whatever research is available. We have to maximize the students' vigorous critical and reflexive participation which requires establishing a context they feel comfortable with and simultaneously engaging them through both the reading material and the class discussion.

Part II: Pedagogy, methodology and reflexivity: building a class that works

In a region where issues of sexuality are so frequently and so vehemently contested, the challenge of developing a module that fully engages these novel issues but does not threaten the uninitiated demands sensitivity and creative teaching methods from the outset. This section of the chapter therefore outlines some of the concerns students have at the start of the module and the specific techniques employed to facilitate their eager participation. The ultimate objective is to equip them with skills appropriate for assessing the applicability of various analytical frameworks to their own cultural and professional contexts. Meaningful discussion and effective analysis is only possible in an environment where any reticence deriving from conventional fears has been overcome, so the start of the course prioritizes establishing an environment conducive to open discussion and learning. Before detailing how this is achieved, it is necessary to illustrate the form and extent that student fear and reticence has taken in the past, as that is instructive in itself.

Meaningful discussion and effective analysis is only possible in an environment where any reticence deriving from conventional fears has been overcome

On the one hand, the students who choose this optional module are self-selecting and therefore evince a certain willingness to confront the challenge that customary taboos around sexuality present. On the other hand, the challenge of actually participating in class discussion remains real. This was clearly demonstrated in 2007 when students, who had initially elected to do the module, switched on the second day of classes to a 'safer' module they found less challenging both in terms of their easy participation in discussion and its uncontested acceptability as a 'normal' subject. Alongside their wariness about the actual content of the module and its discussion, they explicitly articulated a fear that they would suffer through association with the title's reference to 'sexuality'. It subsequently emerged that the mere prospect of the word 'sexuality' appearing in the module titles listed on their final degree transcripts prevents some students from even considering signing up for it. At the start of the module in 2009, students who had elected to do the module reported that other masters students had warned them they were naïve to select this module as its appearance on their degree transcripts would disadvantage them in future job applications, regardless of how good their results might be. Students asked whether we might change the title of the module so that the word 'sexuality' did not appear, pointing out that this would undoubtedly result in more students registering for the module. They also required reassurance that the module was 'relevant' having been told by other students that it was 'a waste of time'.

In addition to the fact that renaming the module was not appropriate since its focus is undeniably on sexuality, gender and law, I suggested that its listing on their degree transcripts might be seen as indicating students' foresight. Future scholars are more likely to be incredulous at the absence of sexuality in any course on gender and the law for while sexuality is a new field of study it has grown enormously in recent years. It has proved to be an extremely productive medium through which to analyze a large number of social, cultural, historical and political dynamics including (but not limited to) relations of gender and race, as well as broader questions of difference and equality, not least in a post-colonial world where these issues are ever more topical. The global ascendance of human rights discourse and conventions, the concomitant development of women's claims to sexual independence, equality and full economic participation, and the imperatives of reproductive and sexual health all give sexuality a pressing relevance. With the regulation of sexuality so central to the construction of gendered identity and relationships, its novelty in African scholarship signals the fact that the students at SEARCWL are present at the start of a field that is already growing. This field will expand significantly and become increasingly valid in the coming years – a prospect that places students at a distinct advantage as the 'pioneers' in their respective fields. This is clearly substantiated by the rapid and extraordinary growth of sexual politics and advocacy organizations (whether related to lesbians/gays, sex workers, violence against women or HIV/AIDS), as well as the significant development of research and academic publications on sexuality that have emerged throughout the southern and eastern African region in the last 10 years.[4]

The global ascendance of human rights discourse and conventions, the concomitant development of women's claims to sexual independence, equality and full economic participation, and the imperatives of reproductive and sexual health all give sexuality a pressing relevance.

Students' concerns are understandable in so far as they reflect their anxiety about the vehement rhetoric that has dominated many of the public debates around sexuality in numerous southern and eastern African countries in the last 15 years.[5] The strength and effect of this rhetoric is signalled by the fact that most students arriving at SEARCWL to do a master's degree in gender and law, have little appreciation of and some resistance to the notion that sexuality (and the laws that patrol it) is significant in regulating gender identities, relationships and structures. This is why students signing up to join the class sometimes attract the curiosity of other students who, in dismissing their selection of

---

[4] The large number of organizations throughout Africa engaging in advocacy and education relating to sexuality in order to combat HIV/AIDS or violence against women are well documented; sex worker advocacy projects and unions now exist in many countries in the region including South Africa, Nigeria, Mali, Democratic Republic of Congo, Kenya and Uganda (to mention just a few). Meanwhile lesbian and gay rights groups are now present and active in Cameroon, Uganda, Zimbabwe, South Africa, Botswana, Namibia, Kenya, Sierra Leone, Algeria, Nigeria, Rwanda, Zambia and many others (for a more comprehensive database on organizations throughout Africa, see www.mask.org.za). Furthermore, developing regional alliances (for example, PanAfrican MSM Network, the Coalition of African Lesbians, the All Africa Rights Initiative) are a measure of growing capacity. For information on sexuality scholarship and research, see footnote 8 in this chapter.

[5] Most notable has been rhetoric concerning homosexuality emanating from Zimbabwe, Uganda, Malawi, Cameroon, Namibia, Senegal and Kenya, as well as some highly publicized trials of homosexuals.

this module as 'naïve' or a 'waste of time', also speculate about whether participation in the module might indicate a student's perversion or prurience. While such a strong reaction is usually tempered by the fact that most students know each other fairly well by this stage and all have great respect for the friendly warmth and open intellectual culture of SEARCWL, there remains an inadequate conception of sexuality as a valid subject of scholarship, even amongst postgraduate students of gender. This reflects an historical neglect of sexuality and resistance to including it in mainstream gender analysis. A more specific result is that subscribing to this module can require particular courage on the part of the students. And yet a constant refrain in students' evaluations at the end of the module is that this should not be an optional module but a foundational element of any course on gender and law, as it has given them a far fuller and more meaningful understanding of gender dynamics. This is best interpreted as sexuality being essential in a comprehensive and meaningful analysis of gender relations (and of the intersection of gender and law).

As this is a seminar-based masters programme with a daily reading list, it is vital that students prepare properly for class and then contribute meaningfully to group discussions. Facilitating class discussions effectively therefore demands a particular sensitivity on the part of the lecturer from the very beginning; a sensitivity that engages with the specific dynamics arising from the inhibitions, concerns and different identities of all those present. This makes it impossible to leave the personal identities of lecturers and students at the door; for in as much as the personal is political, the life histories and experiences of all those in the classroom inevitably inform their engagement with the course material. More directly, they affect the way students judge different theories and concepts, and assess their appropriate application to their own cultural settings. This is not to suggest in any way that the course acts as therapy or as a confessional where anecdotes prevail but to insist that intellectual analysis must fit with lived experience, that the location one speaks from informs the manner in which one hears and the perspective from which one sees. Feminists have long understood the importance of acknowledging personal experience and of doing reflexive research.[6] Engaging effectively with gender analysis requires a consciousness of ones own gendered identity, while examining the relationships of power that patrol sexuality will inevitably beg some scrutiny of one's own sexual narratives and interaction with these relations of power. Such reflexivity is fundamental to gendered research and the experience of this course makes it clear that it is also unavoidable in teaching sexuality.

Customarily, in the first class the lecturer and students introduce themselves and outline any scholarly or professional experience they have relating directly to sexuality as well as the particular experience or interest in the law that has

Facilitating class discussions effectively therefore demands a particular sensitivity on the part of the lecturer from the very beginning

---

[6] See, for example, Roberts (1981).

led them to do a masters. Invariably, none of the students taking this course have studied sexuality before so the first class tends to be characterized by acute embarrassment, mixed with puzzlement about the basic question of how sexuality relates to gender or law. One way to overcome embarrassment while simultaneously illustrating key conceptual links between sexuality, gender and regulation is to engage in an exercise that has proved consistently popular with students (see box below).

EXERCISE
Juno from outer space

The class divides into groups of four to engage in a role play. Each group has to define 'sexuality' and explain its social meaning to a hypothetical alien, 'Juno', who has just landed from outer space (despite her ignorance of human society, Juno conveniently speaks perfect English).

While this may initially appear to be a simple task, in practice it quickly becomes clear that sexuality cannot be contained within any one definition. There are numerous 'meanings', dimensions, values, associations and purposes that can be attributed to sexuality and that need to be mentioned if we are to reflect the true breadth of sexuality's reach.

In trying to pin down a suitable definition for Juno, students volunteer some of the many and varied biological, social and cultural purposes and phenomena associated with sexual behaviour, and thereby rapidly appreciate the extent to which sexuality is implicated in so many different dimensions of our lives.

I encourage students to offer as many possible alternatives as they can imagine to help Juno define sexuality and understand its role in human society. We map these out on a blackboard to highlight some of the tensions and patterns, clarity and confusion, relationships of intimacy and distance that accompany our understanding of sexuality in its many manifestations. Sexuality can be defined by referring to a wide range of anatomical acts and physical behaviour involving one, two or more people. We can relate it to emotional expressions of love, intimacy and desire that can take an infinite variety of forms. Or it can be implicated in the reproduction of social structures and markers through rules and regulations that permit or prohibit specific relations and or acts.

In the end, it emerges that these definitions are far from exhaustive. None of them are adequate on their own but that when considered all together they reflect the multiple ways that sexuality is manifest and impacts on our lives, and that above all, these definitions all consistently involve relations of power.

...by the start of the second day, silent embarrassment has morphed into giggling familiarity and students are noticeably more comfortable discussing matters that the day before seemed unmentionable

The ingredients of 'ideal' masculinity are defined in direct relation to the ingredients of 'ideal' femininity. 'Failing' to reflect those 'ideal' values can lead to accusations of inadequacy or confusion which in turn reinforce the desirability and power of 'ideal' gender stereotypes. Gender power is regulated and rewarded through relationships between different men, or between different women, in addition to relationships between men and women.

The Juno exercise also allows students to discover the differences between their expectations and experiences of sex as men and women, and to do so through the presence of Juno, rather than by revealing themselves. At the same time, they are slowly introduced to speaking out loud some relevant words that they are not in the habit of articulating in public or in mixed company. Students do this gradually, making reference to subjects as and when they feel most comfortable. This means that by the start of the second day, silent embarrassment has morphed into giggling familiarity and students are noticeably more comfortable discussing matters that the day before seemed unmentionable. By the third day, giggles and laughter tend to be less an indication of embarrassment and more a recognition of genuine humour and amazement as students become increasingly at ease with open discussions of sexual behaviours and attitudes. This is a necessary development to initiate more critical and rigorous thinking and encourage students to participate more freely in discussion. They begin to value the contributions that other writers and commentators have made to the field and appreciate the pervasive significance of sexuality in so many different aspects of our lives.

As students develop a deeper understanding of all the structures of power (including both law and custom) that regulate sexual relations and control women's reproductive capacity, they realize that, after an initial focus on women's position, the analysis needs to go further. They need to focus on the role that the law and custom play in maintaining particular sexual relationships and identities for both women and men. The latter structure and reinforce a gendered society wherein women are generally subordinated to men and where particular stereotypes of masculine and feminine sexuality are valorized or censured to reproduce specific hierarchies between genders *and* within genders. Thus, we need to consider how sexuality serves to value some masculine identities over other subordinated masculine identities and how particular concepts of femininity are rewarded or censured to create hierarchies that are both gendered and sexualized. Students are introduced to R.W. Connell's work to better understand the role of subordinated stereotypes of masculinity (for example, the 'wimp', 'nerd' and 'weed') or femininity (for example, the 'tomboy', 'plain girl' and 'whore') in establishing more aspirational stereotypes of idealized masculinity (for example, the 'boss', 'big man' and 'player') and idealized femininity (for example, 'the domestic goddess', 'dutiful mother' and 'obedient virgin'). Students quickly understand how these identities only exist in relationship to each other and that they make up a gender order that maps out 'hegemonic' (ascendant) identities for (and between) men and for (and between) women.[7] This is discussed in more detail later in this chapter.

---

[7] For more see Connell (1987).

Part III: Understanding post-colonial sex: locating historical continuities

The scepticism or seriousness with which students anywhere approach any course is determined by their appreciation of its significance and relevance to the real lives they either experience themselves or they observe around them. And even though all students have a gender (and some experience of sexuality), it is not always immediately or explicitly apparent to them how analyzing sexuality can productively contribute to our understanding of gender or broader social and cultural relations. This is partly because of traditional restrictions on discussing sexuality openly. It is also because these restrictions have frequently been reinforced by any explicit articulation of 'sexuality' being rejected as 'western' or 'imported'. However, as will become clear in this and Sylvia Tamale's chapter, a growing body of regional research on sexuality is increasingly becoming a part of mainstream gender studies.[8] It is therefore important to start by helping students find vivid examples of the centrality of sexuality to gender relations. A key way to do this is to engage with the basic but locally problematic tension between a woman and her family's ownership of her reproductive capacity.

Students immediately relate to this fundamental and direct illustration of the importance of sexual autonomy in daily life. The issue of a woman's capacity to decide with whom and when she consents to sexual relations and to marriage is readily reflected in local legal and historical research. A belief in gender equality implicitly presupposes that a woman should have ownership over her body, her reproductive capacity and her sexuality. This implies not only that a woman should have the right to choose whom she marries and when but also that she should have the right to refuse (or accept) a sexual proposition, and that she should do so on her own terms rather than at the behest of her family or community. Of course in practice individual identity in southern and eastern Africa is deeply implicated in family and community relations and as autonomy *per se* can only be defined in relational terms, the historical disputes about definitions of autonomy and identity persist in altered post-colonial form. So to fully understand regional struggles around sexuality, gender and law, one must consider their location in the shifting boundaries of individual citizenship and allegiance to lineage in the context of customary law and the nation state. This alternating ascendancy of individual citizenship and allegiance to lineage can be related to context by applying numerous

...to fully understand regional struggles around sexuality, gender and law, one must consider their location in the shifting boundaries of individual citizenship and allegiance to lineage in the context of customary law and the nation state

---

[8] See, for example, the following: Marc Epprecht (2004, 2008), Signe Arnfred (2004), Mikki Van Zyl and Melissa Steyn (2005), Charles Gueboguo (2008), Ruth Morgan and Saskia Weiringa (2006), Will Roscoe and Stephen Murray (2001) and see further various works by the module leaders Oliver Phillips and Sylvia Tamale as listed in the bibliography at the end of the chapter.

theoretical frameworks including that of John and Jean Comaroff. They trace the dual overlapping and often contradictory registers of 'primal sovereignty' and 'radical individualism' in analyzing the colonial and post-colonial development of rights (Comaroff, 1997: 193-236). Similarly, Mahmood Mamdani's differentiation of citizen and subject (1996) locates post-colonial Africans within a bifurcated state, offering a parallel framework through which to analyze the dual (urban/rural) quality of belonging in relation to both lineage and the nation state. These frameworks prove useful for an analysis of both law and sexualities because they highlight the tensions that people encounter between their allegiance to and the authority of lineage on the one hand and their rights and responsibilities as individual citizens of the post-colonial nation-state on the other hand. They also traverse the contexts of both colonial and post-colonial southern Africa, situating these tensions in a historical context, while also helping students understand their experience of these tensions in their present-day lives. Students can relate this directly to their own negotiation of a hybrid existence where they are both embedded in the customary relations of lineage and offered the rights to equality and autonomy that attach to citizens through their relationship with the state.

While this remains a key dynamic of post-colonial lives, it is one that was set in motion with the foundation of the colonial state. For where the newly established colonial authorities did not directly contest traditional structures and customary law, they nevertheless had significant effect on their operation and development. The research of Martin Chanock (1985) and others[9] analyzes the impact of the codification, collections and restatements of African customary law to show how colonial authorities drew on the 'authoritative' accounts of older men (deeply interested in securing their own positions of power in a society undergoing serious transition) to concretize relations and practices that had previously been fluid and contextual. In a quest for predictability, a rigid format was applied to customary law, depriving it of fluidity, entrenching positions of (patriarchal, gerontocratic) power, eliding traditional modes of accountability and abrogating key practices (for example, elopement) that had offered women relief from the harshest effects of obligatory marital and sexual arrangements.[10]

Similarly, Diana Jeater's research (1993) is an excellent resource in helping students understand both the tension between the authorities of state and lineage and also the striking continuities between colonial law's regulation of sexual relations and the legal regulation of their sexual lives that students experience today. Jeater provides a vivid and detailed map of a gradual shift from the collective interests of lineage and the gerontocratic patriarchal authority of the 'headman', to a focus on the sins of the individual moral

...colonial authorities drew on the 'authoritative' accounts of older men (deeply interested in securing their own positions of power in a society undergoing serious transition) to concretize relations and practices that had previously been fluid and contextual

---

[9] See also Schmidt (1990) and Jacobs (1984)

[10] See, for example, Gelfand (1975a and 1975b).

citizen and the regulatory authority of the centralized state (Jeater, 1993). This is most explicitly observed in early attempts of the Southern Rhodesian colonial authorities to 'emancipate' African women through the registration of marriages; with the state (rather than the headman) as the central arbiter of marriages, it was possible to promulgate a ban on the pledging of young girls in marriage and to insist on a woman's consent to marriage – both provisions of the Southern Rhodesian Native Marriage Ordinance of 1901. These were only two amongst an array of measures instrumental in usurping the authority of local headmen and asserting the centrality of the newly formed colonial state in the regulation of relationships of gender and sexuality. But paradoxically the waning authority of older chiefs and headmen disrupted the colonialists' ability to administer indirect rule. So soon the colonial authorities were forming alliances with older African men to re-assert traditional patriarchal control and to regain traditional social and cultural capital in the face of challenges from young men newly bestowed with the economic power of wage-earners and young women furnished with new avenues of escape from the obligations of arranged marriages (Mbilinyi, 1988: 1-29).

… soon the colonial authorities were forming alliances with older African men to re-assert traditional patriarchal control and to regain traditional social and cultural capital

While the varied sources and diverse locations of these accounts suggest these broad dynamics were replicated across the region of southern and eastern Africa, this particular alliance of African patriarchs and colonial authority is most famously epitomized by the Southern Rhodesian Native Adultery Punishment Ordinance of 1916 which initiated criminal punishment for adultery that was focused on the body of the married African woman, while the institution of polygyny exempted African men from similar restrictions. Similarly gender-bound and also indicative of the colonial authorities' disingenuous approach to women's emancipation, was the Southern Rhodesian Immorality and Indecency Suppression Ordinance 1917. This criminalized (with extreme penalties) any sexual relationship between black men and white women, yet simultaneously failed to offer any protection to black women from their more frequent predatorial abuse by white men. This legislation was the subject of significant and persistent but ultimately futile campaigns for reform by both black men and white women; it remained an explicit reflection of the direct intersections of racial and sexual identities around which the social hierarchies of colonial Southern Rhodesia and South Africa were constructed. While some of the details and the harsh reinforcement of these hierarchies differed between different colonial and settler states in the region, the overall patterning was often remarkably the same.[11]

I have identified only a few legal interventions that came with colonization or settlement and the scale of this chapter demands that I limit my list to only a few legal measures rather than meticulously marking each of the plethora of

---

[11] See Kennedy (1987) and also Hansen (1989)

social, political, cultural and religious instruments of regulation and censure that were the armoury of the settler and colonial states. But it is already notable that all the above measures go directly to the regulation of sexual relationships with significant impact, whether interfering in the traditional practices of indigenous ethnicities in the name of civilization or attempting to enforce hierarchies that directly reflected their urgent concerns about the intersections of race and sex. It should now be immediately apparent, to any student or reader, that the intersections of law, gender and sexuality are both complex and far-reaching, with implications that reverberate in post-colonial southern and eastern Africa, so that there is much potential for a field of sexuality studies.

Understanding post-colonial sex: identifying imperialism and ideology

As a result of legal measures such as those listed above, the significance of sexuality in post-colonial southern and eastern Africa is considerably compounded. It is evidently not only a topic showered in inhibition and promptly clothed in taboo but it also has a symbolic significance through which colonial authority and anti-imperialist resistance have historically engaged in loud and vividly illustrated battle. Sexuality has provided the fecund terrain for some heated contests central to the definitions of, first, colonial relations and second, the newly formed identities of the post-colonial state.

It is thus hardly surprising that the arguments born out of colonial resistance and implicitly relying on a social constructionist base (for example, 'colonialists/missionaries are corrupting our traditional cultural values') have gradually transposed into dogmatically defensive claims characterized by trenchant essentialism (for example, 'homosexual practices being inherently unnatural are completely unknown in this region').[12] This shift to absolutism is delivered in the heat of rhetorical campaigns whose passionate sloganeering takes them ever further from reasoned analysis, for it clearly confuses the factual possibilities of physical behaviour that exists the world over, with the

---

[12] Since 1995, homosexuality has repeatedly been suggested to be a white man's disease, corrupting the naturally heterosexual virtue of Africans, as President Mugabe has made many well known pronouncements to the effect that homosexuality 'is mainly done by whites and is alien to the Zimbabwean society in general' (President Mugabe, *GALZ* 11, Jan 1994: 13) and that homosexuals are 'behaving worse than dogs and pigs' (*The Herald*, 12 August 1995), as he called for a 'return to our traditional culture that makes us human beings' (*The Citizen*, 12 August 1995). These denouncements, made in Shona, have clear idiomatic implications relating to the notion of *ubuntu* or what makes one a person or *munhu* (in Shona). Alongside similar statements by numerous senior politicians in Zimbabwe and across the region, these have contributed to the more widespread suggestion that homosexuality was unknown to Africans before the arrival of white people, while it is more likely that acts without procreative consequence went relatively unnoticed and it was homophobia (particularly as institutionalized in law) that was imported with colonialism. For more on this see Phillips (2000) and also the work of Marc Epprecht (in particular 2004 and 2009).

social prohibitions and permissions that are specific to particular cultures.[13] Moreover, the virtue of the claim that Africans have a more limited corporeal imagination than any other group on the planet is only matched in ironic folly by the idea that their sexual relations are so 'naturally' ordained that they exist outside social or cultural regulation and management. This retreat into simplistic and dogmatic assertions ironically reproduces the tendency of the colonizing Victorian discourse to reduce all the varied African cultures to one static monolith and to lay claim to disciplined 'civilization' by representing Africans as 'savage' and therefore hypersexual and close to nature.

As writers such as Sander Gilman (1986) and Chandra Mohanty (1991) have since pointed out, these stereotypes of savage hypersexuality, while representing the African or native as licentious and close to nature, simultaneously served to reinforce the elevated image of western women as 'secular, liberated and having control over their own lives' (Mohanty, 1991: 74) .[14] More recent rejections of homosexuality as 'alien' to African cultures might similarly be argued as serving to denigrate as 'immoral' those (western) cultures that accommodate homosexual relations, thereby implicitly claiming a 'higher' morality for more puritanical 'African' values. Ironically, in their rejection of a secular post-enlightenment notion of human rights, these 'African' values are arguably rooted in a Christian and Victorian morality that implicitly relies on and reinforces a notion of sexuality as exclusively and persistently oriented around a homo/heterosexual divide. This binary concept of hetero/homosexuality, whereby all possible variations of sexual orientation are ultimately reduced to differences of biological sex and social gender, is far from any of the African traditions revealed by research and scholarship.[15] It is a classification first developed by late nineteenth-century European 'sexologists'[16] that arguably accompanied the development of an

...recent rejections of homosexuality as 'alien' to African cultures might ... be argued as serving to denigrate as 'immoral' those (western) cultures that accommodate homosexual relations

---

[13] For more on this, see Charles Gueboguo (2008).

[14] See more generally, see Gilman (1986).

[15] Research suggests a multiplicity of different approaches to homosexual practices across Africa, varying from strict prohibitions, to the institutionalization of homosexual practices in rites of fertility and worship, to complete indifference since homosexual acts have no reproductive consequences and so no impact on familial relations. Amongst others see Phillips (2000), Epprecht (2004) and Murray and Roscoe (1998) .

[16] Michel Foucault (1978) locates the rise of the homosexual as 'species' (in place of the sodomite's 'temporary aberration') in the rise of science and its investment in the morphology of the pervert ('Nothing that went into his total composition was unaffected by his sexuality. It was everywhere present in him: ...it was consubstantial with him, less as a habitual sin than as a singular nature') and suggests that Carl Westphal's characterization of homosexuality in his 1870 publication on 'contrary sexual sensations' was 'its date of birth' (1978:43). While the actual invention of the terms 'homosexual' and 'heterosexual' is commonly attributed to the Hungarian writer Karl-Maria Benkert in 1869, they came into more common usage through their inclusion in the 'scientific' categories of sexual types and aberrations put forward by Richard von Krafft-Ebing (1886) and other researchers of that era intent on applying 'scientific method' to their studies of sex (see Weeks, 1985: 61–95).

The Sunday Times (Harare) 4 April 2010

...proclamations by educated, cosmopolitan members of ruling elites denying homosexuality's presence are more a reflection of their desire to reshape contemporary conceptions of traditional culture

individualist, consumerist culture under industrial capitalism. Thus, proclamations by educated, cosmopolitan members of ruling élites denying homosexuality's presence are more a reflection of their desire to reshape contemporary conceptions of traditional culture in line with their aspirations of propriety and property than a reflection of practices that may or may not actually have existed in the past.

In short, issues relating to sexuality are not only clothed in taboo but are buttoned up with deception before being flourished with wilful denialism. Claims and counter-claims concerning sexuality have been paraded through the political arena with such élan that even the most extraordinary myths can become integral to the politics of gender and race in both the colonial and post-colonial states in the region. But once one starts speaking of and investigating sexuality, it does not take long to discover its very particular significance in the history and politics of the region, and to realize this significance is vital to engaging students effectively in its proper study. More significantly, the particularity of this heavily invested cultural history must be incorporated into sexuality scholarship in southern and eastern Africa. Consequently any existing theoretical frameworks for analyzing sexual relations must be critically considered for their relevance and appropriate adaptability to the local context, weighed down as it is by post-colonial memory.

Theoretical frameworks appropriate for regional post-colonial sexualities

The second week of the module is therefore devoted to critically evaluating different theoretical perspectives to filter out those elements that clearly have no purchase in local scholarship. We identify how some approaches exacerbate current tensions surrounding sexual and racial relations and consider which analyses coherently aid students' understanding of gendered relations in their own contexts. Extensive debates among and between analysts of gender and feminism from within Africa, from other developing countries and from 'the north', serve as a platform to start discussing these theoretical positions.

In the struggle against colonial power, twentieth century African nationalism subordinated women's rights to the demands of political and economic independence

In the struggle against colonial power, twentieth century African nationalism subordinated women's rights to the demands of political and economic independence.[17] Gender equality was either expected to develop automatically

---

[17] The lateness of the South African post-colonial movement made the ANC Women's League determined to be a notable exception to this historical subordination, resulting in (amongst other things) the ANC's commitment to reserving 30 per cent of all its parliamentary seats for women (Hoad, Martin and Reid, 2005:20).

with liberation or was dismissed as 'a new form of cultural imperialism'.[18] But in twenty-first century post-colonial Africa an unprecedented array of international and regional legal instruments promise to advance women's rights. As the site of considerable interaction between transnational and local governmental and non-governmental organizations this objective remains vulnerable to accusations of 'western' interference, an all too familiar refrain to the many post-colonial feminists obliged to negotiate the dialectic of local resistance to women's empowerment (as foreign inspired) and universalist presumptions in western feminism (as ignoring local culture).[19] Sexual pleasure and sexual autonomy are often the most contentious areas of dispute in regard to gendered relationships (to the extent that precaution will often demand their neglect). The least contested campaigns for women's rights have frequently been those perceived to be 'above' culture and in the wider national interest, for instance, health-related and reproductive rights (reducing maternal mortality, teenage pregnancy and sexually transmitted infections), overlapping with violence against women through a narrative of sexual harm.[20] Indeed, these areas delivered substantial alliances between feminists from across the world, ensuring greater integration of sexual and reproductive freedoms into women's rights through the Declarations at Vienna (1993), Cairo (1994) and Beijing (1995).[21] As women have developed increasingly global alliances, so they have needed to account more carefully for the differentials of culture and history.

...an unprecedented array of international and regional legal instruments now promise to advance women's rights

> 'As feminism has sought to become integrally related to struggles against racialist and colonialist oppression, it has become increasingly important to resist the colonizing epistemological strategy that would subordinate different configurations of domination under the rubric of a transcultural notion of patriarchy' (Butler, 1993:46).

These 'different configurations' impacted significantly on studies of gender, sexuality and race but the intersection of these (and other markers of identity) was brought into sharpest relief in the cross-cultural debates within feminist politics, bringing about a newly invested reflexivity.

---

[18] This phrase was coined by a spokesman for the ruling Zimbabwe African National Union – Patriotic Front (ZANU-PF) party, as quoted in Seidman (1984: 432).

[19] See for example, Narayan (1997: 1–40) and Menon (2000: 77–100) and, more generally, Gilligan (1993).

[20] Alice Miller (2004: 16–47), while recognizing reproductive rights and sexual harm as key engines in advancing women's rights in the international sphere, critically appraises the limits of these strategic platforms and cautions that the protection resulting from prioritizing them can ultimately privilege 'respectability', reinforcing the gendered hierarchies and undermining the fundamental goals of equality.

[21] World Conference on Human Rights (Vienna 1993), International Conference on Population and Development (Cairo 1994) and the Fourth World Conference on Women (Beijing 1995). For critical appraisal of the specific advances and alliances of these conferences, see Petchesky (2003).

> 'Universal images of "the third world woman" (the veiled woman, chaste virgin and so on) – images constructed from adding "the third world difference" to "sexual difference" – are predicated upon (and hence obviously bringing into sharper focus) assumptions about western women as secular, liberated and having control over their own lives' (Mohanty, 1991).

As a result, definitions of 'feminism', 'gender' and 'sexuality' have been repeatedly interrogated by African women, with some writers such as Amadiume (1997) and Ovewumi (1997) explicitly criticising western gender dichotomies and theories as inappropriate for analysis in Africa. Yet it is these same conceptual categories of gender that are used by governments and non-governmental organizations to deliver formal rights through legal instruments (whether national or international), that are constantly imported through discourses of development and often cited in claims to justice by those ordinary African women unversed in these cosmopolitan, intellectual debates of (feminist?) semantics. The inherent dynamism of cultures, compounded by the post-colonial imperative of reinvention (Hobsbawm and Ranger, 1991), leaves key definitions susceptible to both assertion from above and reinterpretation from below. Consequently, Uma Narayan (1997: 9–10) suggests that third world feminists' critiques of their local culture should be seen as 'just one prevailing form of intracultural critique' whose similarity to western feminism springs from the universal ubiquity of gender inequality and whose particular mobilization will be informed by their own experience of local culture. Students on this module have in the past found Narayan's flexible and grounded approach useful and politically productive, whereas the positions of Amadiume and Ovewumi are more challenging. Their rejection of 'feminism' does not lend itself so readily to establishing alliances within and outside Africa and across the developing world, let alone with women from more powerful countries.

The assured narrative that underscores Narayan's analysis, interweaving the theoretical and the personal as a lived whole, and the accessibility of her language and writing, tend to sit well with students on this course. Narayan offers simultaneous transparency and sophistication in negotiating this post-colonial dialectic of national belonging and feminist critique. But in an analytical exercise that brings to the fore the differences between the specific ethnic cultures that inhabit the entire region and that are represented in the class, two other theoretical frameworks consistently survive the withering critique of students diligently engaged in testing the applicability of different theories to the conditions of their own local contexts (though not without partial losses or local amendments).

The first of these is Gayle Rubin's early (1984) model of sexual hierarchies, where relative values are attached to a hierarchy of sexual behaviours and identities (see figure 11.1 below) so that the further one moves away from the 'charmed circle' of normative relationships, the greater the stigma and punitive consequences mustered to enforce a return to conformity and to that initial 'charmed circle' of acceptability. Most cultures limit this 'charmed circle' to married, heterosexual, reproductive relations in the 'missionary position' that are monogamous in the west but may well be polygynous in an African setting, but in either case are not regarded as promiscuous or unregulated 'free love'.

Figure 11.1: The sex hierarchy: the 'charmed circle' v the outer limits

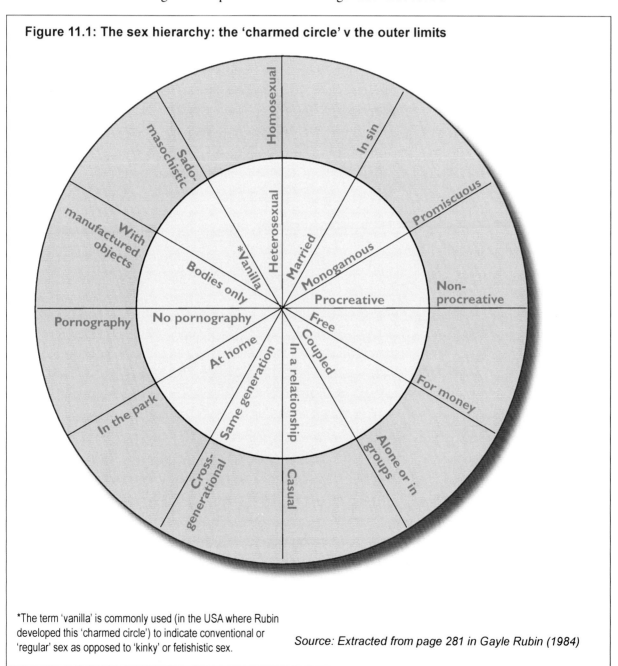

*The term 'vanilla' is commonly used (in the USA where Rubin developed this 'charmed circle') to indicate conventional or 'regular' sex as opposed to 'kinky' or fetishistic sex.

Source: Extracted from page 281 in Gayle Rubin (1984)

Rubin's sexual hierarchies are also reflected through a second diagram (opposite) that illustrates the boundaries between 'good' and 'bad' sex and offers some scope for mapping obstacles and potential transitions between and across these categorizations of 'good' and 'bad'. This second diagram also illustrates Rubin's suggestion that sexual morality has much in common with ideologies of racism (a suggestion that tends to resonate well with students, possibly on account of the regional history of racial and sexual intersections). Sexual morality grants virtue to dominant groups and therefore 'naturalizes' the supremacy of those dominant groups; Rubin contrasts the (often religious) discriminating, moralistic basis of these 'good/bad' categorizations with a 'democratic morality' which would judge sexual acts by the harm or pleasure inherent in the way partners treat one another (the level of mutual consideration, the presence or absence of coercion, and the quantity and quality of the pleasure they provide). Rubin's analysis of this conventional hierarchical stratification of sexuality highlighted the significance of the concept of 'respectability' in preference to more democratic notions of mutual respect and consent, and the hierarchy in 1980s America was therefore represented as shown in the diagram opposite (taken from Rubin, 1984: 282).

While the class at SEARCWL have consistently found these diagrams useful, students find it most interesting and productive to consider how regional cultures might apply Gayle Rubin's model of sexual hierarchies. Students are asked to locate different sexual behaviours, whether conforming to the 'charmed circle' (sex within marriage) or deviating from the mainstream (commercial or homosexual sex, for example) or somewhere in between (transgenerational or transactional sex) in relation to the hierarchies that exist in their own local contexts.

This forces students to consider critically the values, harms and patterns that emerge from analyzing their own cultures. Often for the first time, they find themselves obliged by other members of the group to scrutinize and justify or critique categorizations that they may well have previously taken for granted. Alternatively for some students this offers their first opportunity to voice their long-restrained critique of the sexual restrictions and prejudices that shape their own cultural scenarios. Additionally, this highlights some of the differences that occur within and between regional cultures and requires students to consider their own positions in relation to these categorizations. Obviously the categorizations vary across the region but students tend to agree that there are also some fairly consistent attributions of morality, to the extent that one possible mapping (suggested by the students) of the categorizations that apply across the southern and eastern African region might be as shown in the Figure 11.3 on page 298.

Often for the first time, … [students] find themselves obliged by other members of the group to scrutinize and justify or critique categorizations that they may well have previously taken for granted.

Figure 11. 2. The stratification of sex

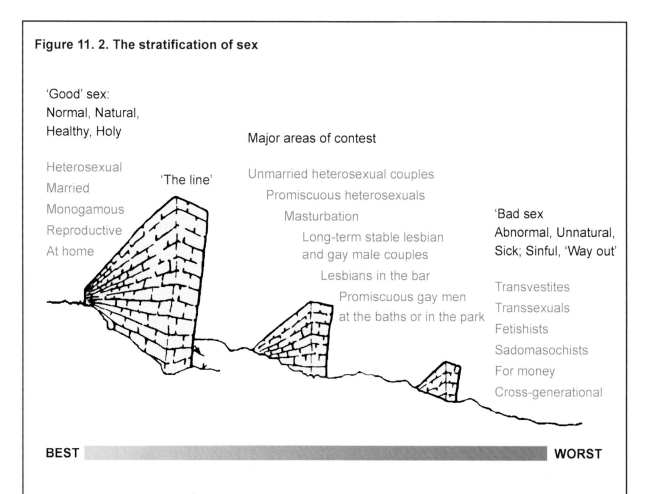

'Good' sex:
Normal, Natural,
Healthy, Holy

Major areas of contest

Heterosexual
Married
Monogamous
Reproductive
At home

'The line'

Unmarried heterosexual couples
Promiscuous heterosexuals
Masturbation
Long-term stable lesbian
and gay male couples
Lesbians in the bar
Promiscuous gay men
at the baths or in the park

'Bad sex
Abnormal, Unnatural,
Sick; Sinful, 'Way out'

Transvestites
Transsexuals
Fetishists
Sadomasochists
For money
Cross-generational

BEST   WORST

'The diagram lists on the left the kinds of sexual relationships and identities which are considered 'good' or socially approved, normal, natural, healthy or in line with dominant religious beliefs.

'It lists on the right the kinds of sexual relationships and identities which are considered 'bad', abnormal, morally wrong.

'In the middle are those relationships and identities which are gaining approval and are not considered completely bad or bizarre but are not fully accepted either.

'The diagram was developed to describe the situation in the United States in the 1980s. The categories may vary according to time and place, however, the key point is not what the categories are or where they are located, but that sexualities are ordered according to a hierarchy' (Esplen, Ilkkaracan and Jolly, 2007).

Figure 11.3: Suggested regional sexual hierarchies

Good sex	Major areas of contest	Bad sex
normal, natural	unmarried heterosexual couples	abnormal, unnatural
healthy, holy	promiscuous heterosexuals (some question of polygynous relations – for example, 'small houses')	sick, sinful, way out
heterosexual, married, monogamous, polygynous (still accepted but also subject to critique, for example, South Africa's President Zuma)	masturbation, active sexual agency by women, possibly long term gay male couples.	transvestites, transsexuals, homosexual men (certainly casual sex, maybe even long term gay relations), lesbians (often incur more disapproval and violence than gay men)
reproductive, at home	sugar daddies, transactional sex, bed hopping, transgenerational sex between adults (older women with younger men is far more problematic than older men with younger women)	sadomasochists, gay men for money, sex with underage youth, sex in public places, pornography, beastiality.

Students suggested the table above (roughly) reflected a basic consensus that could be mapped across the different cultures they originated from in the region. They found a number of differences between the sexual hierarchies specific to their own cultural contexts which tended to relate to the degree of censure attached to some types of 'bad sex'.

Examples of differences that students tend to note fairly consistently include variations in the acceptability of homosexuality, transgenerational sex and informal transactional sex (for example, 'sugar daddies') as well as the different impact that HIV/AIDS prevention programmes have had on behaviours in different cultural and social contexts (for example, the frequency of condom use and the visibility and organization of sex workers).

But on the whole the variations signaled by the students are either too diverse or too culturally specific and often too complex to discuss in detail here.

On this module students also found Ilkkaracan and Jolly's more recent (2007) critical application of Rubin's framework particularly germane to sexual politics in their own regions:

> 'However, what this stratification does not describe is the way that those who do conform, or fit into the socially approved categories of sex, may also lose out. For example, married women may be vulnerable to marital rape which remains unrecognized in many countries. Unemployed married men may feel as if they have failed as men in contexts where they are expected to be the breadwinner. The concept of sexual rights allows us to look beyond categories of socially approved and socially marginalized, to consider how rights for all can be sought' (Esplen, Ilkkaracan and Jolly, 2007).

In the 'Law, gender, and sexuality' module we therefore examine how sexuality and human rights interact, considering critically the productive platform that sexual health and reproductive rights can provide in advancing sexual rights more generally. However, this is not straightforward as a preoccupation with reproductive and sexual health can disguise or conceal the important role of sexual pleasure and the complications of sexual agency. For, while it is clear that developing women's sexual agency is central to the broader growth of reproductive and sexual health, this same growth of women's sexual agency will inevitably challenge the hierarchies of respectability so vividly identified in the application of Gayle Rubin's model of sexual hierarchies.

As is clear in the work of Carole Vance and Alice Miller (2004: 1–47), a key tension in developing sexual rights therefore arises from the contradiction between the significance of agency in sexual equality and the importance of a victim's apparent innocence (and respectability) in determining her ability to lay effective claim to human rights remedies – for women who are active sexual agents are rarely identified as respectable or 'innocent' victims easily deserving of remedies and yet the development of that agency is central to realizing women's sexual rights. This is most clearly illustrated in the person of a woman who has sex outside of marriage – her sexual agency is key to her autonomous control over her reproductive capacity and bodily integrity and yet that same sexual independence is likely to impact negatively on her social standing and reputation. Any lack of respectability will then make it harder to represent her as equally deserving of rights as the figure of the 'good wife'. Conventional discourses of morality tend to portray active sexual agents as 'bad' and inherently less deserving of rights and yet the foundational basis of human rights is that they should apply to all people regardless of marital status.[22] Sex workers too find that their sexual commodification removes them

...women who are active sexual agents are rarely identified as respectable or 'innocent' victims easily deserving of remedies

---

[22] For more on this see Miller (2004) and also Phillips (2009).

from the realm of 'respectability' that attaches more easily to rights claims and yet as sex workers they may well be in the most immediate need of asserting sexual rights claims.

As explained earlier, a second major theoretical framework that students find useful in considering social censure and sexual hierarchies is R.W. Connell's (1983) adaptation of Gramscian theories of hegemony to explain the structures and institutions that sustain ascendant stereotypes and behaviours within and between gender identities. Like Rubin's theoretical framework, Connell's tends also to be easily adapted on this module to students' own contexts. This is possibly because Connell's use of hegemony allows for a clear understanding of how particular behaviours serve to promote or subordinate specific values in relation to masculinity or femininity, so that certain traits are valorized as more ideally masculine or feminine while other, less ideal characteristics are attributed to subordinated masculinities/femininities. Students tend to recognize how different values, ascribed to particular types of manliness or particular types of femininity, offer a nuanced understanding of the construction of gender and particularly of the role of sexuality in the dual process of promoting particular gender types as ideal and subordinating others that fall short of the idealized normativity. Thus, a man who actively pursues women for sex and manifests his cultural and economic power through having multiple wives is regarded as highly masculine; indeed, he is rewarded with the very same accolades that serve to denigrate as powerless and lacking in masculine initiative the man who displays devotion to one wife, particularly if she has independent economic earning power and expresses her own opinions. Such independent behaviour may in turn lead her to be labelled a 'whore' (Seidman, 1984), a label that could equally result from wearing trousers, skirts above the knee or make-up (Runganga and Aggleton, 1998:75). Just as these behaviours all remove her ever farther from the hegemonic stereotype of a 'good wife', it is only possible to define what makes the latter 'good' through simultaneous reference to the characteristics that make a wife 'bad'. This simple but real example of the continuum upon which idealized and subordinated stereotypes of gender behaviour are developed, makes clear to students the role that sexuality can play in regulating relationships both within gender identities and between genders, so that they might readily apply this framework to their own cultural contexts.

Other models and theoretical perspectives are discussed and considered with variable results and while there is limited space for a full reflection of that discussion here, it is notable that Will Simon and John Gagnon's concept of sexual scripting appears to travel effectively across cultural landscapes. It offers students a way to account for the interaction between individual desire and the constraints of social context (at the three levels of cultural scenarios, interpersonal scripts and intrapsychic scripts) (Simon and Gagnon, 2007).

© Cartoonstock

Nerds have always had trouble picking up women

Stereotypes of sexual behaviour are key in empowering particular gender identities. These are regulated through the differential rewarding of different kinds of men ('real' men/'nurds') or different kinds of women (whores/ good wives), as well as through relationships between men and women as a whole.

But in order for students to properly assess the value of these conceptual frameworks for analyzing sexuality, they are also introduced to relevant regional research and scholarship (such as listed in footnote 8), and encouraged to critically consider how this research might reflect their own experience and social contexts. We also spend considerable time critically appraising research and analysis that is specifically African in origin or focus, such as Abdullahi An-Na'im on human rights and Jane Bennet, Pierre de Vos, Marc Epprecht, Charles Gueboguo, Neville Hoad, Kendall, Amina Mama, Patricia McFadden, Graeme Reid, Everjoice Winn and Mikki Van Zyl on cultural relativity and the writings of the class co-ordinators, Sylvia Tamale and Oliver Phillips.

The conceptual frameworks discussed in this chapter are intended to introduce students to some tools with which to analyze the relationship between law, gender and sexuality. This grounding prepares students for the second part of this module where they will have the opportunity to use these conceptual frameworks to analyze specific manifestations of gendered power in the regulation of sexuality, applying these conceptual approaches more directly to current law and politics in the region (see chapter 12 by Sylvia Tamale).

Conclusion: a platform for further development?

This chapter started by highlighting how the module's focus travels a road that is ordinarily patrolled by taboo and licensed with discretion, and is initially faced with trepidation and embarrassment on the part of students. This means that we need to adopt innovative and imaginative methods of teaching to maximize students' participation and engagement in the class. By overcoming their inhibitions and recognizing key gender dynamics we increase the possibility that this class might contribute to establishing a regional knowledge base of sexuality scholarship and equip both students and lecturers with tools to better engage with sexuality in their own professional worlds.

Earlier sections of this chapter outlined the historical and conceptual frameworks we use to establish a platform for analysis of sexual politics in the region, and the techniques and approaches we use to overcome students' initial reservations, issues and embarrassments. One mechanism is to draw on their curiosity and enable them to engage in a more rigorous and productive (but still fun) process of analysis and reflection that allows us all to think of how theory might usefully inform our lives personally, intellectually, politically and professionally. Achieving this has given the lecturers (Professor Tamale and myself) the opportunity to learn from the students' experiences and reflections about the applicability of conceptual frameworks as well as the customs, institutions and structural relationships of other sexual cultures.

Once students have been introduced to relevant historical work on regional sexual politics, have engaged in critically appraising key conceptual frameworks and have participated in the exercises described, they are keen and able to participate in a collective critique (along with the lecturers) of the direction that advocacy might take in relation to sexual politics. They can identify the goals we might advocate for and the utility of different strategies in achieving those goals. One of the most commonly assumed strategies for advocacy at the start of the twenty-first century is the realm of human rights but the many controversies that arise reveal that the relationship between sexuality and human rights cannot be taken for granted. In addition to the arguable limits of the legal framework for empowering women,[23] the assumed universalism of human rights and the cultural specificity of sexual practices and regulations immediately create specific tensions between issues of sexuality and human rights, as highlighted in the work of Alice Miller and Carole Vance discussed earlier. Yet this has not inhibited a massive investment in the discourse of rights the world over, whether by formally trained advocates or ordinary people, including in the realm of sexuality. By the end of the class students are better placed to consider the strategic significance and limitations of the human rights framework in advancing both analysis and advocacy around issues relating to sexuality (and gender) within the region and within students' own social contexts.

...students are better placed to consider the strategic significance and limitations of the human rights framework in advancing both analysis and advocacy around issues relating to sexuality

Many of the students' professional lives involve an explicit engagement with the concept of human rights and we actively encourage all the students to consider how the course material might inform their approach to their own work as criminal justice professionals (whether police or prison officer, magistrate or judge, non-governmental organization consultants, legal counsels, community or health workers or in whatever formal capacity they ordinarily work). They occupy positions where they are able to implement real changes and to directly and effectively apply at least some of the concepts and frameworks discussed in class. Similarly, it is their valuable experience in these capacities that informs the discussion in the class, augments the lecturer's knowledge-base and contributes significantly to the lecturer's own learning experience. This is why both Professor Tamale and I have found this module a powerful factor in our own educations. We both learn enormously, both pedagogically and substantively, from our interaction with the students.

The twin tasks of assessing human rights strategies and professionally implementing change came together most fruitfully in one particular case that clearly illustrates the potential utility of this module. This involved a student who, prior to her arrival at SEARCWL, was a member of her country's

---

[23] For more on the limits of law as a vehicle for empowering women, see Carol Smart (1989).

human rights commission. During her time at SEARCWL she was elected to serve as chair of that commission and at the end of the sexuality module, she commented:

> 'Last year the Human Rights Commission was obliged to deal with an issue relating to sexuality and human rights, and we had no idea how to even start engaging with it, let alone discussing it. Now, I feel confident that the next time such an issue arises, and it is bound to arise, I shall have some very concrete ideas on how we should deal with the question and how we should frame our approach to these issues.'

If the module achieves this level of impact on even an occasional basis, that will be a notable achievement. But even without this direct impact, the mere existence of this module is something to celebrate as an indication of the broader development of a field of sexuality scholarship in the region. It reflects the fact that SEARCWL is part of the growing wave of sexuality scholarship in southern and eastern Africa. The truly regional basis of SEARCWL as an institution is extremely important in creating a trans-national and continental network that lends credibility and strong intellectual support to the growth of sexuality scholarship. Much of this chapter is premised on the need for special attention to be given to the issue of sexuality in analyzing gender and law; the ultimate goal is to do away with that need and to reach a situation where sexuality is embedded as an inherent part of the analysis of gender and law, and beyond that, is recognized as a subject of research and scholarship that has a validity of its own.

Bibliography

Alexander M.J. (2003) 'Not just (any) *body* can be a citizen: the politics of law, sexuality and postcoloniality in Trinidad and Tobago and the Bahamas', pages 174-182 in J. Weeks, J. Holland and M. Waites (eds.) *Sexualities and society: a reader*, Polity Press, Cambridge.

Amadiume I. (1987) 'The politics of motherhood,' in I. Amadiume (ed) *Male daughters, female husbands: gender and sex in an African Society*, Zed Books.

– (1997) *Reinventing Africa: matriarchy, religion and culture*, Zed Books, London.

Amory D. (1997) '"Homosexuality" in Africa: issues and debates', *ISSUE: A Journal of Opinion* 25(1): 5-10.

An-Na'im A.A. (1992) 'Towards a cross-cultural approach to defining international standards of human rights', pages 19–43 in A.A.An-Na'im (ed) *Human rights in cross-cultural perspectives: a quest for consensus*, University of Pennsylvania Press, Philadelphia.

Arnfred S. (ed) (2004) *Rethinking sexualities in southern Africa*, Nordiska Afrikainstitut, Uppsala.

Beauvoir S. de (1949/1984) *The second sex*, Penguin Modern Classics, Penguin, Harmondsworth.

Brittan A. and M. Maynard (1984) *Sexism, racism, and oppression*, Basil Blackwell, Oxford.

Butler J. (1990) *Gender trouble: feminism and the subversion of identity*, Routledge, London.

– (1993) *Bodies that matter*, Routledge, London and New York.

Campbell C. (2004) 'Migrancy, masculine identities, and AIDS; the psychosocial context of HIV transmission on the South African gold mines', pages 144–154 in E. Kalipeni, S. Craddock, J. R. Oppong and J. Ghosh (eds) *HIV/AIDS in Africa: beyond epidemiology*, Blackwell, Oxford.

Chanock M. (1985) *Law, custom and social order: the colonial experience in Malawi and Zambia*, Polity Press, Cambridge.

– (1982) 'Making customary law: men, women, and courts in colonial Northern Rhodesia', pages 53–67 in M. Hay and M. Wright (eds) *African women and the law: historical perspectives*, Papers on Africa VII, Boston University, Boston.

Comaroff J. (1997) 'The discourse of rights in colonial South Africa: subjectivity, sovereignty, sodernity', pages 193–236 in A. Sarat and T.R. Kearns (eds) *Identities, politics and rights*, University of Michigan Press, Michigan.

Connell R.W. (1987) *Gender and power*, Polity Press, Cambridge.

– (1995) *Masculinities*, Polity Press, Cambridge.

Epprecht M. (2004) *Hungochani: the history of a dissident sexuality in southern Africa*, McGill-Queens University Press, Montreal.

– (2008) *Heterosexual Africa? The history of an idea from the age of exploration to the age of AIDS*, University of KwaZulu-Natal Press, Durban.

Esplen E., P. Ilkkaracan and S. Jolly (2007) *Gender and sexuality*, BRIDGE Cutting Edge Pack, Institute of Development Studies, Brighton.

Foucault M. (1978) *The history of sexuality: an introduction*, Peregrine, London.

Fried S. (2004) 'Sexuality and human rights', *Health and Human Rights* 7(2):273–304.

Gelfand M. (1975a) '*Kukanganisa musikana*: seduction in Shona law', *NADA* XI(3):321–27.

– (1975b) '*Kutiza mukumbo* and *kutiziswa mukumbo*: elopement in Shona law', *NADA* XI(4): 443–48.

Gilligan C. (1993) *In a different voice*, Harvard University Press, Cambridge, MA.

Gilman S.L. (1986) *Difference and pathology: stereotypes of sexuality, race, and madness*, Cornell University Press, New York.

Gueboguo C. (2006) 'L'homosexualité en Afrique: sens et variations d'hirer a nos jours', *Socio-logos* 1/2006, available online at: http://socio-logos.revues.org/document37.html.

Hansen K.T. (1989) *Distant companions: servants and employers in Zambia 1900-1985*, Cornell University Press, New York.

Hoad N., K. Martin and G. Reid (eds) (2005) *Sex and politics in South Africa*, Juta and Co., Johannesburg.

Hobsbawm E. and T. Ranger (eds) (1991) *The invention of tradition*, Canto (Cambridge University Press), Cambridge.

Hocquenghem G. (1972/1993) *Homosexual desire*, translated by D. Dangoor, Duke University Press, London.

Holland J., C. Ramazonaglou, S. Sharpe and R. Thomson (2003) 'When bodies come together: power, control and desire', pages 84–94 in J. Weeks, J. Holland and M. Waites (eds) *Sexualities and society: a reader*, Polity Press, Cambridge.

Human Rights Watch, and International Gay and Lesbian Human Rights Commission (2003) *More than a name: state-sponsored homophobia and its consequences in southern Africa*, Human Rights Watch, New York.

Jacobs S.M. (1984) 'Women and land resettlement in Zimbabwe', *Review of African Political Economy* 27/28: 33-50.

Jeater D. (1993) *Marriage, perversion and power: the construction of moral discourse in Southern Rhodesia 1894–1930*, Clarendon Press, Oxford.

Kapur R. (2005) *Erotic justice: law and the new politics of post-colonialism*, Glasshouse Press (Cavendish), London.

Kendall (1998) '"When a woman loves a woman" in Lesotho: love, sex and the (western) construction of homophobia', pages 223–241 in S.O. Murray and W. Roscoe (eds) *Boy-wives and female husbands: studies of African homosexualities*, St Martin's Press, New York.

Kennedy D. (1987) *Islands of white: settler society and culture in Kenya and Southern Rhodesia 1890–1939*, Duke University Press, Durham.

Krafft-Ebing R. von (1886/1999) *Psychopathia sexualis – a clinical-forensic study*, Bloat Books, Burbank CA.

Mamdani M. (1996) *Citizen and subject; contemporary Africa and the legacy of late colonialism*, Princeton University Press, Princeton.

Mbilinyi M. and N. Kaihula (2000) 'Sinners and outsiders: the drama of AIDS in Rungwe', pages 76–94 in C. Baylies and J. Bujra (eds) *AIDS, sexuality and gender in Africa: collective strategies and struggles in Tanzania and Zambia*, Routledge, London and New York.

McFadden P. (1992) 'Sex, sexuality and the problems of AIDS in Africa', in R. Meena (ed), *Gender in southern Africa: conceptual and theoretical issues*, SAPES, Harare.

– (2003) 'Sexual health and rights for African women', in B. Madunagu (ed), *Social and gender justice*, Development Alternatives with Women for a New Era (DAWN), Calabar, Nigeria.

Menon U. (2000) 'Does feminism have universal relevance? The challenges posed by Oriya Hindu family practices', *Daedalus* 129(4): 77–100.

Miller A. and C. Vance (2004) 'Sexuality, human rights and health', *Health and Human Rights* 7(2):5-15.

Miller, A. (2004) 'Sexuality, violence against women and human rights: women make demands, ladies get protection', *Health and Human Rights* 7(2): 16-47.

Mohanty C.T. (1991) 'Under western eyes: feminist scholarship and colonial discourses', page 74 in C.T. Mohanty, A. Russo and L. Torres (eds) *Third world women and the politics of feminism*, Indiana University Press, Bloomington.

Morgan R. and S. Weiringa (eds) (2006) *Tommy boys, lesbian men and ancestral wives: female same sex practices in Africa*, Jacana, Johannesburg.

Murray S. and W. Roscoe (1998) *Boy-wives and female husbands: studies of African homosexualities*, St Martin's Press, New York.

Narayan U. (1997) 'Contesting cultures: "westernization", respect for cultures, and third-world feminists', pages 3–39 in U. Narayan, *Dislocating cultures*, Routledge, New York.

Ortner S.B. and H. Whitehead (eds) (1981) *Sexual meanings: the cultural construction of gender and sexuality*, Cambridge University Press, Cambridge.

Oyewùmí O. (1997) *The invention of women: making an African sense of western gender discourse*, University of Minnesota Press, Minneapolis and London.

Pape J. (1990) 'Black and white peril: the "perils of sex" in colonial Zimbabwe', *Journal of Southern African Studies* 16(4):699–719 Dec 1990.

Petchesky R. (2003) 'Negotiating reproductive rights', in J. Weeks, J. Holland and M. Waites (eds.) *Sexualities and society: a reader*, Macmillan, London.

Phillips O.C. (1997) 'Zimbabwean law and the production of a white man's disease', *Social and Legal Studies* 6 (4): 471–491.

– (2000) 'Constituting the global gay: individual subjectivity and sexuality in southern Africa', in C. Stychin and D. Herman (eds), *Sexuality in the legal arena*, Athlone/University of Minnesota Press, London/Minnesota.

– (2001) 'Myths and realities of African sexuality', *African Studies Review* 44 (2):195–201.

– (2004a) 'The invisible presence of homosexuality: implications for HIV/AIDS and rights in southern Africa', pages 155–166 in E. Kalipeni, S. Craddock, J.R. Oppong and J. Ghosh (eds), *HIV/AIDS in Africa: beyond epidemiology*, Blackwell, Oxford.

– (2004b) '(Dis)continuities of custom in Zimbabwe and South Africa: the implications for gendered and sexual rights', *Health and Human Rights* 7(2): 82–113.

– (2006) 'Gender, justice and human rights in post-colonial Zimbabwe and South Africa', in F. Heidensohn (ed), *Gender and justice: new concepts and approaches*, Willan Publishing, Collumpton.

– (2009) 'Blackmail in Zimbabwe: troubling narratives of sexuality and human rights, *International Journal of Human Rights* 13(2 & 3):345-364.

Rich A. (1999) 'Compulsory heterosexuality and lesbian existence', pages 199–225 in R. Parker and P. Aggleton (eds) *Culture, society and sexuality: a reader*, UCL Press, London.

Roberts H. (1981) (ed) *Doing feminist research*, Routledge & Kegan Paul, London.

Rothschild C. (2004) 'Not your average sex story: critical issues in recent reporting on human rights and sexuality', *Health and Human Rights* 7(2):165–178.

Rubin G. (1984) 'Thinking sex: notes for a radical theory of the politics of sexuality', pages 267–319 in C. Vance (ed), *Pleasure and danger: exploring female sexuality*, Routledge & Kegan Paul, Boston; Reprinted (2007) pages 150–187 in R. Parker, P. Aggleton (eds), *Culture, society and sexuality: a reader*, (2nd edition), Routledge, London.

Runganga A. and P. Aggleton (1998) 'Migration, the family and the transformation of a sexual culture', *Sexualities* 1(1): 63–81.

Saiz I. (2004) 'Bracketing sexuality: human rights and sexual orientation – a decade of development and denial at the UN', *Health and Human Rights* 7(2): 48–81.

Schmidt E. (1990) 'Negotiated spaces and contested terrain: men, women and the law in colonial Zimbabwe, 1890-1939', *Journal of Southern African Studies* 16(4) Dec 1990: 622–648.

Seidman G. (1984) 'Women in Zimbabwe: post-independence struggles', *Feminist Studies* 10(3):432 (Fall).

Shire C. (1994) 'Language, space and masculinities in Zimbabwe', pages 147–158 in A. Cornwall and N. Lindisfarne (eds), *Dislocating masculinities: comparative ethnographies*, Routledge, London.

Simon W. and J.H. Gagnon (2007) 'Sexual scripts', pages 31-40 in R. Parker and P. Aggleton (eds) *Culture, society and sexuality: a reader*, second edition, Routledge: London.

Smart C. (1989) *Feminism and the power of law*, Routledge, London.

– (1995) *Law, crime and sexuality: essays in feminism*, Sage, London.

Tamale S. (2005) 'Eroticism, sensuality and "women's secrets" among the Baganda: a critical analysis', *Feminist Africa* 5, available online at: http://www.feministafrica.org/05-2005/feature-sylvia.htm

Tambiah Y. (1995) 'Sexuality and human rights', pages 369–390 in M.A. Schuler (ed), *From basic needs to basic rights: women's claim to human rights*, Women, Law, and Development International, Washington DC.

Van Zyl M. and M. Steyn (eds) (2005) *Performing queer: shaping sexualities 1994–2004 Volume 1*, Kwela Books, Cape Town.

– (eds) (2009) *The prize and the price: shaping sexualities in South Africa Volume 2*, HSRC Press, Cape Town.

Vance C. (1984) *Pleasure and danger: exploring female sexuality*, Routledge & Kegan Paul, London.

Vos P. de (2004) 'Same-sex sexual desire and the re-imagining of the South African family', *South African Journal on Human Rights* 20 (179).

Weeks J. (1985) *Sexuality and its discontents: meanings, myths and modern sexualities*, Routledge & Kegan Paul, London.

White L. (1990) *The comforts of home: prostitution in colonial Nairobi*, University of Chicago Press, Chicago.

Zalduondo B. de (1999) 'Prostitution viewed cross-culturally: toward recontextualizing sex work in AIDS intervention research', pages 307–324 in R. Parker and P. Aggleton (eds), *Culture, society and sexuality: a reader*, UCL Press, London.

12

Gendered sexualities, power and legal mechanisms in Africa

Interrogating the link: experiences from the lecture room

Sylvia Tamale

Part I: Setting the stage –
'Are we really going to talk about sex?'

Talking about sex in public is taboo in most societies. Therefore when postgraduate (mostly) law students at the University of Zimbabwe Southern and Eastern African Regional Centre for Women's Law (SEARCWL) are confronted with the choices of elective courses, most view the course 'Gender, law and sexuality' (MWL518) and its underlying agenda with a certain amount of unease, curiosity, even suspicion. This is despite the fact that it is a second semester course for graduate students who have previously spent a semester being exposed to theories and perspectives in women's law.

Sexuality as an area of serious scholarship in legal academies in and outside Africa is a relatively new phenomenon. Thus, it is critical to use creative teaching methods that very early on in the course 'break the ice', bridge the lecturer–student divide and create a 'safe environment' for meaningful discussions. An approach that presents fresh, relevant and critical perspectives to sexuality is always a challenge to the lecturer. In the main, students at SEARCWL come from different countries in southern and eastern Africa. Depending on the individuals that enrol for the class, each course group presents its own dynamics, diversities and experiences. Navigating and negotiating such quandaries can sometimes prove to be quite sticky.

This course has two main objectives. The first is to demonstrate how sexuality is instrumentalized and deployed by culture, religion and the law,

...it is critical to use creative teaching methods that very early on in the course 'break the ice', bridge the lecturer–student divide and create a 'safe environment' for meaningful discussions

among others, as a control mechanism for maintaining unequal power relations in African societies. Here, the main focus is on acquiring a deeper understanding of how sex, sexuality and gender are interlinked with the law in its pluralities, and with other sites and structures of power, to regulate sexual relations and to consolidate control.[1] Secondly, we explore sexuality as an alternative and empowering force for challenging gender and power hierarchies. Through an exploration of the linkages between the human body, gender, sexuality and culture, we critically examine the social, cultural and legal constructions of sexuality as they intersect with gender. While we focus a lot on women, the issues traversed are not about women alone; rather, they are about the role that the law plays in maintaining particular sexual relationships and identities for both women and men, structuring and reinforcing a gendered society wherein women are largely subordinated to men.

...we explore sexuality as an alternative and empowering force for challenging gender and power hierarchies

The readings and assignments are selected to challenge students to recognize the intersecting aspects of gender, law, sexuality, culture and identity, and the ways in which individuals and groups have resisted and continue to resist oppression. The course is designed for maximum interaction and vigorous student participation in ways that are comfortable and engaging. As much as possible, examples are drawn from everyday experiences and references to real cases from across the continent are used throughout the course. Fortunately, there is never a lack of media exposure of current stories on issues of sexuality from around the continent. Examples discussed in the 2009 class included:

● The case of the Zambian Editor, Chansa Kabwela, who was arrested and charged with circulating 'obscene/pornographic materials'. She had sent pictures of a woman giving birth in the parking lot of a government hospital (where health workers were on strike) to government officials. The dead baby was in breach position and the graphic pictures showed its legs hanging from its mother's vagina.[2]

● The female Sudanese journalist, Lubna al-Hussein, who was arrested for wearing trousers in public and faced the penalty of flogging for violating an indecency law in that country.[3]

● The case of the South African athlete, Caster Samenya, the 800 metre champion, whose ambiguous sex identity was called into question, raising the issue of whether intersexed individuals have a right to compete in sports.[4]

---

[1] Halley (2006) expresses reservations about the efficacy of feminism in analyzing sexuality and power. Until alternative theories are developed, we maintain that sex and gender currently offer the best frames for analyzing sexuality and power.

[2] See http://www.lusakatimes.com/?p=14633

[3] See www.wikio.com/themes/Lubna+Hussein

[4] See www.mg.co.za/.../2009-09-12-sa-officials-meet-on-semenya

The first module of the course (taught by Dr Oliver Phillips – see chapter 11) introduces students to some key conceptual approaches and historical studies that are useful in considering the relationship between law and culture, as relates directly to sexuality and gender. I present the second module of the course which relates theory to the more specific manifestations of gendered power in the legal regulation of sexuality. By the end of the course we expect students to have acquired the necessary analytical skills to critically question seemingly 'gender-neutral', 'objective' and 'universal' legal concepts and sexual norms. They should leave the course wearing gendered lenses that allow them to perceive and understand the subtle ways – normally hidden – which the law employs to perpetuate gender discrimination through sexuality. At the same time, students who have gone through this course appreciate the positive, empowering aspects of sexuality — reflected through resistance, subversion, negotiation, identity, self-desire, pleasure and silence.

My own inspiration in designing this course was rooted in the glaring gap that existed in legal training for analyzing sexuality. I wished to create a space for law students to conceptualize sexuality beyond the 'funny' rape cases that they encountered in the traditional criminal law classes. The African Gender Institute at the University of Cape Town was critical in crystallizing my motivation and sharpening my scholarship in this area. In 2002 I was actively involved in developing the teaching resources for lecturers in gender and women's studies on the continent. The African Gender Institute organized several workshops with various African feminist scholars to discuss pedagogical and content issues in the area of women's studies.[5] It was here that I honed participative feminist teaching methods, imbibed a rich array of literature (published and unpublished) and developed invaluable linkages with like-minded scholars across the continent. My close involvement in the 'Mapping African Sexualities' research project organized by the African Gender Institute and the Institute of African Studies (IAS) at the University of Ghana in 2003 was the culmination of this learning process and sealed my conviction that this area was of critical importance to emerging academic discourse on the continent.

This chapter discusses the pedagogical issues and methodological tools that I employ in the second module of the course. While the main focus is on its instructional aspects, some non-pedagogical issues that are more conceptual and legal obviously form part of the discussion. Some of the questions that the chapter attempts to address are as follows:

- How do we get over the initial reservations, embarrassments and reticence to involve the class in rigorous, productive and engaging analyses and reflections?

---

[5] For further details see http://www.gwsafrica.org/teaching/

- What skills do I experiment with in trying to link theory to everyday experience as well as to its application to the professional work students engage in?

- What resources are available to demonstrate how legal mechanisms associated with sexuality hinder and/or facilitate social change or transformation?

- What tools do I employ in helping students 'unlearn' deeply embedded knowledge and 're-learn' innovative ways of building new theories of knowledge?

Each year is a new learning process for me and for the students, built and facilitated by our mutual symbiotic synergies.

After this introduction, Part II gives a contextual overview of the course before delving into a pedagogical discussion of some strategies that I employ to break the sexual taboos in the lecture room environment in Part III. Part IV discusses the unlearning and re-learning processes that the course participants experience. Part V reflects on the pedagogical aspects of linking gender/sexuality theory to social, cultural and political practice. In Part VI I explore the transformational potential in transgressive sexuality,[6] illustrating how students learn to question the very categories through which society constructs, regulates and systematizes the sexual. Finally Part VII reflects on the lessons that I have so far learnt from facilitating this course, the challenges encountered and its future prospects.

Part II: Contextualizing African sexualities

Popular understanding of the term 'sexuality' is often limited and closely linked to 'the sex act'.[7] In other words, the physical looms large over the course. Hence one of the first tasks undertaken in the course is to broaden such understanding by showing the way that sexuality is deeply embedded in almost all aspects of human life. The historical, social, cultural, political and legal meanings and interpretations attached to the human body largely translate into sexuality and systematically infuse our relationship to desire, politics, religion, identity, dress, movement, kinship structures, disease, social roles and language.

Using a historical approach to sexualities in Africa is extremely important for this course for three main reasons. First of all, it helps students appreciate the significance of various forces such as colonialism, religion, capitalism and

---

[6] 'Transgressive sexuality' constitutes sexual acts that are seen to defy or violate culturally accepted norms and are described as immoral, defiling and even unnatural.

[7] Not just any 'sex act' but heterosexual, procreative intercourse.

culture in shaping and influencing sexuality on the continent. For example, tracing the history of rape law in common law jurisdictions reveals that it was designed to protect the honour and the 'property' that men (the husband and/or father) had through the victim and not to protect the victim's bodily integrity. It explains why the crime does not fall under 'offences against the person' but under the 'offences against morality' sections of most penal codes that directly imported this crime from former European colonial states. It further explains the law's narrow, restrictive approach to what constitutes rape. The historical analyses also shed light on, say, the exemptions placed on marital rape and why evidentiary rules for rape allow the accused rapist to introduce the sexual history of the victim as a mitigating factor (Coughlin, 1998). The phallocentric nature of the offence is also manifest from the requirement of penile-vagina penetration as a main ingredient of the crime.[8]

The second reason for taking a historical perspective is that this approach reveals the dynamism of the phenomenon of sexuality and how it has continued to unfold over the years. Finally, a historical lens assists students in developing a broader view of contemporary sexual controversies, placing them in their proper contexts. Learning about the sexual diversities and realities that existed on the continent prior to contact with Europeans and Arabs, for example, offers perspectives that recognize the complexity and depth of African sexualities. History will likewise explain the pervasive double standards that govern men and women's sexual morality in Africa.[9] Therein lies the answer to questions like 'Whose morality?' and 'What purpose do such moral codes serve?'.

Delving into the history of African sexualities and engaging with its political economy is usually a new experience for most lawyers in the class. For example, a historical discussion of the case of the Khoisan woman, Saartjie (Sarah) Baartman, the so-called 'Hottentot Venus', is as fascinating as it is shocking to students. Baartman, who was born in South Africa, was forcibly taken to Europe in 1810 and her naked body exhibited on the streets of Britain and France like a zoo animal. Londa Schiebinger reports that Sarah Baartman was 'exhibited like a wild beast' with a focus on her buttocks and genitalia 'which, for an extra charge, viewers could poke and prod' (Schiebinger, 1993: 169).[10] The response to Baartman symbolizes the racist, imperialist and sexist representations of African women's sexuality by colonial powers.

The response to Baartman symbolizes the racist, imperialist and sexist representations of African women's sexuality by colonial powers

---

[8] The irony is that while the colonizing countries have long jettisoned or amended these laws to reflect more equitable gender concerns, most former colonies are jealously holding on to the anachronistic and archaic laws in a bid to maintain a stranglehold over women's lives.

[9] Examples of such double standards are evident in the laws governing criminal adultery, prostitution, monogamy, evidentiary rules, and so on.

[10] Sarah Baartman died in France in 1816, aged 26, where her remains were displayed at the Museum of Mankind until the 1970s. In 2002, her remains were finally returned for a dignified burial in South Africa.

It throws light on the current attitudes towards African women's sexualities (medicalized, maternal, promiscuous, and so on) that stem from colonial policies and institutions. Such stereotypes have been internalized by many Africans and are often repeated in media reports, research reports and popular culture. It also explains the nature of sexual laws in most postcolonial states that aim at suppressing and regulating women's sexuality following the model of Victorian Europe.

Indeed, texts from nineteenth century reports authored by white explorers, missionaries and anthropologists reveal a clear pattern of the ethnocentric and racist constructions of African sexualities. They foisted gross simplifications on extremely complex realities. Narratives equated black sexuality with primitiveness. African sexuality was depicted as crude, exotic and bordering on nymphomania. Perceived as immoral, bestial and lascivious, Africans were caricatured as having lustful dispositions. Their sexuality was read directly into their physical attributes; and those attributes were believed to reflect the essential culture and morality of Africans.[11] By constructing Africans as bestial, the colonialists could easily justify and legitimize the fundamental objectives of colonialism: it was a 'civilizing mission' to the barbarian and savage natives of the 'dark continent.'

By constructing Africans as bestial, the colonialists could easily justify and legitimize the fundamental objectives of colonialism

Furthermore, the fact that laws that govern sexualities in Africa are sourced from various legal systems (cultural, religious or statutory) poses different and extremely complex challenges. The pluralistic legal systems found in most African countries are theoretically governed by a hierarchical paradigm whereby 'modern' statutory law takes precedence over cultural and religious laws. In other words, applicability of the latter is subjected to the 'repugnancy' test, meaning that only those indigenous/religious practices and values that are not repugnant to (colonial) natural justice, equity and good conscience pass the test. And yet a critical examination of students' own experiences and knowledge about human relations (including sexuality) in Africa reveals that it is culture or religion and not statutory law that governs the day-to-day interactions of most African people. Legal tensions around social institutions such as polygyny, bigamy, bridewealth and adultery, and how they relate to gender, power and sexuality are discussed. Hence, the gap between law-in-the-books and law-in-action even when it comes to sexuality is very apparent.

Family structures (and their evolution) present another important contextual feature of this course. Given its rich and diverse cultures, the African continent hosts a range of family arrangements and a plethora of kinship relations. Students from various countries share their cultural practices with the rest of the class. The revelations that come to students during these discussions are always astounding. They discover the range of existing family structures

---

[11] For a critical re-creation of the racism and sexism at the heart of European imperialism, see Chase-Reboud (2003) and also Gilman (1986).

and authority systems — patriarchal, patrilineal or matrilineal, patrilocal or matrilocal, exogamous or endogamous, extended or nuclear, polygynous or polyandrous — and the significance of the impact of these different social systems on gender, sexuality and violence. The link is also made between various 'marriage' arrangements and sexuality. A good example is the practice of *chimutsamapfihwa* among the Shona ethnic group of the Ndaus in eastern Zimbabwe—a type of surrogacy that links the institution of *lobola*, barrenness and reproductive rights (see box 1).[12] Such a traditional concept facilitates the class understanding the delinking of sexuality from reproduction in some African traditions.

Using seminal works such as those by Ifi Amadiume (1987), we explore the historical and ethnocentric conceptualizations of African family structures, tracing their impact on African sexuality discourses. A deeper examination of more contemporary family arrangements that are at odds with the dominant, socially accepted ones (for example, single-parenting, same-sex relations) also helps in unveiling the close relationship between the institution of the (heterosexual) family and the social processes of sexuality control.

For a more nuanced, critical approach we try to avoid situations that encourage what Gordon and Cornwall (2004) describe as 'the tyranny of consensus' whereby no space is created for minority individuals to express difference and to explore personal feelings. A good example is our interrogation with the concepts of 'culture' and 'rights'. Instead of presenting the two concepts as distinct, invariably opposed and antagonistic, we explore the emancipatory potential of culture to enhance the quality of lives in Africa. The potential that culture holds for emancipating women in Africa is often buried, for instance, in the avalanche of literature many feminist scholars devote to the 'barbaric' cultural practice of female genital mutilation. Not only is there an acute lack of sensitivity to and recognition of grassroots and local initiatives undertaken by African groups and activists in this regard but the missionary zeal applied to the enterprise often produces a negative backlash.[13] By taking such an approach, we surface

---

BOX 1

Chigadzamapfihwa – 'one who lights the fire'

Lobola (bridewealth) transferred the woman's total self (productive and reproductive rights) to her husband's family. Once acquired, the woman's sexuality remained a resource for the whole clan and neither barrenness nor death terminated this chain of obligations between the two clans.

In the event that the wife was not able to bear children, her family would organize a young woman from her brothers' offspring who would go and stay with the barren woman and bear children for her with no additional transfer of *lobola*. The young woman (*chigadzamapfihwa* — the one lighting a fire where there was no fire) can remain in the family and be the man's second wife and continue to bear children for him.

…we explore the emancipatory potential of culture to enhance the quality of lives in Africa

---

[12] As told to the class by Rebecca Magorokosho (class of 2009).

[13] While culturally-sensitive, holistic approaches to the elimination of the practice of female genital mutilation condemn its rights violations and the health risks associated with it, they acknowledge its positive aspects, for example, the celebration of the rite of passage and rite of 'being' which is crucial for people's identity and culture. Alternative rites of passage have been successfully adopted in countries such as Kenya to maintain the underlying positive social value that the practice represents.

the limitations that stem from holding culture and rights as binary opposites on our strategic interventions for transforming society (Tamale, 2008).

Finally, a human rights perspective provides an excellent framework for contextualizing African sexualities. Speaking the language of rights to lawyers and activists is relatively easy because it has become hegemonic in the search for equality for the marginalized. Although 'sexual rights' as a concept has not yet been fully embraced by the international community, we explore the various rights incorporated in existing national bills of rights that relate to human sexuality. These include: respect for bodily integrity; protection from violence; the right to privacy; the right to decide freely the number, spacing and timing of children; the right to sexuality education; equal protection of the law; and non-discrimination.[14] By discussing sexuality, sexual health and reproductive health as issues of human rights, we shed new light on issues such as abortion, prostitution, homosexuality and HIV/AIDS. In particular, we attempt to demonstrate the centrality of 'bodily integrity' (in other words, the control of ones sexuality and reproductive capacities) to the emancipation of African women. Exploring the connections between sexuality and citizenship and what it means to be a 'sexual citizen' against the backdrop of imported colonial sex laws, rising fundamentalisms (cultural, religious, economic), political dictatorship and militarization helps unravel the challenges associated with realizing such rights.

The whole discussion of sexual rights is conducted with the sensitivity to the tensions inherent in the conceptualization of sexuality within the framework of rights. Alice Miller and others have articulated the paradoxes that burden the context of 'rights' when it comes to sexuality (Miller and Vance, 2004): one cannot simultaneously use the language of sexual rights to police 'harm' (for example, freedom from rape or tackling homophobia) *and* to demand 'privacy' (for example to defend the sexual pleasure of consenting adults). The contradictions can be seen further in claims for the 'right to privacy' while at the same time you speak of 'freedom from marital rape' or the awkwardness of claiming the 'rights' of people to sell/make images of sexual activity and simultaneously claim that people should be 'protected from' sexual objectification.

By discussing sexuality, sexual health and reproductive health as issues of human rights, we shed new light on issues such as abortion, prostitution, homosexuality and HIV/AIDS

---

[14] This discussion is conducted in the context of 'cultural relativism' and the limitations of fitting all sexuality issues within the framework of rights claims.

Part III: Transversing stigmatized boundaries, breaking with sexual taboos

As stated earlier, it is an enormous challenge for us to create a relatively free and safe space where students can shake off all inhibitions and feel comfortable enough to have a frank and meaningful intellectual discourse and engaging discussions on a range of sexuality topics (Muchera, 2004). Finding ways of lifting the shroud of secrecy, taboos and silences that engulfs sexuality matters and breaking through the hegemonic moral code that associates sexuality with shame and guilt requires skillful creativity and resourcefulness. Sensitive, uncomfortable subjects such as masturbation, menstruation, orgasms, same-sex erotics, incest, abortion, wet dreams, sadomasochism, infidelity, sexually transmitted diseases, aphrodisiacs, erotic fantasies, oral sex, cyber sex, pornography and so forth are brought into public discourse. Direct reference to male and female genitals without use of sanitized euphemisms is also encouraged. Such strategic 'disruptions' of the social constructions of sexuality are integral to the students' unlearning and relearning curve.

Carefully thought-out strategies and tools are employed to help students open up and shift their attitudes beyond the stigmatized subject matter of sexuality. This is extremely important in order for us to achieve our objectives and to spice up the sessions so that students get emotionally charged and engrossed in the subject matter. For example, I make use of the 'question basket' technique whereby students anonymously place 'embarrassing' questions for class discussion at an appropriate time.[15] A candid discussion of a range of hitherto taboo topics on sexuality provides a means of empowering students on the journey towards informed choices, better control of their lives as well as the skills to challenge hegemonic sexuality discourse.

A candid discussion of a range of hitherto taboo topics on sexuality provides a means of empowering students on the journey towards informed choices, better control of their lives as well as the skills to challenge hegemonic sexuality discourse

On day one of the course, it is important for the class to formulate some basic ground rules that will operate through the duration of the course. Involving students in setting these standards means that they will 'own them' and therefore feel more obliged to honour them. Usually the rules are along the following lines: respect other people's views and opinions even when you are challenging them; tolerate differences, including diverse identities, lifestyles and sexual orientations; confidentiality—private or sensitive stories shared in class should not be broadcast outside; allow others to contribute by not interrupting and/or dominating discussions; allow individuals to 'pass' when they are unwilling or not ready to speak; exercise your right to ask questions as there are no 'stupid' questions; avoid disparaging stereotypes that fuel

---

[15] An example of a question that keeps turning up in this basket is: 'How do lesbians have sex?'

BOX 2
Moons waiting[16]

Many a woman know the feeling
Of intercourse, then overdue moons
The waiting, anxiety, desperation…

Crouched on the hard bench of the lab
The acrid smells pricking my nostrils
Like a convict in a dock
I waited for the verdict

The results hit like a sledgehammer
P-o-s-i-t-i-v-e!

I had just turned nineteen
A fresher at the university
My future bright and promising
Not ready to become a mother
I had to restore my moon cycle

'Thou shalt not take the life of the unborn'
Said Mr Law
'Will you take care of it when it's born?"
I asked Mr Law
'Of Course Not'

The abortion was swift and efficient
Or so I thought
Two days later I lay in the Intensive Care Unit
They had been twins,
One remained rotting inside me
To save my dear life,
It had to be flushed out…
Together with my womb

An eternal end to moons waiting

[16] I was inspired to write this poem after one of my students at Makerere University related her own true story to me .

different types of –isms, for example, racism, ageism and sexism; and prepare for class by reading assigned materials.

As much as possible, we avoid long lecture sessions, preferring instead an interactive seminar environment where students actively participate through large/small group discussions, role play skits, visual clips, debates, poetry, personal testimonies, case studies and peer reviewing. Participatory, interactive learning is a major tenet of feminist pedagogical strategies (Hooks, 1989; Omolade, 1993). As lecturer, I take on the role of a mere *facilitator* of students' learning and not the 'expert' know-it-all who transmits information in a one-directional flow (Freire, 1986). For example, the use of the poem, 'Moons waiting' (see box 2 on page 316) has offered students the opportunity to confront the otherwise difficult topic of abortion in very useful ways. Allowing students to actively participate in their own learning holds several advantages: firstly, a sense of community is built within the lecture room that allows for free expression, trust and respect; secondly, students have the opportunity to be reflexive and critical of oppressive structures and practices; thirdly, encouraging their participation in the various activities, allowing their voices to be heard and developing the sense that their views are valued, can be extremely empowering for students; finally, it provides a rich learning experience for everyone (including the lecturer) from the diverse experiences and knowledge represented in the class. When we were discussing reproductive health and rights four years ago, for example, the professional nurse in the class enriched the conversation with her practical experiences from the field. During a discussion of diverse sexualities, she made the connection between the intransigent cases of yeast (*candidiasis*) infections among her female patients and heterosexual anal sex.

However, if not handled with sensitivity, experience has also taught us that feminist pedagogical methods may have a down side. For example, sometimes the discussions may get hijacked and sidetracked from the main issue, leading to petty squabbles and insecurities. This usually happens during discussions of the controversial moral debates, say regarding same-sex desire. Somehow the dialogue always veers to a discussion about the sexuality of animals: 'even animals know better than to engage in unnatural sex…'. On such occasions, it is important to redirect the discussion and ensure that the objective of the class is realized. For instance, citing case studies that have proved homosexual pair bonds among animals and challenging the class as to whether 'unnaturalness' equals immorality and whether homo sapiens should be looking to animals for moral standards. The brief lecture sessions at the start of each session are mostly used to introduce topics and to provide a theoretical backdrop on which to hook subsequent discussions. Indeed, caution has to be applied to ensure that 'classroom liberalism' does not become counter-productive to the learning process.

Use of humour and appropriate icebreakers is an excellent way to reduce anxieties and to create a friendly, relaxing atmosphere. If used appropriately, humour has the ability to bridge intercultural, interfaith, interpower and intergenerational divides when all other forms of communication fail. Here we do not refer to jokes that elicit loud laughter but rather to conceptual humour that facilitates the students' learning process. For example, I often borrow Stephen Law's stimulating debate on homosexuality by having two students play the roles of God and the protagonist, Mr Jarvis (Law, 2003). Another example is through a dramatization of the famous Kenyan case of a 67-year-old female activist who married a 25-year-old man;[17] we are able to clarify some important issues regarding sexuality in family law. The use of the French phrase '*la petite mort*' (meaning 'a little death') in reference to sexual orgasm also adds a light touch to the uneasy topic. Furthermore, sharing of personal experiences, including those of the lecturer gives the discussions a 'human face' and helps in cultivating a sense of trust.

Once students feel comfortable enough to discuss taboo topics, reticence is replaced with excitement and enthusiasm to learn new things. They exchange knowledge about various 'exotic' practices in their different cultures which become the subjects of intellectual discourse. Take the cultural aesthetic practice of elongating the inner folds of the labia minora among several Bantu-speaking communities of eastern and southern Africa, for example, the Baganda (Uganda) the Tutsi (Rwanda), the Basotho (Lesotho), the Shona (Zimbabwe), the Nyakyusa and Karewe (Tanzania), the Khoisan of southern Africa and the Tsonga (Mozambique).[18] Or the Kenyan versions of male circumcision among the Masai and Kikuyu which involves partial circumcision, allowing the lower part of the foreskin to remain attached in a 'bib' of atrophied flesh (Romberg, 1985). Ostensibly the 'bib' works to enhance the pleasure of sexual intercourse for both partners. The specific form of 'outercourse' from Rwanda and parts of Uganda is another practice that always generates a lot of interest among students, especially its associations to female ejaculation.[19] The dialogue on positive sexuality usually translates into an empowering, life-changing experience for most students.

The dialogue on positive sexuality usually translates into an empowering, life-changing experience for most students.

---

[17] This case demonstrates one woman's defiance against patriarchal sexual norms that limit and oppress women. See Wanjiru Kariuki (2005).

[18] A lively debate always ensues among students whether such elongation qualifies as 'female genital mutilation' in the definition provided by the World Health Organization. See Tamale (2005).

[19] The local names for this practice include *kachabali* (Tamale, 2005) and *kunyaza* (Bizimana, 2010).

Part IV: Unlearning and re-learning for transformational sexuality

Part of the introductory session of the course emphasizes the importance of keeping an open mind in a class of this type ('minds, like parachutes, only work when open!'). Individuals with open minds are less likely to be judgemental. A rigid, closed mind on the other hand, limits one's intellectual potential and is less likely to lead to transformational change. But transformative learning can only be achieved through a process of unlearning and relearning. This cognitive process has proved to be a huge challenge for many students who have gone through colonial and postcolonial educational systems—systems that limit their instruction to rote learning and grossly neglect honing the skill of unlearning.[20] Without being equipped with the art and science of unlearning, it is extremely difficult for us to question unjust frameworks, let alone to challenge them. Under such circumstances, it is important for us to facilitate the students wading through the layers of normative assumptions that many have never been able to question or to challenge.

Unlearning requires students to leave their comfort zones and abandon deeply entrenched beliefs and practices. It calls for confronting prejudices, shifting attitudes and even turning around their mindsets. All this involves serious discomfort and disequilibrium. Relearning, on the other hand, requires acquiring new knowledge and/or reorganizing the old (Soto-Crespo, 1999; Gordon and Cornwall, 2004). It explains why sexual stereotypes that intersect with gender, race, religion and culture and are deeply embedded in social and individual consciousness, become extremely difficult to overcome.

Discussions on sexuality can be extremely controversial and we often have lively, impassioned debates in class. Inevitably individuals have strong views about divisive issues such as abortion, sex work and homosexuality. Even when students 'unlearn' the dominant sexuality discourses, several express the huge dilemma they wrestle with in reconciling their religious beliefs with their newly acquired sexuality discourses. These are never simple issues to tackle and we spend a lot of time discussing feminist theology, issues of re-interpretation and contextualization of the scriptures, drawing parallels with racist interpretations of the holy word, and so forth.

students ... express the huge dilemma they wrestle with in reconciling their religious beliefs with their newly acquired sexuality discourses

On some occasions individuals, in their ardent bid to voice their views, break the ground rules, crossing the line of respect and appropriate behaviour

---

[20] Even outside the formal education systems, the informal cultural instruction that we receive in most of our African family and community circles reinforces the uncritical, unquestioning pedagogy. Both formal and informal education thus largely emphasize learning in dualisms and absolute truths (right-wrong, good-bad, moral-immoral, inclusion-exclusion, male-female, and so on), doing little to foster reflective and critical thinking.

towards their colleagues. At times like those as lecturer I momentarily retreat (not physically but vocally) and let the class deal with such situations. This tactic encourages students to sharpen their critical thinking and expressive skills, drawing on the knowledge acquired from the class. It has the additional advantage of showing that the lecturer's views are not being imposed on the students. Such lecture room discussions usually spill over to residential halls where students engage colleagues who are not enrolled in this class. Sometimes we also invite guest speakers from organizations such as Gays and Lesbians of Zimbabwe (GALZ) to have a discussion with students.

Prior to joining the programme, generally and in this class in particular, very few students would have questioned taken-for-granted images that patriarchal societies construct for us regarding femininity, masculinity, motherhood, fatherhood, desire, non-procreative sex, multiple sexual partners, same-sex erotics, rape, sex work, abortion, menopause, decency and sexual morality. The cultural definitions and meanings that are attached to these issues are rarely questioned and even less so their links to power and dominance. So we spend many hours in the lecture room unpacking the 'blocks' used to construct and give meaning to these concepts, analyzing the role of the law in creating, sustaining and reproducing these blocks and how individuals, groups and communities subvert hegemonic sexual norms and values. An effective way of engaging with all these issues is to theorize the various ways that sexuality norms are institutionalized and how these are interwoven into the social fabric of students' everyday experiences, knowledge and social relationships. Theory then helps students make the connections between seemingly disparate concepts and to answer the why and how questions relating to sexuality. In their course evaluations, many students have positively rated the course using words such as, 'informative', 'an eye-opener' and 'life-changing'.

Part V: Linking theory to everyday experiences

Having attempted to create a feminist lecture room environment, it is important to surface the connections between theory and practice in order for students to expand and deepen their understanding of the linkages between gender, inequality and sexuality. Hence, theory is the overarching contextualizing factor in the course. The process of theorizing sexuality begins from the simple awareness that sexuality (like race and gender) is a social construction. To a large extent, the human body enters the world as a blank slate. Thereafter, the social world promptly begins to infuse meanings and interpretations to it, turning it into a sexed body, a cultural body, a gendered body, a classed body, a religious body, a racial body, an ethnic body. These social inscriptions — which are normalized and naturalized — are engraved on our bodies by the

The process of theorizing sexuality begins from the simple awareness that sexuality (like race and gender) is a social construction

dominant social class using the nibs of culture, law, politics, media, education, morality and religion. In Africa, such nibs inscribe with the bold influence of colonialism, neo-colonialism and patriarchy. It is an effective way of maintaining unequal power relations. Hence, the inscribed rules, images, symbols and even hierarchies that give shape and character to the bodies of African women and men become an important tool for sustaining patriarchy and capitalism.

Indeed, women's bodies constitute one of the most formidable tools for creating and maintaining gender roles and relations in African societies. While the texts that culture inscribes on African women's bodies remain invisible to the uncritical eye, it is in fact a crucial medium for effecting social control. The inscriptions that are encoded onto women's bodies have sexuality writ large; through the regulation and control of African women's sexualities and reproductive capacities, their subordination and continued exploitation is guaranteed. The theory of sexual scripting makes the important link between individual interactional behaviour on the micro level and the larger social forces of the macro level (Gagnon, 2004).

The theory of sexual scripting makes the important link between individual interactional behaviour on the micro level and the larger social forces of the macro level

The theoretical readings that we assign to students are interdisciplinary in nature, authored by a mix of scholars from the global north and the global south (Pereira, undated). Conceptualizations of sexuality and desire, heteronormativity, representation, sexual scripting, performance and performativity, are explored using feminist jurisprudence, post-structural theory and postcolonial theory. Some of the theorists we use in class include: Sigmund Freud, Chandra Mohanty, Uma Narayan, Ifi Amadiume, Catharine MacKinnon, Gayle Rubin, Michel Foucault, John Gagnon, Judith Butler and Patricia McFadden. We are keenly aware of the dangers of uncritically using theories that are constructed from the global north to explain African societies. However, existing western theories cannot be completely ignored for three main reasons. First, much of the contemporary sexual morality code and most of the laws in the statute books of postcolonial countries are rooted in the history and tradition of the former colonizing European nations. This means that western theoretical perspectives, to a certain extent, define the underlying rationale and practice of the legal regime governing sexualities in Africa.

The second reason for not ignoring western theories is that sexuality scholarship on the continent is relatively new; the conceptual development in this area is still in its infancy.[21] Hence, existing theoretical frameworks (for example, Foucault's conceptualization of sexuality in terms of power relations or Butler's views on the subversive potential in gender performativity) can be extremely useful in analyzing sexualities in Africa—as long as this is

---

[21] The relative paucity of published materials in this area by African scholars has spurred me into developing a *Reader on African sexualities* (forthcoming 2011).

done with the continental specificities in mind. Finally, and most importantly, gendered sexualities, whether in the west or in Africa, are primarily based on *similar predictions*, namely labour, authority and performance (Bennett, 2000). In other words, the hierarchical constructions of sexuality in either context are linked by the force of gender to labour, authority and performance within the context of capitalism and patriarchy (in their multiple variants). Hence there is no need to reject or dismantle western 'theoretical scaffoldings' as they provide useful tools for students to reflect upon and develop insights concerning social relationships.

...there is no need to reject or dismantle western 'theoretical scaffoldings' as they provide useful tools for students to reflect upon and develop insights concerning social relationships

Having said that, theorizing African sexualities would differ from western ones in nuanced specificities because of certain ideologies and practices unique to the continent (Helle-Valle, 2004). For example, one cannot ignore those aspects of cultural ideology that are widely shared among Africans (the communitarian, solidaritarian and *ubuntu*[22] ethos), just as one must pay attention to the common historical legacies inscribed in cultures within Africa by forces such as colonialism, capitalism, imperialism and globalization. Take the self-identifying terms 'gay', 'lesbian' and 'transgendered' that have emerged from western societies, which differ quite markedly from the descriptors for some same-sex relations found on the continent.[23] Neither do same-sex relations in Africa always necessarily involve sexual desire. One example would be the woman-to-woman marriages among the Nuer of southern Sudan, the Nandi of Kenya, the Igbo of Nigeria and the Zulu of South Africa. The primary goals behind such relationships are not necessarily sexual but to bear children (for barren women) and provide companionship and security.[24]

In the same vein, it would be foolhardy for anyone theorizing women's sexuality to ignore the machinations of Africa's 'structurally adjusted' economies and the attendant 'feminization of poverty' to women's involvement in commercial sex work and the heightened prevalence of HIV/AIDS. It is also necessary to make the philosophical link between institutionalized, state-inspired homophobia and Africa's autocratic and dictatorial regimes;[25] by constantly attacking homosexuals, attention is conveniently diverted from the national issues that the population is suffering from. In Uganda, the Minister of Ethics and Integrity condemns homosexuals at every opportunity but he is conspicuously quiet, say, when parliament is openly bribed to change the constitution to lift presidential term limits. In February 2005, when four

---

[22] The African concept of *ubuntu* (humaneness) refers to understanding diversity and the belief in universal bond and sharing. See Ramose (1999).

[23] For example, see Jane Kendall (1998), Sylvia Tamale (2003) and Ifi Amadiume (1987).

[24] See, for example, Njambi, Wairimu and O'Brien (1998); Evans-Pritchard (1945); and Gluckman (1970).

[25] Well aware that legalized homophobia in Africa was a direct import by colonial powers.

Ugandan women's rights groups organized the staging of Eve Ensler's play, *The vagina monologues*, in Kampala, government, through the Media Council, was quick to slap a ban on the play. They argued that the title was 'offensive to cultural sensibilities' and that the content was 'too obscene' and 'promoted lesbianism in Uganda'. In fact the purpose of the play is to celebrate female sexuality as well as to spotlight sexual violence against women.[26]

Before students leave their home countries, we request that they collect sexuality-related materials, legislation, newspaper clips, and so on, and bring them to use in class. Grounding sexuality concepts in real-life experiences is crucial to the process of knowledge production among students. One technique found useful over the years in getting students to appreciate gender/sexuality theoretical explanations is to make extensive use of analogies to racism. African students—especially male ones—more readily appreciate theories on and comparisons with racism than they do gender or sexuality theories. When we explain discrimination and oppression from the analogous ground of 'racism' and 'otherness', the pieces begin to fall into place for most students. The oppressive structures that underlie racism, sexism, genocide, homophobia, xenophobia and such doctrines are all legitimized through 'naturalized' norms that dehumanize, infantalize, disempower and disenfranchise people. Therefore, by invoking the justifications pandered by some racist theorists, students begin to appreciate analogous experiences of 'otherness'.

When we explain discrimination and oppression from the analogous ground of 'racism' and 'otherness', the pieces begin to fall into place for most students

Viewing inequalities through the lens of 'gendered sexualities' facilitates students' understanding of sexual laws and policies. This in turn aids their capacities to challenge and critique institutions, laws and policies that reinforce such inequalities (Cornwall and Jolly, 2008). For example, most students enter the course with deeply embedded prejudices against commercial sex. But an illumination of the connections between class/gender inequalities and the control of women's desire and sexual activity usually facilitates the 'light bulb' moments for students regarding their appreciation of the dynamics of sexual work and its criminalization.

---

[26] See Media Council ruling: *In the Matter of the Press & Journalists Act* and *In the Matter of the Media Council* and *In the Matter of a Play, 'The Vagina Monologues'* (unpublished), February 16, 2005. For an analysis of the ruling see Apollo Makubuya (2005) and Frederick Jjuuko (2005). Also see Wasike and Wafula (2005) and Ahimbisibwe (2005).

Part VI: Social transformation via resistance and subversion

Talking about the positive, pleasurable aspects of sexuality is a major component of realizing the objectives of the course. It goes against the prescribed cultural morality of the oppressive structures that operate in Africa. Such discussions have undoubtedly proved to be an empowering resource for students whose incapacitated world view is radically transformed by the end of the course. Many students have, for example, found Audre Lorde's eloquent words empowering:

> 'There are many kinds of power, used and unused, acknowledged or otherwise. The erotic is a resource within each of us that lies in a deeply female and spiritual plane... In order to perpetuate itself, every oppression must corrupt or distort those various sources of power within the culture of the oppressed that can provide energy for change. For women, this has meant a suppression of the erotic as a considered source of power and information within our lives' (Lorde, 1984: 53).

One student told the class that Lorde's essay, 'Uses of the erotic: the erotic as power', was such an eye-opener for her that it completely transformed her marriage and sexual life. This student had never conceived of her sexuality as a source of power.

Therefore, even as women's sexualized bodies represent powerful constraints in Africa, sexuality also holds positive, empowering possibilities for them. The 'body politics' for African women is also possessed of an empowering sub-text, reflected through resistance, negotiation, identity, self-desire, pleasure and silence. There is a legitimate silence surrounding African women's sexuality, a silence that is unengageable and ambiguous. Here, 'silence' is different from the 'western' feminist approach that names it as a total blank while valorizing 'voice'. In many African cultures while speech is necessary and empowering, in sexuality, silence can be equally powerful. For instance, silence may serve as a tool for the rejection of externally imposed projections of African women's sexuality.

In many African cultures while speech is necessary and empowering, in sexuality, silence can be equally powerful

Sexual initiation traditions across the continent that are espoused by erotic cultures such as the *Ssenga* among the Baganda of Uganda, the *Tete* among the Shona of Zimbabwe, the *Alangizi* among the Yao of Malawi and the Chewa/Nyanja of Zambia, the *Mayosenge* among the Bemba of Zambia and the Lawbe women of Senegal, all carry some empowering messages for young girls and women embedded in intricate sexual practices and traditions. Most of these positive erotic cultures have survived and endured the repressive regime of foreign laws and religions that tried to smother them.

Analyzing gendered sexuality against the backdrop of the HIV/AIDS pandemic in Africa has significant implications for subversive transformation. Not only has the scourge opened up African women's bodies and sexuality to public scrutiny, it has also forced open a public debate on women's sexualities, vulnerabilities and power. The sheer volume of financial and scientific interest in HIV/AIDS has meant that the authors in the mainstream story have not always been African women.[27] However, women living with and affected by the pandemic have persisted in defining, reframing and articulating their needs and rights, and in rewriting the script.[28] Hence, even as the pandemic has created new hierarchies of domination and exploitation, it has at the same time built bases of empowerment for African women by spurring a new kind of political consciousness and self-organization.

Debates around the issues of sexual harassment, dress codes and gender discrimination as well as the processes through which such oppressive structures are maintained opens up ideas for discursive techniques that can be deployed to resist them. The common stereotypes and misconceptions that students hold regarding issues such as sexual advances, the *hijab* and nudity are debunked and deconstructed in transformative ways.

Part VII: Lessons, challenges and future prospects

Not all students that enroll for this module have an interest in a transformatory agenda when they first join the class. As stated earlier, some join the class out of sheer curiosity, others because they see career opportunities in the subject area, and so forth. However, regardless of the initial motive for joining the class, by the end of the course not only do the majority of students understand the links between sexuality and women's status but they also appreciate the intellectual place of sexuality within gender and the law. It is astounding to observe the lecture room climate transform over the days from 'giggles' to serious discussions, dialogue and serious interrogation. By the end of the first week both male and female students get over the embarrassment and begin dialoguing into mature discussions of where they come from. Analyzing the law through gendered lenses affords students the opportunity to critically examine the relationships between law, gender, identity and oppression. It is gratifying to hear changed voices committing to return home and become agents of transformation in their own small ways. As one criminal defence lawyer put it at the end of the 2009 course: 'I'm totally ashamed of what I've been doing to all those rape victims in court during cross examination.'

---

[27] For example, see Cohen (2000) and Caldwell (2000).

[28] For example, see Adomako Ampofo (1999), Sisulu (2000) and Obbo (1995).

In many ways this course is an exercise in self-discovery, personal growth, healing and empowerment. Some students have been so stimulated by the course that they have gone on to develop research proposals in the area of gender, law and sexuality. Excellent dissertations have been written on exciting topics such as 'Traditional marriage counsellors and HIV/AIDS',[29] 'Sex education in schools',[30] 'Abortion in rape situations',[31] and 'Sex tourism'.[32] In all these studies, one can clearly see the influence of the course deeply interwoven in the analysis and conceptual understanding of the issues under discussion.

Analyzing and negotiating the complex terrain of sexuality in a lecture room environment necessarily means that there are several ambiguities, contradictions and intersections that we do not get to address fully in class. This is especially so given that we have a period of only four weeks within which to cover this subject. Just as most students are beginning to feel at ease with the subject matter, the course comes to an end and they have to prepare for examinations. It is at this 'liberated' stage, for example, that most are willing to confront the numerous contradictions between their inner desires and the social norms to which they are supposed to comply.

We face further challenges: getting students with various academic and social pressures to read and internalize the assigned materials is never guaranteed. Only a handful of them seem to take the time to quickly browse through the readings and the common evaluation comment on this issue returned every year is that the assigned readings are 'too much'. It is therefore important to think about ways of motivating students to critically read and analyze the assigned texts.

Course evaluations are extremely useful in educating us about students' expectations, interests and fears, and about the effectiveness of the course. Some of the consistent feedback in this regard reveals that students appreciate the mixing of lectures with other interactive methods. Not only does it provide the necessary balance in bridging the gap between theory and practice but it also creates the informal and safe environment needed for discussing sexuality.

---

[29] See Martha Mapala (2004) 'Traditional marriage counsellors and HIV/AIDS: a study of Alangizi National Association of Zambia in Lusaka'

[30] See Anastasia Otieno (2006) 'Gender and sexuality in the Kenyan education system. Is history repeating Itself? An exploratory study of information on sexuality within Nakuru town.'

[31] See Netty Rusere (2006) 'Justice delayed is justice denied: the experiences of applicants for termination of pregnancy in rape situations under the Termination of Pregnancy Act in Zimbabwe'.

[32] See Annette Mbogoh (2008) '*Bangaiza na mzungu*: a critical analysis of laws and policies and their effectiveness in the prevention, suppression and punishment of sex tourism involving the youth in Mombasa, Kenya'.

Many students have also observed in their evaluations that this course is so central to 'women's law' that it should cease to be an elective. Below is one example of such recommendations:

> 'Very essential… This course is a must for all MWL [Masters in Women's Law] students... It lays foundations of how the law issues impacts on gender and sexuality... Should be part of the introductory lectures to MWL maybe soon after the sex and gender topic; it should not be an option.'

In future we hope to expand the curriculum to lay more emphasis on topics such as 'sexuality and disability' and 'sexuality and masculinities'. We further plan to integrate one or two field visits into the course, allowing students to get 'hands-on' experience with groups such as sex workers, sexual minorities, traditional sex trainers, and so on. Use of films and other audio-visual materials in analyzing the issues should further enrich our pedagogical repertoire. Needless to say, we are eager to learn from colleagues elsewhere about teaching skills that have been successful in conducting similar courses.

Bibliography

Adomako Ampofo A. (1999) 'Nice guys, condoms and other forms of STD protection: sex workers and AIDS protection in West Africa', pages 561-90 and 559-88 in C. Becker, J. Dozon, C. Obbo and M. Touré (eds) *Vivre et penser le Sida en Afrique / Experiencing and understanding AIDS in Africa*, CODESRIA, IRD, Karthala, PNLS, Dakar and Paris.

Ahimbisibwe F. (2005) 'Vagina play dropped', *New Vision,* 18 February.

Alexander J. and C. Mohanty (eds) (1997) *Feminist genealogies, colonial legacies, democratic futures*, Routledge, New York.

Amadiume I. (1987) *Male daughters, female husbands: gender and sex in an African society*, Zed Books, London.

– (1997) *Reinventing Africa: matriarchy, religion, culture*, Zed Books, London.

Bennett J. (2000), 'Thinking sexualities', *African Gender Institute Newsletter* 7.

Bizimana N. (2010) 'Another way for lovemaking in Africa: *Kunyaza*, a traditional sexual technique for triggering female orgasm at heterosexual encounters', *Sexologies* 19(3): 157–162 July-September, doi:10.1016/j.seol.2009.12.003.

Caldwell J. (2000) 'Rethinking the African AIDS epidemic', *Population and Development Review* 26(1): 117-135.

Cohen D. (2000) *Poverty and HIV/AIDS in sub-Saharan Africa*, UNDP/SEPED, New York.

Cornwall A., S. Jolly and S. Correa (eds) (2008) *Development with a body: sexuality, human rights and development*, Zed Books, London.

Coughlin A. (1998) 'Sex and guilt', *Virginia Law Review* 84(1): 1–46.

Chase-Reboud B. (2003) *Hottentot Venus*, Doubleday, New York.

Evans-Pritchard E.E. (1945) *Some aspects of marriage and the family among the Nuer*, the Rhodes-Livingstone Institute, Livingstone, Northern Rhodesia (Zambia).

Freire P. (1986) *Pedagogy of the oppressed*, Continuum, New York.

Gagnon J. (2004) *An interpretation of desire: essays in the study of sexuality*, University of Chicago Press, Chicago.

Gagnon J. and W. Simon (1973) *Sexual conduct: the social sources of human sexuality*, Aldine Publishing, Chicago.

Gilman S. (1986) 'Black bodies, white bodies: toward an iconography of female sexuality in late nineteenth-century art, medicine, and literature', in H.L. Gates Jr (ed), *'Race', writing, and difference*, University of Chicago Press, Chicago.

Gluckman M. (1970) 'Kinship and marriage among the Lozi of Northern Rhodesia and the Zulu of Natal', pages 175-190 in A.R. Radcliffe-Brown and D. Forde (eds), *African systems of kinship and marriage*, Oxford University Press, Oxford.

Gordon G. and A. Cornwall (2004) 'Participation in sexual and reproductive wellbeing and rights', *Participatory Learning and Action* 50: 73-80.

Halley J. (2006) *Split decisions: how and why to take a break from feminism*, Princeton University Press, Princeton.

Helle-Valle J. (2004) 'Understanding sexuality in Africa: diversity and contextualized dividuality', in S. Arnfred (ed), *Re-thinking sexualities in Africa*, Nordic Africa Institute, Uppsala.

Hooks B. (1989) *Talking back: thinking feminist, thinking black*, Sheba Feminist Publishers, London.

Jjuuko F. (2005) 'To ban or not to ban? A critique of the Media Council ruling', *East African Journal of Peace & Human Rights* 11(1): 172-181.

Kariuki W. (2005) 'Keeping the feminist war real in contemporary Kenya: the case of Wambui Otieno', *Jenda: A Journal of Culture and African Women Studies* 7, available online at: http://www.google.fr/search?q=africaresource.com%2Fjenda%2Fissue7%2Fkariuki.html&ie=utf-8&oe=utf-8&aq=t&rls=org.mozilla:fr:official&client=firefox-a

Kendall J. (1998), 'Looking for lesbians in Lesotho', pages 223–242 in S. Murray and W. Roscoe (eds) *Boy-wives and female husbands: studies in African homosexualities*, Palgrave, New York.

Law S. (2003) *The philosophy gym: 25 short adventures in thinking*, Headline Book Publishing, London, available online at: http://stephenlaw.blogspot.com/2007/03/whats-wrong-with-gay-sex.html?showComment=1174406580000

Lorde A. (1984) 'Uses of the erotic: the erotic as power', in *Sister outsider,* first edition, The Crossing Press, New York.

Ly A. (1999) 'Brief notes on eroticism among the Lawbe, Senegal', *CODESRIA Bulletin* 3 & 4: 46-48.

McFadden P. (2003) 'Sexual pleasure as feminist choice', *Feminist Africa* 2: 50 -60.

Machera M. (2004) 'Opening a can of worms: a debate on female sexuality in the lecture theatre', in S. Arnfred (ed), *Rethinking sexualities in Africa,* Nordic Africa Institute, Uppsala.

Makubuya A. (2005) 'The "Vagina monologues" saga and free expression in Uganda: exploring the limits', *East African Journal of Peace & Human Rights* 11(1): 165-171.

Mapala M. (2004) 'Traditional marriage counsellors and HIV/AIDS: a study of the Alangizi National Association of Zambia in Lusaka', masters dissertation, SEARCWL, Harare.

Mbogoh A. (2008) '*Bangaiza na mzungu*: a critical analysis of laws and policies and their effectiveness in the prevention, suppression and punishment of sex tourism involving the youth in Mombasa, Kenya', masters dissertation, SEARCWL, University of Zimbabwe, Harare.

Miller A. and C. Vance (2004) 'Sexuality, human rights and health', *Health and Human Rights* 7(2): 5-15.

Njambi W. and W. O'Brien (1998) 'Revisiting "woman-woman marriage": notes on Gikuyu women', *National Women's Studies Journal* 12(1): 1-23.

Obbo C. (1995) 'Gender, age and class: discourses on HIV transmission and control in Uganda', in H. Brummelhuis and G. Herdt (eds), *Culture and sexual risk: anthropological perspectives on AIDS,* Gordon and Breach, Amsterdam.

Omolade B. (1993) 'A black feminist pedagogy', *Women's Studies Quarterly* 15: 32-39.

Otieno A. (2006) 'Gender and sexuality in the Kenyan education system. Is history repeating itself? An exploratory study of information on sexuality within Nakuru town', masters dissertation, SEARCWL, University of Zimbabwe, Harare.

Pereira C. (undated) *Bibliography on sexuality*, Gender and Women Studies in Africa Teaching Resources, available at: http://web.uct.ac.za/org/gwsafrica/teaching/charmaine%27s%20essay.html#1.

Ramose M. (1999) *African philosophy through ubuntu*, Mond Books, Harare.

Romberg R. *(1985) Circumcision: the painful dilemma*, Bergin and Garvey, South Hadley, MA.

Rusere N. (2006) 'Justice delayed is justice denied: the experiences of applicants for termination of pregnancy in rape situations under the Termination of Pregnancy Act in Zimbabwe', masters dissertation, SEARCWL, University of Zimbabwe, Harare.

Sisulu E. (2000) 'A different kind of holocaust: a personal reflection on HIV/AIDS', *African Gender Institute Newsletter* 7.

Soto-Crespo R. E. (1999) 'The bounds of hope: unlearning "old eyes" and a pedagogy of renewal', *Thresholds in Education*, 2 & 3: 42-46.

Schiebinger L. (1993) *Nature's body: gender in the making of science*, Beacon Press, Boston.

Tamale S. (2008) 'The right to culture and the culture of rights: a critical perspective on women's sexual rights in Africa', *Feminist Legal Studies* 16 (1): 47-69.

– (2005) 'Eroticism, sensuality and "women's secrets" among the Baganda: a critical analysis', *Feminist Africa* 5: 9-36.

– (2003) 'Out of the closet: unveiling sexuality discourses in Uganda', *Feminist Africa* 2: 17-29.

Wasike A. and E. Wafula (2005) 'Government opposes "Vagina monologues"', *New Vision,* February 11, 2005.

THEME

FOUR

Linking legal form
to lived realities

13

Pathways to real access to land-related resources for women

Challenging and overturning dominant legal paradigms

Patricia Kameri-Mbote, Anne Hellum and Pauline Nyamweya

Part I: Background and objectives of the course

Access to resources is a key theme in the discourse on women's rights and naturally occupies a central place in the exploration of the status of women in society. Independent and effective rights to natural resources for women have been identified by researchers and policy makers as vital for family welfare, food security, gender equality, empowerment, economic efficiency and poverty elimination. Women make up half the world's population, own less than 10 per cent of the world's property and produce 60–80 per cent of the food in developing countries. The starting assumptions are that these gender injustices arise when gender-neutral international, regional and national laws and policies on property and environmental and natural resources meet with the reality on the ground where access to and control of resources are highly gendered. We explore the gendered interface of life and law with a view to improving women's access to, control and ownership of resources. The overall objectives of this course include:

Access to resources is a key theme in the discourse on women's rights

- Analyzing feminist discourses related to access to resources with emphasis on ecofeminism;
- Conceptualizing the relationship between access, control and ownership of environmental and natural resources;
- Exploring the relationship between gender-neutral laws and gendered relationships, customs and beliefs informing access to, control and ownership of environmental and natural resources;
- Analyzing the international, regional, national and local laws, policies and practices impacting on women's access to, control and ownership of environmental and natural resources;

- Linking access to environmental and natural resources to the human rights to water, food, health and education;
- Facilitating the evolution of appropriate investigative, methodological and analytical techniques for analyzing the relationship between gender-neutral laws and gendered access to, control and ownership of resources.

Through discussion of ongoing research the students are encouraged to situate their course work and dissertations in areas that need to be explored. As a result a number master dissertations have contributed to new knowledge in the field.

...

The course is divided into two main parts, presented by three instructors in the forefront of women's law research in this field. The course is research based, taking students through ongoing research carried out in the region. Through discussion of this research the students are encouraged to situate their course work and dissertations in areas that need to be explored. As a result, a number of masters dissertations have contributed to new knowledge in the field.

Part I, which provides the overall theoretical framework, is taught by Patricia Kameri-Mbote who has a background in environmental law, property law and women's law. Part II situates women's access to, control and ownership of resources within the rights-based approach to development. The emphasis is on the interrelatedness between the human right to food, water, health and education. This part of the course makes extensive use of empirical examples from the different countries in southern and eastern Africa. The rights-based approach to water and land is taught by Anne Hellum who, in her teaching and research, has one foot in law and one in anthropology. Using her regional research experience in the field of land and water she addresses fieldwork as a method of studying women's access to resources in the intersection of international, national and local law. Pauline Nyamweya, who in her work as a consultant has evaluated a variety of programmes based on a human rights approach, presents a series of empirical research reports that speak to problems related to its operationalization.

Interestingly, when the course was first offered, the instructors had difficulty carving out their niche in the entire Masters in Women's Law course because of the interlinkages between access to resources and other areas covered in other courses such as commerce, education and access to law and legal resources. The purview of the course was considered too wide, necessitating a refashioning of core issues to be covered. Having offered it four times, the course has now coalesced around access to land and related environmental resources such as wildlife, forests, minerals and water. Because these resources are accessed through mediated channels and relationships (UN HABITAT and Benschop, 2002) we explore how access to resources for women is influenced significantly by factors like the marital status of women and education levels.

Selected topics in the overall course include: ownership, control and access to community resources such as forests, wildlife and water; the impact of new technologies on access to resources; access to water for different purposes; and the interrelatedness of the human rights to education, health and land with access to resources specifically focusing on HIV/AIDS. It explores the situation of women in different social strata (professionals, peasantry, decision-makers, home-makers).

Since this course is taught by three different lecturers with different research and teaching experiences a great deal of time has been spent defining the basic thematic, legal, theoretical and methodological foundations of the course. We have arrived at the four main pillars of the course, namely:

1   Ecofeminism;
2   Women, environment and development;
3   Gender justice;
4   Women's human rights and legal pluralism.

The three parts of the course are taught using a diversity of methods. Firstly, in the introductory session, the students indicate what their expectations are in taking the course. Secondly, the instructor and the students go through the general content of the course and assess the extent to which the students' expectations are addressed. Audio-visual teaching aids are used in the delivery of the lectures and presentation of expectations including flipcharts and Powerpoint presentations. Students are expected to make presentations as individuals drawing from their country experiences, especially with regard to land and natural resources. Thirdly, students are expected to present a critical analysis to the class of selected readings from the course outline.

In each of these methods, the following happens:

●   **Collaboration and power sharing**

The instructors and students engage in a collaborative learning environment where the students' ideas, as much as the lecturer's, count as contributions to knowledge. The instructor's role is limited to providing additional background information not present in the readings and most of the time the class is loosely structured to accommodate discussion, group activities and exploratory writing. This approach ensures that individual students are responsible for their understanding of the course materials and for their own learning. Power becomes shared as students assume more responsibility for teaching and teachers for learning.

Power becomes shared as students assume more responsibility for teaching and teachers for learning.

●   **Using personal voice, diversity and experience**

The course and especially the case studies emphasise personal lived experiences and validation as the basis for analysis, activism and research. Students are expected to speak up in class and share their thinking. So the instructors too have to open up and explore their own personal views and attitudes. Such a perspective results in several positive outcomes, including increased respect, enhanced empathy, better critical thinking skills and a liberated classroom where the students learn to respect each other's differences rather than fear them.

This chapter essentially describes the engagement with theoretical concepts pertinent to the course taught by Patricia Kameri-Mbote. It then moves on to explore the use of concrete case studies as taught by Anne Hellum and Pauline Nyamweya and how these build on to the pillars that form the core of the course.

Part II: Course delivery – engaging with foundational pillars and theoretical constructs

Patricia Kameri-Mbote

A Charting the parameters for engagement

The starting point of the course is to seek to identify, engage and challenge the dominant paradigms. A research-based method is adopted by using concluded or ongoing research to illustrate what the dominant paradigms are (Kameri-Mbote, 2002). Over the years that I have taught the course, opportunities to explore these paradigms have presented themselves in different researches and I use these in class to illustrate dominant paradigms at different levels (Kameri-Mbote, 2002, 2004). I define 'paradigm' as a view of the world; a frame of reference. Paradigms represent the way we see the world and, in gender terms, how we perceive, understand and interpret maleness and femaleness from different paradigmatic points of view. We determine through personal reflection and discussions that our socialization, education and experiences in life colour the lenses through which we look at the world and that we may look at the same thing and see different things and all be right. We ask the question: *What determines our paradigmatic stance?* We then collaboratively identify our identity as African women as determining our view of the world. We proceed to unpack 'African women' using Everjoice Win's article (Win, 2004) by asking ourselves whether we fit into the typology of the 'poor, powerless and pregnant' African woman. Given the consensus that access to resources for women is not optimal, we ask ourselves how we can get optimal access to resources for women.

We finally discuss how we can change the paradigms. We identify law as one possibility

EXERCISE

The challenges to access

These are identified as:

● Patriarchy

● Dominant paradigms – scarcity of resources and struggle therefore contestations for bastions of authority

● Law: we ask ourselves what law? We also ask whether law is based on a particular paradigm.

● Theory: Whose theory? Is it devoid of paradigmatic biases?

● Other interventions? Are these devoid of paradigmatic biases?

Other interventions identified

- *Promulgating and implementing laws* that promote women's access to resources

- *Identifying and mobilizing allies* in the quest for women's access to resources

- *Seeking access as groups* as opposed to as individuals – the role of women's groups in providing institutional support and social capital

- *Education* – some unlearning (challenging the norms) and some learning (taking a fresh look and adopting new perspectives)

- *Using windows of opportunity and alleys of hope* – 'And who knows but that you may have come to royal position for such a time as this.'[1]

- *Changing dominant discourse:*
  - Challenging, overturning, rebelling, overthrowing
  - Engagement, discussion, negotiation, mediation
  - Images and autobiographies, for instance, Wangari Maathai's autobiography: *Unbowed: One woman's story*
  - Life stories of women and women's groups and their contributions and endeavours in claiming space
  - Stories and documentaries of women's struggles – no story is too small or insignificant:

    In many African communities, certain parts of animals or chicken are reserved for men. These include gizzards and some parts of goat. Eating this meat as a woman can be liberating. We share our examples of breaking the shackles by eating what we are forbidden to eat.

- Deconstructing myths – Wangu wa Makeri stories

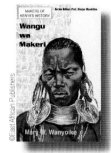

Wangu wa Makeri is a woman born into traditional Gikuyu society who rose to the position of 'headman', as the first and only female to do so in the entire colonial period.

She is portrayed as a ruthless and loose woman who provoked men to rise up against her rule in a way that also illustrated gender power. All of the men impregnated their wives to disable them from resisting male assumption of power. With the women pregnant, in childbirth or nursing, it is said that the men easily assumed control in an unusual, bloodless coup that toppled Wangu (Wanyoike, 2002).

- **Lobbying and advocacy**
- Social engineering
- Socialization
- Espousing different paradigms

---

[1] Esther 4:14, *The Holy Bible*, new international version. In 2007 we had a student from Cameroon named Esther who was very religious and this statement was coined to capture her role in furthering women's access to resources.

and human rights features prominently. Law can provide for human rights entrenched in constitutions as a way of dealing with gender discriminatory customary law. It could proscribe discrimination generally, except in personal law matters, as some constitutions have done or make customary law subject to the right to equality. We agree that despite the fact that gender discriminatory aspects of customary law feature prominently, we should not 'throw the baby out with the bath water'. We need to capture positive 'living' customary law aspects.

We need to capture positive 'living' customary law aspects

We also agree that success stories of women who have access to resources are a powerful way of moving from the world view that 'women cannot have' to 'women can have'. Most students in the class give examples of themselves or women they know and the difference that resources make in their lives. For instance, many cite the ability to leave home and come for the course as an aspect of autonomy born out of having access to resources. It is also important that the individual identities of women are separated from community identities to provide for avenues though which women can access resources.

B   Engaging with ecofeminism

I turn to feminist theory that addresses the manifestations of women's oppression, its causes and consequences as well as hopes for change. Ecofeminism is one such theory which seeks to bring about an ecological revolution and ensure human survival on earth, by bringing a radical change in relations between women and men and between humans and nature. Two ecofeminisms – essentialist and cultural – inform our discussions. The essentialists perceive the women-nature connection as a result of intrinsic and biological attributes of women while the cultural ecofeminists believe that the connection is socially constructed (Fox-Genovese, 1991).

Ecofeminism as discussed by Merchant (1990) and Spretnak (1990) forms the springboard of our interrogation. Merchant seeks to have feminism inform environmental discourses while Spretnak argues that ecofeminism has philosophical, political activism and spirituality aspects. In her view, ecofeminists can use all these to question the male biases in environmental movements and development models and campaign for animal rights and against reproductive technologies. The use of radical feminism to illustrate the similarities between male disregard and abuse of nature and women is discussed in depth. The students' reaction to the readings is invariably shock and distancing their experiences from those used, which centre mainly on pornography and sexual exploitation.

The use of radical feminism to illustrate the similarities between male disregard and abuse of nature and women is discussed in depth.

I use the writings of Vandana Shiva (Shiva and Mosser, 1995) to explore ecofeminism as 'connectedness and wholeness of theory and practice'. This helps us to introduce concepts of sustainable development and the importance of protecting 'Mother Earth from the vagaries of modern science and technology'. The use of the term 'mother' introduces the exploration of the reproductive role of the ecosystem and how it has been devalued like that of women (Shiva, 1994).

I also use Bina Agarwal's work (1997) to elaborate the woman/nature relationship, especially her description of the four overlying precepts in ecofeminism:

1   Gender oppression and environmental degradation are mainly caused by male western dominance.

2   Men are more related to culture and women are related to the environment. Culture is seen as superior to the environment and hence both women and the environment have been subjugated by men and share a common inferior position.

3   Oppression of women and the oppression of nature have occurred simultaneously and thus women have a responsibility to stop male domination over both.

4   Ecofeminism seeks to combine feminism and ecological thought, as they both work towards egalitarian, non-hierarchical structures. Ecofeminists argue that both women and nature could be liberated together.

I broaden the victims of patriarchal domination, exploitation and mistreatment beyond women and nature to include children and minority groups in the world. I also get the students to explore ecofeminists' work with grassroots organizations and Green political movements that oppose the concentration of power and wealth in the hands of a few corporations (Mies, 2003). For instance, the Chipko movement in India started in the 1970s was organized by women resisting the destruction of forests. The women would hug the tree to prevent loggers from cutting them down (womeninworldhistory.com, 2010).

Christopher Stone's seminal article written in 1970 entitled 'Should trees have standing?' is a useful bridge between feminist and environmental rights discourses. In his article, he analogizes the quest for the rights of trees to that for women's rights and explains the resistance that such quests elicit from the entities that have the power to bestow rights (Stone, 1972). He explains the resistance from the point of view that 'until the rightless thing receives its rights, we cannot see it as anything but a thing for the use of us. It is hard to see it and value it for itself until we can bring ourselves to give it rights' (Stone, 1972). While most students have no problems advocating for the rights of women, they have problems with tree rights. I use this example to show how difficult it is for those with rights to concede to new entities getting rights and thus one can understand how patriarchy is perpetuated and nurtured.

...'until the rightless thing receives its rights, we cannot see it as anything but a thing for the use of us. It is hard to see it and value it for itself until we can bring ourselves to give it rights' (Stone, 1972)

In one of the previous classes, a student averred that 'ecofeminism is more of a philosophy that has been left at an abstract level'.[2] However, other students have used ecofeminism in their research for their dissertations. For instance, Makanatsa Makonese, in her study on Zimbabwe's forest laws, policies and practices and implications for access, control and ownership of forest resources by rural women, notes:

> 'The ecofeminist approach was also used to explore the consequences of environmental degradation on women's everyday lives as they seek substitutes or alternative coping mechanisms for environmental resources that should otherwise be abundantly available within their communities were it not for the degradation of the environment. I used this approach in analyzing the environmental degradation that has occurred in one of the research areas, Domboshava, and how the resultant lack of environmental resources like firewood has led to the oppression and suffering of women in the area.'

C   Engaging with women, environment and development

Since the early 1980s, various theories explaining underdevelopment have emerged as well as approaches to understanding the roles and status of women in the development process. I use women, environment and development concepts to conceptualize women's access to resources. Dianne Elson's work (Elson, 2006) is a point of departure for discussion of male bias in the development process. Women, environment and development concepts emphasize the special bond that exists between women and the environment: women are seen as the privileged bearers of a special knowledge imparted to them by nature. According to this view, women are assumed to be caring, nurturing and selfless beings committed to both future generations and the environment. In the words of Diamond and Orenstein (1990):

Women, environment and development concepts emphasize the special bond that exists between women and the environment

> '[B]ecause of women's unique roles in the biological regeneration of the species, our bodies are important markers, the sites upon which local, regional or even planetary stress [is] played out. Miscarriage is frequently an early sign of the presence of lethal toxins in the biosphere.'

We explore the special case of indigenous women who draw on a complex knowledge base as they are familiar with ecosystems, geographic features, climate, weather and tides. They understand the ecological succession, habitats and life cycles of resource species. They have detailed knowledge of all kinds of plants and animals, their habitat requirements, means of reproduction, nutritive values, as well as knowledge of various types of tinder

---

[2] Ndangariro P. Moyo, class of 2005.

and fuel, foods and medicinal herbs (Turner, 2003). They have also acquired cultural knowledge and understanding – including about important plants and animals – and rules relating to resource use, sharing and acquiring knowledge in culturally appropriate ways. Since such women operate in a context where their groups are seeking recognition, they are not at the forefront and gender issues are rarely a priority in the discourses (Hellum *et al,* 2007). Women consequently suffer intersectional discrimination on account of being members of a marginalized community as well as being women. Barriers for women in these contexts seeking to access justice are insurmountable as the seemingly more urgent and nagging community concerns take centre stage (Banda and Chinkin, 2004). We also look at the extent to which 'external protection' (Kymlicka, 2005) through human rights instruments plays out for women.

> *Women ... suffer intersectional discrimination on account of being members of a marginalized community as well as being women*

D   Defining access, control and ownership

Before we get into the substantive discussions on access to land and environmental resources, we unpack the definitive terms: *access*, *control* and *ownership*. The students name what they understand each term to mean and get consensus on what definition approximates closest to what we understand each term to stand for. In each definition, students are challenged to identify the gendered aspects of these terms. We note that while ownership is in most instances a legal concept denoting entitlements that are backed by legal sanctions (Dukeminier and Krier, 1993), control and access are determined by relationships between owners of resources and users of the resources. The owners have control of resources. They also determine who has access to resources. Land as the resource we focus on is a site for gender contest in most of the countries represented.

To understand our territory, we start by asking ourselves what access, control and ownership mean. It is immediately clear that many people confuse these terms and that ownership as a legal concept is sometimes ascribed to instances where there is only access. We look at pointers to ownership in formal legal terms in contradistinction to customary and living law pointers. We define ownership as a legal, social and economic construct constituting the overall right to property. Property has an individual and a social side. A community can own property as can an individual. In community ownership, the perception is that the entire community owns the land but it is clear that the entity that has control can exercise rights akin to ownership to the detriment of other members of the community. In a gendered context, we discuss how this can disadvantage women members of communities.

EXERCISE

How gender plays out in different countries in ownership of resources.

- How many women own land?
- What prevents women from owning land?
- How does not owning land impact on access to other resources?

We then look at access as being the permissions that people who are not owners have with regard to a resource. We note that access to property in many traditional societies is predicated on three things, namely: membership to a given society, functions relating to the property and the performance of reciprocal obligations owed to others in the society. The socially-constructed roles of men and women are integral to the delineation of access rights. In discussions with the students, it is clear that in many countries women's access to land is only via a system of vicarious ownership, through men as husbands, fathers, uncles, brothers and sometimes sons (UNHCS, 1999). Such access is not legally protected and may be severed by divorce or death. In Rwanda, for example, a daughter rejected by her husband or his family could be given a portion of land in the centre and south or in the northwest from lands held in reserve by the patrilineage for such emergencies (Pottier, 1997). Similarly, a woman who never married and did not bear children could also receive an allocation of land from the lineage holdings (Burnet, undated). According to Pottier (1997), a woman would have access to it for as long as she was deemed in need, if necessary, for life. After her death however, the land would be reclaimed by her late husband's nearest patrikin.

Control, we agree is the power to distribute and redistribute ownership and access rights. In patriarchal settings, the role is vested in older male members of a community. We also discuss the interplay between access, control and

STUDY

Women and property rights in Kenya

This study was conducted on behalf of the International Federation of Women Lawyers in Kenya (FIDA-Kenya) among selected farming communities in Kenya whose core business was cash and food crops. It aimed to inform revisions to the law on matrimonial property in Kenya.

The issue of how production is carried out in these economies raised questions about planning and management for optimal production. Ownership, access and control over resources emerged as key variables in rational economic decisions relating to savings and investment and allocation and distribution of benefits. FIDA sought to explore the forms of property among the communities, how women relate to them, the factors influencing their rights over productive resources and also what can be done to harness and sustain these rights, not only for the intrinsic value of gender equity but also for social and economic development and justice.

The study was carried out in Nyeri, Kisumu, Nyando and Keiyo districts. Data was collected from both primary and secondary sources. Conventional research methods and techniques were used to generate the report. These included library research, survey interviews, indepth key informant interviews and focus group discussions.

ownership, noting that the rights of access may be limited by the person that owns or has control of property. Ownership and control of land, for instance, constitute essential validation of social, economic and political autonomy for individuals as well as communities. I use a study on women and property rights in Kenya, 'A study on trends in ownership, control and access to land and productive resources in agricultural communities in select districts' (Kameri-Mbote and Mubuu, 2002) to illustrate how these issues play out practically (see box on page 342).

E   Demarcating subject matter coverage: access to what resources?

As noted above, it became clear after the first class in 2003 that we needed to narrow down the range of resources addressed in the course. We decided on land and environmental resources. Land is important as it constitutes the condition for community identity and is akin to territorial sovereignty for states. Control of land constitutes an essential validation of social and political autonomy. Access to, control over and ownership of land is influenced by diverse factors which include gender, age and marital status. Land is mainly controlled by male household heads on the assumption that the rights are held in trust for all in the household. I pointed out above that women have access or usufruct rights to land in many African countries. To that extent, their autonomy in the social, political and economic realms is limited by their lack of control over land.

Land is mainly controlled by male household heads on the assumption that the rights are held in trust for all in the household.

This is significant taking into account that land represents the vehicle through which women can move from the reproductive (private and non-valued work) realm to the productive (public and valued work) realm. Land is also habitat for other resources such as forests/trees, livestock, wildlife and water. Indeed access to water is linked closely to land ownership or access.

We discuss and note that gender-neutral laws on land and environmental resources have not resulted in more women owning these resources because of structural barriers such as access to credit and the prevalence of the myth that women cannot own land. Women are under-represented in institutions that deal with land and environmental resources.[3] Their rights under communal ownerships and 'group ranches' are not defined and this allows men to dispose of family land freely. Few women have land registered in their names. Similarly, state control of environmental resources has not resulted in equitable access to the resources for all. In instances where resources such as grazing areas and forests are vested in communities, equal access for all members of the community is not always guaranteed.

---

[3]   Most of the institutions dealing with environment and natural resources have few women representatives with some, such as wildlife and forest agencies, being predominantly male. See Ruto, Kameri-Mbote and Muteshi (2009).

ASSIGNMENT

Women, access to resources and the law assignment

● What are your expectations of the course?

● What are the most critical resources for women in carrying out their roles in your country? Indicate in what ways these resources are critical.

● Outline briefly how law has facilitated/constrained/ignored women's access to resources.

● How would you have law impact in the area of women's access to resources – domestically, locally, nationally and internationally?

F   The role of law – gender and law

...we discuss how legal equality may result in substantive inequality where the prevailing situation of legal subjects is not taken into account.

Since the students have already studied theories of women's subjugation and have interrogated legal pluralism, we start by exploring the role of law and how law can facilitate or constrain access to resources for women. Students are encouraged to discuss experiences from their countries. With the aid of their answers to an assignment (see example above) we discuss how legal equality may result in substantive inequality where the prevailing situation of legal subjects is not taken into account. We also share how the social ordering in different African countries tilts access to resources in favour of male members of society, emphasizing the point that laws intended to grant equal access for men and women yield very different outcomes upon application in gendered contexts (Dahl, 1987).

We discuss how constrained access to resources, lack of ownership rights and vesting control of land and resources in men has implications for women's performance of their duties (Meinzen-Dick *et al.*, 1997; Rocheleau and Edmunds, 1997). In similar vein, we discuss how women's ways of managing land and environmental resources[4] are marginalized, outlawed or demeaned. We also look at how the introduction of technologies that obliterate women's roles impacts on their work and political leverage as they become more dependent on new forms of knowledge that are owned and controlled by others (Thomas, 2003). We interrogate Seager and Hartmann's assertion that gender mediates environmental encounter, use, knowledge and assessment; and, secondly, that gender roles, responsibilities, expectations, norms and the division of labour shape all forms of human relationships to the environment (Seager and Hartmann, 2005).

---

[4]   Saving seed, shifting cultivation and slash and burn agriculture.

What law?

The methodological foundation of the course combines a women's law and legal pluralist approach (Hellum, Stewart, Ali and Tsanga, 2007). How the human rights system is responding to environmental, social and economic challenges is dealt with through discussions of recent legal developments, such as the evolving right to water and protection of informal property rights. We explore how the concept of equality and non-discrimination in CEDAW and the Protocol to the African Charter on the Rights of Women responds to the gendered uses of land and water on the ground. We question the legal centralist 'one size fits all' approach with reference to the need to do justice to women embedded in a wide variety of relationships, for example, matrilineal and patrilineal marriage and inheritance systems. Our course is premised on the assumption that while the nation-state is the main duty bearer under international law, it is in practice not the sole regulatory mechanism. To engage with the theory of legal pluralism we present students with a complex situation where women's rights to access, control and ownership of resources are negotiated at the intersection of plural sources of regulatory norms, giving rise to practical problems and dilemmas. They are encouraged to critically explore the potential of local knowledge and institutions as part of the search for ways to combine economic growth, poverty alleviation and more equitable distribution of natural resources between men and women and rich and poor.

Our course is premised on the assumption that while the nation-state is the main duty bearer under international law, it is in practice not the sole regulatory mechanism.

DISCUSSION

Introspectives

This discussion helps the students and I to look introspectively at our own lives and how we have fitted into the dominant paradigm or engaged and challenged it. We ask ourselves questions such as:

- Would we eat gizzards, eggs or other things if our families or communities forbid us from eating them when we know they are good for our health?
- Do we own land as individuals? What are the experiences around that ownership?
- When we contribute to purchasing land that is jointly owned with our spouses, do we insist on having our names on the deed?

We begin to identify small ways in which we can challenge and change the dominant paradigm in our own lives and in our communities.

By asking students and discussing what they understand to be law and listing the different sources of 'legal authority', we identify different normative and institutional regimes influencing ownership, control and access in the countries represented. The concept of legal pluralism that the students are already familiar with is useful in this discourse. While all the students are familiar with international, regional and national laws on women's rights, not many understand environmental laws. Unpacking the international, regional and national laws to identify and excavate the intersections between women's rights and access, control and ownership of land and environmental resources is an exciting exercise interjected by 'Aha' from the students as the light bulbs on connections at personal and local levels flash in their minds.

The Nairobi Forward Looking Strategies, the Beijing Platform for Action, the Convention on the Elimination of all Forms of Discrimination Against Women (1979), the African Charter on Human and Peoples' Rights (1986) and the Africa Protocol on Women (2003) serve as important starting points in identifying the standards for women's access, control and ownership. We look at how international, regional and national environmental and land laws address women's access to resources. We also look at the international geopolitical/political economic terrain and its implications for women's access to resources. In this regard, Maria Mies provides insights into the interconnections between the community of nations and how changes at any level reverberate at the lowest levels (Mies, 2003: note 11). We also note how bilateral donors purvey norms that directly or indirectly impact on access to land and related resources. At each level, we discuss how different instruments are used by polities at different levels to allocate resources and power. We discuss gender and generation factors that influence access, involvement, representation and input in decision-making processes.

At each stage, students are challenged to identify the dominant paradigm in all these regimes and to rationalize some of the beliefs, myths and ideas in the discourses on women's access to resources.

At the national level, we unpack statutory, religious and customary norms and the intersections and interactions between them and with international and regional norms. Myths and taboos at local and household levels help us appreciate how norms develop that colour women's access to resources. At each stage, students are challenged to identify the dominant paradigm in all these regimes and to rationalize some of the beliefs, myths and ideas in the discourses on women's access to resources. In most cases, we discover confluence between the different normative regimes in limiting women's access to resources.

Part III: Linking lived realities to legal form – empirical studies

To link lived realities to legal form we make extensive use of empirical studies. The empirical studies that are addressed in the second part of the course are based partly on first-hand experiences from field work in different parts of the region (Anne Hellum), partly on evaluations of rights-based programmes in the region (Pauline Nyamweya) and partly on the students' personal or professional experiences, including their masters dissertations.

A rights-based framework emphasizing the indivisibility and inter-relatedness of civil and political and social and economic human rights, in laying a foundation for the protection of women's access to and control of livelihood resources, has little meaning unless linked to everyday life. A bare-bones assessment of women's human rights entitlements is a sterile exercise without understanding the relationships which have a bearing on women's access to resources, their life choices and their capacity to pursue their options. The overall aim of our course is to enable the students to engage international and national legal frameworks with knowledge about women's actual access, control and ownership of natural resources on the ground. We further aim to provide students with the tools to deconstruct legal form and address underlying relationships that create, uphold or change the unjust distribution of resources between women and men, and between rich and poor. We actively encourage students to contribute to existing research through their masters dissertations. Through oral and written assignments, we make them engage with areas that need more research.

The overall aim of our course is to enable the students to engage international and national legal frameworks with knowledge about women's actual access, control and ownership of natural resources on the ground.

We teach the empirical studies in two parts. The first part, presented by Anne Hellum, shows how social and economic rights have a bearing on women's access, control and ownership of resources and focuses on the relationship between food, land and water, and education. The second part, presented by Pauline Nyamweya, addresses the relationship between social and economic, and civil and political rights with particular reference to statistical gender inequalities.

A   Access to resources: the interrelatedness of the right to food, water and land

Anne Hellum

Concrete case studies offer an opportunity to link broader theoretical issues to methods of data collection and analysis. In my engagement with the students, I use case studies as the hands-on approach to the grounded theory underlying women's law methodology (Bentzon *et al.*, 1997). As a lawyer and anthropologist I have used field work extensively in my study of women's social and economic human rights in context. In class, I share my research experiences with the students, using them as an entry point for further exploration of the student's experiences through group discussions, individual presentations and written assignments.

CASE 1:

The right to water in international law and local custom

Water's centrality for basic needs led the United Nations Committee on Economic, Social and Cultural Rights in General Comment 15 to address the human right to water as part and parcel of the right to an adequate standard of living in article 11 of the International Covenant on Economic, Social and Cultural Rights (the Covenant). The Committee states that water is a human right contained in article 11.1 of the Covenant defining the right to an adequate living standard 'including adequate food, clothing and housing'.

STUDY

The human right to water

While the human right to water was a site of legal contestation, local norms and practices in Zimbabwe point to a right to water that is more clearly defined than in international human rights law. This was demonstrated by a study of local water management that I carried out in Mhondoro communal lands with a research team for the Centre for Applied Social Studies (CAS) and Michigan State University.

In this study, by observing everyday practice but also studying cases of contestation and relevant statements made by the villagers, we explored the content and outreach of the norms underlying local water management. To supplement our own field observations, our research team drew on a series of Zimbabwean monographs on natural resource management, including water, wetlands, forests and land.

All these sources pointed to a consistent practice over time and space in upholding the norm that no one can be denied clean drinking water. The obligation to share drinking water, we observed, extended to all water sources, including those on private land. It extended to boreholes constructed for principally commercial or dedicated use and cut across kinship and village borders.

A factor upholding the right to clean drinking water was most villagers' strongly held view that they risked having the water source poisoned if they did not share it (Hellum, 2007).

The term 'including', in accordance with the Committee's dynamic interpretation, indicates that the catalogue of rights encompassing the right to livelihood in the legal text is not exhaustive but must be adapted to changing social and economic concerns such as the global water crisis. The 'Guidelines on the realization of the right to drinking water and sanitation' were passed by the Sub-commission on the Protection and Promotion of Human Rights in 2006.

I give students an assignment that requires them to explore the relationship between the human right to water, local water management practices and the Dublin Statement on Water and Sustainable Development of 1992. This statement was commended to the world leaders assembled at the United Nations Conference on Environment and Development held in Rio de Janeiro in June 1992. The Dublin Principles have been the main axiom for water reform in Africa, as elsewhere. Defining water as a social and economic good, the Dublin Principles represented a shift from supply to demand-driven water management systems based on the user-pay principle.

The students usually bring a wealth of comparative evidence to the table that links legal knowledge to local experience. A Malawian student's presentation of the Malawian water policy, for example, gave rise to a discussion of measures to make governments and non-governmental organizations comply with international human rights standards. In line with the Dublin Principles, Malawian water management was decentralized, local water user associations were formed and user fees introduced. Poor women in the student's home area could not afford the membership fees. They found the community wells locked and had to resort to unsafe water. The student concluded that this practice was not in consonance with local custom, nor with the human right to water. As a result of these discussions, several students have incorporated the issue of how women's access to water is constituted in the intersection of local use and municipal, national and international regulations in their dissertations.

The research questions discussed in the course seminars are often pursued in the students' masters dissertations. Over the years different aspects of water reforms in Mozambique, Malawi, Kenya, Zimbabwe and Ethiopia have been addressed.[5]

ASSIGNMENT
The Dublin Principles

In response to the Dublin Statement on Water and Sustainable Development, most African states have put regulatory systems focusing on water permits and water levies in place.

- What are the principles underlying water reform in your country?
- Is the right to water embedded in constitutions, laws, policies or local practices?
- How have the human right to water and the user-pay principle been balanced?
- How has water reform affected poor women?

---

[5] For example, the following SEARCWL masters' dissertations focused on this theme: Mekonnen (2004), Afonso (2004), Katsande (2006), Odeny (2006), Mchaju-Liwewe (2008) and Nyongesa (2008).

CASE 2:
The right to livelihood – the indivisibility of land and water

As an integral part of the right to an adequate standard of living embedded in article 11 of the Covenant, the right to water demonstrates the interdependence of a cluster of mutually constitutive rights such as the right to health and the right to food. Water's centrality for basic needs led the United Nations Committee on Economic, Social and Cultural Rights in General Comment 15 to emphasize the interdependence of human rights in general and between access to water and the right to health in article 12. 1, the right to food in article 11 and the right to life and human dignity enshrined in the International Bill of Human Rights. The 'Guidelines on the realization of the right to drinking water and sanitation' do not include water for subsistence agriculture.

STUDY
Women's gardens

I use a study of women's gardens in three villages in Mhondoro communal land in Zimbabwe which I conducted with researchers from the Centre for Applied Social Studies at the University of Zimbabwe and Michigan State University to demonstrate the mutual importance of land and water in ensuring rural livelihoods (Hellum, 2007). Here, as elsewhere in Africa, land and water uses are interwoven through highly gendered patterns of use.

While irrigated cash crop agriculture is often controlled by men, women, assisted by their children, are usually in charge of hand-irrigated vegetable gardens. They collect water from nearby rivers, self dug shallow wells or use borehole water. The produce in these gardens is used for family consumption and sale. Women, who usually control this income, use the money to pay school fees or buy medicine or food.

This use of land and water is often overlooked when policies and investment plans are made, resulting in investment in irrigating commercial crops, controlled mostly by men, while water for gardens is overlooked.

Right: One of the women's gardens we visited in Mhondoro

ASSIGNMENT

Water policies and water rights

- How does the human right to water embedded in article 11 of the Covenant on Social, Cultural and Economic Rights relate to women's use of water for vegetable gardens? Is use of water for food that is necessary to prevent disease and starvation a part of the human right to water described in General Comment 15 or in the 'Guidelines on the realization of the right to drinking water and sanitation'?

- How should water programmes and policies be constructed so as to put women's land and water uses on an equal footing with forms of agriculture that are dominated by men?

- What are the potential conflicts between the human right to water and environmental concerns? How should women's quest for equal access be balanced against environmental concerns?

The women's gardens case study is a departure point for discussion of broader legal and socio-legal issues through assignments requiring students to interrogate the issues of rights to water and the policies or principles employed.

The water policies and water rights assignment usually brings out a wealth of experiences. Most students grew up in rural areas and have memories of their mothers' gardens. According to one student, her mother's garden was the main source of the family's economic wealth. Their home was on the edge of a wetland where all kinds of vegetables and fruits were grown and sold in the market:

'Unlike the other families we always had milk and sugar in our tea and we all went to school thanks to the cash income she provided.'

One student told me, when we met a year later, that the course had opened her eyes to a wide range of issues she had previously not perceived of as women's rights issues. Being aware of urban gardens and their significance for the day to day survival of poor families, she had now started to explore how municipalities' regulations were affecting access to land and water.

CASE 3:

The right to water and to education: a girl-child perspective

Women and girl-children's right to gender equality is intimately linked to their social and economic rights. A crosscutting theme of discussion is how social and economic rights can contribute to gender equality. Students explorations of the interdependence of rights have resulted in important contributions to existing research. How girl-children's right to education is affected by the interplay between lack of accessible water and norms and practices placing a duty to fetch water on the girl-child is illustrated by Irene Afonso's masters dissertation addressing water management in rural Mozambique (Afonso, 2004).

...girl-children's right to education is affected by the interplay between lack of accessible water and norms and practices placing a duty to fetch water on the girl-child

The study was conducted in 2004 in four rural districts in the southern regions of Maputo, 180 kilometres from the capital. Six school areas were visited – two where no pumps or boreholes were installed, two which had one borehole and two with several boreholes and pumps. With some exceptions, group interviews with teachers brought out that the girls in the area had the duty to fetch water. Girls often came to school late because they were fetching water or they were absent-minded because they were thinking about where they would fetch water and many girls went straight to fetch water on leaving the school. An 11 year old girl who was interviewed at the school said:

> 'We are eight members in the family. I have three brothers and two sisters. We don't have water at home. We used to get water at a natural hole named Fussekan, a place that is very far from where I live. I go to school at 7 o'clock. Early in the morning, at about 4 o'clock, I go to fetch water and come back home at about 6 o'clock or half past. When I reach home I take my books and go to school. I am late for school and I do not have time to review my lessons. When I come back from school I go back to fetch water. I only read during the weekend when I am free. My brothers do not fetch water because they are boys. My sisters are very young and can't help me. My mother died. I live with my stepmother. She does not help me either. Only I fetch water for the family' (Afonso, 2004).

Group discussions with women and men in the local communities brought out the stereotyped views that informed these practices. One woman in her forties, for example, stated:

> 'A girl can go to school but, after all, she has to be taught housework before she gets married. I will not be at her house when she gets married. She must know the housework including fetching water so that she can become a good wife for her husband. She must provide water and food for him. What can she do with her education if she does not know the housework? Her husband does not eat paper from school' (Afonso, 2004).

The study, however, indicated that measures in line with article 5(a) of CEDAW, obliging states to take measures to eradicate stereotyped gender roles underlying discriminatory practices, are gradually being put in place by women's organizations. In a group discussion with youth in Kassimate the girls and boys responded:

> 'We were taught by the Mozambican Women's Organization that women and men are equal and both must do all the housework. There is no specific work for women and men' (Afonso, 2004).

CASE 4:
Balancing individual and communal rights

A contested issue in contemporary policy discourse in Africa is how individual and communal property rights should be balanced. The intersection of individual women's right to equality on the one hand and protection of a group's right to resources on the other, is often a site of contestation. The complex and differentiated relationships underlying group rights are explored through empirical case studies.

STUDY

South Africa's land restitution

A study of South Africa's land restitution process illustrates how local tensions as to how a fair balance between communities, households and individuals may be reached, have received inadequate attention by law and policy makers (Hellum and Derman, 2010). In the planning processes, local communities were seen as undifferentiated, with common interests, and therefore inadequate attention was paid to their complexity in terms of gender and class.

The post-restitution experiences speak to the need to deconstruct the notion of common community interests so as to come to grips with deep-seated patterns of gender and social differentiation. Interviews the researchers had with members of communal property associations in communities that had successfully claimed their land back in Limpopo Province indicated tensions as to how individual and communal rights should be balanced.

Out of the 69 members interviewed, 36 per cent favoured individual and household benefits. In this grouping, the majority of women favoured the individual whereas the men preferred household payments. Those who thought that the community alone should receive the benefits accounted for 29 per cent of the total, three quarters of whom were men. Women were far more supportive of individual benefits than men who supported household or community benefits.

ASSIGNMENT
Forming a communal property association

You are working for a non-governmental organization assisting local communities who have taken ownership over an irrigation scheme previously owned by the state. The community are under an obligation to form a communal property association and to draft a constitution.

What would your advice be in terms of drafting a constitution that ensures women equal participation and equal access to resources?

Most students are astonished that there are actually ways of reconciling women's rights as group members with their rights as individual citizens. From this follows a discussion on how common property systems based on customary law may be made more sustainable by securing fair and equal treatment of each and every beneficiary as opposed to a quest for abolition of customary law.

To further explore how common property regimes may be constructed to work to the benefit of women and the poorer members of the community by specifying the individual rights of the beneficiaries, the students do an assignment on a communal property association.

CASE 5:
Balancing indigenous rights, environmental rights and women's rights

Preserving the environment is often seen as opposing indigenous and local use rights. In the light of the difficulties that preserving the environment poses to women who depend on natural resources for their sustenance, the concept of sustainable use is introduced with emphasis on how to strike a balance between environmental and human development.

Students who had worked in environmental organizations welcomed the sustainable use approach in the light of a common perception among environmentalists that women's dependence on the environment led to over-exploitation of the environment with resultant degradation. Makanatsa Makonese's dissertation (2008) on Zimbabwe's forest laws, policies and practices and implications for rural women's access, control and ownership of forest resources was written to dispel this myth and show that women are natural environment managers because of their relationship with the environment. I use the example of forest produce to explain the implications of the various natural resources with a view to coming up with recommendations that encourage sustainable use of forest resources by rural women.

CASE 6:
Formalizing local use – the case of matrilineal land rights

Establishing and clarifying land and water rights has become a key issue in development policies aiming to promote more productive use of resources for women and the poor. The most recent policy initiative is the United Nations Commission on Legal Empowerment of the Poor. Against the background of a wide range of studies and policy initiatives, it outlines four interrelated pillars of legal empowerment of the poor that relate to women's access, control and ownership of resources. These are access to justice and the rule of law, property rights, labour rights and business rights. An overall concern is the uncertainty over legal ownership of forests, swamplands and sources of water – most of the rural poor depend on access to these for their livelihoods (Commission on Legal Empowerment of the Poor, 2008:36). The Commission assumes that legal empowerment of women and the poor can be achieved by formalizing the rights, and that women and the poor should be able to use their property as collateral to obtain loans and use these funds for further investment.

Whether and to what extent formalizing informal property rights, as advised by both the World Bank and the United Nations Commission on Legal Empowerment of the Poor, will benefit everyone within groups and communities is an open question. Human rights actors often assume that it is not possible to realize women's human rights in local practice or custom, and we can only offer alternatives offered in national legislation. To challenge this assumption, theoretical and empirical research demonstrating potential opportunities in collaboration between human rights activists and community members committed to social and legal change is presented. In the article, 'Are local norms and practices fences or pathways? The example of women's property rights', Celestine Nyamu-Musembi, based on a local study in Kenya, addresses features that facilitate and diminish the possibility of realizing gender equal property rights at the local level (Nyamu-Musembi, 2002).

Human rights actors often assume that it is not possible to realize women's human rights in local practice or custom, and we can only offer alternatives offered in national legislation.

STUFF

STUDY

The Ogiek in Kenya

A study of the Ogiek in Kenya interrogated the gendered perception of the group's relationship with the state, the forest and its resources underlying the indigenous group's quest for recognition of their indigenous land rights. The analysis reveals that men, in a situation where the Ogiek have taken their land claims to court with the support of the non-governmental organization community, represent the generic community's voices while women's concerns as users of the land are not articulated. The case of the Ogiek demonstrates how the quest for cultural rights, unless situated in its gendered context, can result in a restatement of patriarchy and the entrenchment of patriarchal norms of dominance over women (Kameri-Mbote and Odour, 2007).[6]

---

[6] The article is based on Odour's original masters dissertation on the Ogiek (2004).

Conflicting concerns, such as economic growth, democracy, equality and secure livelihoods, are currently reflected in formalization initiatives across the African continent. These processes are influenced by a wide range of international actors ranging from the World Bank, United Nations agencies, donor agencies, governments and non-governmental organizations. A crucial challenge lies in ensuring that formalization does not result in inequality between women and men. A human rights based approach requires that mechanisms protecting women against direct and indirect discrimination are put in place. Towards this end a dynamic and context-sensitive human rights approach is needed, where knowledge about local practices and principles is employed in a continuous dialogue with the evolving equality and non-discrimination standard.

A crucial challenge lies in ensuring that formalization does not result in inequality between women and men.

Linking lived realities to legal form, we present empirical case studies showing how seemingly gender-neutral laws and policies often result in indirect discrimination because they overlook the gendered uses of land and water on the ground (Ikdahl *et al.*, 2005). These case studies demonstrate the need to explore the power of women to negotiate in differing social, economic and political contexts. Particular attention is given to the ongoing erosion of women's customary land rights embedded in matrilineal principles and practices.

The students do an assignment to explore how these processes are unfolding in their own countries. This assignment usually brings a wide

STUDY

Water users associations in Malawi

A study examining the transfer of two smallholder irrigation schemes to water user associations in Domasi in Malawi illustrates how unequal power relations between men and women in practice make their mark on formalization processes (Ferguson and Mulwafu, 2008). The study observes the interface between long-standing customary practices and implementing new water laws and policies. The scheme is located in an area where women have gained access to plots on the basis of appeals to cultural traditions recognizing matrilineal inheritance of land. Most farmers interviewed by the researchers had no clear understanding of what their rights to land and water uses would be once the transfer of the scheme to the new water users associations was accomplished. According to the research team, it was highly uncertain how the new laws and policies that proposed to make inheritance more equitable by not recognizing either customary or matrilineal inheritance practices would affect women's rights to valuable irrigated land.

range of cases to the table which often give rise to students conceptualizing their research topic. Research methodology is thus part of the case-work component. A dissertation from the 2007–2008 programme, based on a second study of two water user associations in Domasi in Malawi, highlights the potential outcome of this integrated teaching method.

Students are encouraged follow up their research through engagement with non-governmental organizations and international and national law and policy makers. Authoring the 2010 gender and human development report in Malawi, Olivia Mchaju-Liwewe was able to translate the research findings from her masters dissertation (see details in the box below) into policy recommendations.

The report recommends that:

'Development programmes and legal provisions in Malawi need to recognize the relevance of the customary rights of women and use them as a platform for development. There is a compelling need to recognize matrilineal women's land rights today, instead of acting in violation of them, which forces women into greater poverty instead of moving them out of it' (Mchaju-Liwewe, 2003).

ASSIGNMENT
Formalization programmes

Describe and discuss formalization programmes that have been carried out in your country. Give an assessment of how women have fared in the light of the equality and non-discrimination standards embedded in CEDAW and the Protocol to the African Charter.

DISSERTATION
A history of diminishing returns: the paradox of women's land rights in small-scale irrigation reform in matrilineal societies in southern Malawi

Struggling to come to grips with equality and non-discrimination principles relating to women's land rights embedded in matrilineal and matrilocal principles and practices, Olivia Mchaju-Liwewe (2008) decided to re-study the two water user associations in Domasi in Malawi, previously studied by Ferguson and Mulwafu.

Her new study showed how the disruption of matrilineal land rights, which came with the government's transfer of ownership to the users, had eroded women's customary land rights. Neither the new Land Act nor government policy recognized women's customary land rights deriving from matrilineal and matrilocal principles and practices.

Revealing a conceptual silence in both CEDAW and the Protocol to the African Charter, the study calls for a rethinking of the equality and non-discrimination standard with a view to respecting and protecting women's customary rights embedded in matrilineal principles.

B Access to resources: the interrelatedness with the right to education and health

Pauline Nyamweya

Overview

This part of the course is motivated by my consultancy work on the correlation between the economic empowerment of women and the removal of structural inequalities that exist in the non-economic sphere, particularly those that prevent the equal opportunities of women to education and health.[7] It aggregates information from several surveys and studies and this allows for generalizations on the gendered reality in applying and enjoying these rights. It illustrates the interrelatedness of human rights in the resources arena, informed by the concrete case studies in Anne Hellum's section. In this part we also focus on the more statistical data illustrating the skewed distribution of resources.

This section has been taught since 2005 when it explored the interrelationship between women's access to a wide range of resources and access to land. Resources that were examined from a gender perspective were access to financial resources, employment, education, health care and legal resources. Since 2007, we have narrowed the focus of the case study to the interrelated nature of the rights to education, health and access to land, with specific emphasis on HIV/AIDS.

We use a collection of researches and narratives, mainly from eastern and southern Africa, to illustrate the impact of HIV and AIDS on women's property rights and livelihoods.[8] These studies also serve to expose discriminatory laws and practices. For example, a summary of a narrative taken from Kaori Izumi (2006:34–37) which tells one woman's story, is given on page 359.

We focus on two main areas, health and education which draw heavily on the students' prior exposure to gender concepts, analytical frameworks and methodologies and on their own socialization and lived realities.

---

[7] For example we examine an evaluation undertaken of 'Gender equality in Swedish Development Cooperation' (Sida Evaluation Series, 2010:1). In the Nyanza roads programme in Kenya, the effectiveness of gender equality measures was more limited in Kuria district which has suffered from a long history of structural marginalization and high levels of poverty. Gender relations and status were not fundamentally altered by the temporary infusion of employment opportunities and income connected to roads construction, yet at the same time concrete specific benefits to women at an individual level such as access to education for girls, skills training, access to health services and family planning were observed as a result of the income they got from the road construction.

[8] The key case studies and narratives that are examined are Kaori Izumi (2006), Michael Aliber and Cherryl Walker (2006) and Scott Drimie (2002/2003).

NARRATIVE

AIDS took my son and my property

This narrative outlines Beatrice Wanjiru Muguiyi's life experiences, revealing the struggles she experienced in claiming her most basic rights. This account was put together by her daughter, Lucy Muguiyi Njuguna, from interviews in Nairobi, January 2005 and is published in a collection entitled *Reclaiming our lives: HIV and AIDS, women's land and property rights and livelihoods in southern and east Africa, narratives and responses* (Izumi, 2006).

Beatrice had been fortunate as a child, as she says:

> 'I was lucky to be sent to school at the early age of eight years. ... My father was humiliated because of me. Other men would not allow him to participate in their talks or attend their parties, but his mind was set. I passed and was admitted to Alliance Girls High School. I was the first girl to go to high school in the whole district.'

However, although her education gave her a secure career, it subsequently caused tension in her relationship with her husband and she found herself responsible for her husband's extended family as he refused to contribute to the family maintenance:

> 'Life was extremely difficult because the salary was now stretched and yet [her husband] kept talking ill of "educated women"'.

While she was able to purchase land and invest in a secure home for the family, this situation was turned upside down when her eldest son died of AIDS and her husband sought a new heir with a new wife he installed in the family home.

> 'The death of my son was a double tragedy in that it also heralded the loss of the home I loved.'

While her efforts to reclaim her home were unsuccessful in the courts, she finally succeeded in her quest some months later:

> 'I sought the help of community leaders and peacefully walked into my home. I made it clear to my husband that the home was rightfully mine and I had come back.'

Sample of some pertinent issues for discussion:

- Society's attitudes to education for girls – have they changed?

- A need for a shift in the male paradigm?

- How effective is a just law in a society where unjust attitudes persist?

- Was AIDS really the culprit?

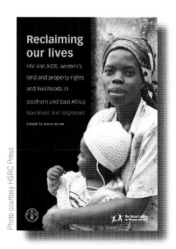

Photo courtesy HSRC Press

ASSIGNMENT
Women's rights to education, health and land

In group sessions and individual presentations, students:

- Discuss the interrelatedness of women's rights to education, health and land, as illustrated by various researches and narratives, and the household, cultural and structural factors that affect women's access;

- Identify key strategies a rights-based approach can employ to address the gendered power relations and roles that are manifest in the case studies and narratives.

We begin by examining the substantive contents of the rights to health (with specific emphasis on HIV/AIDS) and education as embodied in various international and regional human rights instruments.[9] The objectives of this are three-fold:

- To provide the normative basis and arguments for women's right to education and health;

- To examine and discuss in greater detail the normative content of these rights as a first step in analyzing the gendered enjoyment of the same;

- To illustrate the interrelatedness of these rights to access to land.

We then move on to explore the divergence between the substantive rights and the lived realities of women, by demonstrating, statistically, the various disparities that exist between men and women when it comes to the enjoyment of these rights, and their effect on women's access to land resources. The students also engage with the concept of equality by addressing the structural bases of women's inequality in their assignments. These exercises aim to interrogate the disadvantages suffered by women and how they are created and maintained irrespective of the normative prohibition of discrimination.

1 Health, HIV/AIDS and women's access to land

The students discuss the right to control one's health and body, including sexual and reproductive freedom and the state's duty to provide health protection which provides equality of opportunity for people to enjoy the highest attainable level of health. An important element we stress is that the right to health is an inclusive right extending not only to timely and appropriate health care but also to the underlying determinants of health, such as access to safe and potable water and adequate sanitation, an adequate supply of safe food, nutrition and housing, healthy occupational and environmental conditions, and access to health-related education and information, including on sexual and reproductive health.

...the right to health is an inclusive right extending not only to timely and appropriate health care but also to the underlying determinants of health

---

[9] A key resource in addition to the international and regional human rights instruments is found in Eide (1995).

SUMMARY TABLE

Institutional, cultural and legal issues affecting women's health: the case of Tanzania

INSTITUTIONAL ISSUES	CULTURAL ISSUES	LEGAL ISSUES
● Geographic inaccessibility has a significant impact on use of health facilities. In Tarime rural district, health centres are unevenly located and very far from the people so travel time to health services is long for rural women. The roads are gravel and during the rainy season they become slippery and in some places not navigable at all. Therefore, both distance and travel time have a significant impact on use of health services because most of the women are poor, and have no money for transport.	● Married women are supposed to seek permission from their husband to use family planning. Many men are reluctant to allow their wives to use contraception either on religious grounds or for other reasons, such as wetness of the vagina. This affects women negatively as high fertility puts women at risk of malnutrition and maternal mortality. ● Female genital mutilation is practised and in unhygienic situations. Tools used are often not properly sterilized. ● Some community members believe in witchcraft and myths and this results in more health problems for women – an example is the myth that raping a virgin will cure HIV/AIDS or that infection with HIV/AIDS is the result of being bewitched (by a wife or by women witches).	● Section 151 of the Penal Code restricts abortions. This is dangerous for women's health because many of them opt to use illegal methods which sometimes cost them their lives. ● Section 10 of the Marriage Act recognizes polygamy and since this involves multiple sexual partners, female spouses in this practice face a higher risk of HIV infection.

Students explore the many ways in which women carry an extra burden in health matters through structured class discussions, group discussions and in question and answer sessions. Some of the issues they look at are:

● Women are the last to be given resources and the last to benefit from health schemes because of discrimination and disparities in access to resources.

● Women's roles in child bearing and child rearing mean that many health problems are unique to them. Fulfilling their roles as carers and food producers puts strains on women's health and also on their nutritional status. For example, repeated pregnancies and caring for large families can take its toll on their health.

● Son preference disadvantages women's health from birth in terms of poor nutrition, neglect, abandonment and infanticide.

Some of the issues that arise from the group and individual presentations on factors affecting women's health and access to resources are captured in the summary table on page 357 which focuses on the situation in Tanzania.

In the discussions on access to health, we acknowledge that within any given social setting, an individual's access to health services is determined by general factors such as distance, availability, affordability as well as the appropriateness and adequacy of services as perceived by the users. While these factors affect both women and men, there are important differences by sex and gender that cut across social groups.

In discussing the interrelatedness of the right to health and access to land, the starting point is acknowledging that access to health services is a function both of the resources at the overall disposal of a society or community and of its distribution across social groups and individuals. Thus, wealthier nations and more powerful groups within countries are likely to have greater availability of health services and better access to these services. Health therefore has a cause and effect relationship with other resources, including access to land:

● Resources are essential for the right to health to be realized;

● Health also has a socio-economic impact. Good health is essential to leading a productive and fulfilling life, and the right of all women to control all aspects of their health, in particular their own fertility, is basic to their empowerment as well as in access to land and related resources.

We explore the additional effects of HIV/AIDS and the vulnerabilities that women are exposed to as a result of this pandemic. HIV/AIDS generates and exacerbates poverty as people lose housing tenure and productive employment. Various studies expose the scale of the economic impact of HIV/AIDS (Aliber and Walker, 2006; Drimie, 2002). Students have access to this documentation that traces the rapid transition from relative wealth to relative poverty among

SURVEY
Measuring HIV/AIDS and women's vulnerabilities

The Food and Agriculture Organization (FAO) carried out qualitative and quantitative research in communities in Namibia, Uganda and Zambia. As stated in the abstract of the study report:

> *'Although the relationships among gender, food security and rural livelihoods have been acknowledged in the growing literature on HIV/AIDS impacts, relatively few studies provide adequate focus and empirical evidence on the gender aspects of these interrelationships among vulnerable rural households. Such gender aspects of these relationships have been explored in detail by FAO in Namibia, Uganda and Zambia'* (Curry et al., 2006: abstract).

The sampled households (a mix of those affected and those not affected by the HIV/AIDS pandemic) were asked about changes in area of land cultivated within the five years before the study and what they considered the reasons for this. All households had experienced reductions in the land they cultivated. Changes were highest in the Uganda sample (minus 10 per cent) and lowest in the northern Zambia sample (minus 2.2 per cent). Male-headed unaffected households had the lowest reduction with only a 2 per cent loss in area cultivated. In the Uganda and southern Zambia samples, reductions in cropland were patterned more along gender lines; on average female-headed households reduced cropland by about 10-15 per cent more than male-headed households in Uganda and about 4 per cent more in southern Zambia.

In order to provide some measure of wealth status for households in the studies, an asset index was constructed using data on asset ownership. It was assumed that household wealth is the main source of variation in asset ownership levels and, therefore, levels of asset ownership could provide an indication of the level of financial capital of the household.

In general, female-headed households in the samples made up a higher proportion of households in the lowest asset index category than households headed by men. In Namibia, nearly one-third of the affected female-headed households were in the low asset category, while nearly half of the affected female-headed households in Uganda were similarly asset-poor. In southern Zambia, the proportion in the lowest asset category reached nearly two-thirds for female-headed households, regardless of whether they were affected or not by the HIV/AIDS pandemic. In northern Zambia, female-headed households made up between 36 and 44 per cent of households in the low asset category; female percentages are nearly twice as high as for their male counterparts.

However, the studies exposed the difficulties of conducting research which includes an overt HIV/AIDS component. Due to the perceived stigma attached to the illness, interviewees' responses were not always reliable. Also, answers were affected by people's expectation that they may be able to receive aid. Future studies would need to take a broader view, linking health, agricultural production and poverty surveys using a much larger sample base.

Source: Curry, Wiegers, Garbero, Stokes and Hourihan, October 2006.

TABLE
Gender-disaggregated data on HIV/AIDS prevalence (Adults 15–49) 2007/2009

Country	HIV prevalence rates	
	Male	Female
Ethiopia	1.6	2.4
Eritrea	1.0	1.5
Kenya	4.3	8.0
Uganda	4.3	6.6
Tanzania	5.0	7.6
Rwanda	2.3	3.2
Burundi	1.6	2.4
Cameroon	3.9	6.3
Mozambique	10.0	14.9
Zimbabwe	12.2	18.7
Zambia	12.4	18.0
Malawi	10.2	13.5
Botswana	18.9	28.9
Lesotho	19.4	27.1
South Africa	14.4	21.8

Source: Population Reference Bureau, 2010

AIDS-affected households in urban and rural areas. In communities where customary land tenure is based on the active use of the land, households suffering AIDS-related losses of labour and reduced productive capacity may lose their rightful access to land as their level of production declines or their land lies fallow.

The reality of HIV/AIDS in many African countries provides students with the background to relate their experiences and examples of how they have personally observed the linkages between HIV/AIDS, education and access to resources for women. Gender is an inextricable part of the HIV/AIDS equation. Young women are disproportionately vulnerable to infection; elderly women and young girls are disproportionately affected by the burden of care-giving in the epidemic's wake. In addition gender inequalities fuel the epidemic in rural areas and often exacerbate gender inequalities in workloads, poverty and rights to land.

2 Education and women's access to land

This section illustrates how education determines entry into the labour market – whether through wage-labour or self-employment – and so it also determines access to the resulting important economic returns. These include income, ownership and control over assets such as land and housing which in turn provide economic security and access to credit and opportunities and incentives for growth. Furthermore, education also empowers women, and men, to question traditions and cultural norms and take action against discriminatory practices that perpetuate inequity.

The interrelatedness between education and access to land and other resources is also evident from the experiences that the students share during group work discussions. We examine the strong, empirically verifiable, positive relationships across all societies between the wages and salaries people receive at work and the level of education they have attained. It has also been shown that the earnings of the self-employed, including those in urban and informal sector activities, are higher for the educated than for the uneducated.

We therefore focus on the gender disparities in access to education and examine the reasons for these persistent inequalities in the context of both national and international legislation purportedly promoting the equal right to education.

The World Bank Gender and Development Group commissioned the International Centre for Research on Women to carry out a study on the impact of investments in female education on gender equality. The study, undertaken by Anju Malhotra, Rohini Pande and Caren Grown in 2003, reviewed existing empirical literature from a variety of social science and health disciplines. The report concluded, however, that while education was an essential ingredient for change, it could not make a difference without concomitant changes in societal attitudes and structures. An extract from the executive summary from their report which captures the essence of their findings, is presented in the box below.

REPORT
The impact of investments in female education on gender equality

'While the benefits of educating girls and women for societies, in general, and their families, more specifically, are well-understood, the case for education serving as a catalyst in reducing gender inequality, or benefiting women themselves, is less clearly established. ...

'Our review indicates that education is a necessary, but not sufficient investment for achieving gender equality or improving women's wellbeing. Of the twelve indicators we examined in the four themes (*Health and wellbeing*, *Position in family and society*, *Economic opportunities and returns* and *Political participation*) education has a consistently favourable impact on women's wellbeing and gender equality for only two outcomes, namely, maternal health and women's mobility. For all the other aspects that we examined, the empirical literature suggests that a range of underlying social and economic conditions needs to be favourable in order for female education to have a beneficial effect on gender equality and women's wellbeing. Female education is most beneficial to women in settings which are already less patriarchal, where women have access to services, options and opportunities, and where market and social conditions favour positive returns. The review also indicates that often it is only secondary or higher levels of schooling that lead to improved options, opportunities and outcomes for women.

'For policymakers, this suggests that investments in education often need to be accompanied by investments in improving the enabling conditions within which schooling has the greatest payoff for girls and women. This requires improvement in provision of services and opportunities, and more fundamentally, shifts in social and economic structures and gender norms.'

An extract from the executive summary of the report, Impact of investments in female education on gender equality (Malhotra, Pande and Grown, 2003:1).

Conclusion

Teaching the course has been a source of great joy and intellectual inspiration. It has given us the platform to share our research with the students and each other. It has also enabled us to interrogate our own understandings of feminist and ecological discourses. Most significantly, it has opened a whole new area of research on women and sustainable development for us as researchers[10] and for students.[11] Several of the students who have completed the course have recently been accepted for the SEARCWL doctoral programme and are now conducting further research in this field.

As an expansion of research-based teaching we have embarked on a joint research programme on gender, human rights and water governance with research teams from Kenya, Malawi, Zimbabwe and South Africa.[12] Another research project that has been informed by the course is on access to land and land-based resources among women in pastoralist and forest-dwelling communities in East Africa. This project is exploring multiple exclusions and their impacts on women's citizenship. As part of these research projects we have doctoral students in Malawi, Zimbabwe and Nairobi working on different aspects of women's access to resources.

The research-based character of our course has enabled us, firstly, to move the grounded theory between the classroom and the field and use lived realities of women as examples. Secondly, the research results will be useful case studies for the course in the future. Thirdly and most importantly, the doctoral students working on gender and access to land, water and environmental resources will be the future instructors on the course, leading to inter-generational succession that is vital for the course's continued growth and dynamism.

We have been challenged to look at the issues of environmental justice for women and noted that there is resistance from African women's rights activists to embrace ecological discourses for fear that the latter will mask the former. This fear also resides in the environmental rights activists.

We have also learnt that changing dominant paradigms takes one and every woman 24 twenty four hours a day, seven days a week

We have also learnt that changing dominant paradigms takes one and every woman twenty four hours a day, seven days a week. Because of our discussions with the students and engagements with our reflexive selves, we have also realized that learning happens in the most mundane ways, such as by interrogating everyday activities and asking the next (often unasked and sometimes rhetorical) question.

---

[10] See Kameri-Mbote (2006, 2007a, 2007b, 2008 and 2009) and Kameri-Mbote and Oduor (2007) all of which are the result of teaching this course.

[11] See, for example Makanatsa Makonese (2010) and Elisabeth Rutsate (2010).

[12] 'Gender, human rights and water governance'; *Funder:* Global Partner Gender Programme of the Norwegian Research Council; *Research leader:* Anne Hellum; *Principal researchers:* Patricia Kameri-Mbote, Ngeyi Kanyangolo, Ellen Sithole and Barbara van Koppen.

Bibliography

Afonso I. (2004) 'Access to clean water in the southern region of Mozambique and its implication for girls' education', masters dissertation, SEARCWL, University of Zimbabwe, Harare.

Agarwal B. (1997) 'Environmental management, equity and ecofeminism: debating India's experience', *Journal of Peasant Studies* 25 (4):55-95.

Aliber M. and C. Walker (2006) 'The impact of HIV/AIDS on land rights: perspectives from Kenya', *World Development* 34(4): 704–727.

Banda F. and C. Chinkin (2004) *Gender minorities and indigenous peoples*, Minority Rights Group International, London.

Benschop M. (2002) *Rights and reality: are women's equal rights to land, housing and property implemented in East Africa?*, UN Human Settlements Programme (UN-HABITAT), Nairobi.

Bentzon A.W., A. Hellum, J. Stewart, W. Ncube and T. Agersnap (eds) (1997) *Pursuing grounded theory in law: south-north perspectives in women's law*, Tano-Aschehoug and Mond Books, Oslo and Harare.

Burnet J. (undated) *Women's rights in Rwanda*, Rwanda Initiative for Sustainable Development, Kigali, available online at: http://www.law.emory.edu/wandl/WAl-studies/rwanda.htm (accessed 20 March 2011).

Commission on Legal Empowerment of the Poor (2008) *Making the law work for everyone, Volume I*, UNDP, New York.

Curry J., E. Wiegers, A. Garbero, S. Stokes and J. Hourihan (2006) *Gender, HIV/AIDS and rural livelihoods: micro-level investigations in three African countries*, Research paper 2006/110, UNU-WIDER, Helsinki.

Dahl T.S. (1987) *Women's law: an introduction to feminist jurisprudence*, translated by Ronald L. Craig, Norwegian University Press, Oslo.

Diamond I. and G.F. Orenstein (eds) (1990) *Reweaving the world: the emergence of ecofeminism*, Sierra Club Books, San Francisco.

Drimie S. (2002) *The impact of HIV/AIDS on land: case studies from Kenya, Lesotho and South Africa*, Human Sciences Research Council, Pretoria, also published in *Development Southern Africa* 20(5) December 2003.

Dukeminier J. and J.E. Krier (1993) *Property*, 3rd edition, Little Brown, Boston.

Eide A., C. Krause and A. Rosaset (eds) (1995) *Economic social and cultural rights: a textbook,* Martinus Nijhoff Publishers, Dordretcht.

Ferguson A. and W. Mulwafu (2008) 'If governments fail how are we to succeed?', in B. van Koppen, J. Butterworth and I. Juna (eds), *Community-based water law and water resources management reform in developing countries*, Cabi publishers, Oxford.

Fox-Genovese E. (1991) *Feminism without illusions: a critique of individualism*, University of North Carolina Press, Chapel Hill and London.

Hellum A. (2007) 'Human rights encountering gendered land and water uses. Family gardens and the right to water in Mhondoro communal land', in A. Hellum, J. Stewart, S.S. Ali and A. Tsanga (eds), *Human rights, plural legalities and gendered realities; Paths are made by walking*, Weaver Press, Harare.

Hellum A. and B. Derman (2008) 'Historical justice and socio-economic development: tensions in South Africa's land restitution programme', *Forum for Development Studies* 1.

– (2010) 'The making and unmaking of unequal property relations between men and women: shifting policy trajectories in South Africa's land restitution process', *Nordic Journal of Human Rights* 28(2).

Hellum A., J. Stewart, S.S. Ali and A. Tsanga (2007) 'Paths are made by walking. Introductory thoughts' in A. Hellum, J. Stewart, S.S. Ali and A. Tsanga (eds) *Human rights, plural legalities and gendered realities; Paths are made by walking*, Weaver Press, Harare.

Ikdahl I. with A. Hellum, R. Kårhus, T.A. Benjaminsen and P. Kameri-Mbote (2005) *Human rights, formalization and women's land rights in southern and eastern Africa*, Studies in Women's Law No.57, Institute of Women's Law, University of Oslo, Oslo.

Izumi K. (2006) *Reclaiming our lives: HIV/AIDS, women's land and property rights and livelihoods in southern and eastern Africa – narratives and responses*, Human Sciences Research Council, Pretoria.

Kameri-Mbote P. (2002) 'The impact of traditional/religious institutions on gender relations and gender discriminative practices and scope for changing the negative trends: a case study of select pastoral communities in Kenya', report prepared for the Netherlands Organization for International Development Cooperation (SNV), The Hague.

– (2002) 'Proprietary status of women in Kenya: towards greater recognition of ownership rights', paper prepared for the National Conference on Women, Land and Property Rights in Kenya to input into the Presidential Commission on Land, 11-12 March 2002, Garden Hotel, Machakos.

– (2005) *Achieving the Millennium Development Goals in the drylands: gender considerations*, IELRC working paper 2005-8, available online at http//www.ielrc.org/content/w0508.pdf.

– (2006) 'Women, land rights and the environment: the Kenyan experience', *Development* 49 (3) September.

– (2007) 'Women and sustainable environmental management', *Agenda* 72: 36–46.

– (2008) 'Gender, rights and development: an East African perspective', *Forum for Development Studies* 1 (August), Oslo.

– (2009) 'Engendering environmental management for sustainable livelihoods', in S. Ruto, P. Kameri-Mbote and J. Muteshi (eds), *The promises and realities: taking stock of the Third International Women's Conference*, African Women and Child Feature Service and Ford Foundation, Nairobi.

Kameri-Mbote P. and J. Onyango Oduor (2007) 'Following God's constitution: the gender dimension in the Ogiek claim to the Mau forest complex', in A. Hellum, J. Stewart, S.S. Ali and A. Tsanga (eds), *Human rights, plural legalities and gendered realities; Paths are made by walking*, Weaver Press, Harare.

Kameri-Mbote P. and K. Mubuu (2002) 'Women and property rights in Kenya: a study on trends in ownership, control and access to land and productive resources in agricultural communities in select districts', paper documenting findings of a study commissioned by FIDA (Kenya) as a background to a revised Matrimonial Causes Bill.

Katsande R. (2006) 'Women's access to potable water and sanitation as a human right: a case study of Alaska and Shackleton settlements in Chinhoyi, Zimbabwe', masters dissertation, SEARCWL, University of Zimbabwe, Harare.

Kymlicka W. (1995) *Multicultural citizenship*, Clarendon Press, Oxford.

MacKinnon C. (2005) *Women's lives, men's laws*, Harvard University Press, Cambridge MA and London.

Makonese M. (2010) 'Zimbabwe's post independence land reform laws and policies and their impact on women's right to agricultural land: a critical analysis of the fast track land reform programme from 2000 and beyond', masters dissertation, SEARCWL, University of Zimbabwe, Harare.

Mchaju-Liwewe O. (2008) 'A history of diminishing returns: the paradox of women's land rights in small scale irrigation scheme reforms in matrilineal societies in southern Malawi', masters dissertation, SEARCWL, University of Zimbabwe, Harare.

– (2010) *Gender and human development in Malawi – 2010. Women and the potential of achieving the Millennium Development Goals*, UNDP Malawi, Blantyre.

Meinzen-Dick R.S., L.R. Brown, H.S. Feldstein and A.R. Quisumbing (1997) 'Gender, property rights and natural resources', *World Development* 25(8):1303-1315.

Mekonnen H. (2004) 'Gendered implication of access to clean water on the girl child: a case study in two rural villages in Ethiopia', masters dissertation, SEARCWL, University of Zimbabwe, Harare.

Merchant C. (1990) 'Ecofeminism and feminist theory', in I. Diamond and G.F. Orenstein (eds) *Reweaving the world: the emergence of ecofeminism*, Sierra Club Books, San Francisco.

Mies M. (2003) *Patriarchy and accumulation on a world scale: women in the international division of labour*, Zed Books, London.

Nyamu-Musembi C. (2002) 'Are local norms and practices fences or pathways? The example of women's property rights', in A.A. An-Na'im (ed), *Cultural transformation and human rights in Africa*, Zed Books, London.

– (2008) 'Breathing life into dead theories about property rights in rural Africa. Lessons from Kenya', in B. Enlert and E. Daley (eds) *Women's land rights and privatization in eastern Africa*, James Currey, London.

Nyongesa G. (2008) 'Right to land, clean water, food and shelter: a case study of the gendered effects on squatters of the constitution's failure to address these rights in Mogotio, Kenya', masters dissertation, SEARCWL, University of Zimbabwe, Harare.

Odeny M. (2006) 'Privatization, commercialization of water services and its implication for women's access and control of water: a case study of Njoro Community Water Project', masters dissertation, SEARCWL, University of Zimbabwe, Harare.

Pottier J. (1997) S*ocial dynamics of land reform in Rwanda, past, present and future*, Department of Sociology, University of London, London.

Rocheleau D. and D. Edmunds (1997) 'Women, men and trees: gender, power and property in forest and agrarian landscapes', *World Development* 25(8):1356.

Rutsate E.L. (2010) 'All that glitters is not gold! A critical analysis of the impact of illegal gold mining on women's right to a healthy and sustainable environment: a focus on women in Ngorima communal lands of Chimanimani district, Manicaland province, Zimbabwe', masters dissertation, SEARCWL, University of Zimbabwe, Harare.

Seager J. and B. Hartmann (2005) *Mainstreaming gender in environmental assessment and early warning*, UNEP/DEWA, Nairobi.

Shiva V. (1994) 'The seed and the earth: biotechnology and the colonization of regeneration', in V. Shiva (ed) *Close to home: women reconnect ecology, health and development worldwide*, Library Company of Philadelphia, Philadelphia.

Shiva V. and I. Mosser (1995) *Biopolitics: a feminist and ecological reader*, Zed Books, London.

Spretnak C. (1990) 'Ecofeminism: our roots and flowering', in I. Diamond and G.F. Orenstein (eds) *Reweaving the world: the emergence of ecofeminism*, Sierra Club Books, San Francisco.

Stone C. (1972) 'Should trees have standing? Toward legal rights for natural objects', *Southern California Law Review* 45(1972): 450-501.

Thomas S. (2003) 'Saving seed, shifting cultivation and slash and burn agriculture', Nuffield Foundation (United Kingdom) paper prepared for the Gender Advisory Board, United Nations Commission on Science and Technology for Development, Geneva.

Turner N. (2003) 'Passing on the news: women's work, traditional knowledge and plant resource management in indigenous societies of north-western North America', in P. Howard (ed) *Women and plants*, Zed Books, London.

UNHCS (1999) *Women's rights to land, housing and property in post-conflict situations and during reconstruction: a global overview*, Land management series 9, UNHCS, Geneva.

Wanyoike M.W. (2002) *Wangu wa Makeri*, East African Educational Publishers, Nairobi.

Win E.J. (2004) 'Not very poor, powerless or pregnant: the African woman forgotten by development', *IDS Bulletin* 35(4): 61–64.

Women in World History (undated) *The Chipko movement: India's call to save their forests*, Today's heroes – linking present to past, available online at: http://www.womeninworldhistory.com.

World Bank (2006) *Gender equality and economic growth in the World Bank*, World Development Report, New York.

14

Women, labour,
social security and law

Ngeyi Ruth Kanyongolo and Munyaradzi Gwisai

'Women, labour, social security and law' is one of the optional courses offered under the Masters in Women's Law at SEARCWL. Employment is one of the critical resources in society and plays a fundamental role in the social and psychological wellbeing of its members.

Traditionally the focus in legal academia has been on formal employment with little attention paid to the informal sector and the connection between the two. In reality the majority of people in Africa, especially women, are in the informal sector or engaged in unpaid work. A narrow focus on formal employment therefore fails to reflect the lived realities of most women and makes the subject less relevant to their lives.

A narrow focus on formal employment ... fails to reflect the lived realities of most women

At the same time, the importance of social security, although a relatively new area of study in Africa, cannot be underestimated in the context of increasing levels of poverty, on the one hand, and increasing calls for recognition of women's labour and redistribution of resources on the other. The extent to which the law engenders processes of social security and insecurity on the basis of one's labour justifies our examination of the course not only from a feminist perspective but also from a legal perspective. This is the focus of the 'Women, labour, social security and law' course which we discuss in detail in this chapter.

The course has undergone considerable evolution over the years. It was a small component of the first semester courses – it then developed into a full optional course in the Masters in Women's Law programme. When it started as a postgraduate diploma course in the mid 1990s, it was entitled 'Women, employment and the law'. The emphasis then was on the legal regulatory framework of formal employment and how this impacted on women.

After 2005, in order to ensure that it adequately related to women's lived realities, we decided to broaden the course to cover labour beyond formal employment and more importantly to link labour to the benefits accruing from one's labour, such as social security. The course was accordingly renamed.

We confronted a number of challenges as we sought to re-engineer the course. These have included drawing the boundaries between formal and informal work and catering for the diversity of our classes. Since its inception the course has tended to be monopolised by students with a legal background and from only two or so countries. Our challenge is therefore to develop a course that is attractive to students from a multi-disciplinary background and one that draws on a broader diversity of country case studies in the region.

Course objectives and expected outcomes

In this course we explore and critically analyze the theoretical and practical role of law in regulating labour and social security with a focus on women in the formal and informal sectors. At the end of the course we expect students:

- To show an understanding of the historical and current context of labour and social security in southern and eastern Africa;
- To be able to critically analyze various factors that impact and influence labour and social security developments in relation to women;
- To show an appreciation of the different approaches, perspectives, theoretical foundations and principles of labour and social security generally and specifically in relation to women and the law;
- To identify and critically analyze the general legal and regulatory framework of labour and social security and how it impacts on women;
- To show an understanding of patterns of women's participation and recognition in institutional structures for the administration and funding of labour and social security and their potential to influence change and reforms;
- To show evidence of independent critical reflection on the emerging issues from the course and vision for reform.

We aim to meet these expectations through research, in-depth discussion and critical analysis of the various topics by both lecturers and students. We use a combination of methods for each topic for a total coverage time of eight hours per topic on average.

Part I: Definitions and conceptual framework

Under this topic we explore the political economy of work and social security at the general level and from a gendered perspective. At the general level we seek to explore the centrality of the process of labour in the evolution and development of human society. Students are given readings of contrasting materials on the special role of the family and the oppression of women.[1] We also look at the relationship between labour and social security in times of shocks in life, especially with reference to the centrality of the male-dominated formal labour sector in the attainment of meaningful social security. Students are asked to reflect on their personal experiences and discuss common shocks and risks faced by men and women in their society.

Based on the readings and the experiences, we then analyze the various definitions of social security starting with the International Labour Organization (ILO) definition:

> 'Social security refers to the protection which society provides its members through a series of public measures against the economic and social distress that would otherwise be caused by the stoppage or substantial reduction (brought on) by certain contingencies' (ILO, 1994).

The critique focuses on a gendered analysis of the various definitions and notes how in most cases social security is defined in relation to employment and therefore covers only the limited number of women who are in the formal labour market, whilst excluding those in the 'informal sector'. The International Labour Organization definition of the latter is used as a working definition:

> 'The term "informal sector" refers to very small-scale units producing and distributing goods and services, and consisting largely of independent, self-employed producers in urban areas of developing countries, some of whom also employ family labour and / or a few hired workers or apprentices; which operate with very little capital, or none at all; which utilize a low level of technology and skills; and which generally provide very low irregular incomes and highly unstable employment to those who work in it' (Mhone, 1996).

Literature by such scholars as Olivier (2001, 2002) and Kaseke (Olivier, Mpedi and Kaseke, 2004) assist in this gendered analysis. In order to critically analyze various definitions and conceptions of core terms and examine the

---

[1] Readings include: Loutfi (2001); Democratic Socialist Party (2008); Engels (1979); German (1989).

practical implications of these for women and therefore their relevance, we provide students with diverse literature on the core concepts of the course. The core of the readings are included in a compiled materials case-book given to every student.[2] We assign students readings to work on and the chosen papers are debated in class for students to engage with the issues and identify appropriate definitions and analytical frameworks. We then pair the students in teams of countries of choice in the southern and eastern African region to research and investigate the situation of women in the labour market and social security from a perspective of the identified and debated definitions and analytical framework.

After this conceptual critique, we begin to look at the different types of social security, analyzing social protection, social insurance, social assistance and traditional safety nets. The discussion allows more gender issues to emerge. These have included issues of: how women contribute towards social security, especially within the care economy and traditional safety nets; how women are excluded from social insurance due to lack of ability to make contributions; and how social protection systems exclude women's interests.

The lesson then moves on to look at the direct but often ignored link between labour and social security and how particular (mis)conceptions of this link contribute towards excluding women from the benefits of social security.

A reading of Kasente (1996) initiates the debate on how particular conceptions of labour focusing more on paid and less on unpaid labour in the process offer better social security benefits to those in paid labour. The majority of these are men. The discussion shows how a more inclusive approach which values unpaid labour would easily recognize women's interests in relation to social security (Dekker, 2001:247–268).

The outcome of the matrix exercise (on the right) has been very informative. In almost all cases, students begin to articulate how women are differently situated, how the various systems that women resort to for survival are interdependent and how experiences of shocks cut across gender, race and age. At the same time the students independently begin to distinguish the different levels of vulnerability. This analysis grounds the course in women's real experiences, as observed by the students themselves.

EXERCISE
A matrix: shocks and risks

Discuss and draw a matrix from the following questions.

- What shocks and risks do people suffer from time to time? Are any of these specific to women?

- How do people/ women survive each of the risks?

- If they are unable to survive on their own, who or what do they rely on for survival?

- What factors determine the type of reliance?

- How is the reliance system regulated?

---

[2] The key readings here are Torres, 'Labour markets in southern Africa', available at: http://www.fafo.no/pub/rapp/257/257-innm.pdf and Loutfi (2001).

EXAMPLE

The right to health

In one exercise students produced a complex matrix of how a sick woman may access health care:

- If she is employed in the formal labour market, she accesses health care from the workplace on the basis of employment law;

- She can access the state hospital on the basis of the constitutional right to health care;

- She also accesses community and family care on the basis of the informal rules of care and reciprocity.

The exercise is followed by an analysis of the role and nature of law in regulating the process of work and social security and it being a key site of struggle and conflict in the engendered and class character of work. The debate is premised on legal pluralism and the gendering power of law. In this regard, students look at and discuss literature by Smart (1992: 29–44), Manji (1999: 435–455), Griffiths (2002) and Hellum (2000), among others. These readings engage students with the complexity of legal plurality and how women navigate through the different legal systems.

The conclusions that follow from a discussion of these readings usually clearly illustrate how the students become empowered by the different frameworks for analyzing issues from a legal perspective. The different individual student conceptual standpoints also become evident and students start to respect each other's scholarly opinions.

In a 2009 class one student made the following comment:

> 'I think I understand (X) better now because she seems to articulate her views from a liberal feminist perspective. I am more radical and would associate myself with marxist legal theories. I now appreciate our differences in opinions since we seem to have different theoretical perspectives on most issues.'

Overview and historical context of labour and social security in southern and eastern Africa

In order to properly contextualize the position of women and role of law in labour and social security from a historical perspective, we ask students to explore the various factors that have influenced particular conceptions and developments in labour and social security over time. The analysis takes a historical perspective and students are taken through the varying stages capitalism has gone through, from the colonial to the post-colonial and from welfare capitalism or state capitalism through to free-market neo-liberal capitalism. The focus is on how at certain points in history the law has reinforced particular conceptions of work, labour and social security with gendered differences between men and women.

There is also discussion of other factors including economic, social and biological. The historical analysis begins with the general global picture and moves to specific attention to southern and eastern Africa in the pre-colonial, colonial, independence and now globalization eras. Some of the texts that guide this discussion include Bevan (2001), Bailey (2004), Cliff (1984) and German (1989). The former writers have critically analyzed the historical development of labour and social security.

We provide students with the above core readings in advance. At least two students are asked to lead the discussion after the introductory lecture. The class then identifies trends and major factors that influence developments in each era. This has proven important in contextualizing current debates and highlighting the enormity of the issues affecting women.

Students have been amazed at how a detailed scrutiny of history from a specific focal point brings out a unique understanding of issues. This was evident from a comment made by one student in the 2009 class:

> 'I have studied history so many times and I enjoy the subject. Having read the literature again with a focus on women, I now appreciate gender construction and its impact on women better, especially in relation to labour and social security' (Josephine Mandangu).

Part II: Analytical approaches and theoretical frameworks

Under this section we build on the compulsory course on feminist jurisprudence that students do in the first semester. The emphasis here is to analyze, compare and contrast the different major theories of labour relations and legal philosophies on the gendered and discriminatory labour market and social security systems. In the introductory lecture, we outline the broad division into the classical and traditional non-interventionist theories and the interventionist theories and philosophies. Students revisit the principal general points of feminist legal theories. This is contrasted with an introduction and summary of the classical and traditional theories including:[3]

- Classical labour relations theories: unitarism; state corporatism and pluralism
- Classical jurisprudential legal philosophies such as: natural law theories, positivist and sociological and historical theories.

Student groups select two theories of their choice, one from each broad category, and compare and contrast them using the following set of questions:

---

[3] Materials selected from: Finnemore (1999); Davies and Freedland (1983); Ruwanpura (2004); Anker (1997) Loutfi (2001) Gwisai (2006).

EXERCISE
Personal reflection

After students have presented and discussed the various theories and the questions we asked, they do a personal reflection.

This is the most interesting part when the students identify a theory or theories that better explain the situation of women and law for them.

This has proved to be an important self discovery exercise which helps students take personal responsibility for the analysis and the necessary future interventions.

● What are the causes of the gendered fragmentation of the labour market and social security systems?

● Is such fragmentation legitimate and functional?

● What is the most appropriate agency for addressing any deficiencies?

● What is or should be the role of the state and law in correcting any identified deficiencies?

In the final plenary lecture, we summarize and contrast the broad positions of the theories and philosophies as well as highlight emerging underlying principles and values in the formal and informal systems. Emerging principles and values have included:

– Solidarity and *umunthu*, *ubuntu*, *harambee* and *ujamaa*

– Ethics of care (Sevenhuijsen, 2003)

– Human rights.

Solidarity can be conceptualized as a value or merely in relational terms, as a characteristic of social relations important for social cohesion (Van Oorschot and Komter, 1998:5-24). In the analysis, the emphasis on solidarity is how its conception and the way it is translated in practice has serious differential implications for survival of risks between and among men and women and hence for their social security. Another important value that is closely associated with solidarity in the context of social security is referred to in the vernacular as *umunthu* in Malawi (Chigona, 2002), *ubuntu* in South Africa (Olivier, 2001: 27), *unhu* in Zimbabwe and *ujamaa* in Tanzania (Tungaradza in Olivier, Mpedi and Kaseke, 2004). In South Africa the concept of *ubuntu* has been recognized in the context of social security as an important value of solidarity (Oliver 2001: 27):[4]

> 'The concept [of *ubuntu*] is of some relevance to the values we need to uphold. It is a culture which places some emphasis on communality and on the interdependence of the members of a community.'[5]

We also look at one interesting study by Sevenhuijsen, Bozalek and Minnaar (2003:299–321) which critiques the concept of *ubuntu* using the ethic of care concept. It interrogates the importance of care through its gendered divisions

---

[4] *Umunthu* and *ubuntu* have been recognized as having similar meaning and are used in this chapter interchangeably in some cases.

[5] Judge Langa in the case of *S v Makwanyane* 1995 3 SA 39(CC); 1995 6 BCLR 665 (CC) para 224.

and how it can be manipulated to reinforce normative assumptions about the position of women and exclude them from enjoying social security benefits.

This is highly instructive on the need to subject values to critical gendered analysis especially in relation to women's labour and social security.

Human rights have also been used as a basis for provision of social security and labour. Other than South Africa, most countries in Africa have not expressly recognized social security as a right.[6] There are, however, a number of legal provisions which implicitly and cumulatively recognize some aspects of social security and labour as human rights.

This part of the course has proved popular with students. Firstly, the debate is made to emerge from students' own analysis of women's lived realities. Secondly, the discussion focuses on traditional values which have not really received much attention in academia. The interface between these and the now more conventional human rights approaches brings the course much closer to reality:

...the discussion focuses on traditional values which have not really received much attention in academia

> '*Unhu* is a traditional value which is very central in our everyday life in Zimbabwe. We talk about it in many situations. It is actually a strong basis for people's interdependence especially in times of need. However, I have never thought about it and its relevance for women and development in the way that we have just done in this course. I am excited about its potential for articulation of women's issues and I hope to explore it further within programmes I will run when I go back to work' (Tsitsi Mariwo, 2007 class).

Part III: Regulatory and legal framework

The objectives of this section are three-fold, namely:

- For students to gain a broad understanding of the dualistic and inter-related nature of the regulatory frameworks for labour and social security systems between the formal and informal or traditional sectors;

- To identify and summarize the principal forms, levels and sources of regulation of labour and social security under both the formal and informal sector systems, followed by a comparison of the strengths and weaknesses of each system in relation to the lived reality of women in the process of work and social security;

- To begin to link the above with underlying theoretical and conceptual frameworks that students will have studied in the first part of the course.

---

[6] Section 27 (1) Constitution of the Republic of South Africa 108 of 1996.

In this topic we focus on a detailed analysis of the formal regulatory frameworks through tutorials, class presentations and lectures. The section is introduced by a discussion on the different analytical categories in which legislation and international law may be divided, looking at contrasting approaches, including Strydom (2004), Rycroft and Jordaan (1992) and Kiseylov (1988). This is followed by a lecture on the various regulatory frameworks at the international and national levels. We look at international law at the level of general international and regional human rights instruments which have a bearing on women, work and social security.[7] This is followed by lectures on specific labour and social security instruments at the international level with emphasis on the role and nature of the International Labour Organization as well as a summary of the main ILO conventions and recommendations pertaining to the area of women, work and social security. We include the most important of these in a handbook on international labour and social security standards which we provide to the students.[8] The international instruments provide benchmarks against which national policies and legislation are measured (Olivier *et al.*, 2003:623).

We introduce students to the main national frameworks including: national constitutions, general legislation, labour legislation, collective bargaining agreements and the common law. After this introduction, students do group tutorials, as outlined on the next page. The tutorials are designed to ensure that students have a grasp of the principal frameworks as well as a comparative analysis of their strengths and weaknesses.

Following the students' tutorial presentations and class discussions we give an overview of the critical and emerging issues in relation to the regulatory and legal framework. Major areas covered include:

● The relationship and application of the different levels of instruments, including the incorporation of the international and regional instruments into domestic laws;

● Legal plurality and how women negotiate their survival in the different legal arenas;

---

[7] The main instruments we look at include: the United Nations Universal Declaration of Human Rights (1948), the International Covenant on Economic, Social and Cultural Rights (1966), the Convention on the Elimination of all forms of Discrimination Against Women (1979), the African [Banjul] Charter on Human and People's Rights (1981), the Protocol to the African Charter on Human and Peoples' Rights on the Rights of Women in Africa (2003), the Charter of Fundamental Social Rights in SADC; and the SADC Declaration on Gender and Development (1999).

[8] Including: M. Gwisai *et al*, 'An outline of fundamental labour rights under international laws, national constitutions and Zimbabwean constitutional norms', *Kempton Makamure Labour Journal 71* (2009); and S. Mombeyarara and S. Barangwe, 'An outline of fundamental gender rights under international and regional and national constitutions' *Kempton Makamure Labour Journal* 2(88) (2009).

TUTORIALS
Regulatory frameworks

1   Identify and summarize what you consider to be the four most important labour and social economic rights under international and regional instruments.

2   Discuss two potential strengths and weaknesses of international law as a source of regulation of labour and social security for women at work.

Identify, compare and contrast labour and social security provisions pertaining to women in the constitutions of any two countries of your choice in the southern and eastern African region and discuss the extent to which international law is applicable in such jurisdictions as well as the extent of compliance with labour standards in international and regional instruments.

3   Discuss the potential strengths and weaknesses of constitutions as sources and regulators of labour and social security in a manner that realizes women's rights.

Of the above constitutions which one do you consider to provide the most favourable and the least favourable framework for realizing women's rights?

4   Discuss two potential strengths and weaknesses of the following platforms of regulation of labour and social security in relation to women in the formal and informal sectors:

●   National labour legislation

●   Collective bargaining agreements

●   Common law

Why do some authors argue that the dichotomy between formal and informal-traditional systems is false and not useful in the southern and eastern Africa context?

Do you agree?

- Compatibility, conflicts and normative tensions within and between the various instruments and laws. For instance with regard to national constitutions and legislation, the following issues arise:

  - Whether the constitution has both vertical and horizontal application, that is its applicability in the public and private domains. Many constitutions in the region only provide for vertical application, thereby excluding the private sector and the family/private place where most women work;

  - The status provided to adverse customary practices viz women's equality rights;

  - Locus standi: whether the constitution provides for class action or group locus standi or is individually based;

  - Class and gender composition of constitutional courts and commissions;

  - Within national labour legislation, pertinent issues include: the application to atypical contracts and the informal sector, definition of 'employee' and the multiplicity and conflict within legislation;

  - The integration of formal and informal labour and social security systems.

Part IV: Discrimination law and equality in labour and social security markets

From the general discussion on the legal framework we move to a detailed discussion on discrimination laws and to what extent these have managed to address the issue of the gendered labour and social security markets. We discuss this in relation to the following topics:

- Definition of discrimination and the distinction between direct and indirect discrimination.
- Justifiable defences and efficacy of remedies.

Our introductory lecture discusses and compares the different definitions of discrimination from a direct and indirect gendered perspective, under general international and ILO instruments. Article 1 of CEDAW provides:

'... the term "discrimination against women" shall mean any distinction, exclusion or restriction made on the basis of sex, which has the effect or purpose of impairing or nullifying the recognition, enjoyment or exercise by women, irrespective of their marital status, on a basis of equality of men and women, of human rights and fundamental freedoms in the political, economic, social, cultural, civil or any other field.'

Article 11 of CEDAW further elaborates grounds of discrimination against women in relation to work, namely: marital status, marriage, maternity, pregnancy and family responsibility.

Article 1 (1) (a) of the ILO Convention number 111 provides:

'… the term "discrimination" includes – (a) any distinction, exclusion or preference made on the basis of race, colour, sex, religion, political opinion, national extraction or social origin, which has the effect of nullifying or impairing equality of opportunity or treatment in employment or occupation.'

We also discuss the concepts of direct and indirect discrimination using examples drawn from regional instruments and decided case law, regionally and internationally.[9] We ask students to identify the anti-discrimination provisions in the national constitutions and labour legislation of their tutorial group countries and compare these to the international provisions. Two general trends are evident amongst national constitutions and legislation, with the older constitutions usually incorporating the older traditional definition which merely referred to grounds of 'sex' or 'gender', whilst more recent constitutions tend to incorporate the more elaborate definition under CEDAW which specifies grounds such as pregnancy, marital status and family responsibility. A similar dichotomy is evident between national constitutions and labour legislation definitions.

Indirect discrimination and justifiable defences

A comparative analysis of international, regional and national instruments and laws shows the universal existence of gender equality legislation prohibiting *de jure* discrimination against women. The real issue in most areas now pertains to the area of indirect discrimination. A number of issues come up for scrutiny in this area:

● We discuss and identify possible practices, criteria and features that have or can be used to ground indirect discrimination, including, for example, height, weight and part-time contract status.

● We compare and contrast the efficacy, limitations and underlying jurisprudential basis of the various tests that have evolved, as reflected in judicial precedents and legislation, to deal with issues such as the burden of proof, the standard of fairness, the standard of proof and locus standi in establishing unlawful discrimination.

---

[9] Including cases like: *Bradwell v Illinois* 83 US 130 (1873) (USA); *Incorporated Law Society v Wookey* 1912 AD 623 (South Africa); and *Wazara v Belvedere Teachers College* 1997 (2) ZLR 508 (H) (Zimbabwe).

● We explore the relationship between the different tests and different theoretical and jurisprudential schools to investigate how the former are in fact influenced or determined by the latter. On the one hand, we explore the relationship between the non-interventionist theories – whether classical, modern or liberal feminist – and tests and practices that restrict the broader application of discrimination laws and result in emphasis on equality in opportunity and formal equality rather than substantive equality. And, on the other hand, we examine the relationship between interventionist theories – including classical sociological and historical and modern radical and socialist feminist theories – and tests and practices that allow a broader application of discrimination laws in a manner that emphasizes substantive equality or results rather than formal equality and equality in opportunity.

Finally we investigate the justifiable defences to discrimination with focus on the concept of 'special measures' and the bona fide occupational qualification or inherent occupational requirement defence and how this has been a minefield that has allowed hostile major inarticulate premises to influence the restricted application of anti-discrimination legislation.

CASE

Griggs v Duke Power Company

Prior to Title VII of the Civil Rights Act of 1964, the defendant company had openly discriminated against blacks by consigning them to one of its five departments, the Labour Department, which had the lowest salary grades at the company. After the 1964 Act was passed, the defendant introduced new requirements for employees being placed in any of the departments other than Labour or to be promoted to the other departments.

These requirements included passing a standardized general intelligence test and having a high school diploma. The result of these requirements meant that a substantially higher rate of blacks failed than whites. Of the company's 95 employees, 14 were black and all were in the Labour department.

The issue before the court was whether an employer was prohibited by the new Act from requiring such test and diploma qualification when it was shown that:

a   the test and qualification were not proven to be significantly related to successful job performance;

b   both requirements operated to disqualify a disproportionately higher rate of blacks than whites;

c   the jobs in question had formerly only been filled by whites.

The court held the practices to be discriminatory holding: 'The Act proscribes not only overt discrimination but also practices that are fair in form, but discriminatory in operation. The touchstone is business necessity.'

We look at the above issues in detail, drawing from examples from the United States, United Kingdom and South Africa where they have been dealt with exhaustively. Two examples of cases we examine are provided below.

What emerges is that the nature of the tests, onus and burdens used can be decisive in determining whether anti-discrimination provisions result in mere formal equality or substantive equality. For instance, to restrict the impact of anti-discrimination laws, courts may:

a   require a high and strict level of linkage or causation between specific practices and the alleged discrimination; or

b   require comparison with a comparator pool of qualified persons as opposed to the general population; or

c   where disparate impact is proven, still allow an employer to escape liability by merely proving a legitimate business justification as opposed to a strict essential business requirement.

CASE

Price Waterhouse v Hopkins

The Respondent was a senior manager at an office of the Appellant who applied for a partnership position. Her application was initially held over to the following year and subsequently denied. She sued the Appellant for unlawful gender discrimination in violation of Title VII of the Civil Rights Act of 1964.

At the time, of the 662 partners at the firm, seven were women. Of the 88 persons proposed for partnership that year, only one – the Respondent – was a woman. Forty seven candidates were admitted into partnership, 21 rejected and 20, including Hopkins, were held over for reconsideration in the following year.

Subsequently, the following year Hopkins was denied admission despite evidence of sterling work performance including that none of the other partnership candidates 'had a comparable record in terms of successfully securing major contracts for the partnership' and strong client and staff evaluations that she was 'a highly competent project leader'.

The Respondent argued that she had been overlooked because of impermissible sex stereotyping by many of the partners that she was too aggressive for a lady. Some of the comments included that: she 'over-compensated for being a woman', another partner advised her to 'take a course at charm school', whilst another partner recommended that: 'she should walk more femininely, talk more femininely, dress more femininely, wear make-up, have her hair styled, and wear jewellery'.

It was held that an employer who acts on the basis of a belief that a woman cannot be aggressive, or that she must not be, has acted on the basis of gender. That 'once a plaintiff shows that gender played a motivating part in an employment decision, the defendant may avoid a finding of liability only by proving that it would have made the same decision even if it had not allowed gender to play such a role.'

TUTORIALS
Anti-discrimination laws

1   Compare and contrast the cases of *Griggs v Duke Power Company 401 U.S. 424 (1971); Wards Cove Packing Co. v Atonio 109 S.Ct. 2115 (1989);* and *Price Waterhouse v Hopkins 109 S.Ct. 1775 (1989)* in relation to:

   a   Who has the burden to establish unlawful discrimination?

   b   What is the appropriate test to establish unlawful discrimination and what is the comparator pool used in the cases?

   c   What evidence is necessary to establish discrimination?

   d   What are the appropriate defences available to an employer where there is disproportionate impact on women or a protected group?

2   In the above cases do the standards, tests or defences adopted or endorsed by the court make it easier or harder to establish unfair discrimination – why do you think the court took such a position?

3   Analyze the anti-discrimination provisions in the constitution or labour legislation of your tutorial group country and discuss whether these provide for an accommodating or restrictive framework in relation to proving unlawful discrimination against women.

The method we use to explore the above issues and concepts is analysis and discussion of case authorities and textbooks using the tutorial guidelines shown above (see box).

Effectiveness of anti-discrimination laws and alternatives

Finally we discuss how effective anti-discrimination laws are as tools for addressing gender inequalities in the formal and informal labour markets. Students refresh the data profiles of their tutorial group countries in relation to the position of women in the labour markets and social security regimes.

We end this topic by examining why, despite decades of anti-discrimination laws, women remain desperately disadvantaged. Students explore the issue by comparing and contrasting materials from at least two different theoretical approaches. On the one hand, radical feminists like O'Regan point out the limitations of anti-discrimination laws. For example, they require symmetrical treatment, resulting in a focus on treatment rather than impact. Yet programmes aiming to redress historic disadvantages by treating protected groups like women differently do not qualify as symmetrical treatment (O'Regan, 1994; Dupper, 2004:4–8; Gwisai, 2004:64–73). This contrasts with the marxist class contention that effective transformation of gender inequities in the labour and social security markets requires a fundamental overhaul of the institution of the family and the property relations of society, as forcefully argued by Dupper and the Democratic Socialist Party:

> '...unless a commitment to the implementation of affirmative action measures and the redistribution of wealth and resources to the disadvantaged accompany the prohibition of discrimination, patterns of inequality will remain untouched' (Dupper, 2004:4).

> 'The struggle for women's liberation poses the problem of the total reorganization of society from its smallest repressive unit – the family – to its largest – the state. The liberation of women demands a thoroughgoing restructuring of society's productive and reproductive institutions in order to maximize social welfare and establish a truly human existence for all. Without a socialist revolution, women will not be able to establish the material preconditions for their liberation' (Democratic Socialist Party, 2008: 16).

We end by discussing some experiences from the region and the global south that have gone furthest in providing for both affirmative action and wealth or natural resources redistribution, focusing on Zimbabwe, South Africa, Bolivia and Venezuela (Simbi, 2009:99). We conclude with a survey of regional trends in selected national jurisdictions of some of the major issues discussed .

Part V: Specific conditions: managing differences

In this section we look in detail at a variety of specific labour and social security conditions, benefits and rights and duties in relation to the formal and informal gendered labour markets. We begin by identifying the key conditions and provisions in terms of international and regional instruments. We refresh students' knowledge of the main theoretical and jurisprudential foundations of the specific provisions, focusing on the special role of the institution of the family in the gendered nature of labour and social security markets.

The traditional patriarchal family has economic, social, psychological and ideological functions that places it at the centre of the marginalization, oppression and exploitation of women in the process of work. There are different jurisprudential conceptions on the origins, role and functions of the family in society in general and work in particular. We analyze the institution of the family by contrasting two major philosophies, namely *idealism*, especially natural law theories, versus *materialism*, especially historical and dialectical materialist philosophies.[10] This is done through tutorials, chosen from those shown in the box on page 386.

---

[10] For a summary of these refer to: Gwisai (2006:8–16); Democratic Socialist Party (1997: 17–25) and Harman (1999).

TUTORIALS

The role of the family

SET A

1 Compare and contrast idealist and dialectical and historical materialist conceptions on the origins of the family and the role of women therein.

2 Identify and discuss three functions of the family in modern society and how such functions inhibit or promote the participation of women in formal work.

3 How do the emergence of capitalist industrialization and neo-liberal globalization contain contradictory features, positive and negative, in relation to the institution of the family and women's effective and equitable participation in paid social work?

SET B

1 Analyze the lyrics of Steven 'Dhongi' Makoni's song, 'Handiende', and answer the following:

   a What are the principal reasons stated by the woman for refusing to be divorced and what alternatives does she offer?

   b Are her reasons and alternatives justifiable or a violation of the husband's fundamental human right to dissolution of marriage when mutual consent no longer exists?

2 Consider the following different families at Anglo-Pinnacles and Sons (Pvt) Ltd, a manufacturing concern in a country in southern Africa, and answer the questions that follow:

● Pinnacles, the factory owner and his family of a wife and children;

● Nzingo, the female finance director at the factory and her family of a lawyer husband and children;

● Shingai, an artisan in the factory and his family of a full-time housewife and children;

● Trymore, an informal sector vendor who, with his wife, Bongi, and daughter, sells food and refreshments to workers at the factory gate; and

● Kudakwashe, the brother to Shingai who stays and works in agriculture at the family rural home, with his family, including his wife, Onai.

   a Compare and contrast the different functions and roles of the family in the above families – highlight the main similarities and differences.

   b Which family unit(s) amongst the five families is likely to be the biggest and smallest? Give reasons.

   c Which of the above families are likely to be most stable or durable and which ones are likely to be most vulnerable to a break- up? Why?

   d Which family unit is likely to be most accommodating or liberating for women and work?

A summation lecture follows the tutorials, including a summary of the two highlighted major worldviews. Idealist theories presuppose a 'transcend-all', metaphysical, religious or natural basis for the origins of the family, which is seen as made up of a male and female(s) and as playing a fair and just role in society, hence the need for its special protection.[11] Women are viewed as subordinate to men and the 'natural' second and weaker sex.[12]

Dialectical and historical materialism on the other hand sees the family as a historical institution whose emergence is intrinsically linked with the emergence of private property, class exploitation and women's oppression about 10,000 years ago. Its primary function is the promotion of the class rule of the economically dominant male élite groups.

The family has undergone changes historically but its basic function as a pillar of class rule and exploitation has remained the same.

Following the above jurisprudential analysis of the central role of the institution of the family in the organization of work under capitalism, we proceed to analyze a select number of specific provisions and conditions of social security law and general labour law. We rely here on various national statutes and constitutions as well as textbooks and journal articles on labour law and social security law.[13] Some of the areas covered include:

Social security
- Maternity, paternity and pregnancy and reproductive care
- Child care, flexi-time, family support and family responsibility
- Unemployment and retirement
- Sickness; disability

General labour law
- Establishment and variation of employment and employment provisions
- Remuneration and the living wage
- Equal pay for work of equal worth
- Occupational safety and health and sexual harassment
- Termination of employment and unemployment

---

[11] For instance, the story on the origins of humanity from Adam and Eve in the Garden of Eden postulated in *Genesis* in the Bible and article 16 of the Universal Declaration of Human Rights (3).

[12] See for instance the reference in *Genesis* of women (Eve) being created out of one rib of a male (Adam) and the case of *Bradwell v Illinois* 83 US 130 (1873) where it was held that 'women's unique capacity for child-bearing and house-making renders them unsuitable by nature to the vicissitudes of the world of industry and trade'.

[13] These include: Strydom (2004), Grogan (2007), Gwisai (2006), Murray (1994) and Pittar (1988).

We introduce each of the areas listed through an introductory lecture on the substance of the provisions at general international and regional law as well as specific ILO conventions and recommendations. Through class discussions we explore the extent of application, coverage and adequacy of the provisions to redress gender inequities in the formal and informal labour and social security markets as well as underlying jurisprudential influences.

After the general plenary lectures and discussions, we divide students into groups dealing with three broad categories of national systems. Those countries which have undergone significant legal and social interventionist experiences such as South Africa, Malawi and Uganda; countries still exhibiting traditional conservative and patriarchal value systems such as Kenya, Botswana and Zambia; and those countries in between like Zimbabwe and Namibia. All tutorial groups deal with the question on maternity, paternity, family responsibility and child care and in addition one area each from the social security and general labour law categories.

A plenary discussion follows in which the different groups report back and we identify and discuss emerging common issues and differences. We conclude with a lecture on overarching themes and issues.

TUTORIAL
Sample questions on national systems

- Identify the rights and provisions covered at national level for the specified condition in the formal, informal and traditional sectors, in terms of the constitution and labour laws of two countries in the region.

- Analyze the extent to which the coverage in both countries is compliant or better than the regional and international norms.

- Identify possible factors, reasons and underlying jurisprudential influences, including the role of the family institution, behind the extent or lack of coverage.

- Summarize, analyze and compare the maternity, paternity, family responsibility and child-care provisions in the national constitution and labour legislation of any two countries of your choice in the region in relation to:
  - benefits granted
  - the extent of coverage to women in the formal, informal and traditional agricultural sectors
  - the extent to which such provisions are consistent with regional and international laws and norms
  - the appropriate underlying jurisprudential philosophy and/ or conceptions on the role of the family

Part VI: Administration, funding and reform

In this section we look at the areas of enforcement, administration and funding of gender, labour and social security rights and provisions. Mainly looking at international and national legislative instruments, students seek to identify the players involved in the provision, administration and funding of women's labour and social security rights and examine how and the extent to which women participate in and benefit from these institutions. Tutorial groups choose from a list of questions to assist them in this process (see box below).

The course concludes with a discussion and summary of the emerging issues and challenges in achieving gender equity in labour and social security markets. This part intends to engage students in independent critical reflection on how the labour and social security systems could best serve the interests and needs of society generally and women in particular. It looks at current reform efforts at all levels – national, regional and global.

TUTORIAL

Provision, administration and funding: sample group questions

1   Identify and summarize the principal methods for administration, enforcement and funding of gender equity provisions under CEDAW, two ILO conventions of your choice, the Protocol to the African Charter on Human and Peoples Rights on the Rights of Women in Africa and the SADC Declaration on Gender and Development.

2   Discuss to what extent the above instruments are effective in redressing gender inequities in labour and social security markets, with special emphasis on the informal and traditional agricultural sectors.

3   Identify, summarize and compare and contrast the methods for administration, enforcement and funding of gender equity provisions in labour and social security frameworks of any two countries of your choice in the southern and eastern African region.

4   Discuss to what extent such national provisions are compliant with international and regional norms and their degree of effectiveness as tools and platforms for redressing gender inequities in the labour and social security markets, with special emphasis on the informal and traditional agricultural sectors.

It also looks at challenges to standard setting and harmonization, including:

● The utility and limitations of the law, the state and reforms in redressing gender inequities in the context of a hostile political economy base of capitalism and the institution of the patriarchal family.

● The impact of neo-liberal globalization and the uneven global division of labour between the global north and global south.

● The efficacy, feasibility and experiences of alternatives based on classical reformism as in feminism; radical reformism as has happened in societies like Mozambique, Tanzania, Cuba, Venezuela and Bolivia; and revolutionary socialism as in the experiences of the 1871 Paris Commune and the 1917 Russian revolution.[33]

We then ask each student to independently reflect on how they would propose to reform at least two major issues that have emerged from the course for the better protection and improvement of women's lives.

Conclusion

The evolution and development of this course has been greatly influenced by student evaluation, peer review during the programme's biannual colloquium and the co-lecturers constant internal and external reflection. The essays that students write on the various topics covered in this course have also assisted as a reality check considering that most of the students carry out grounded research. The writing of this chapter offered another rare opportunity not only to share experiences and strengthen thematic links between and among courses but to further reflect on the methodologies in the teaching and learning of the course and its interface with research.

The above has serious implications for the future teaching, learning and research of the course and other similar courses. The interactive approach to teaching and learning needs strengthening. This would mean serious planning and preparation for lectures and activities by both lecturers and students. It should also include collection of relevant materials. Commitment, adequate time and financial resources are necessary for this to be properly done. In case of research, students writing dissertations on topics related to the course need to be directly linked with and supervised by the course lecturers concerned and offered assistance in in-depth interrogation of issues. This would feed back into the development of the course. We will continue to focus our research on the emerging issues from the course. This will ensure availability of up to date materials.

Bibliography

Anker R. (1997) 'Theories of occupational segregation by sex: an overview', *International Labour Review* 136(3): 315–39.

Bailey C. (2004) *Extending social security coverage in Africa*, ESS paper 20, Social Security Policy and Development Branch, ILO, Geneva.

Boston S. (1980) *Women workers and trade unions*, Davis-Poynter, London.

Brooks B. (2001) 'Some recent international developments in employment dispute settlement', *International Journal of Comparative Labour Law and Industrial Relations* 17(2): 199–209.

Cediey E. (2001) 'Getting equality to work: the South African Employment Equity Act', *Safundi* 2(1)1–15, available online at: http://www.informaworld.com/smpp/content~db =all~content=a778351868~frm=titlelink

Cliff T. (1984) *Class struggle and women's liberation: 1640 to the present day*, Bookmarks, London.

Commission on Gender Equality (1998) *Working women's manual*, Commission on Gender Equality, South Africa, available online at: http://www.cge. org.za/index.php?option=com_docman&task =doc_ details&gid=123&Itemid= (accessed 20 March 2011).

Davies P. and M. Freedland (eds) (1983) *Kahn-Freund and the law*, Stevens and Sons, London.

Davis A. (1981) *Women, race and class*, The Women's Press, London.

Dekker A.H. (2001) 'Social security for those who work informally and informal (community and family based) solutions to social protection', in M.P. Olivier, E. Kalula, J. Van Steenberge, Y. Jorens and W. Van Eeckhoutte, *The extension of social security protection in South Africa: a legal inquiry*, Siber Ink, South Africa.

Democratic Socialist Party (1997) *Feminism and socialism: putting the pieces together*, Resistance Books, Broadway, Australia.

Dupper O.C. (2004) 'Preliminary remarks', in O.C. Dupper *et al.* (eds), *Essential employment discrimination law*, Juta, Cape Town.

Ellingsaeter A.L. (1999) 'Women's right to work: the interplay of state, market and women's agency', *NORA – Nordic Journal of Feminist and Gender Research* 7(2 and 3) September:109–123, available online at: http:// taylorandfrancis.metapress.com

Engels F. (1979) *The origin of the family, private property and the state*, Pathfinder, London.

Finnemore M. (1999) *Introduction to labour relations in South Africa*, Butterworths, Durban.

Geest W. van der and R. van der Hoeven (1999) *Adjustment, employment and missing institutions in Africa: the experience of eastern and southern Africa*, ILO and James Curry, Geneva and Oxford.

German L. (1989) *Sex, class and socialism*, Bookmarks, London.

Griffiths A. (2002) 'Legal pluralism', in R. Banakar and M. Travers (eds) *An introduction to law and social theory*, Hart Publishing, Oxford and Portland.

Grogan J. (2007) *Work-place law*, Juta, Cape Town.

Gwisai M, (2006) *Labour and employment law in Zimbabwe: relations of work under neo-colonial capitalism*, Zimbabwe Labour Centre and Institute of Commercial Law, University of Zimbabwe, Harare.

Gwisai M. *et al.* (2009) 'An outline of fundamental labour rights under international laws, national constitutions and Zimbabwean constitutional norms', *Kempton Makamure Labour Journal 71*.

Hartman H. (1979) 'The unhappy marriage of Marxism and Feminism', *Capital and Class* 3(2):1–33.

Hellum A. (2000), 'Human rights and gender relations in postcolonial Africa: options and limits for the subjects of legal pluralism', *Law & Society Inquiry* 25(2):635-655.

Holt A. (ed) (1977) *Selected writings of Alexandra Kollontai*, translated with commentary, Allison & Busby, London.

International Labour Organization (1994) *Introduction to social security*, ILO, Geneva.

– (2000), *Gender issues in social protection*, ILO, Geneva.

Kasente D. (2000) 'Gender and social security reform in Africa', *International Social Security Review* 53(3):27–41.

Kiseylov I. (1988) *State-monopoly capitalism and labour law*, Progress Publishers, Moscow.

Lachaud J. (1995) *The labour market in Africa*, ILO, Geneva.

Leavy J. and H. White (undated) 'Rural labour markets and poverty in sub Saharan Africa', Institute of Development Studies, Sussex University, Brighton, available online at http://www.google.fr/search?q=Rural+Labour+Markets+ and+Poverty+in+Sub+Saharan+Africa&ie=utf-8&oe=utf-8&aq=t&rls=org.mozilla:fr:official&client=firefox-a (accessed 20 March 2011).

Lissagaray P. (1976) *History of the Paris Commune of 1871*, translated from the French by E. Marx, New Park Publications, London.

Littleton C.A. (1987) 'Restructuring sexual equality', *California Law Review* 75(1987):1279–1337.

Loutfi M. (2001) 'Women, gender and work – an overview', in M. F. Loutfi, *Women, gender and work: What is equality and how do we get there?*, ILO, Geneva.

Madhuku L. (2001) *Gender equality in employment: the legal framework in the case of Zimbabwe*, ILO, Geneva.

Manji A. (1999) 'Imagining women's legal world: towards a feminist theory of legal pluralism in Africa', *Social & Legal Studies* 4: 435–455.

Mhone G.C.Z. (1996) *The informal sector in southern Africa: an analysis of conceptual, research and policy issues*, SAPES Books, Harare.

Mombeyarara S. and S. Barangwe (2009) 'An outline of fundamental gender rights under international and regional and national constitutions', *Kempton Makamure Labour Journal* 2(88).

Murray C. (ed) (1994) *Gender and the new South African legal order*, Juta, Cape Town.

Olivier M. *et al.* (eds), *The extension of social security protection in South Africa: a legal inquiry*, Siber Ink, South Africa

Olivier M. (2002) 'Social protection in the SADC region: opportunities and challenges', *International Journal of Comparative Labour Law and Industrial Relations* 18(4):337–402.

Olivier M., E. Kaseke and G. Mpedi (2004) 'Formulating an integrated social security response – perspectives on developing links between informal and formal social security in the SADC region', paper presented at the EGDI and UNU-WIDER Conference, Unlocking Human Potential: Linking the Informal and Formal Sectors, 17–18 September 2004, Helsinki, Finland.

O'Regan C. (1994) 'Equality at work and the limits of the law: symmetry and individualism in anti-discrimination legislation', in C. Murray (ed) *Gender and the new South African legal order*, Juta, Cape Town.

Pittard M.J. (1988) 'Affirmative action programmes for private and public sector employees', *Australian Journal of Labour Law* 1:85 (1988).

Rae M. (1986) *Women and the law*, Longman, London.

Reddi M. (1994) 'Sexual harassment', in C. Murray (ed) *Gender and the new South African legal order*, Juta, Cape Town.

Ritich K. (2004) *Vulnerablity at work: legal and policy issues in the new economy*, Law Commission of Canada, Ottawa.

Rothstein M., A. Knapp and L. Liebman (1991) *Cases and materials on employment law*, The Foundation Press, New York.

Ruwanpura K. (2004) 'Quality of women's employment: a focus on the South', study report, Decent Work Research Programme, International Institute for Labour Studies, Geneva.

Rycroft A. and B. Jordaan (1992) *A guide to South African labour law*, Juta, Cape Town.

Sevenhuijsen S., G. Bozalek and M. Mcdonald (2003) 'South African social welfare policy: an analysis using the ethic of care', *Critical Social Policy* 23(2003):299-321.

Siphambe H.K. and M. Thokweng-Bakwena (1992) 'The wage-gap between men and women in Botswana's formal labour market', *Journal of African Economies* 10 (2):127.

Smart C. (1992) 'The woman of legal discourse', *Social & Legal Studies* 1(1992):29–44.

Strydom E.M.L. (ed) (2004) *Essential discrimination law*, Juta, Cape Town.

Tamale S. (2004) 'Gender trauma in Africa: enhancing women's links to resources', *Journal of African Law* 48(1):50–61.

Thomas E. (1966) *The women incendiaries*, Haymarket Books, London.

Tomasevski K. (1998) 'Rights of women: from prohibition to elimination of discrimination', *International Social Science Journal* 50(158):545–558.

Tørres L. (1998) *Labour markets in Southern Africa*, Fafo Institute for Applied Social Science, Oslo, available online at: http//:www.fafo.no/pub/rapp/257/257-innm.pdf

Tripp A. (2001) 'Women's movements and challenges to neopatrimonial rule: preliminary observations from Africa', *Development and Change* 32:33–35.

Trotsky L. (1973) *Women and the family*, Pathfinder Press, Atlanta.

Van Oorschot W. and A. Komter (1998) 'What is it that ties...? Theoretical perspectives on social bonds', *Sociale Wetenschappen* 41e jaargang (1998):3 .

15

Awakening potential

A feminist pedagogical approach to teaching and research

Rosalie K. Katsande, Sheillah Kanyangarara, Julie Stewart and Anne Griffiths

> 'Our wealth is built on the breadth and choice of the markets we can sell to – or buy from. For many people economic poverty is rooted in their inability to trade.'
>
> DFID, 2009

The main objective of this course is to facilitate the development of innovative exploratory theoretical and methodological approaches to analyzing the socio-legal aspects of women's participation in commercial activities in Africa with particular emphasis on southern and eastern Africa. To achieve this, bearing in mind that the field of commerce is predominantly a gendered area, we use teaching methods and methodologies that enhance students' skills in identifying legal, social, cultural and other barriers that affect women's capacity to participate in commerce. These are pedagogical approaches that focus on critical thinking and inquiry, promoting a dialogic approach to teaching and collaborative learning (Shackelford, 2003). To this end, the teaching methods of the course are heavily influenced by feminist pedagogy and critical pedagogy. Feminist pedagogy is a methodology that strives to make the classroom more hospitable to women by drawing on examples from their lives, acknowledging the broad range of their accomplishments and drawing examples from their life experiences. While critical pedagogy is a teaching approach that attempts to help students question and challenge domination and the beliefs that dominate (Watkins, 1989).

Due to the vast nature of issues in commerce that call for different expertise, the 'Women, commerce and the law' course is divided into four thematic areas taught by different lecturers. This chapter is thus in four parts where each lecturer chronicles the teaching methods and methodologies used and how these, fused with the content of the course, achieve the ultimate objective of developing students' critical consciousness with regard to women's participation and involvement in commerce.

Part I: Raising the issues

Rosalie K. Katsande

It is insightful to state where I am coming from in the teaching of the course. The 'Women, commerce and the law' course was first taught in 2005. I was then a student in this first class. Prior to undertaking a Masters in Women's Law, I had been a lecturer in commercial and entrepreneurial law in the Faculty of Commerce at Chinhoyi University of Technology in the Mashonaland West Province of Zimbabwe.

The very first lecture was thought provoking. We started by brainstorming on the issues that affect women in commerce. Coming from a strictly commercial law background with its rigid rules where a transaction is a transaction regardless of who the parties are, let alone their gender, issues were raised that I had never thought of as a commercial lawyer. All I was concerned about was that 'an agreement is a contract' as long as all the essential elements of a valid contract are present.

Take, for example, a basic contract of sale. The essential elements of such a contract are the *merx* (the property to be sold) and the *pretium* (the price at which the property is being sold). Once the parties to the contract agree on these there is a valid contract of sale. I never really went as far as analyzing which 'gender', for instance, owned the property to be sold and which 'gender' had the money to buy the goods. I ignored the identity of the parties to the contract and the clearly evident fact that the laws in commerce are gender neutral, bringing out *de jure* equality yet producing *de facto* discrimination. It became clear to me that most women by the nature of their status in society are rarely part of such commercial transactions. If they are, it is on a much lower scale and most of the time they do not realize that they are entering legally binding contracts. We looked at the example of a woman who was a small-scale tomato farmer. We analyzed the various contracts she entered into on a daily basis from the very day she planted her tomatoes to the day she took them to the market. We were all amazed by the legal obligations this woman would have exposed herself to without even knowing. To her all was normal as these were her day to day gender-ascribed roles and part of her efforts to fend for her family.

This first lecture gave ...me an opportunity to critically examine how women entrepreneurs operate and what challenges they face in competing effectively in a male-dominated area of power

This first lecture gave new meaning to entrepreneurship and entrepreneurial law. It gave me an opportunity to critically examine how women entrepreneurs operate and what challenges they face in competing effectively in a male-dominated area of power.

The example of the woman small-scale tomato farmer made me realize that women are more than willing to take the calculated risks that entrepreneurs take. In the words of Emile Loza, 'women make the tough and necessary choices to integrate the hard work of entrepreneurship with the hard work of parenting and running a household. They have the "smarts", guts and ambition to succeed as entrepreneurs' (Loza, 2008). Regardless of all this effort, a small minority of women make it to the top. The question is why. The why question remained with me throughout the course. We raised more questions than answers so when I graduated and took up the challenge of co-teaching on the 'Women, commerce and the law' course, the 'why' question remained my focus. It informs my teaching and the methods and methodologies I use with the objective of devising and prompting students to devise interventions that will see more and more women participating in commerce and benefiting from trade in their own right.

To kick-start the course I give the students the task on gender sensitivity (see box below) to do individually, in pairs or as a group, depending on the size of the class. This task is important as a starting point as it gives me the opportunity to get to know the students and their particular interests as far as women's participation in commerce is concerned. It also reveals their various backgrounds in some depth. In tackling the task, students are expected to employ experiential data. The answers and pursuant discussions on this task pave the way for the discussion on gender mainstreaming in all commercial sectors.

EXERCISE

Why gender sensitivity?

Step 1

Choose an area in commerce and consider the following within the chosen area:

Step 2

Does it have a different impact on women and on men and on different groups of women and men?

Step 3

If there are significant differences in the impact between women and men what are the implications of these differences?

Step 4

What can be done to ensure equality for women and men in this area?

Step 5

What might be the wider consequences of failing to adopt a gender sensitive approach?

Gender mainstreaming

The questions we explore under this heading are what gender mainstreaming involves and, in mainstreaming gender in commerce, where and how do we start. In tackling these questions, I am guided by the *EQUAL Guide on gender mainstreaming* (EQUAL, undated). Gender mainstreaming has been defined as a strategy for making women as well as men's concerns and experiences an integral dimension of the design, implementation, monitoring and evaluation of policies and programmes in all spheres with the ultimate goal of achieving gender equality. Thus, it challenges mainstream policies and resource allocations by recognizing the strong interlink between women's relative disadvantage and men's relative advantage. The ultimate goal of gender mainstreaming is to reduce poverty by boosting economic growth and strengthening citizenship. This can be achieved by targeting major economic and social policies that deliver major resources. Thus it is imperative to mainstream gender in commerce.

> *The ultimate goal of gender mainstreaming is to reduce poverty by boosting economic growth and strengthening citizenship*

Why mainstream gender in commerce?

We brainstorm on the clear benefits that accrue to women in commerce when gender mainstreaming is adopted as a strategy. These benefits, among others, are that gender mainstreaming:

- exposes the social problem of gender inequality in commerce;
- gives an insight into ways of addressing the needs and interests of different groups of women as well as those of different groups of men in the commercial arena;
- makes full use of human resources by recognizing women and men with similar capacities and opportunities – acknowledging that women have a place in commerce; and
- promotes a better understanding of family conditions as they relate to the demands of commerce.

Gender mainstreaming and the international dimension

Analysis of the potential benefits of gender mainstreaming in commerce is facilitated using the Millennium Development Goals, the Convention on the Elimination of all forms of Discrimination Against Women (CEDAW) and Beijing Plus 5 as frameworks. The question we explore is whether these injunctions alert us as to the critical needs in achieving genuine gender mainstreaming.

For example, CEDAW is the most comprehensive and detailed international agreement on women's rights. It establishes rights for women in areas not previously subject to international standards, most notably in personal and

family life. CEDAW is based on two principles – the principle of non-discrimination and the principle of state obligation – thus it raises key issues and standards that are essential for gender mainstreaming. An adjunct to CEDAW is the Beijing Declaration and Platform for Action which is notable for placing great importance on gender mainstreaming in development cooperation. It upholds CEDAW and builds upon previous strategic frameworks and policy commitments at the international level.

The Millennium Development Goals constitute an agenda for poverty reduction and improving livelihoods worldwide. Goal 1 is on eradication of extreme poverty and hunger and Goal 3 is about promoting gender equality and empowering women. Although these goals are not specific to any particular sector or issue, they are of particular interest to women in commerce since effective participation in commerce reduces poverty. On the other hand, gender equality and women's rights underpin any progress women can make in commerce, bearing in mind that it is a male-dominated field.

Women's access to and control over commercial resources

For women to participate fully and effectively in commerce there is urgent need for them to access the requisite resources. The first thing we do is define and identify the resources that women need to participate effectively in commerce. We look at the issues of access and control – which of the two do women have? We examine the implications of having one without the other – whether women sometimes have access without control or whether they have different forms of access. We look at what legal frameworks, if any, are in place for women to both control and access commercial resources. If they exist, are the frameworks working and, if not, what needs to be done? To answer these questions, we do a comparative analysis of an ordinary business and of a specifically woman-owned business using the guide on the right. Students link the guide to their own personal experiences and the legal set-up in the various countries they come from.

The students' observations and country examples lead into the discussion on entrepreneurship.

Challenges faced by:	business in general	women-owned business
Access to finance	-	
Access to markets		
Access to training		
Access to infrastructure		
Access to technology		
Access to law and policy makers /input into trade law and policy		

Adapted from Commonwealth Secretariat (2002)

Masculine	Feminine
Objective	Chancers
Logical	Illogical
Analytical	Intuitive
Outer-focused	Dualistic
Rational	Irrational
Decisive	Indecisive
Competitive	Contented
Action-oriented	Talkers not doers
Explicit and assertive	Passive
Tough	Weak
Unemotional	Emotional
Qualitative	Quantitative solutions
Reductionists	Surface scratchers

Gender economic stereotypes

Source: Gherardi (1995)

Entrepreneurship

Entrepreneurship relates to developing a business and translating ideas into achievable business opportunities. The word 'entrepreneur' is derived from a French root '*entreprendre*', meaning to undertake. Research has shown that the percentage of women entrepreneurs worldwide is still low in relation to male entrepreneurs and in relation to the percentage of women in the population. A Global Entrepreneurship Monitor study of more than 100,000 people in 40 countries found that while women entrepreneurs often exhibit similar patterns of behaviour to men, a gender gap nonetheless exists for entrepreneurial activity across the globe due to gender stereotypes (see box below). On the left are examples of economic gender stereotypes that we discuss in class. The objective is to question and challenge domination and the beliefs that dominate. Students also bring in their personal experiences as far as these stereotypes are concerned.

In line with the French feminist Simone de Beauvoir's argument of the 'otherness' of women and their relegation to the position of the second sex, female entrepreneurs are viewed as the 'other' in terms of how the male entrepreneur is defined. These gendered attitudes towards entrepreneurs make women and their businesses invisible. As such, an argument of 'think manager – think male' has been advanced since males

STUDY

Measuring entrepreneurial activity

The Global Entrepreneurship Monitor (GEM) 2006 study described and analyzed entrepreneurial processes from different countries, using data collected by 40 country teams. It also sought to uncover factors determining the levels of entrepreneurial activity and to identify policies that may enhance the level of entrepreneurial activity.

While the study measured entrepreneurial activity by men and women and across all income groups, one of its concerns was the differences in entrepreneurial activity between men and women. Its main conclusions on the gendered aspect of entrepreneurship were that women entrepreneurs are found in every country under all circumstances whether involved in early stage activities or in established business. However a significant and systemic gender gap exists in entrepreneurial involvement and business ownership with men leading by between 27 and 45 per cent, depending on the size of the business. Interestingly, for 'necessity entrepreneurship', there was no difference between the men and women (Allen, Langowitz and Minniti, 2007).

are said to be task focused and strive to get the job done while women are said to be concerned with the welfare of others above everything else (Hines, 1992: 42). Institutions such as the media do not help the situation as they still cling to the old gender stereotypes in their representation. To illustrate this, below is a caption from a local Zimbabwean newspaper, *The Herald*.

August 30-September 5 2009   business

Market for the big boys
. . . as foreign investors snap big counters

This headline clearly shows the gender bias of the media when it comes to reporting business news. We can interpret the article heading as meaning that, according to the media, business is primarily a male domain.

In the media, women entrepreneurs are described mainly in relation to family businesses and in terms of the family role. A constant theme is the difficulties women entrepreneurs face in balancing work and domestic duties, thus reinforcing and perpetuating the assumption that women's natural place and their primary responsibility is the family. According to the bread-winner and home-maker code, bread-winning is considered a masculine role and home-making a feminine one. Entrepreneurship however departs from these social norms by giving women space in the public sphere of business and the workplace.

In the media ...a constant theme is the difficulties women entrepreneurs face in balancing work and domestic duties

We thus explore the barriers the women entrepreneurs face which hinder them from achieving their full potential.

Socio-cultural barriers

Unpacking socio-cultural forces that mediate women's lives and economic activities is a core component of the course. In class we examine the primary role of women, encompassing family and domestic responsibilities, which are seen as inhibiting women's entrepreneurial credibility. There is a commonly held belief that women's entrepreneurial skills are merely an extension of what has been naturally learnt through gender socialization. This also requires challenging perceived patterns and forms of women's entrepreneurship which are depicted as reflecting the reproductive life cycle of interruptions and discontinuities even in the business field (Gherardi, 1995: 14).

For example, there is a perception that all tasks related to a family's support are the responsibility of women. This is extended in the cultural and traditional thinking that a woman's physical presence in the home is a question of survival for her family. Women thus may feel under pressure to divide their time between their work and productive role and their 'family reproductive role' and to try to balance these competing demands. Consequently time is valuable for women since their livelihoods depend largely on their ability to fulfil the multiple demands of the household and the marketplace. We encourage students to find out through research whether, in spite of the remarkable importance of women's participation in commerce, their enterprises are considered as 'extra income' to help the family survive or simply to improve their living conditions. One consideration that needs to be emphasized when conducting such an analysis is the way these social and cultural stereotypes of women affect development planning and the roles of men and women in pursuing development initiatives.

One postulation that arises from such analysis is that there is likely to be a sharp difference in relations, obligations and expectations within the family when women enter the commercial arena as opposed to when men are the ones working, even if it is the same job or task. We also postulate that there are different effects on the girl or boy child depending on which parent is working in the commercial arena, or when both are doing so.

The exercises that students tackle are designed to elicit these differences. Students are asked to draw on experiential data in responding to the questions posed in the tables on next page 401. The first exercise is on the implication for women when men enter the commercial arena. The second example is on the implications for men when women enter the commercial arena.

Using both tables allows a comparison between male and female roles within the family and shows how there is often little change in women's overall domestic roles while for men domestic work remains relatively minor. This then facilitates a comparative assessment of the value given to male and female roles and contributions to the family. This also highlights ways to revalue women's contributions in matrimonial and family related matters.

Technical barriers

Information gaps concerning business law, financial management and marketing inhibit the development and growth of women's businesses. Since generally men have no reproductive roles to worry about, they can interact in clubs, business breakfast meetings and other business fora. This is where they get the latest information about new and profitable business ventures, new markets and emerging low interest financiers. This is an opportunity women entrepreneurs often lack due to family care obligations and household responsibilities that eat into their daily schedules. This is worsened by women's ignorance of

TABLE 1

Implications for women when men enter the commercial arena

	Home care work	Home chores	Trading / selling obligations	Family business related tasks	Remun-eration?	Other labour obligations	Leisure
Wives							
Monogamous unions	✓		✓	✓	✗	✓	✗
Polygynous unions	✓		✓	✓	✗	✓	✗
Daughters							
Under 5							
5-10	✓	✓					
11-16	✓	✓					
16-21	✓						
Over 21	✓	✓					

TABLE 2

Implications for men when women enter the commercial arena

	Home care work	Home chores	Trading / selling obligations	Family business related tasks	Remun-eration?	Other labour obligations	Leisure
Husbands							
Monogamous unions			✓	✓		✓	✓
Polygynous unions			✓	✓		✓	✓
Sons							
Under 5	✗						
5-10	✗						
11-16	✗	✓	✓				
16-21	✗	✓	✓				
Over 21	✗						

These are the kinds of responses one expects when the charts are filled in but one cannot generalize. Students are encouraged to relate their decisions to actual situations rather than make broad assumptions so they don't fall into the trap of depending totally on their own intuition. However, the girls would traditionally have heavier home-based obligations.

entrepreneurial law. Entrepreneurs who wish to go into business have the choice of carrying out their business as sole traders, forming a partnership, incorporating a company or incorporating a public business corporation. In a mini-research I did when I was still a student on this course (Katsande, 2006), I discovered that most entrepreneurs – both men and women – could not distinguish between these various business entities. They viewed formal business as registering a company yet there are other legal entities requiring much less complicated registration processes. This lack of information is a serious cause for concern as more and more entrepreneurs remain in informal business rather than graduate to formal businesses protected by the law.

Financial barriers

We discuss both macrofinance and microfinance but we pay more attention to microfinance as it is more accessible to women. We explore why microfinance should focus on women and the reasons for promoting women's participation in microfinance programmes. In focusing on women and the potential benefits of microfinance we also probe how microfinance is accessed and controlled. Available evidence from many jurisdictions shows that a significant number of women who may have access to finance may not have control over it (Sebstad and Chen, 1996:8). Thus to sharpen students' critical thinking skills we use a Bangladesh case study which found that about 63 per cent of women's loans are actually invested by male relatives while women bear the formal responsibility for repayment (Hunt and Kasynathan, 2002).

Another study in Bangladesh discovered that of 140 loans granted to women by Action Aid, about 50 per cent were used for men's produce activities. Given the patriarchal nature of African society, African women are likely to be treated in a similar way by husbands.

We also look at two African case studies (see box on page 403). The first is entitled 'Women and informal credit: lessons from Moretile, South Africa' (Kongolo, 2007). Students undertake a critique of this study and do presentations in class linking it to their personal and home country experiences.

The second case study, entitled 'Macro promises of micro credit – a case of a local *esusu* in rural Ghana' moves a step further by looking at the macro gains of micro credit (Norwood, 2005). The study concluded that micro credit organizations have great potential to enhance the lives of rural women. The study notes that while micro credit cannot reduce absolute poverty at national levels, it can relieve the temporary pains associated with abject poverty. Micro credit organizations can be safe havens for women entrepreneurs. We however remain aware that micro credit alone does not lead to women's businesses growing from the informal sector into the formal economy. Macro credit offers women more opportunities for growth.

TWO CASE STUDIES

Informal credit in Moretile, South Africa

This study established the important role of informal credit in urban and rural development in South Africa. Informal credit involves lending, generally in the short-term, among friends, relatives, kin members, landlords, neighbours, village moneylenders and other local income groups. It includes various traditional non-institutional ways of accumulating and extending credit.

Informal credit markets exist in urban areas but the term generally refers to rural markets where institutional credit facilities are absent or insufficient. Informal credit is supplied, at little or no interest, to farmers, local people, various marginal entrepreneurs, relatives and friends. Traders, large landowners and moneylenders usually dominate as the suppliers of informal credit.

Informal credit gives disadvantaged poor men and women access to financial services and helps increase their earning opportunities.

The study findings suggested that informal credit impacts positively on the lives of many rural women by enabling them to become self-employed through self-chosen economic activities (Kongolo, 2007).

Microfinance and women's empowerment

The study involved interviews over three weeks with village women's groups and staff from three non-governmental organizations in Bangladesh and one based in Bihar in India. The organizations provided microfinance to women as a primary strategy for addressing poverty and empowerment. The study argued that development agencies committed to empowering women needed to question the nature of the link between access to credit and the transformation in gender relations needed for empowerment and equality. To understand changes in gender relations and the contribution of microfinance to women's empowerment, the study tried to answer the following questions:

● Who controls decision making regarding the use of credit?

● Who manages enterprises supported by credit and whose paid or unpaid labour is used?

● Who controls the purchasing of inputs for these enterprises and the marketing of products?

● Who keeps, decides on and uses any income generated?

The findings of the study indicated that only a minority of women who received credit from poverty-oriented microfinance programmes were controlling their loans. Many women were merely 'postboxes', passing on the full amount of their loans directly to their husbands, sons or sons-in-law. They had little or no access to the income generated and received back only enough money to make weekly loan repayments. In other cases, loan management and control within the family was more complex, with some women keeping part of their loans for their own enterprises and passing on the remainder to men (Hunt and Kasynathan, 2002).

Market barriers

In class we explore the need for women to actively upgrade their technology and technological skills through the use of information communication technology. This was prompted by the realization that the ability to tap into new markets requires expertise, knowledge and contacts. We question whether women lack access to training and experience in participating in the market place and as a result are unable to market goods and services strategically. We ask whether women-owned enterprises are often unable to take on both the production and marketing of their goods. Students investigate the extent to which women have been exposed to the international market and whether they lack knowledge about what is internationally acceptable. Is it because women fear or face prejudice or sexual harassment, thus restricting their ability to travel to make contacts? Further, has market liberalization complicated women's marketing dilemmas? It has led to increased competition that demands swifter responses to the market. African women's small corporations may struggle with competition from transnational corporations as well as from efficient low cost producers in the developed countries. The question we ask therefore is whether information communication technology can provide a way of addressing women's relative immobility and lack of opportunities.

Information communication technology

The United Nations Development Fund for Women's southern Africa regional office undertook an information communication technology baseline survey in Zambia, Zimbabwe, Swaziland and South Africa in 2002 (UNIFEM, 2002). The study was launched to help bridge the gender digital divide in Africa. It sought to identify women entrepreneurs' awareness, access, knowledge and use of information communication technology in business, the constraints they face and the opportunities available to them through this technology. The study revealed that few women were aware of the potential for information communication technology to improve their economic activities and increase their access to information. Information communication technology can link women to important information for entrepreneurs, for example on:

- supply (obtaining inputs)
- demand (new and existing customers)
- finance (business management and obtaining additional finance)
- knowledge of the environment in which they are doing business
- business skills

According to Hafkin (2002) technology has historically been a male preserve suggesting that women's approach to technology is a political project they must fight for. Women negotiate for access to technology and negotiation is a power issue.

The power relations around the use of technology thus require intervention so that women have equal access to technology. We therefore interrogate the power issues in the use of technology from a feminist standpoint using feminist theories. The questions we ask are whether information technology is gender neutral and if women and men were given equal access to it, would they use it in the same way? There are other questions about the nature, form and presentation of information technology that have raised feminist debates. Ellen Kole (2001: 155–179)[1] has written extensively on this debate. We focus on how such technology can and needs to be adapted to women's needs, realizing that it is critical for women to look at development in technology in the context relevant to Africa.

To explore the gains women can make through the use of technology and to prompt deeper diagnosis and analysis among the students, we use the case study generated by Touch Screen Technology and the telecentres of Nakaseke in Uganda (ITU, 2001) This study explores the experiences of women at grassroots level who have access to information technology and are taking advantage of it in enhancing their entrepreneurial ventures.

> ### EXAMPLE
> **Access to technology?**
>
> The sociologist Njeru (2009) wrote about his father who had a tiny, much-prized radio in the 1970s. His mother had no leisure to listen to the radio and was never allowed to join the men as they sat around outside the house, listening to it.
>
> When his father left for the city, he took the radio with him or tucked it away somewhere, waiting for his eventual return. His father joined the Guerrilla movement for many years and his radio waited in its safe place for his long return.
>
>

Women in management

Not only do we focus on women running their own businesses, be they in the informal or formal economy, we also locate women in commerce at management levels in the corporate world and the challenges they face in cracking the glass ceiling.

Women entrepreneurs can be divided into two groups, namely intentional entrepreneurs and corporate climbers. Intentional entrepreneurs, also referred to as 'born to be' entrepreneurs, are women who always wanted to start their own businesses but worked initially for others to gain business experience (Buttner and Moore, 1997:37). On the other hand, corporate climbers intended to stay in corporate careers but ended up leaving due to negative factors in the work environment. This gives them an unexpected business opportunity.

---

[1] For her doctoral study, Ellen Kole investigated how the internet was introduced to African non-governmental organizations within the framework of international cooperation. Her study involved three case studies in the African region. The main objective of the study was to develop a model on internet and development that supports the socio-political objectives and the practical needs of the technology recipients: African non-governmental organizations and their grassroots constituencies.

This group of women would have been unable to move beyond the glass ceiling.[2] In 1986, two *Wall Street Journal* reporters coined the phrase 'glass ceiling' to describe the invisible barrier that blocks women from the most senior positions in the corporate world. For the 'Women commerce and the law' course, the issue of the glass ceiling is of paramount importance because a sizeable number of women in the corporate workplace who are in middle management find themselves stuck, unable to find room at the top and these negative push factors force them to opt for entrepreneurship (Buttner and Moore, 1997:37). To help students connect theory and practice we explore the issues raised in the 'Corporate glass ceiling' study (ICMR, 2002) which deals with the glass ceiling concept that prevents women from reaching top management positions in the corporate world. The study explains the concept in detail and examines the various reasons why women are prevented from reaching top management. The case gives several examples of women who have reached top management position in the United States and India. Students are required to critique this case study in the African context by bringing out what they consider to be the various factors that prevent women from rising through the ranks in the corporate world. They are also required to come up with possible ways to overcome the obstacles.

The discussion on the factors that push and pull women into entrepreneurship builds up to the globalization debate and the World Trade Organization (WTO) interventions. Globalization and international trade issues have a direct bearing on women's effective participation in commerce.

---

[2] The term 'glass ceiling' refers to situations where the advancement of a qualified person within the hierarchy of an organization is stopped at a lower level because of some form of discrimination. This situation is referred to as a 'ceiling' as there is a limitation blocking upward advancement, and 'glass' (transparent) because the limitation is not immediately apparent and is normally an unwritten and unofficial policy.

Part II: Globalization and international trade

Sheillah Kanyangarara

The globalization and international trade module focuses on women's experiences in the face of globalization. We examine international trade law, seeking to 'locate' women in international trade. The objectives of the module are to facilitate a general knowledge of norms, structures and actors in international trade law and to apply a women's law analytical framework to international trade law. We do this by broadly exploring multilateral, regional and bilateral trade agreements, examining the impact of trade agreements in relation to women as well as revisiting theoretical perspectives in law and economics. The subject is covered through a combination of lectures and seminars as well as videos and directed research.

Informing experiences

When I first participated in teaching on the 'Women commerce and the law' course, I constantly asked myself if the 'traditional' centralist approach that had been applied when I studied law at undergraduate level is mutually exclusive in applying a women's law approach. My dilemma in this area is best captured in the classic question of which came first, the egg or the chicken? Do I deal first with the general area of international trade? I wondered whether it was possible to apply a women's law approach to exploring an area of knowledge without imposing personal views on the subject. I remembered how it had been difficult for me at times, at undergraduate level, to distinguish between the personal views of some lecturers and the content of some subjects. The dominant theoretical framework at the time was Marxist-Leninism. After some lectures I wondered whether we had learnt any real law or if we had been through Marxist-Leninist indoctrination! In some subjects, I had to read around the content of the law after graduation, in order to apply the law in the real world.

...it had been difficult for me at times, at undergraduate level, to distinguish between the personal views of some lecturers and the content of some subjects

On the other hand there were some lecturers who, while they had been clearly persuaded by a particular world outlook, managed to teach the content of the law as well as encourage critical thinking around the subject from different angles. As I began working in different capacities around the improvement of the status of women in society, I came across some people who, though passionate about improving the position of women, could not sustain an argument on the impact of some laws on women beyond the rhetoric of 'the marginalization of women in a patriarchal system'. For example, statements like 'inheritance laws suppress women' were liberally aired in arguments for the reform of inheritance laws. As an advocate liaising with parliamentarians, such statements were not necessarily self explanatory. The then Minister of Justice declared that he would only listen to solid arguments that he could use to convince fellow parliamentarians to accept the proposed revolutionary changes.[3] He emphasized that the majority of the parliamentarians were men who would want to protect their property from 'uncustomary' beneficiaries. The lesson I took away from that meeting was that while one liners are good for newspaper headlines, they would not be good enough to sustain bedrock shattering discussions on the position of women.

...one liners are good for newspaper headlines, they would not be good enough to sustain bedrock shattering discussions on the position of women

My experiences as a student and a practitioner have shaped my approach to teaching. I seek to strike a balance between in-depth exploration of substantive areas of law and analyzing the concepts within that field from women's perspective. 'Women, commerce and the law' is undertaken at postgraduate level in the second part of the programme and this greatly influences my teaching approach. I proceed on the assumption that by the time students take the elective, they are equipped with the theoretical and analytical skills pertaining to women's law. The challenge is therefore to facilitate an exploration of the area of international trade and globalization from a women's perspective. Theoretical perspectives in women's law are couched as questions relating to the issues under consideration.

Introducing the subject matter

From food choices to lifestyle preferences, we experience globalization and trade on a daily basis. The challenge faced in teaching this module is to relate these everyday experiences to an area of substantive law. To facilitate this transfer of information, students are invited to share their experiences and knowledge of contemporary issues around international trade and globalization. Topical venues or words associated with issues on trade and globalization are suggested to probe students' awareness of the issues, for example, Cancun, Seattle, G7, G20 and the World Economic Forum. Students are asked about their preferred brands of drink, cereal and clothing and their favourite movies and actors. They are invited to note common preferences despite their different geographical backgrounds. Though this might appear simplistic, the exercise serves to highlight the impact of globalization.

Students are invited to share their experiences in 'attending' televised world events. In one session we discuss the personal impact on students of

---

[3] The proposed law sought to give spouses the right to inherit residential property in the absence of a will. Previously, wives did not have the right to inherit residential property from their husbands unless there was a will to that effect. The eldest male child inherited residential property to the exclusion of the current wife.

global events like the attack on the World Trade Centre in New York. Another follows the death and televised memorial of Michael Jackson. Students speak enthusiastically of international soccer teams they support, almost as if they are local. Such experiences illustrate how seemingly distant events can have local and personal impact. From that realization, students are invited to think through how other global events have impacted on their lives and on the lives of women at local and personal levels.

Using questions directed at specific students, the class is able to learn more about personal experiences in relation to globalization and trade. A student from Kenya was invited to share Kenyan experiences related to the establishment of South African chain stores in Kenya. A Zimbabwean was asked about the impact of Chinese imports on the local market. Students from Uganda shared the difficulties that a local brand of fruit juice was facing in the light of competition from imported brands. Students are asked what, if anything, law has to do with their experiences.

Globalization is taken to imply the opening out beyond local and nationalistic perspectives to a broader outlook of an interconnected and inter-dependent world

We adopt a common definition of globalization. For the purposes of this module, globalization is taken as the worldwide movement towards economic, financial, trade and communications integration. Globalization is taken to imply the opening out beyond local and nationalistic perspectives to a broader outlook of an interconnected and inter-dependent world with free transfer of capital, goods and services across national frontiers.

Substantive issues

Globalization has necessitated a paradigm shift in gender analysis from an exclusively domestic paradigm to seeking to understand the relations between and amongst global actors (Shiva, undated). The module therefore explores the perception of women as purely domestic actors, working within the home or within national boundaries, in contrast to women operating at a regional and international level. The subject matter we cover includes:

- Principles of international trade law
- Contentious issues in international trade law
- Frameworks for enforcing international trade law
- Identifying the role played by women as regulators, traders and consumers

Women as global actors and participants

'By focusing on the woman and her relationships with men and with other women and the society in which she is embedded, we may uncover the norms, expectations and social and economic forces which influence problem solving and dispute resolution.'

Bentzon, 1998:99

This module seeks to identify and examine women's relationships in globalization as well as how such relationships influence and shape norms across countries. Women's actions are driven by various interests at different levels of interaction with other women, men and society in general. Students are invited to identify various trade relationships at domestic, community, country, regional and international levels. A table is drawn up on the board and students suggest actors in global trade. Examples of such actors include governments, multinational corporations, non-state actors and local corporations. From this list of actors, students firstly identify whether any of the actors are women and secondly we discuss the role women and other actors play at all these levels. From the discussion, women are identified as consumers and manufacturers or traders of products and services and as administrators within various trade facilitation bodies. This exercise highlights the complex role of women as drivers and beneficiaries in an international trade system. It also highlights that women are both passive and active participants in globalization as well as willing and sometimes unwilling ones.

...women are both passive and active participants in globalization as well as willing and sometimes unwilling ones

Another exercise explores the conflicting and complementary interests of women operating in the various roles. For example, students are asked to examine the interests of a woman trading in goods and the interests of the woman consumer of those goods. As an illustration, we raise questions relating to women who sell cosmetic products that have been banned to protect consumers. The women obtain such products in one country where the laws are different and smuggle them to sell to other women in their own country, in spite of the local laws and the potentially negative health impact. The point for consideration is whether women participate in such transactions as purely economic actors, uninfluenced by the nature or interests of their consumers?

Women negotiating trade agreements on behalf of their countries bring another dynamic into the discussion. The discussion centres on whether such negotiators would look out for the interests of women in another country where there is a likelihood of conflict with the interests of women or men in the home country. Examples are drawn from countries in the region where women hold influential political positions. For example, students from Malawi and Tanzania identified women members of parliament from their countries who were known to be interested in advancing women's interests. As a class we look

at the trade interests of fisherpeople and people living around Lake Malawi on the Tanzanian and Malawian side. The students discuss how fisherpeople on either side would want the maximum benefits from the fishing industry. They note how the fisherpeople are likely to be affected by any regulation that would give them an unfair advantage on either side. In the event of a conflict in interests, we note that each parliamentarian is driven by national interest first because as a politician, her accountability would be to the country's electorate and parliament and not to women of another country.

Complex, conflicting and sometimes confusing roles played by women in all the rule-making processes are examined. We discuss the complex position of women as shareholders or executives in corporate organizations who have a vested financial interest in the outcome of trade negotiations on one hand and the interests of women as consumers together with women in government as facilitators of trade. We note that, unlike in some situations where one can identify a woman or man's issue with little difficulty, in trade, women are affected differently and their responses are dependent on the financial or political gains to be made in the circumstance and not necessarily on the basis of sex or gender.

The World Trade Organization agreements are products of various rounds of trade negotiations. The current round, the Doha round, is the ninth in a series of such negotiations which began in Geneva in 1947 (Stiglitz and Charlton, 2005:41).[6] This process of rule making and norm creating at international level is explored with a focus on strategies traditionally employed to ensure inclusion of women-sensitive international and national rules. We consider the role played by prominent international conferences like the Beijing Platform for Action or the annual Commission on the Status of Women meetings held in New York, in drawing attention to women's issues. We ask whether students know of any international conference that has sought to bring public attention to the impact of globalization or international trade on women. Students who are active in women's

EXERCISE
South African interests and women politicians

In one session we considered the economic strength of South Africa versus the aspirations of women traders from South Africa's neighbours. We noted that South Africa's minister of foreign affairs[4] and deputy president[5] were both women at that time, powerful positions in any government.

We considered whether such legislators would approach a trade discussion with any other country as women or merely as technocrats with vested national interest. We considered whether they would seek to open their country's borders to women from other countries who may want to import goods into South Africa at concessionary rates at the expense of their own country's revenue and industry?

The exercise showed that women's lives are complex and may not be improved by simplistic measures of putting women in positions of power and that women are not a homogeneous group.

---

[4] Dr Nkosazana Dhlamini Zuma, Minister of Foreign Affairs 1999–2009.

[5] Pumzile Mlambo-Ngcuka, Deputy President 2005–2008.

[6] Other rounds were Geneva 1947-8, Annecy 1949, Torquay 1950-1, Geneva 1966, Dillon 1960-2, Kennedy 1963-7, Tokyo 1973-9, Uruguay 1986-93, Doha 2001-present

empowerment movements are asked if they have attended any such international conferences as well as how they funded their attendance. We briefly explore the link between sources of funding for various women's causes and various other causes. It is noted that most funds that capitalize the consideration of women's issues are state aided. The question is posed whether a state capitalized donor fund would finance a developing country delegation that is likely to oppose its national interests? This is raised in the context of multilateral trade negotiations where consumers in, for example, the United Kingdom, would have different interests from women producers in Mozambique. Usually there are negative responses. It is agreed that any country would ideally want to promote the interests of its nationals, based on the best quality products at the most affordable prices. The best price for the woman producer would not be in the interests of the purchasing woman consumer. The challenge posed is therefore how can women's interests be brought to the international trade agenda in the absence of independent sources of finance to attend international trade negotiations?

Women's methods of acquiring and sharing information on international trade are considered, looking at cross-border trading on the one hand and formal corporate international trade on the other. Students are invited to share their personal experiences of either importing or exporting goods from outside their home countries. Zimbabwean students shared how they had tried to export Zimbabwean cereals to Mozambique and Zambia to benefit from the different exchange rates between the countries. They also shared the challenges of getting visas for South Africa in order to go to that country to buy goods for resale. Zambian students shared their experiences of importing clothing from Dubai. All students spoke of some unpleasant experiences regarding immigration or customs in different countries. They were requested to examine where and how they had acquired information on how to fill in customs declaration forms. The response was almost unanimous – information had been obtained from people in the queue. In some cases regarding immigration, some had resorted to the internet but they verified such information with people in the queue or those who had visited other countries. Students noted that even the educated rely on informal sources of information in relation to international trade unless such trade is conducted within the corporate framework. The impact of informal sources of knowledge on the nature and extent of women's involvement in international trade is also considered. It is noted that women are either consciously or unconsciously involved in smuggling when it came to declaring goods. Students also share stories they have heard of informal traders seeking access to other countries to sell their wares and human trafficking to the detriment of other women.

On the basis of the stories shared, I invite students to relate their experiences to the principles in international trade being explored. For example, we discuss

...even the educated rely on informal sources of information in relation to international trade

the challenges related to exporting mealie-meal or rice from Malawi in times of drought. These experiences are related to principles in the Agreement on Agriculture which permits countries to set limits on the quantities of produce that can be exported or imported in times of surplus or shortage.

In relation to challenges that women face in securing visas to sell goods or to seek employment in foreign countries, I highlight the principles enshrined in the General Agreement on Trade in Services (GATS) which permits countries to set minimum qualifications for entry or minimum qualifications for people who may be employed in specific sectors. Students who have tried to seek employment in foreign countries vent their frustrations at the rigidity of the entry requirements into some countries. We also look at the experiences of people we know who have emigrated, what they are doing and why they are in those jobs. The experiences and frustrations are then used as a basis of discussions on shortcomings in the General Agreement on Trade in Services, especially from the perspective of women. Relating the international agreements to everyday experiences enables the class to explore seemingly complex international agreements.

In pairs or groups, depending on class size, the class examines a bilateral trade agreement. Ideally, students examine trade agreements involving their own countries for an in-depth analysis.[7] However, in the absence of such country-specific agreements, we have examined the Zimbabwe–Mozambique agreement. From the issues covered in the agreements, students are invited to examine what sectors of production impact on women in the various capacities previously identified, namely, as consumers, producers and administrators. The question we ask is how women obtain information about trade and how they use such information in their trading. The objective is to establish whether the agreement takes into consideration the reality of women's lives and, if not, whose interests the agreement caters for. Students are invited to identify ways of improving the agreement for the benefit of women. Some of the improvements proposed have included finding ways of ensuring the participation of women in the negotiating process, raising negotiators' awareness of sectors that impact on women, raising awareness of the agreements, improving the availability of information in the vernacular and making the information more accessible.

---

[7] In the past a request made through the office for students to bring such agreements was communicated after the students had already left their home countries so we were unable to look at country-specific agreements. Unfortunately, most countries are yet to make agreements available online. And it is also difficult to secure such agreements from outside the countries.

Impact of teaching methods

The combined seminar and lecture approach to exploring globalization and international trade is essentially relaxed and almost informal. This enables an in-depth exploration of an otherwise complex and lengthy subject area in a short timeframe. Sharing stories heard or personal experiences reveals areas of knowledge that would otherwise have been excluded because they are not documented in published materials. Considering the dearth of published information on women in globalization and international trade, this approach enriches learning by generating issues for further research and helping us organize the documentation processes.

We rely heavily on the internet as a source of information. Content of international trade agreements can be downloaded or referred to both for personal research and in video presentations. The internet is also a valuable source in summarizing the work of international organizations like the World Trade Organization, the Common Market for Eastern and Southern Africa (COMESA) and the Southern African Development Community (SADC). We are able to identify their current areas of focus and obtain insights into their work in relation to women by accessing their official home pages.

Newspapers and magazines are also useful sources of information for the purposes of discussion and we pay attention to the advertisements as well as the reported stories. Advertisements help to raise our awareness of local availability of goods manufactured in various parts of the world, highlighting the globalization of tastes and preferences dictated by availability. Examining labelling on goods obtained from a local supermarket also enables students to identify the global presence of some transnational corporations.

Part III: Expanding the terrain

Julie Stewart

I did the groundwork to launch this course when it was first offered and it has grown and blossomed under Rosalie Katsande's management and is meeting the theoretical and methodological expectations that I had for it under her careful and enthusiastic guidance.[8]

As a continuation to the globalization and international trade debate, one poignant topic in this course is that of women and indigenous knowledge and its exploitation and protection. It is an old saw that women have passed on from generation to generation, across continents and civilizations – knowledge based in daily management and productive arenas. Women are aware of and expert users of medicinal plants, especially in rural areas, they are experts in craft making, weaving and pottery, and skilled in designing and decorating clothes and artifacts. Women currently supplement family incomes with skilled work, work that is often snapped up by middle persons for minimal prices to the original craftswoman, then marketed vigorously by a variety of entrepreneurs who make significant profits.[9] The craftswoman may part with her work for a pittance because of economic constraints, lack of knowledge of the market or logistical problems in marketing the product. One of the exercises here is to replicate the supply and contractual chain discussed earlier in this chapter and to consider how and at what point intellectual property rights could be invoked and applied to aspects of indigenous knowledge. Article 14 of CEDAW becomes significant at this juncture as although it deals with rights of rural women in general issues related to protecting and marketing effectively, their skills and products are clearly a part of dealing with rights over indigenous knowledge and skills.

Women are aware of and expert users of medicinal plants, especially in rural areas, they are experts in craft making, weaving and pottery, and skilled in designing and decorating clothes and artifacts

© Ed Wilmsen

However, many of the countries students come from have not adopted intellectual property provisions that protect indigenous knowledge, indigenous products or indigenous skills. In those countries that have such provisions there is a profound lack of knowledge on the part of those needing protection of the existence of such protection. If they have some inkling that such provisions exist, they often do not know how to obtain protection from them. Costs are invariably a factor in filing for protection.

---

[8] I am pleased that she still sees fit to engage me to do a small part of the course despite being one of the victims of my initial attempt to get the course off the ground.

[9] It is not just women who suffer in this way and it is implicit in this discussion that the same analysis can be used with men.

For example, although Zimbabwe has legislation that addresses rights in folklore works, little if anything is known of it and more or less nothing by potentially affected communities.[10]

This is a relatively new aspect of the course and requires greater development. However, it is likely that we will carve some space from the course to do more on this topic in the future and an expert in the area, a former student on the course, will be engaged to present this topic.

Manipulating women and women's bodies in commerce

The other contribution that I make to this course is to examine how women's bodies and women's sexuality are used as marketing tools aimed at both men and women.

To consider how to deal with gender stereotyping and its adverse consequences we have to ascertain and scrutinize its sources. Although the use of sexually explicit advertising may be controlled and regulated in mainstream media, a considerable amount of highly gendered and gender role reinforcing advertising takes place in all forms of media. To tackle the role of the media in sex and gender stereotyping, we need to tackle advertising – a commercial activity. I created an exercise to alert students to the way sex and gender are used in the commercial world. The exercise is simple and involves watching television, shopping with gender lenses, reading magazines and newspapers and reporting back to the class. I buy a bundle of glossy magazines which target different audiences – men, girls, women in general and women with families. I distribute these fairly carefully around the class to get a sex and gender balance as well as, where possible, age and ethnicity representations. The exercise (see box on page 417) is self explanatory and the readings selected prime the students on what they are looking for although, as usual on the programme, they are to a certain extent on their own.

Having completed the exercise and filled in a chart (page 418) they report back. Most are amazed at the different perspective that they have on the various materials and sources when considered from a sexed and gendered angle.

One of the significant outcomes of this exercise is that students appreciate how gender and sex stereotyping processes go far beyond the family and the school and they realize that if we want to effectively curb their influence we will need to include them in paradigm-shifting interventions.

It is significant for our reconceptualizing of women and commerce in Africa that such topics are drawn together in one course that explores women and commerce, revisits women as entrepreneurs and examines how women are conceptualized at all levels of commercial enterprise.

---

[10] S80 Copyright and Neighbouring Rights Act, Chapter 26:05

EXERCISE

The gender dimensions of advertising and marketing strategies

This exercise is designed to help you identify the sexed and gendered dimensions of marketing and advertising strategies.

1   You have each been given one or two magazines or newspapers and/or been assigned to watch television or listen to the radio to identify various sex and gender based marketing/ advertising strategies. Look at where advertisements are placed in magazines and newspapers and the types of magazine or newspaper they are. In the case of TV and radio adverts look at the type of programme and the flighting times .

2   Record your findings in relation to various aspects of life (see chart on page 418). Use the chart to record examples you found, what they were about, who they targeted and the sexed and gendered elements in the strategy (as you see it).

Hint: It is largely about how sexuality and sex appeal are used to market products or about gendered roles such as homecare/housework, child care, work and work related products.

3   Who do particular kinds of advertisements target and what are the modes of targeting – for example, woman as carer, nurturer, nurse or man as provider, defender, public persona. Also look at children's sections in magazines and see how the 'emerging consumer' is groomed.

Hint: It is also about the sexed and gendered messages and images which define women and men's realms and their assumed interests – ask yourself how these messages and images affect definitions of male and female.

5   Are there any advertisements in which there is no connection between the product and the images used – for example where women and their bodies are used to attract male attention or vice versa?

6   During the forthcoming week, also consider how sex and gender are used in marketing products in stores, supermarkets, restaurants and bars. When you go out just be aware of the role of sex in advertising – even advertising signs on the streets are part of the scenario.

Suggested background reading

Allen R. (1992) 'Analysing representations', in Bonner et al.(eds), *Imagining women, cultural representations and gender*, Polity Press, Stafford.

Benyon J. (2002) 'The commercialization of masculinities: from the "new man' to the 'new lad'", in J. Benyon, *Masculinities and culture*, Open University Press, Buckingham.

Roberts N. (1993) *Whores in history: prostitution in western society*, pages 353-358, HarperCollins, Hammersmith.

Leggett T.(2003) *Rainbow vice: the drugs and sex industries in the new South Africa*, pages 169–187, Zed Books, London.

Durham M.G.(2002) 'Girls, media, and the negotiation of sexuality: a study of race, class and gender in adolescent peer groups', pages 332–348 in Williams and Stein (eds), *Sexuality and gender*, Blackwells, Oxford.

Loe M. (2002) 'Working for men: at the intersection of power, gender and sexuality', pages 221–238 in Williams and Stein (eds), *Sexuality and gender*, Blackwells, Oxford.

CHART

Marketing, advertising, sexed and gendered terrains – an exploration

Product, service, life event that is the basis for the marketing and how women are targeted.	Magazine Newspaper Website TV/Radio Which?	Product/s	Marketing Advertising strategy, sex gender, class, ethnicity, other targets	Product/s,	Marketing Advertising strategy, sex gender, class, ethnicity, other targets	Product/s	Marketing Advertising strategy, sex gender, class, ethnicity, other targets	Product/s	Marketing Advertising strategy, sex gender, class, ethnicity, other targets
		Food/ nutrition		Clothing		Cosmetics Perfume Jewellery Personal grooming		Equipment, Computers Vehicles Furniture	
Birth									
Children/ growth & nurturing									
Marriage									
Home life									
Housework									
Food									
Health									
Education									
Work									
Leisure									
Sports									
Animals/ pets									
Entertainment									
Investment									
Banking									

Part IV: Research

Anne Griffiths

As part of the course work, students undertake a mini research project. The research is done in Harare and the surrounding areas. My contribution is to get students to apply the skills and knowledge they have developed during the programme to implementing research in the field. Thus my input to this course is aimed at encouraging students to apply the analytical and theoretical skills that they have acquired in devising and designing a mini research project over a two-week period. The mini research is extremely important because of the dearth of empirical material in this area. The studies may be very limited in scope given the timeframe for the research but they represent a step towards pursuing vital information on how women and law intersect in a commercial environment on the ground.

My part of the course aims to get students to move from the abstract and broader concerns of women's law to a more specific and detailed focus on research in action with regard to a particular topic. This requires them to apply and adjust their critical and theoretical insights from a macro to a micro level, in terms of establishing a small, self-contained local project. Interrogating law at a number of different levels is important. Given that the module in the course before deals with the impact of globalization, it is crucial to be able to move from an international and transnational form of analysis to exploring the impact of these regulatory frameworks at a local level, in terms of people's, especially women's, lived experiences.

This is essential as, in acquiring a holistic picture of how law operates, students need to be aware of how law is mobilized from an array of perspectives, including the strategies employed in selecting and using differing normative orders. This information highlights the complex ways in which local forms of knowledge and organization are constantly being reworked in interaction with changing external conditions. It demonstrates how power operates in different places and is transformed to provide for the emergence of new identities and alliances within specific populations. Part of this analysis involves acknowledging the central role that gender plays in this process, particularly in an African context. This reinforces the need for gender mainstreaming to be made an integral part of the research design process, as well as a consideration in implementing, monitoring and evaluating programmes and policies that are planned or in operation. It is essential to take account of how these interventions affect both women and men.

The first week of my part of the course involves students identifying themes that have arisen from the course and selecting a topic for the subject of their research. Once students have selected a few topics, for example, 'women as

...it is crucial [for students] to be able to move from an international and transnational form of analysis to exploring the impact of these regulatory frameworks at a local level, in terms of people's, especially women's, lived experiences

© Ed Wilmsen

Interviews in the field, Botswana, 2010

market traders' or 'the challenges women entrepreneurs in the farming sector face in accessing and using the internet', they form groups and spend the rest of the week designing a concrete research project that could be the subject of future field research.

The idea is to make students move from more general, abstract propositions to concrete realities in the context of a specific research topic. They build on the general theoretical and critical forms of analysis highlighted in the first part of the course and also on the first semester courses on 'Theories and perspectives in women's law' and 'Research methodologies and methods in women's law'. This requires them to apply their knowledge to a defined problem area and to include the possibilities and limitations of a socio-legal perspective in action.

In this process, students draw on their experiences of carrying out field work in the first semester and this encourages them to address the advantages as well as the limitations of data collection in the field. Thus, the exercise helps them to reflect on past experience, including the positive and negative aspects of data collection, while looking forward to their fieldwork for their dissertation at the end of the course. As a result the exercise develops their practical research skills in a way that will be useful to them when it comes to their more extended field research for the dissertation.

Students have to design a feasible, manageable research project that can identify and circumvent potential difficulties and remain flexible

This is achieved by reinforcing their skills through practice. Students have to design a feasible, manageable research project that can identify and circumvent potential difficulties and remain flexible, allowing for modification during the research process. Students are encouraged to reflect on their first experience of doing a mini project in the field and how this experience required them to modify or change their research objectives, assumptions and questions in the course of their brief exposure to data collection.

At the end of the first week each group does a twenty minute presentation of their project to the class (see box on page 419 for details).

At the beginning of the first week the topics selected by the class are generally very broad. They acquire a more narrowly defined focus when developed by students for their individual research projects carried out in the second week. Given the students' different academic and professional backgrounds, some time is given over to exploring possible lines of research that are of particular interest to the students who make up the class. After the students have picked their topics they divide themselves into groups and go away to work on their communal project. I make myself available to each group if they want to discuss any matters with me and I regularly go round each group to observe how they are getting on. I do not, however, participate in their discussions at this stage unless consulted or asked to do so. On days four and five in the first week, the groups come together to make their presentation to the class as a whole.

EXERCISE
Group research project presentations

At the end of the first week, the groups present their research project plans and are required to include the following information:

- Topic
- Research objectives
- Research assumptions
- Research questions
- Sources of data
  - International, regional and national human rights instruments, country-specific constitutions, national legislation, case law, customary law and practices, cultural, social, political, economic and environmental factors
  - Actors, for example, women in informal or formal businesses, men in informal or formal businesses, officials dealing with credit, government officials dealing with economic development, city council officials, and so on.
  - Structures, for example, the family and status of women within the family (married/unmarried/divorced/ widowed), Ministry of Small and Medium Enterprises, Ministry of Youth, Gender and Employment Creation, City Council, Chamber of Commerce, and so on
- Research methodologies (theories and methods applied to research design)
- Timeframe and budget for project
- Potential constraints or difficulties in conducting the research and strategies for dealing with them
- Literature review
- Findings and their relationship with the research objectives, assumptions and questions
- Recommendations or strategies for action, including formulating policy and multiple forms of intervention

Given students' previous experience of this type of exercise and exposure to the theoretical and methodological approaches adopted by women's law, at this stage they are generally quite proficient in making sure that the links between the research objectives, assumptions and questions are clear and coherent. Where students may need more careful scrutiny is when it comes to sources of data. There is a tendency to put down 'semi-autonomous social fields' as a source of data without adequately explaining what these are and why they are relevant to the particular project in hand. Timeframes for the project also tend to be somewhat unrealistic, being given six or nine months for a study that would in reality take one or two years. It is important to get students to think about this as tailoring their research design to square with the time available for implementation is an essential component of the research exercise. Too often students ignore this aspect yet it is a crucial component that can make or break a research project in the field.

Working as a group involves a participatory form of scholarship that empowers students to take the lead in helping one another to develop their capacities and skills. Working in groups represents a form of collaborative learning where students can work in a supportive environment. This is one which enables them to assist one another in enhancing their critical faculties by producing a research product that embodies the outcome of a collective process. This process allow for a less directive form of instruction since my role as a teacher is more one of facilitator, rather than lecturer pursuing more directed forms of knowledge production derived from rote learning or rehashing what is in the books.

Students have to design a feasible, manageable research project that can identify and circumvent potential difficulties and remain flexible

Given the tools of women's law, students are free to explore their ideas within a structured framework that allows them to be creative. They are free to make their presentations in whatever form they consider appropriate, using Powerpoint overheads, flipcharts, printed summaries, posters, stick up cards or video clips. Innovative methods in presenting their information are welcomed.

The strength of this approach is that students do not feel that they are put on the spot as individuals or singled out for criticism where there are problems with the research design. They learn to work with one another in a productive way that builds up their self-confidence. This is especially important for the weaker, more tentative members of the class who need to gain self-assurance and be encouraged to develop and express their ideas about what is relevant to the project.

On a number of occasions I have observed how members of the class support one another where there are gaps or problems with a group's presentation that requires its members to reformulate their research assumptions, objectives or questions, or rethink their research methodologies and sources of data. The same is true for the individual presentations that form part of the group's overall project. Each member of the group is responsible for presenting a section of the project, for example the research objectives or sources of data or recommendations for action. Where individual students falter or have difficulties with their presentations, other members of the group or class are quick to come to their assistance, helping them to think through their part of the research design and to revise their data.

In this supportive environment students are able to express their concerns about or difficulties with any part of the research design without being made to feel foolish or inadequate. This fosters a spirit of genuine intellectual curiosity that is geared to exploring the research design as far as it can be taken and testing its limits. This provides a basis upon which each member of the class can build in selecting and developing a more narrowly defined aspect of a group project for their individual research design.

In this supportive environment students are able to express their concerns about or difficulties with any part of the research design

Thus the second part of my module that takes place over three weeks involves each student producing their own mini-project. This follows the framework set out previously for the group project. So students have a chance to re-engage with topics and research objectives already touched on in the context of group work but honed down to focus on a more limited and confined aspect of the research. This enables them to strengthen the skills they have acquired in week one by re-applying them in week two in the context of their own design projects. Repeating the process helps them to reaffirm what they have learned. It is rather like peeling the layers of the onion for the first group project represents a broader and more abstract proposition which is then taken one step back to an inner layer which represents a less abstract more concrete research proposition. This process can be repeated until the onion is completely unpeeled and the research design has moved from a wide-ranging set of hypotheses to a tightly constructed and highly specific, concrete study.

These topics provide a varied range of research projects that mark an important beginning in building up a databank of information in this area. Some examples of past topics are shown in the box on the next page. Having followed the research design for a second time within a short time period students were generally more confident and assured in their presentations.

What has emerged from the presentations (oral and written) is the need to maintain flexibility in the research design. For example, the study of pre-schools was originally intended to cover several sites within the city but ended up being limited to Belvedere because the student unexpectedly had 'to attend a workshop on judicial training' and 'had no time to focus the research on other areas'.

Dealing with potential problems associated with the research design was given attention in the course of the group presentations. This included, for example, how to find ways of dealing with a situation where the researcher fails to acquire a sufficient number of interviewees. However, students still found

EXAMPLES

Topics chosen for individual research projects

- The role of women in family enterprises: a case study of women in a pre-schools business in Belvedere

- A comparative analysis of the socio-economic impacts of water and electricity cuts in Harare on women entrepreneurs from high and low income suburbs of the city: a study of Dzivarasekwa and Mabelreign suburbs

- The Zimbabwean 'look east' policy and its effects on women entrepreneurs in the clothing industry

- Challenges faced by women in accessing and marketing edible forest fruits: a case study of women at the Mbare market in Harare, Zimbabwe

- Trade liberalization and its impact on women in the flea-market trade in Harare

- An evaluation of women's empowerment groups and their relevance to women in business

- An analysis of strategies developed and adopted by women in senior management in the corporate world to deal with sex and gender discrimination

- An analysis of the challenges women entrepreneurs in the farming sector face in the access to and use of the internet.

A lively focus group discussion with the potters Botswana, 2010

© Ed Wilmsen

this a challenging aspect of carrying out research in the field. One student reported being disconcerted when a male market vendor refused an interview because he bluntly informed her 'I do not have time for you. Can't you see I'm busy?' This left the student feeling 'dejected' but she was able to make up for this gap through the use of focus group discussions. Through interviewing one woman trader at the market 'fellow vendors became inquisitive…and ended up contributing [to discussions]'.

Other problems encountered by students included conducting research during winter which was the 'wrong season' for dealing with the harvesting of forest fruits that takes place in 'the rainy season between August and November'. Further problems included potential interviewees who backed out of interviews when they discovered that the researcher could not pay them or because they considered that 'the government was powerless to bring any positive change'.

Students learned that it is important to carefully plan their research according to their budget. As one of them observed, her 'research was done on a very tight budget'. This hardly covered the cost of transportation and as a result this 'limited the number of times I could go out for field work' with the result that 'I could not go to the rural areas to contact fruit gatherers'.

Overall, this research module that forms part of the course gets students to develop their skills in connection with research in action and in a specific and focused course. It also helps to create a bridge between their experience of fieldwork in the first semester and their forthcoming dissertation, which is based on a more detailed and extended version of field research.

State and international interventions
The ultimate goal of the course is for students to be able to devise law reform strategies and, where appropriate, to implement law reform measures that would enhance women's full and effective participation in local, national, regional and international commercial activities. To achieve this students do the 'Improving women's access to real commercial opportunities' exercise shown on pages 424 and 425..

Conclusion

The 'Women, commerce and the law in Africa' course has been taught three times since the inception of the women's law programme. The course is still being developed and will continuously be reviewed with changing times. Our teaching methodologies change as our careers progress, thus the course will periodically be updated in order to keep current with the progress in the commercial arena and to give the lecturers a regular opportunity for self-reflection.

EXERCISE

Improving women's access to real commercial opportunities: possible sites, options and forms for intervention

In this exercise, students identify the actors needed to facilitate change and areas for action.

The vertical column lists areas in commerce needing intervention, for example, law and policy. The horizontal column lists the actors needed to effect change, for example, the World Trade Organization.

Students are required, for example, to establish gender and legal issues that should be considered by international bodies like trade-based organizations when developing trade policies or how these bodies can make gender a core element of all the programmes they work with.

Areas of intervention	International bodies UN, AU etc	International organizations, trade based – WTO, etc	Governments – national & other, G8, etc
Policy development			
Gender /gender mainstreaming Specific interventions			
Legal – nature and form of regulation/ interventions			
Governance and governance structures			
Financial – levels of regulation			
Market creation			
Market regulation			
Trade facilitation			
Trade regulation			
Information			
Personnel needs			
Training			
Other ??			

The same applies to other actors like the universities, private companies, and so on. This exercise enables students to reflect on the content they have covered in the course. They use this to identify gaps either in law or policy and to come up with interventions needed to build the technical capacities of women in commerce and interventions that will give women the desired opportunities to realize their full potential.

Educators, universities, poly-techs, schools etc	Civil society	Private enterprise	Private individuals	Media etc

Rosalie K. Katsande, Sheillah Kanyangarara, Julie Stewart and Anne Griffiths

Bibliography

Allen I.E., N. Langowitz and M. Minniti (2007) *2006 Report on women and entrepreneurship*, Global Entrepreneurship Monitor (GEM), London.

Beauvoir S. de (1972) (first published in French in 1949), *The second sex*, translated by H.M Parshley, Penguin, Harmondsworth.

Bentzon A.W. *et al.* (1998) *Pursuing grounded theory in law: south–north experiences in developing women's law*, Tano-Aschehoug and Mond Books, Oslo and Harare.

Buttner E.H. and D.P. Moore (1997) 'Women's organizational exodus to entrepreneurship: self reported motivations and correlates with success', *Journal of Small Business Management* 35:34–46.

Commonwealth Secretariat (2002) *Commonwealth business-women: trade matters, best practices and success stories*, Commonwealth Secretariat, London.

Department for International Development (DFID) (2009) Website preamble on booklet entitled, *Trade matters*, available at: http://webarchive.nationalarchives.gov.uk/+/http://www.dfid.gov.uk/tradematters/default.asp

EQUAL (undated) *EQUAL Guide on gender mainstreaming*, European Commission, available online at: http://ec.europa.eu/employment_social/equal/about/key-doc_en.cfm

Gherardi S. (1995) *Gender, symbolism and organizational cultures*, Sage, London.

Goetz A.M. and R.S. Gupta (1996) 'Who takes the credit? Gender power and control over loan use in rural credit programmes in Bangladesh', *World Development* 24(1):45–63.

Hafkin N. (2002) *Gender issues in ICT policies in developing countries: an overview*, United Nations Division for the Advancement of Women Experts group meeting, Information and Communication Technologies and their Impact on and Use as an Instrument for the Advancement and Empowerment of Women, Seoul, Republic of Korea, 11-14 November 2002.

Hines R. (1992) 'Accounting: filling the negative space', *Accounting Organizations and Society* 17 (3):314-41.

Hunt J. and N. Kasynathan (2002) 'Reflections on microfinance and women's empowerment', *Development Bulletin* 57:71-75.

ICMR (2002) *The corporate glass ceiling*, case study, available online at: http://www.icmrindia.org/casestudies/catalogue/Human%20Resource%20and%20Organization%20Behavior/HROB019.htm

International Telecommunications Union (ITU) (2001) *The internet in an LDC: Uganda case study*, ITU, available online at: http://www.itu.int/ITU-D/ict_stories/themes/e-rural.html

Katsande R. (2003) 'Barriers to women entrepreneurial development: an analysis of the laws and procedures of small business registration in Zimbabwe', masters dissertation, SEARCWL, University of Zimbabwe, Harare.

Kole E. (2001) 'Appropriate theorizing about African women and the internet', *International Feminist Journal of Politics* 3(2): 155–179.

Kongolo M. (2007) 'Women and informal credit: lessons from Moretile, South Africa', *Journal of International Women's Studies* 8(4 May 2007):121–132.

Loza E. (2008) 'Starting up: women entrepreneurs face unique challenges in the business world', available online at: http://www.idahotechconnect.com/Home/TechBlog/e_135/TechNews/2008/7/StartingupWomenentrepreneursfaceuniquechallengesinthebusinessworld.htm

Njeru S. (2009) 'Information and communication technology (ICT), gender and peace building in Africa: a case of missed connections', *Peace and Conflict Review* 3(2):32–40.

Norwood C. (2005) 'Macro promises of micro credit – a case of a local *esusu* in rural Ghana', *Journal of International Women's Studies* 7(1 November 2005).

Sebstad J. and G. Chen (1996) *Overview of studies on the impact of microenterprise credit*, AIMS, USAID, Washington.

Shackelford J. (2003) 'Feminist pedagogy: a means of bringing critical thinking and creativity to the economics classroom', *American Economic Review* 82(2):570–76, available online at: http://www.stou.org/view/00028282/d.976313/97p0129410

Shiva V. (1995) 'The effects of WTO on women's rights', *Third World Resurgence* 61/62 Sept/Oct, available online at: http://www.twnside.org.sg/title/women-ch.htm

Stiglitz J.E. and A. Charlton (2005) *Fair trade for all: how trade can promote development*, Oxford University Press, Oxford.

UNIFEM (2002) *Information communication technology baseline survey in Zambia, Zimbabwe, Swaziland and South Africa*, UNIFEM, New York.

Watkins G. (1989) 'Toward a revolutionary feminist pedagogy', in bell hooks, *Talking back: thinking feminist, thinking black*, South End Press, Cambridge, MA, accessed online at: http://www.chss.montclair.edu/english/classes/stuehler/engl105/hooks.html

APPENDIX I: Regulations: Masters in Women's Law (operational from 2011)

1. Introduction

1.1 The Southern and Eastern African Regional Centre for Women's Law hereinafter referred to as SEARCWL and the University of Zimbabwe being aware of the professional, social and family constraints that affect women's capacity to pursue postgraduate studies on a full time basis away from their home countries have endeavoured to provide a flexible programme format which permits women candidates, in particular, to balance these components of their lives in their pursuit of postgraduate studies.

1.2 These Regulations should be read in conjunction with the General Academic Regulations for Masters Degrees by Coursework (hereinafter referred to as the General Regulations).

2. Qualifications for admission

To be eligible for admission to the Masters in Women's Law, a candidate must have obtained a first degree in Law of an appropriate standard from this or another University, normally at second class level or above, provided that candidates with a lower academic ranking but who have a proven work record and/or research experience in women's law and related issues may still be considered. Candidates with first degrees in other disciplines may be considered if they have achieved the appropriate academic standard and have relevant postgraduate experience in areas related to women and law.

In the selection process the candidate's post graduation work and other experience in areas related to women and the law will be taken into account.

3. Programme duration and structure

The programme will normally commence in January of each alternate year and will run until May of the following year.

3.1 The first semester (17 weeks) will focus on theories, and methodologies in women's law and inter-related human rights. The first semester will be comprised of lectures, seminars, fieldwork and research methodology practicals. The courses in this semester, which are all core courses are:

Theories and perspectives in women's law	MWL 501	20 units
Research methodologies and methods in women's law	MWL 502	20 units
Practical paper	MWL 503	20 units
Human rights and women	MWL 504	20 units

The first semester will normally be conducted from January to May in the year in which the programme begins, although the University reserves the right to vary the time when the programme commences.

3.2 The second semester which will run for 15 weeks, normally commencing in mid June of the year in which a programme commences. In this semester candidates will:

3.2.1 take two options from the list of optional courses offered in the MSWL programme, which are:

Women, access to resources and law	MWL 511	20 units
Masculinities, gender and law	MWL 512	20 units
Women, commerce and law in Africa	MWL 513	20 units
Women, law reform and social justice strategies	MWL 514	20 units
Women and the criminal justice system	MWL 516	20 units
Women, family, social realities and law	MWL 517	20 units
Gender, law and sexuality	MWL 518	20 units
Woman, labour and social security law	MWL 519	20 units

3.2.1.1 The SEARCWL shall determine which optional courses will be offered in each programme.

3.2.1.2 The SEARCWL may prescribe the maximum number of students who may take an optional course, the normal upper limit per optional course being 10 students. The SEARCWL may also prescribe the minimum number of students required for the mounting of a course, which would normally be not less than 4 students.

3.2.2. During the second semester candidates will determine their dissertation topic for the third semester and develop their dissertation proposal and field work methodology and methods under the guidance of supervisors approved by the Departmental Board of the SEARCWL and appointed by the Director of the SEARCWL.

3.3   In the third semester each candidate shall conduct field research and present for examination a 20,000-25,000 word dissertation in a selected field in human rights and women's law (see 3.2.2.1 above). The research for the dissertation should be carried out in the candidate's home country, the writing up will, normally, be conducted at the SEARCWL, University of Zimbabwe.

4.   Scheme of assessment/examination

4.1   The scheme of assessment for each course in the course work components of the degree shall be a combination of different forms of assessment:

4.1.1 Semester 1

Theories and perspectives in women's law	MWL 501
Human rights and women	MWL 504

In each of the above courses candidates will be required to submit one or two written assignment which will constitute 35% of the total marks for the course. And write an eight (8) hour research examination which will constitute 65% of the total marks for the course.

4.1.1.1 Research methodologies and methods in women's law   MWL 502

There shall be two components to this course:

1   Exploring research methodologies and methods which shall be assessed as follows:
By two written assignments which shall constitute 25% of the marks for the course; and
A six hour research examination which shall constitute 50% of the marks for the course

2   ILS/ITC which shall be assessed as follows:
By practical/course work component which shall constitute 10% of the marks for the course and a two hour examination which shall constitute 15% of the marks for the course.

4.1.1.2 Research examinations

Candidates will be given the question paper for the research examination at 9.00 on the morning of the examination and will be required to hand in their completed paper by 17:00 on the same day. (Provided that in the Research methodologies and methods in women's law the research paper shall be of six (6) hours duration.) Candidates may write such examinations anywhere designated by the Director of the SEARCWL as an examination venue within the SEARCWL premises.

4.1.1.3 Practical paper   MWL 503

The Practical paper shall be comprised as follows: 75% of the marks shall be awarded based on assessment of the candidate in the fieldwork component of the first semester programme, 25% of the marks shall be determined by a two hour practical examination at the end of the first semester in the planning of a research or funding proposal or similar document.

Candidates in the Practical shall be required to submit with their field report a consolidation of their findings and a recommended action plan, which together shall not exceed in length one thousand (1,000) words and which shall comprise 10% of the marks awarded for the field report.

4.1.2 Semester 2

In each optional course offered the mode of assessment shall be a combination of assessment of seminar presentations, written assignments, practical exercises and an eight (8) hour research examination. The research examinations shall follow the format prescribed in 4.1.1.

The Departmental Board of the SEARCWL shall advise candidates, in writing, at the end of the first semester what form the assessment for each of the optional courses on offer in that academic year in the second semester shall take. However, normally, the assessment will be constituted as follows:

Seminar presentations	–	15%
Written assignment	–	20%
Practical exercise	–	15%
Research examination	–	50%

4.1.3 Evidence of independent work

In all presentations, assignments and practical exercises, regardless of the course being pursued, each student shall be required to submit a separate written assignment or separate evidence of work carried out for presentations or practical exercises even if the initial preparation and consultations were carried out in the form of group work.

4.1.4 Semester 3

Dissertation   MWL 560

Candidates shall submit a dissertation between 20,000–25,000 words on an approved topic (see 3.3 above), normally, not later than 30 April in the year after that in which they enrol for the Masters in Women's Law. Provided that where the timing of the course is altered an alternative submission date will be set for the dissertation. Candidates shall be required to submit with their dissertation a consolidation of their findings and a recommended action plan which together shall not exceed in length one thousand (1,000) words in length and which shall comprise 10% of the marks awarded for the dissertation.

Candidates shall submit one printed copy of the dissertation and an electronic copy of the dissertation. The dissertation and the electronic copy shall be prepared using such word processing programme/s as is, from time to time, prescribed by the Director of the SEARCWL

5. Determination and notification of results

In determining the results of each candidate the following shall apply:

5.1 The coursework components of the degree shall be given a weighting of 60%, with each course work component having equal weight with the other course work components, the dissertation shall be given a weighting of 40% in the computation of the overall classification of the degree.

Candidates must pass each course to be awarded the degree. Provided that where a candidate fails a single course he or she may rewrite that course when it is next on offer, and shall do so at his or her expense.

5.2 In all other respects results shall be published and degrees awarded in accordance with the provisions of the General Regulations.

6. Syllabi

In accordance with the provisions of the General Regulations detailed syllabuses for subjects/courses do not form part of the General or Faculty Regulations but shall be submitted to the Faculty Board for approval. Copies of the detailed syllabuses shall be maintained in the Faculty Office for reference.

APPENDIX II: **Masters in Women's Law programme outline**			
SEMESTER 1 17 weeks			
12 weeks – three courses integrated (10 weeks – swot week – exam week) – 2 x 8 hour research exams and 1 six hour exam			5 weeks – group field research and write up
Theories and perspectives in women's law	Research methodologies and methods in women's law – includes 2 hr ICT and 6 hr methodology exam	Human rights and women	Practical paper (2 hrs) – includes research design and field research for a 'mini' dissertation
SEMESTER 2 15 weeks			
Optional courses 1 (select 1) 6 weeks (2 weeks, reading and course work week, 2 weeks reading, course work and exams) 8 hour research exam			
Women, law reform and social justice strategies	Women and the criminal justice system	Women, family, social realities and law	Women, commerce and law in Africa
Optional courses 2 (select 1) 6 weeks (2 weeks, reading and course work week, 2 weeks reading, course work and exams) 8 hour research exam			
Women, access to resources and the law	Masculinities, gender and law	Gender, law and sexuality	Women, labour and social security law
Research design for dissertation 3 weeks			
SEMESTER 3 19 weeks			
Dissertation – home based research Home based supervision from SEARCWL 10 weeks		Analysis and write up at SEARCWL 9 weeks	

Index of cases

Index of instruments and documents